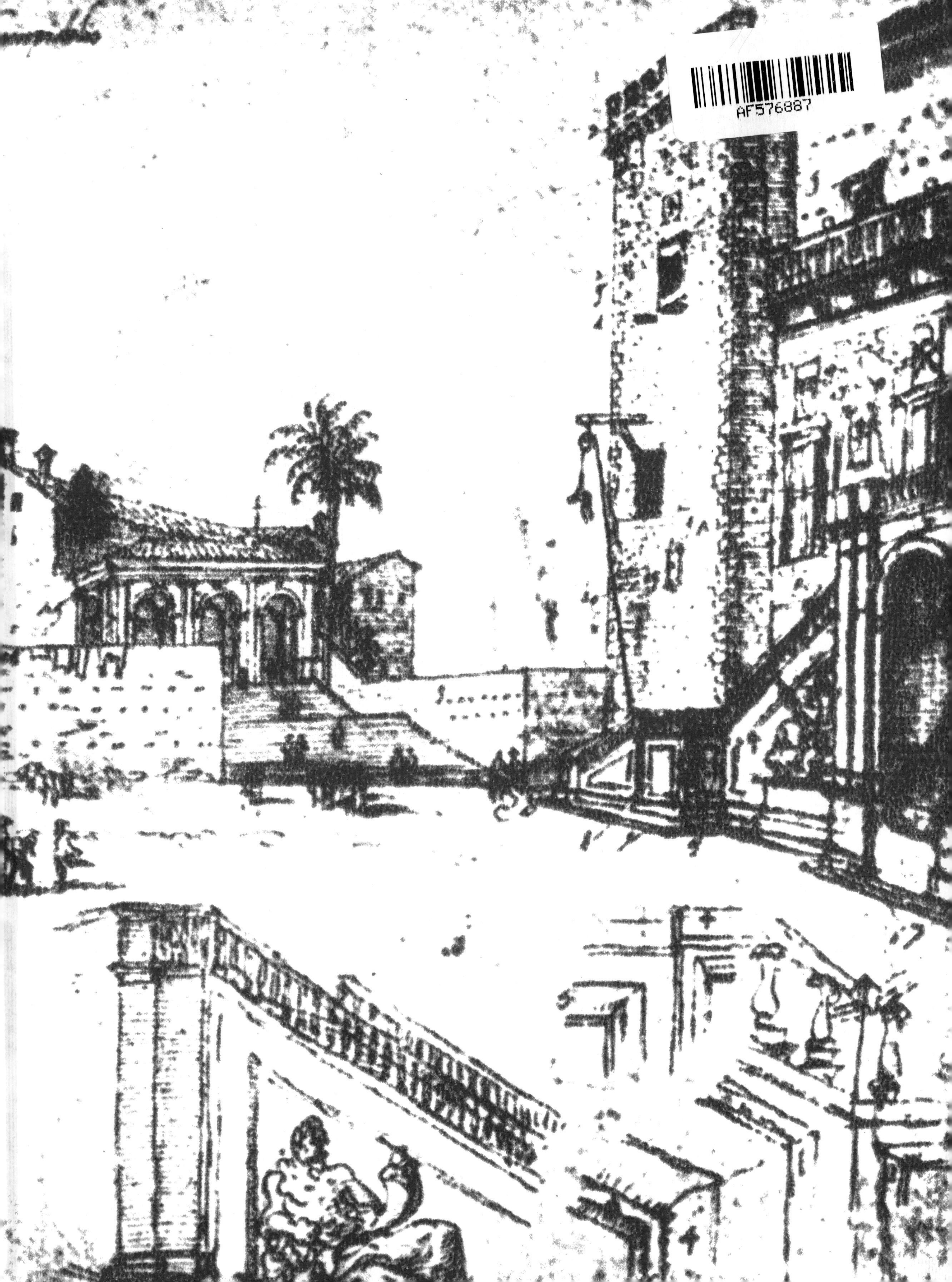

# Campidoglio

# Campi

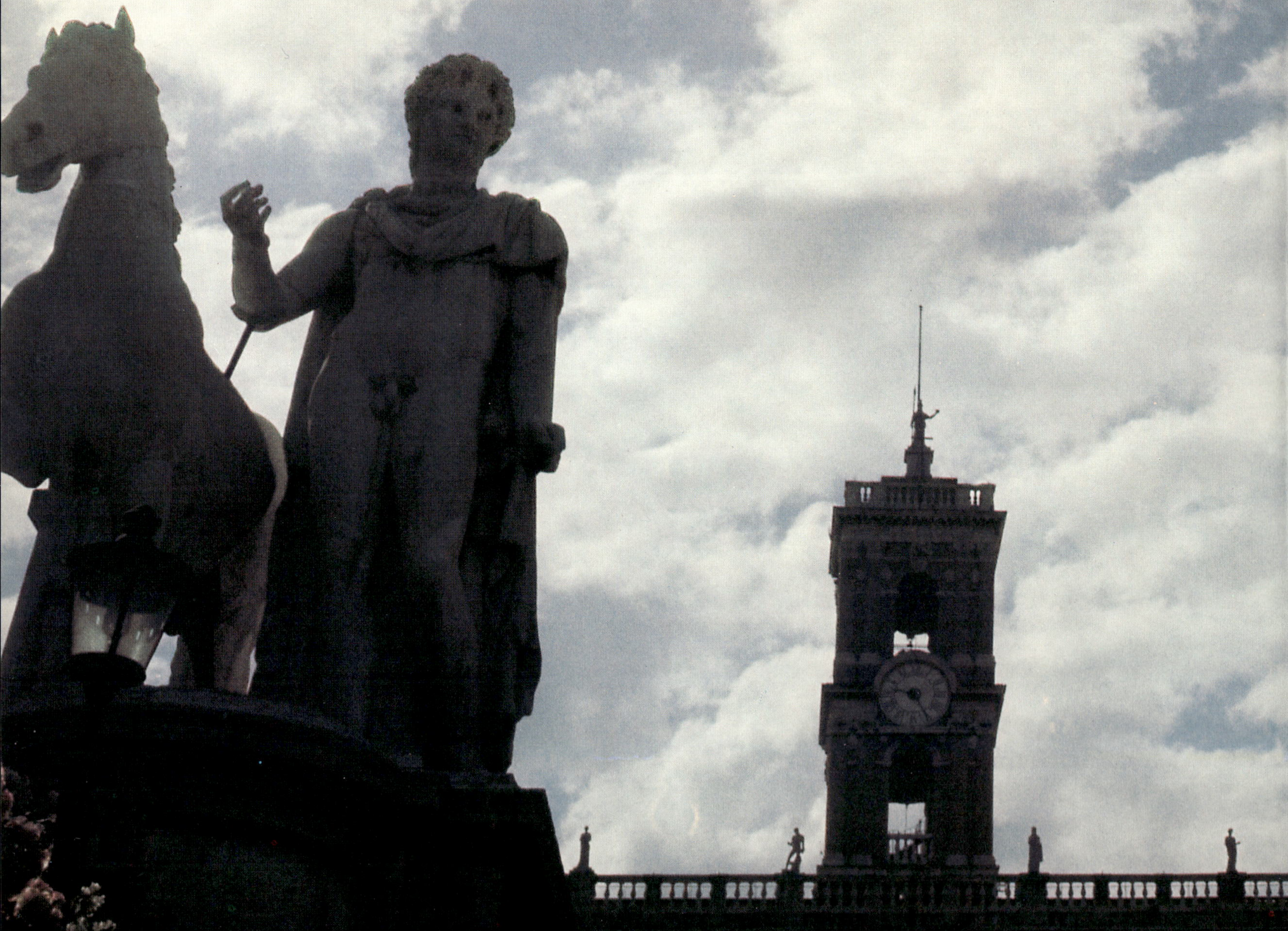

PHOTOGRAPHS BY
ALEXANDER LIBERMAN

# doglio

## MICHELANGELO'S ROMAN CAPITOL

WITH AN ESSAY BY
JOSEPH BRODSKY

Random House

**To Melinda, my wife**

# Acknowledgments

My profound gratitude to my friend S. I. Newhouse, Jr., the Chairman of Condé Nast Publications, for his constant, unwavering support of this enterprise of many years. My thanks to Harold Evans, the President and Publisher of Random House, for his enthusiasm for the project: his editorial decisiveness finally allowed this book to be born. To Andrew Wylie, who protected the endeavor with energy and faith. I am deeply indebted to Sharon DeLano, Senior Editor at Random House, whose care and overall editorial judgment I valued constantly. Also, I want to thank Diane Kelder, Professor of Art History, for her historical and artistic judgment and for information that added great richness to the photographs. My very special gratitude to my assistant, Crosby Coughlin, who has been intimately involved in the selection and organization of the book: to his constant vigilance and overall vision I owe so much. And to the great Joseph Brodsky all admiration for the nobility of thought in his magisterial essay on Marcus Aurelius. My very deep appreciation and admiration to my friend Lucy Sisman for her inspired boldness in the design of the book. Many, many thanks to Danny Berger from the Metropolitan Museum, who so often in Rome arranged difficult permissions and even obtained a cherry picker that allowed rare close-up images of the statue. To Edmund Winfield, who stewarded and organized the photography in the early years. To Denise Otis, who thoughtfully and understandingly edited my introduction. And finally to Lorna Caine and Maura Thompson, who were so helpfully involved in the progress of this project through the years.

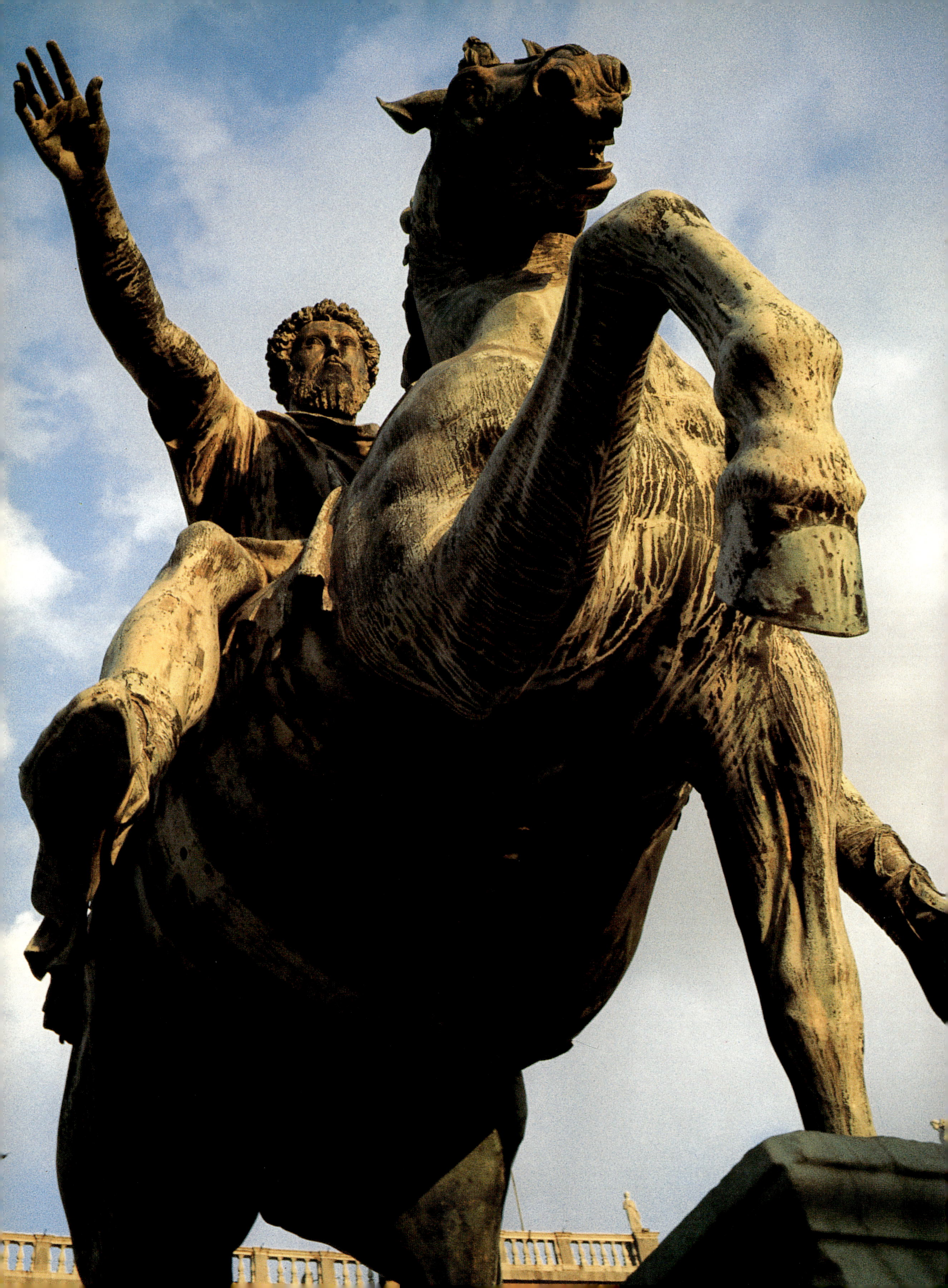

# Contents

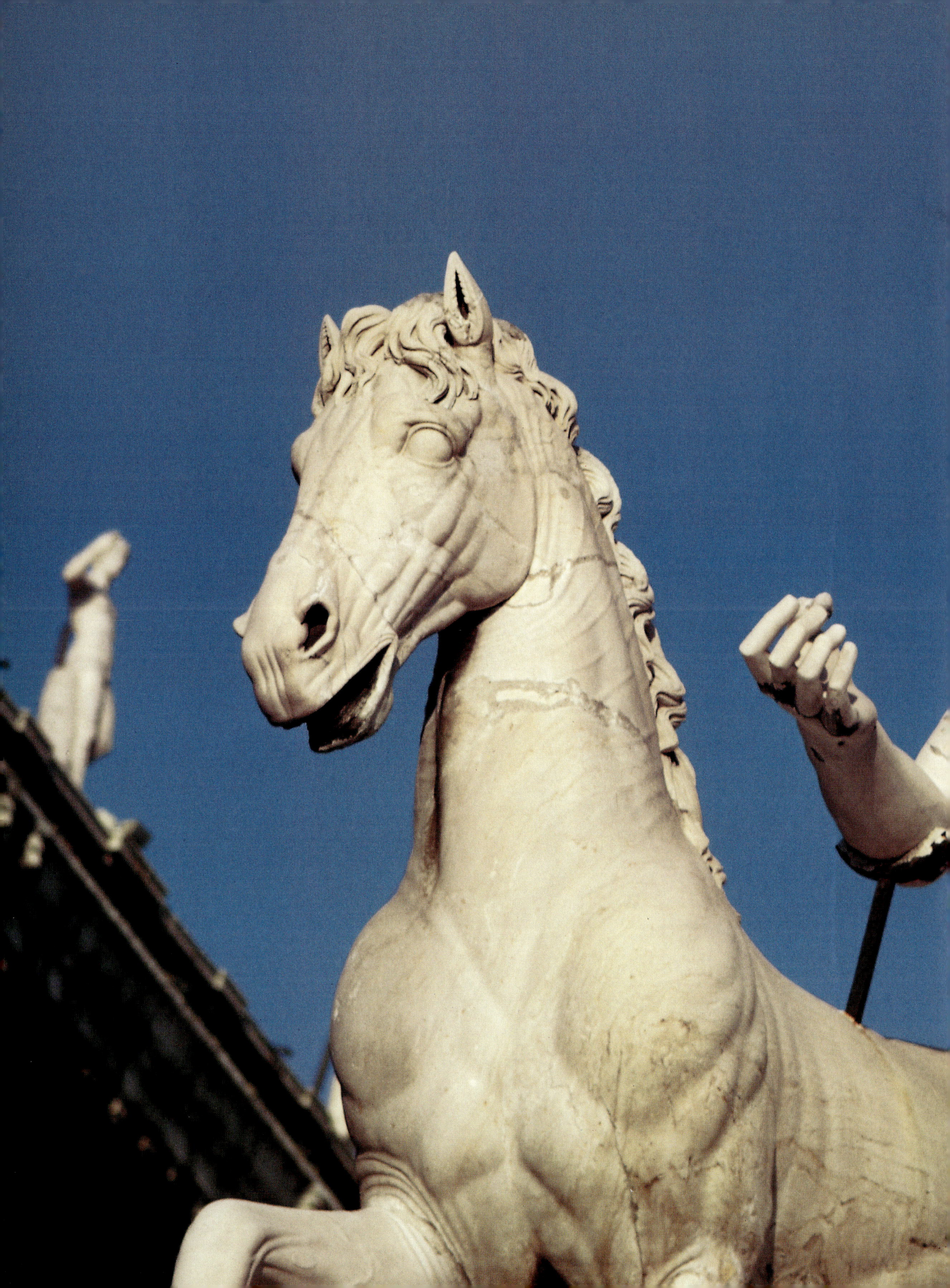

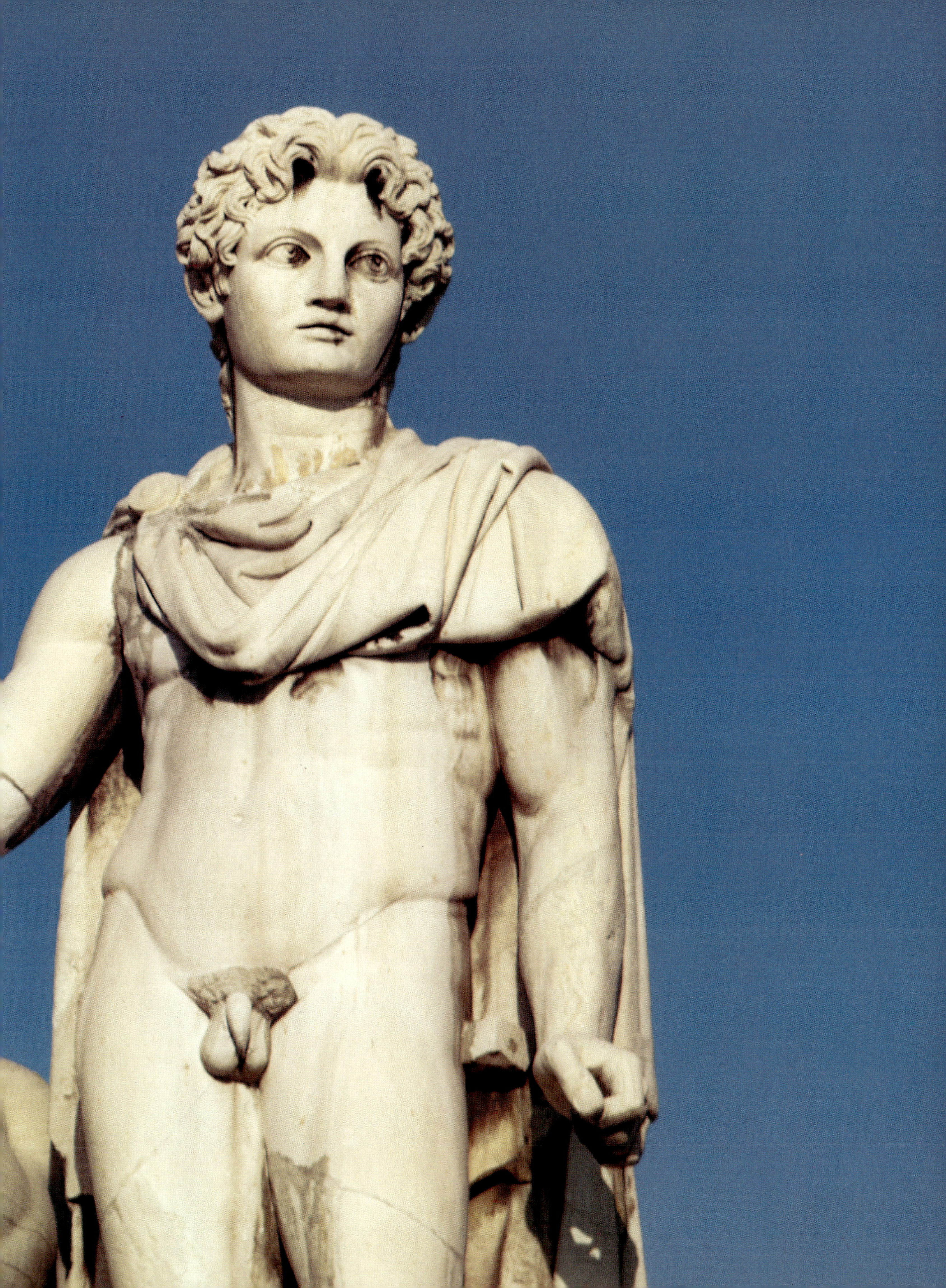

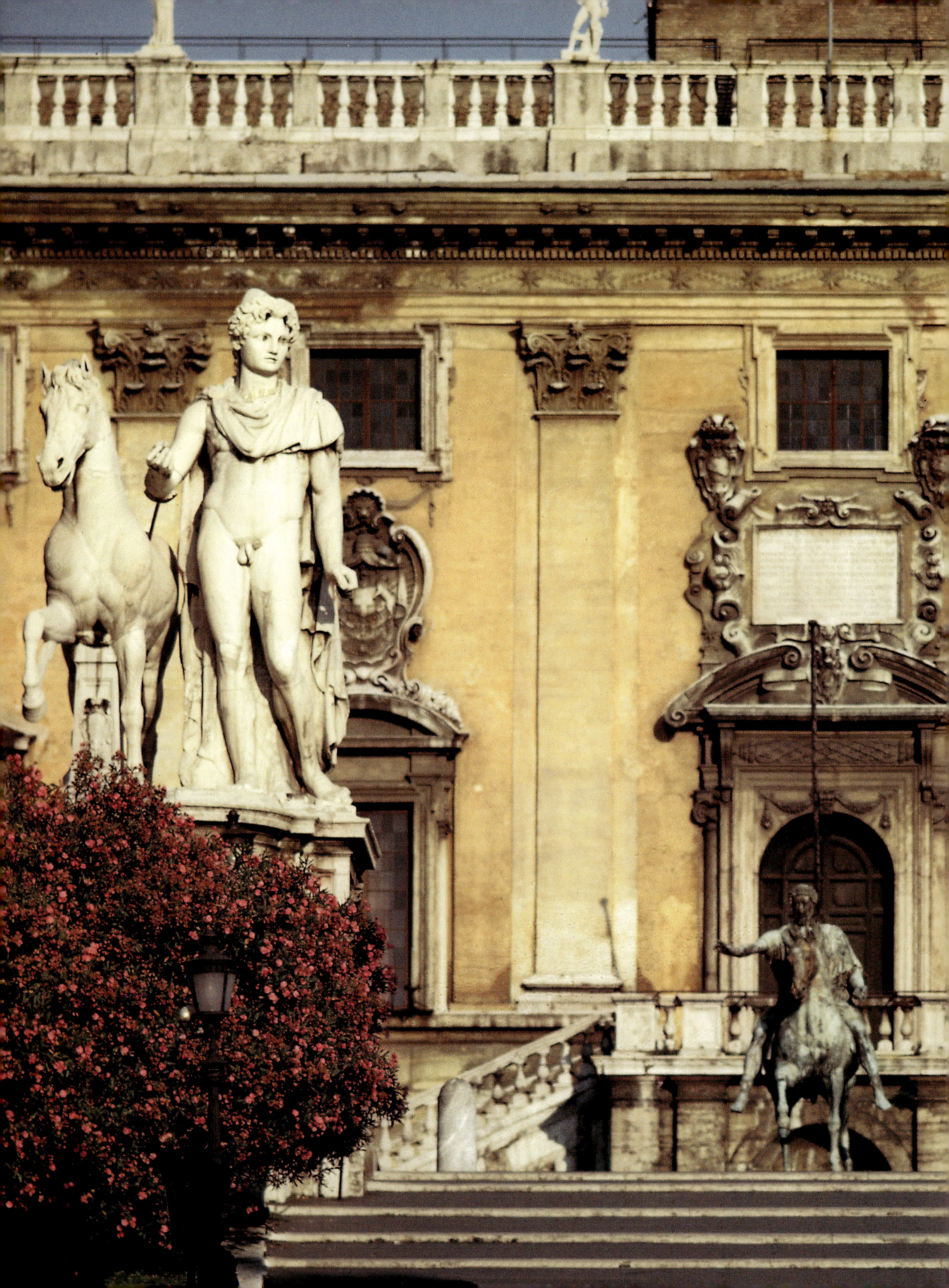

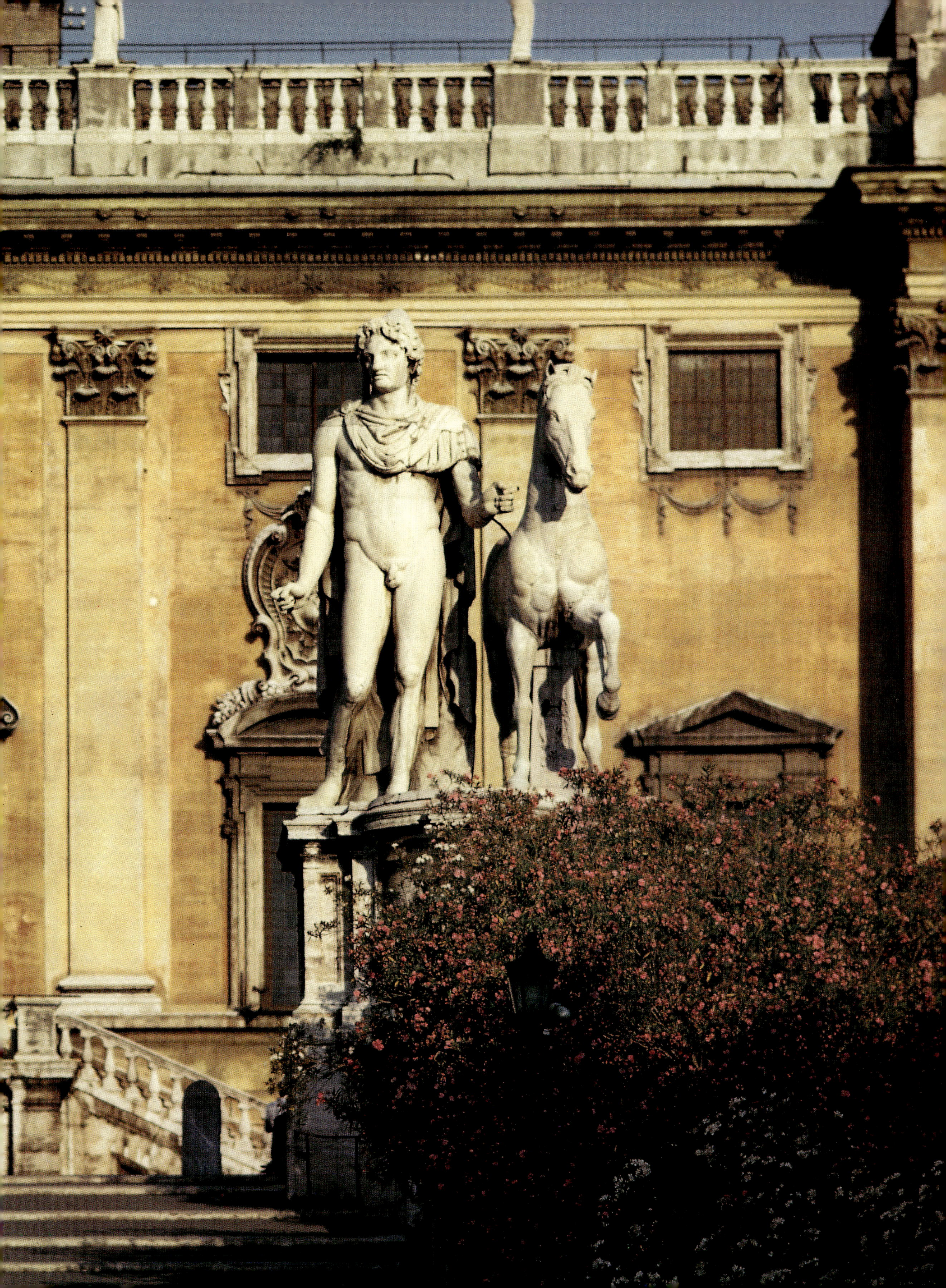

# Experiencing the Cam

by ALEXANDER LIBERMAN

I first saw the Piazza del Campidoglio on a hot summer day. I was stunned and overwhelmed by its power. At the same time, I felt a very quiet sense of grace, of pure beauty—a beauty serene and noble, yet rich and forceful. From that day, any free moment I had in Rome I would go back and try to capture on film the changing light, the changing moods of this unique sculpture and the architecture surrounding it. These pictures were taken over a period of twenty years. There is a curious enrichment of vision as the eye becomes more and more accustomed to the subtle changes and vital transformations cast by light.

I became fascinated with the willed combination of grace and strength in the statue. There are no weak areas. The horse is in motion, its raised leg counterpoints the stirrupless foot of the man. The underbelly gives the animal a crude dimension, a primitive reminder of earthiness and labor. This is not an elegant, courtly, well-mannered creature. In the snarl of its bridled lips one senses a rebellious attempt

# pidoglio

to unseat the rider. Horse and rider seem to and do belong to a rougher, earlier culture than the Baroque ornamentation of the surrounding buildings, with their hints of an already too-refined taste that make the essential nobility of the monument all the more vivid.

The first approach to the enchanted square is up a magnificent flight of steps. On either side, two nude white-marble Dioscuri with their mounts seem to herald the wonders beyond. The symmetrical orchestration of the overall plan brings one's eye to the statue, which accentuates the central axis. At the far end is the Palazzo del Senatore, with a pair of symmetrical stairs sweeping up to its main entrance. This dominant central palace is painted a glowing Roman ochre and at sunset each little pane in its tall windows throws off sparks of light. The sun's rays bring out a special brilliance in the sculpture, giving it a glow of gold. The buildings, too, take on a radiance. The whole becomes a sumptuous re-creation of a golden mythological city.

The Campidoglio holds many treasures discreetly hidden so as not to intrude on the main design. In the palaces there are vast inner court-yards. In one, a Neptune reclines in a moss-covered fountain. On the right side, in the Palazzo dei Conservatori, are the monumental broken-up remains of a colossal statue of Constantine the Great: a giant head, a hand with a symbolic, uplifted finger, a foot that dwarfs the human scale.

I have attempted to document everything that caught my eye. When I photographed the great artists for my book *The Artist in His Studio,* I never gathered information ahead. And when I plunged into the Campidoglio, I came on it in total ignorance, so that the eye was my guide. This is not a scholarly project. I have tried to achieve a kind of visual poem, to capture through juxtapositions and changing light the power and the glory of this treasure unique in the world.

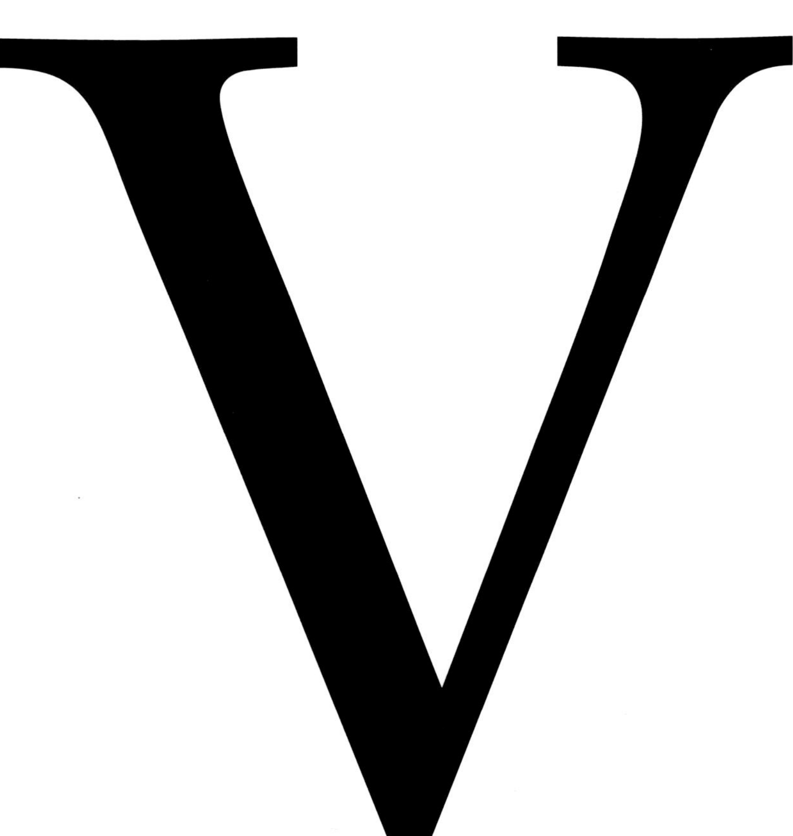

incent Scully puts his finger on one aspect of the magic of the Campidoglio. "Only Michelangelo, perhaps, was far beyond it all in whatever art he chose to employ. His Campidoglio in Rome is a demonstration far beyond the resources of painting of what architecture and sculpture fundamentally, unequivocally, are. He affirms that architecture is a space, an environment. The buildings are pushed back to shape that space, to bring it into being. But sculpture is in the center. It is active; it seems to push the solid buildings back. It says that the human act creates the environment, shapes the human world."

In my life as a sculptor, I have had to consider the way public sculpture is experienced. Here, I wanted to go deeper, and maybe discover the secret of this magical symbiosis of art and environment. Perhaps by focusing on every detail I could reconstruct the wondrous whole. In contemporary sculpture there is a strange and debatable inclination to abolish the pedestal. Here, the graceful marble pedestal designed by Michelangelo himself lifts the statue off the ground, giving it a commanding stance. Raising it is essential to its function as an emblem of power and respect. The master designer of the whole also conceived a miraculous design for the pavement. A vivid compass star radiates from the sculpture in all directions, as if to project the great thoughts of a noble mind into the universe beyond their assigned earthly limits.

Analyzing why this statue works so excitingly in space, one realizes the importance of the outstretched arm. It extends horizontally straight away from the powerful total mass, creating a visual experience that suggests the limitless beyond. Just below the arm, the horse's right leg is raised as if pawing the air. The sculptor knowingly bent it so that the eye is brought back to the main body of the sculpture—the outward thrust of the hand countered by the animal's curved leg, and both movements balanced by the vertical of the man's downthrust leg.

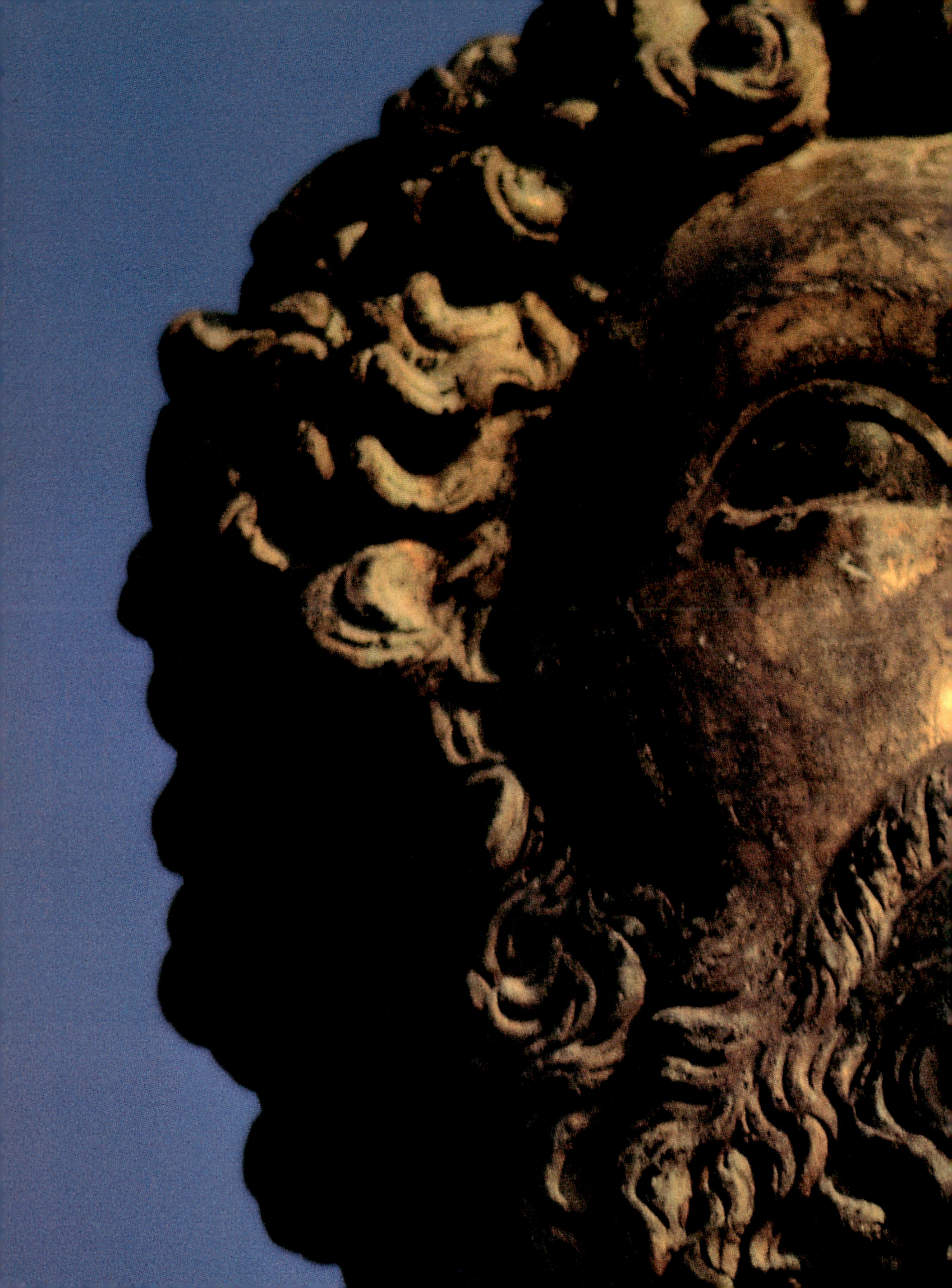

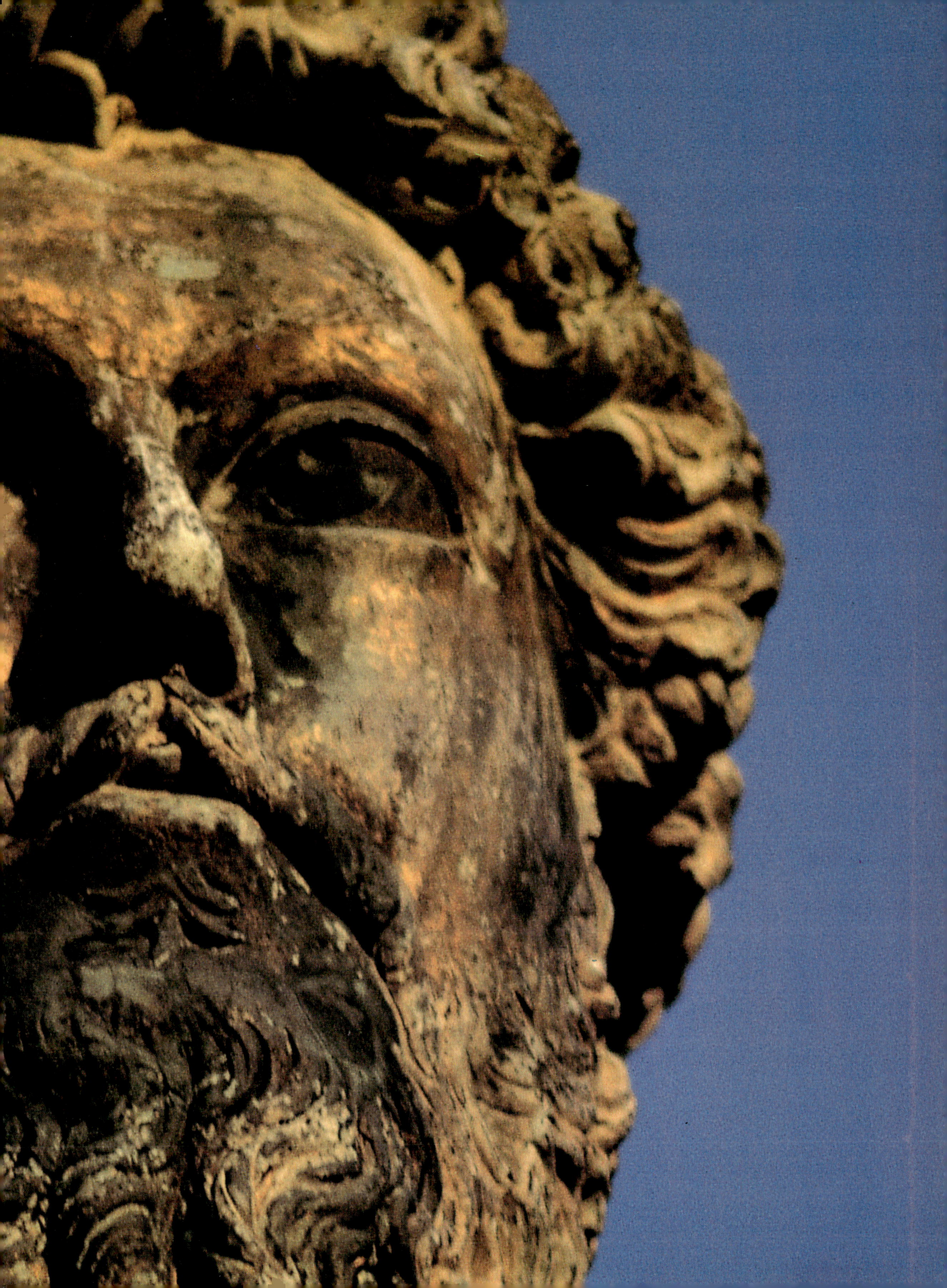

These flights of shapes in different directions animate and bring a soaring life to this unique and monumental work.

After years of contemplation, I felt a bond, a moral direction that was ever present in my own work—the underlying spirituality of the whole. Mies van der Rohe was fond of saying that "God is in the details." Every detail here counts, has its meaning. The sculptural elimination of the unimportant gives an overall grandeur. But the telling, the essential accents are there: the head, vital and serene with a distant, idea-full gaze, powerful but not cruel, a knowing grandeur in the expression. After all, this is a philosopher-emperor. The curls around his head are a nimbus, not of sainthood but of glory. The horse's snarling nostrils and violent, grimacing mouth bring barbaric contrast to the serene self-command of its master. In the head of the horse there is a hint of the legendary animals of Chinese sculpture. Here then is a blending of opposites into a meaningful whole, like all great art the resolution of contradictions into a final masterpiece.

The majesty and the peace in the commanding yet forgiving gesture of the arm extended toward the modern city below seems an eternal link between the past and the present. Rome is full of religious glories, but in this pagan decor there blows a wind of ennobling spirituality.

What adds to the awesome presence is the site, dominating the Eternal City from the Capitoline Hill. Michelangelo respected and admired the unearthed, unharried-by-time, miraculous creation of a past civilization. In his plan, he surrounded it with buildings at an awed, respectful distance, and with a pavement design that encircles and directs the eye to the central focal point. This whole splendor of art, architecture, design, and form is at the same time powerful and intimate. I thought of a setting for *Don Giovanni,* with the Commendatore in the center of it all, the unforgettable, doomsaying voice ringing in my ears.

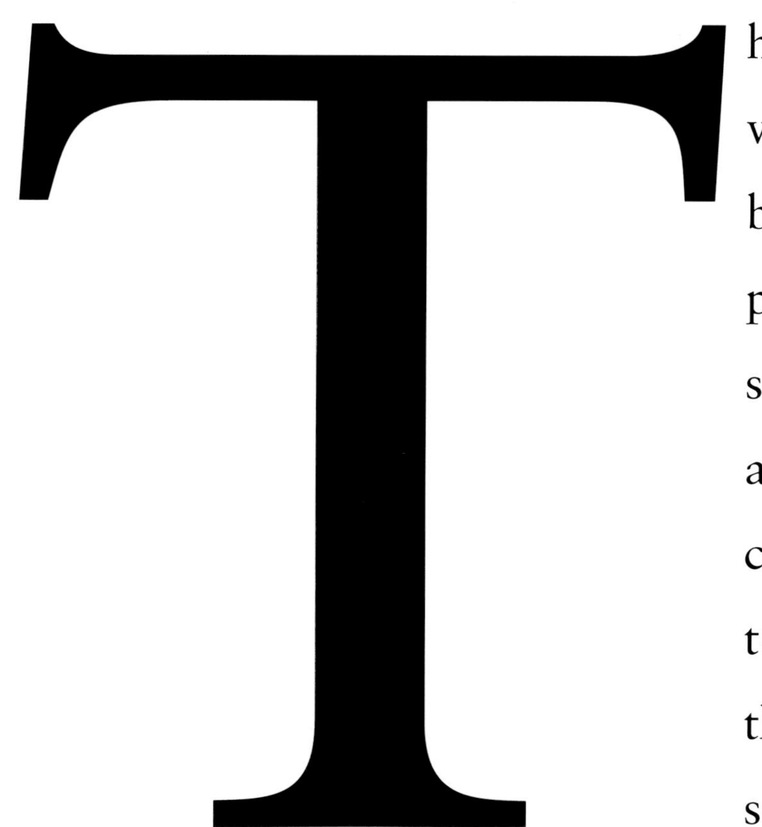

The flow of ages has deposited visible scars of survival on the buildings and statue. Very ancient, patinaed by time, the green bronze still flecked by gold, this sublime achievement of the sculptor's art catches all the different subtle textures—the sensuous folds of the toga, the leather of sandals and saddle, the curls of the hair, the metal of the harness—and fixes them for all time. Sculpture can, if rarely, achieve an awesome effect, magically infusing a quivering tremor of life into inanimate metal, communicating the invisible through the more than real. The presence of the great mystery of creation is the true residue of an overwhelming visual experience. Sit on the steps and contemplate the whole, especially at dusk when, surrounding the plaza, street lights blaze up and transform the reality of the day into a theatrical illusion. The statue—dark, foreboding—becomes a black hole in this constellation. The awakening of man and horse from centuries of silence seems to draw us into a dreamlike transition from an unknown past to a surprising new life.

Now the rider and his horse have been removed, victims of modern pollution. For their own protection they are exhibited in the Capitoline Museum on the left side of the Piazza. Our destructive civilization has done its damage: suddenly, all seems to die without the principal in center stage. True, a replica will soon occupy the center of the Piazza. What cannot be replicated is the authentic patina of centuries. The Campidoglio will become a heartbreaking sight to those who still remember. How paradoxical and cruel to awaken marvels from their buried, ancient sleep, then let our time damage and destroy that which gave us a seemingly permanent inspiration and deep joy.

In this book I have tried to enshrine a triumphant vision in the history of human creation, a true union of sculpture, architecture, and site.

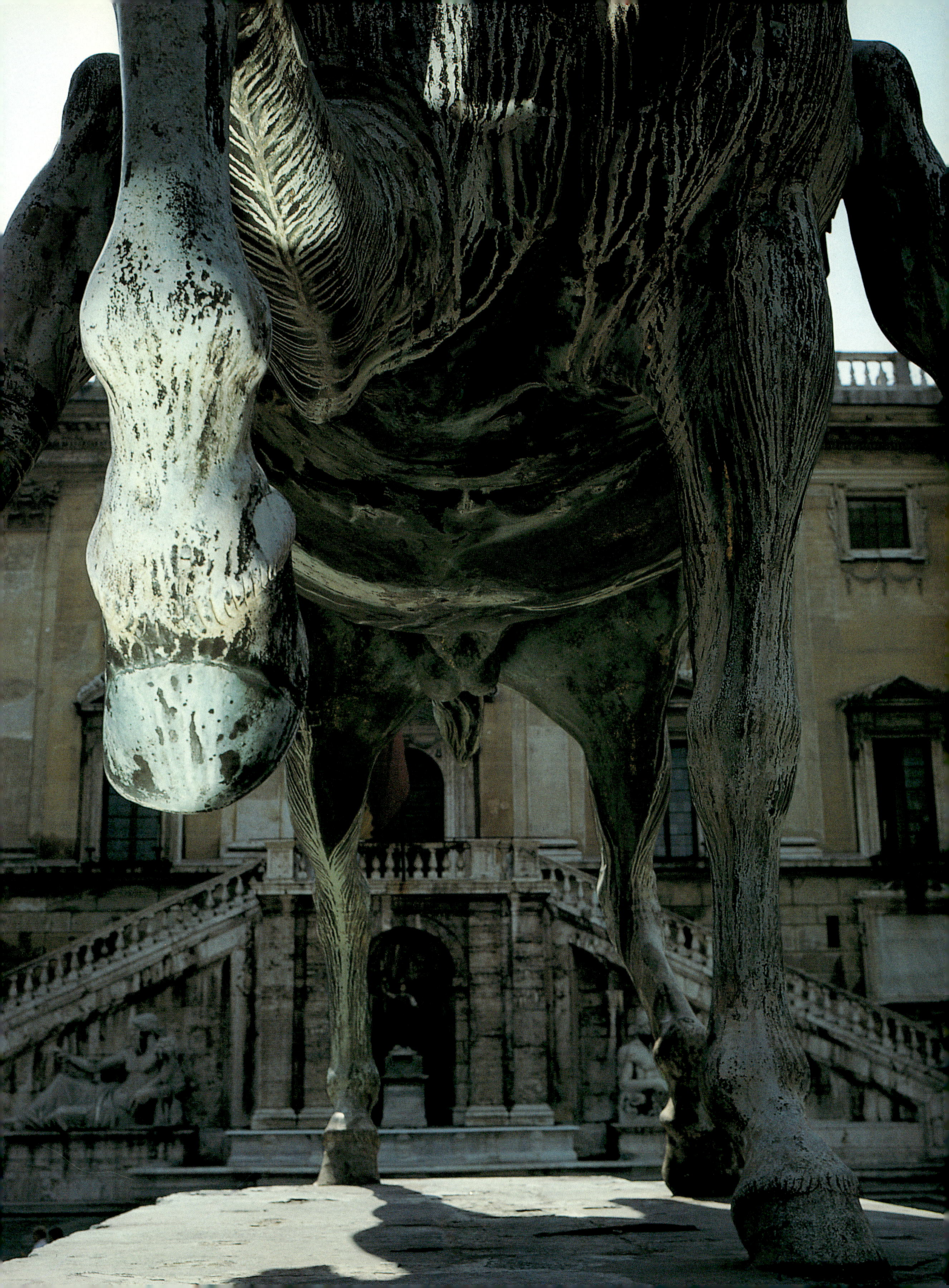

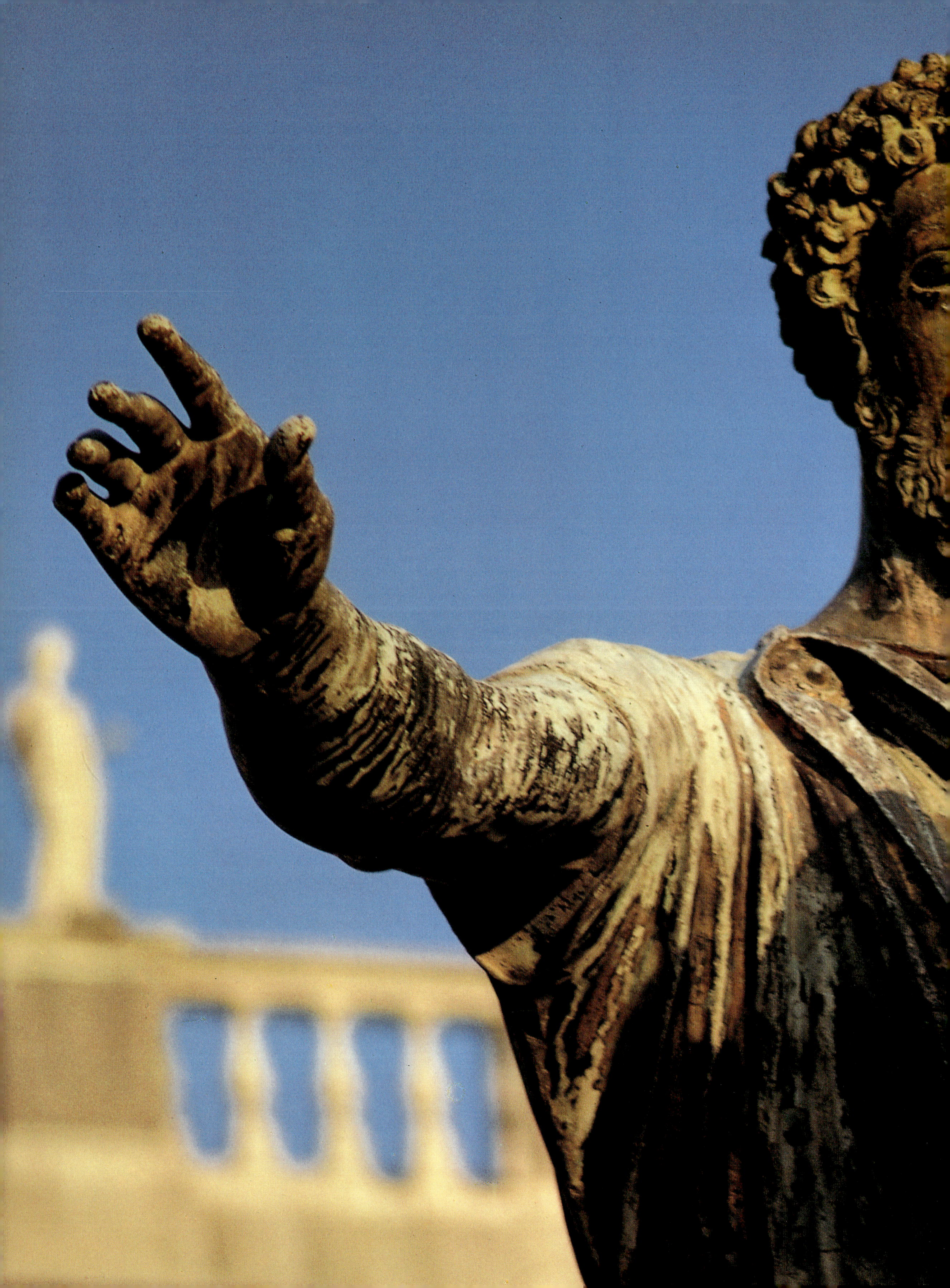

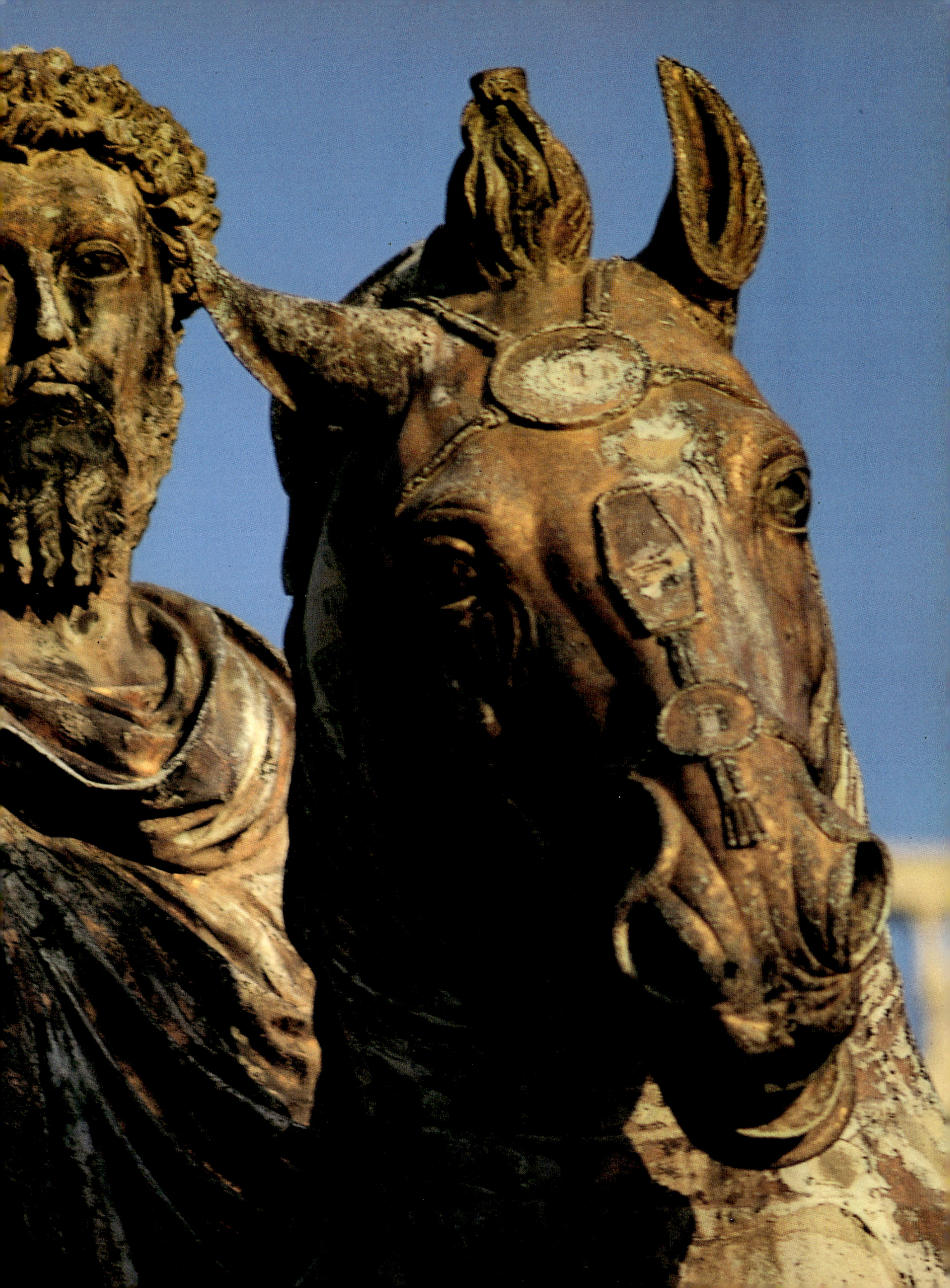

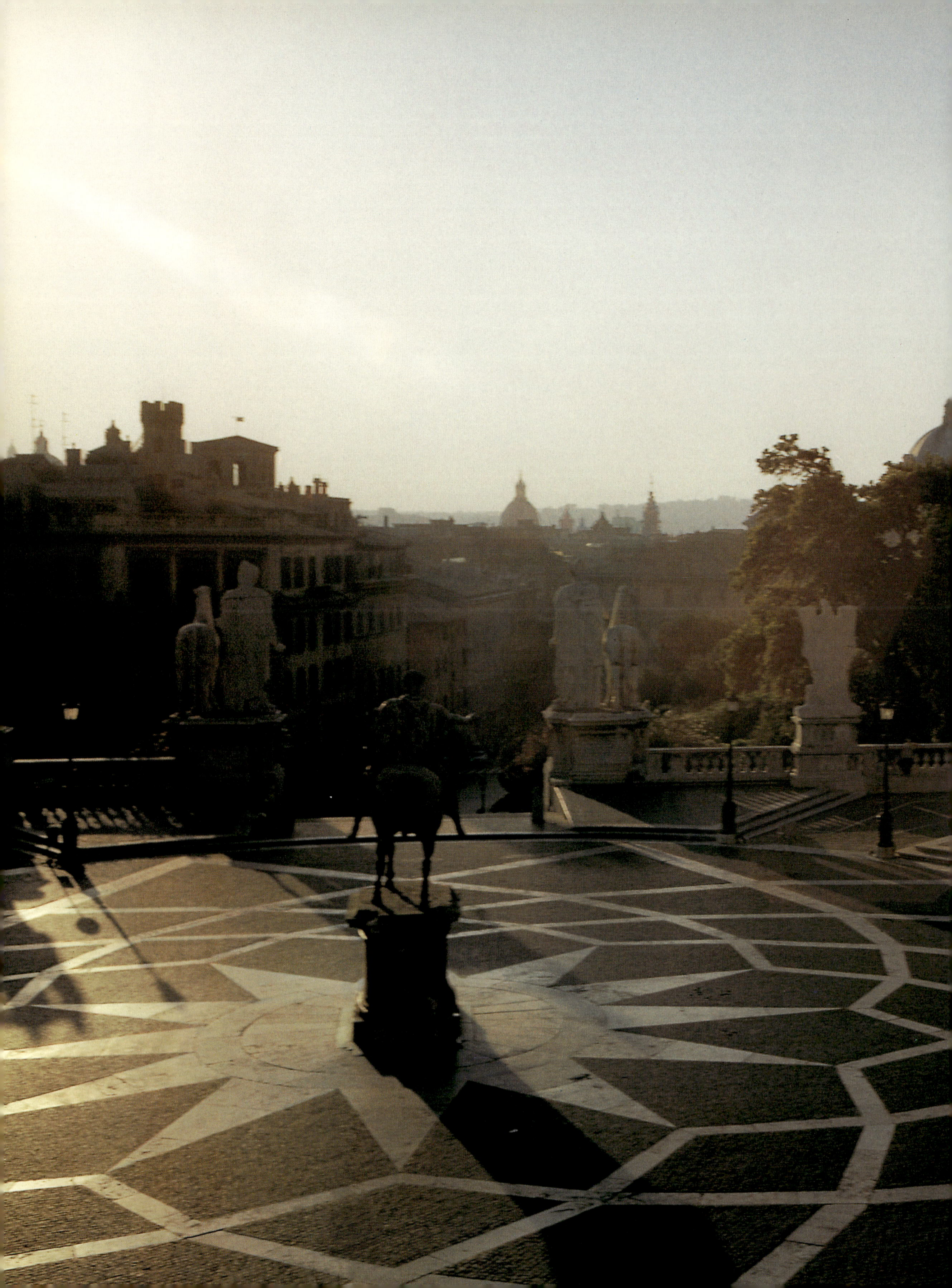

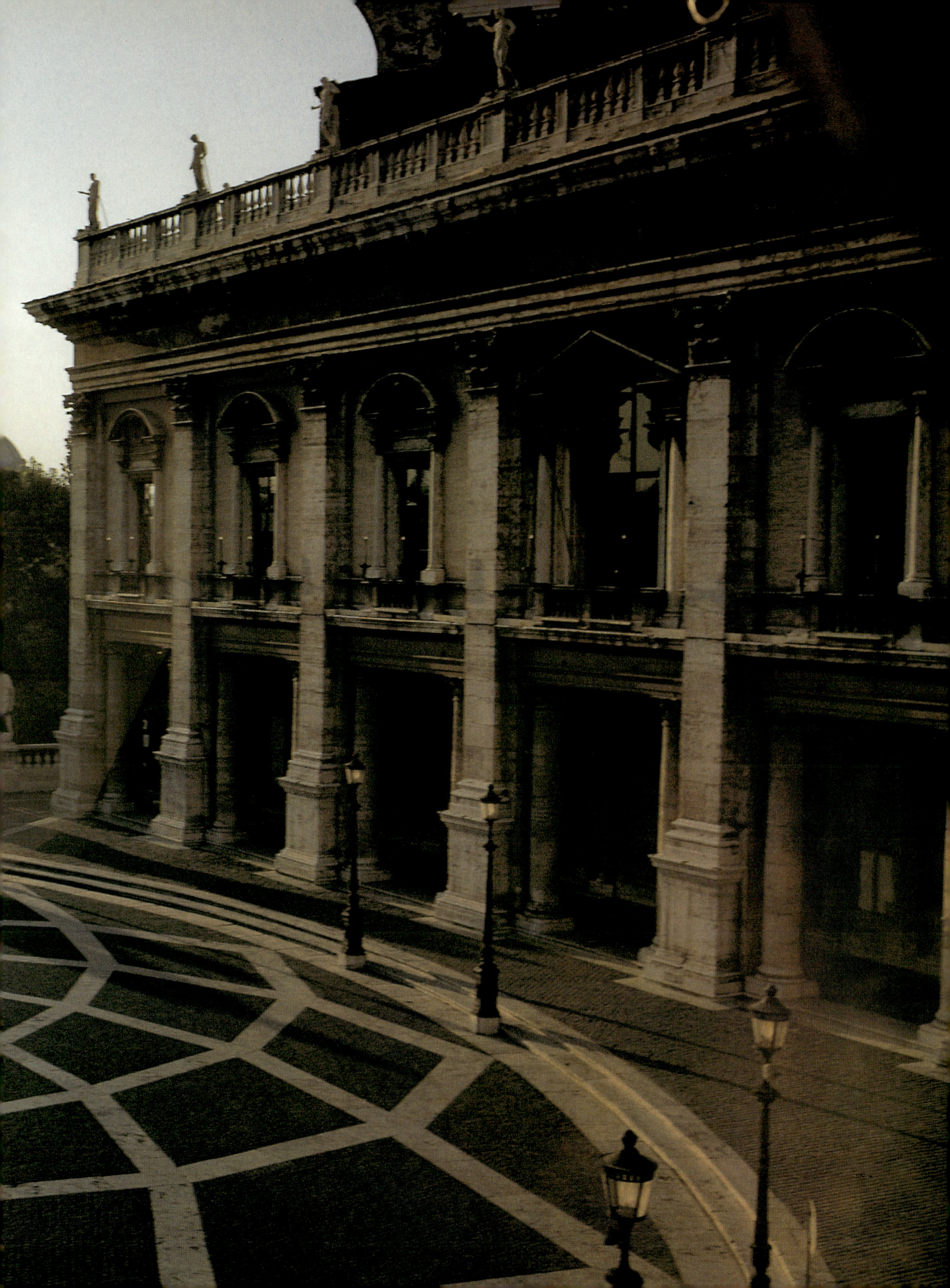

# Marcus

# Homage to Aurelius

by JOSEPH BRODSKY

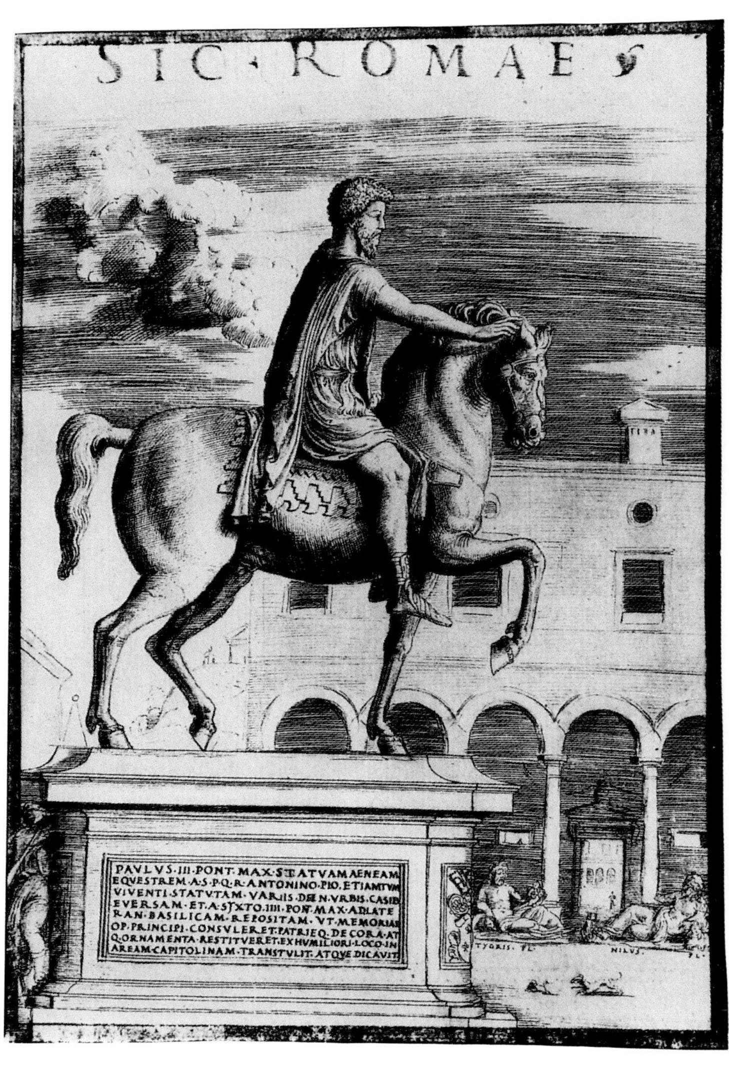

# I

While antiquity exists for us, we, for antiquity, do not. We never did, and we never will. This rather peculiar state of affairs makes our take on antiquity somewhat invalid. Chronologically and, I am afraid, genetically speaking, the distance between us is too immense to imply any causality: we look at antiquity as if out of nowhere. Our vantage point is similar to that of an adjacent galaxy's view of ourselves; it boils down, at best, to a solipsistic fantasy, to a vision. We shouldn't claim more, since nothing is less repeatable than our highly perishable cellular mix. What would an ancient Roman, were he to wake up today, recognize? A cloud on high, blue waves, a woodpile, the horizontality of the bed, the verticality of the wall—but no one by face, even if those he encountered were stark naked. Finding himself in our midst, he at best would have a sensation similar to that of a moon landing, i.e., not knowing what is before him: the future, or the distant past? a landscape or a ruin? These things, after all, have great similarity. Unless, of course, he saw a horseman.

# II

The twentieth is perhaps the first century that looks at this statue of a horseman with slight bewilderment. Ours is the century of the automobile, and our kings and presidents drive, or else they are driven. We don't see many horsemen around, save at equestrian shows or races. One exception is perhaps the British consort, Prince Philip, as well as his daughter, Princess Anne. But that has to do not even so much with their royal station as with the name "Philip," which is of Greek origin and means "philo-hippoi": lover of horses. It is so much so that Her Royal Highness was married—until recently—to Captain Mark Phillips of the Royal Guards, an accomplished steeplechaser himself. You may even add to that Prince Charles, the heir to the British crown, an avid polo player. But that would be it. You don't see leaders of democracies or, for that matter, the few available tyrannies, mounted. Not even military commanders receiving parades, of which these days there are fewer and fewer. Horsemen have left our precincts almost entirely. To be sure, we still have our mounted police; and there is perhaps no greater *Schadenfreude* for a New Yorker than to watch one of these Lochinvars in the saddle issuing a traffic ticket to an illegally parked car while his hackney is sniffing at the victim's hood. But when we erect monuments to our leaders and public heroes these days, there are only two feet resting on the pediment. Well, too bad, since a horse used to symbolize quite a lot: empires, virility, nature. Actually, there is a whole etiquette of equestrian statuary, as when a horse for instance rears up under the rider, it means that the latter died in battle. If all of its four hooves rest on the pediment, that suggests he died in his four-poster. If one leg is lifted high up in the air, then the implication is that he died of battle-related wounds; if not so high up, that he lived long enough, trotting as it were through his existence. You can't do that with a car. Besides, a car, even a Rolls, doesn't bespeak one's uniqueness, nor does it elevate one above the crowd the way a horse does. Roman emperors in particular used to be depicted on horseback not in order to commemorate their preferred mode of transportation but precisely to convey their superiority: their belonging, often by birth, to the equestrian class. In the parlance of the time, "equestrian" presumably meant "high up" or "high born." An equus, in other words, in addition to carrying an actual rider, was saddled with a lot of allusions. Above all, it could represent the past, if only because it represented the animal kingdom and that's where the past came from. Maybe this is what Caligula had in mind after all when he introduced his horse to the Senate. Since antiquity seems to have made this connection already. Since it had far more truck with the past than with the future.

# III

What the past and the future have in common is our imagination, which conjures them. And our imagination is rooted in our eschatological dread: the dread of thinking that we are without precedence or consequence. The stronger that dread, the more detailed our notion of antiquity or of utopia. Sometimes—actually, all too often—they overlap, as when antiquity appears to possess an ideal order and abundance of virtues, or when the inhabitants of our utopias stroll through their marble well-governed cities clad in togas. Marble is to be sure the perennial building material of our antiquity and utopia alike. On the whole, the color white permeates our imagination all the way through its extreme ends, when its version of the past or the future takes a metaphysical or religious turn. Paradise is white, so are ancient Greece and Rome. This predilection is not so much an alternative to the darkness of our fancy's source as a metaphor for our ignorance, or simply a reflection of the material our fancy normally employs for its flight: paper. A crumpled paper ball on its way to the waste basket could easily be taken for a splinter of a civilization, especially with your glasses off.

## IV

I first saw this bronze horseman indeed through a windshield of a taxi some twenty years ago, almost in a previous incarnation. I'd just landed in Rome for the first time, and was on my way to the hotel, where a distant acquaintance of mine had made a reservation. The hotel bore a very un-Roman name: it was called "Bolivar." Something equestrian was already in the air, since the great *libertador* is normally depicted atop his rearing horse. Did he die in battle? I couldn't remember. Presently we were stuck in the evening traffic in what looked like a cross between a railroad station's square and the end of a soccer game. I wanted to ask the driver how far we had to go, but my Italian was good only for "Where are we?" "Piazza Venezia," he blurted, nodding to the left. "Campidoglio," a nod to the right. And with another nod: "Marco Aurelio," followed by what was no doubt an energetic reference to the traffic. I looked to the right. "Marco Aurelio," I repeated to myself, and felt as if two thousand years were collapsing, dissolving in my mouth thanks to the Italian's familiar form of this emperor's name. Which always had for me an epic, indeed imperial, sway, sounding like a caesura-studded, thundering announcement by history's own major-domo: Marcus!—caesura—Aurelius! The Roman! Emperor! Marcus! Aurelius! This is how I knew him in high school, where the major-domo was our own stumpy Sarah Isaakovna, a very Jewish and very resigned lady in her fifties, who taught us history. Yet for all her resignation, when it came to uttering the names of Roman emperors, she'd straighten up, assuming an attitude of grandeur, and practically shout, well above our heads, into the peeling-off stucco of the classroom wall adorned with its portrait of Stalin: Caius Julius Caesar! Caesar Octavian Augustus! Caesar Tiberius! Caesar Vespasianus Flavius! The Roman Emperor Antoninus Pius! And then—Marcus Aurelius! It was as though the names were bigger than she herself, as though they were swelling up from inside to be released into a far greater space than her own body, or, for that matter, the room, the country, the times themselves could contain. She reveled in those odd-sounding foreign names, in their unpredictable succession of vowels and consonants, and that was, frankly, contagious. A child loves this sort of thing: strange words, strange sounds, and that's why, I suppose, history is best taught in childhood. At the age of twelve one may not grasp the intrigue, but a strange sound suggests an alternative reality. "Marcus Aurelius" certainly did to me, and that reality proved to be quite vast: larger, in fact, than that emperor's own. Now apparently came time to domesticate that reality; which is why, I suppose, I was in Rome. "Marco Aurelio, eh?" I said to myself, and turned to the driver: "Where?" He pointed to the top of a huge waterfall of marble steps leading uphill, now right in front of us, and as the car sharply swerved to gain some miniscule advantage in the sea of traffic, I momentarily beheld a floodlit pair of horse's ears, a bearded head, and a protruding arm. Then the sea swallowed us up. Half an hour later, at the entrance to the Bolivar, my valet-pack in one hand, my money in another, I asked the driver in a sudden surge of fraternity and gratitude—after all, he was the first person I had spoken with in Rome and he had also brought me to my hotel and didn't even overcharge me, or so it seemed—his name. "Marco," he said, and drove off.

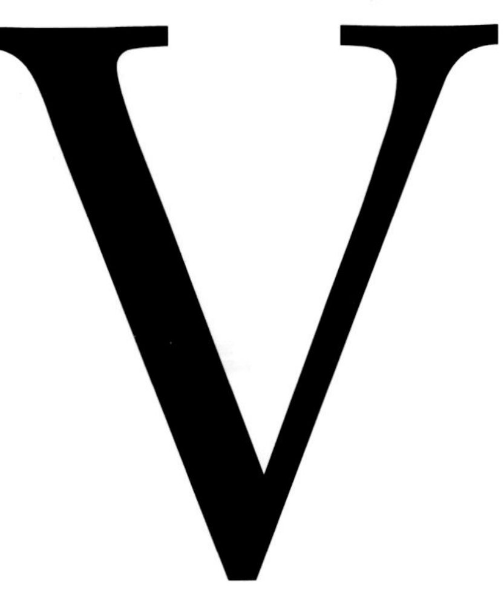

The most definitive feature of antiquity is our absence. The more available its debris and the longer you stare at it, the more you are denied entry. Marble negates you particularly well, though bronze and papyri don't fall too far behind. Reaching us intact or in fragments, these things strike us of course with their durability and tempt us to assemble them, fragments especially, into a coherent whole, but they were not meant to reach us. They were, and still are, for themselves. For man's appetite for the future is as limited as his own ability to consume time is, or as grammar, this first casualty of every discourse on the subject of the hereafter, shows. At best, these marbles, bronzes, and papyri were meant to outlast their subjects and their makers but not themselves. Their existence was functional, which is to say, of limited purpose. Time is no jigsaw puzzle, because it is made up of perishing pieces. And though perhaps objects-inspired, the idea of the afterlife wasn't an option until quite late. Anyhow, what is before us are the leftovers of necessity or vanity, i.e., of considerations always near-sighted. Nothing exists for the future's sake; and the ancients couldn't in nature regard themselves as the ancients. Nor should we bill ourselves as their tomorrow. We won't be admitted into antiquity: it was well inhabited, in fact, overpopulated, as it was. There are no vacancies. No point in busting your knuckles against marble.

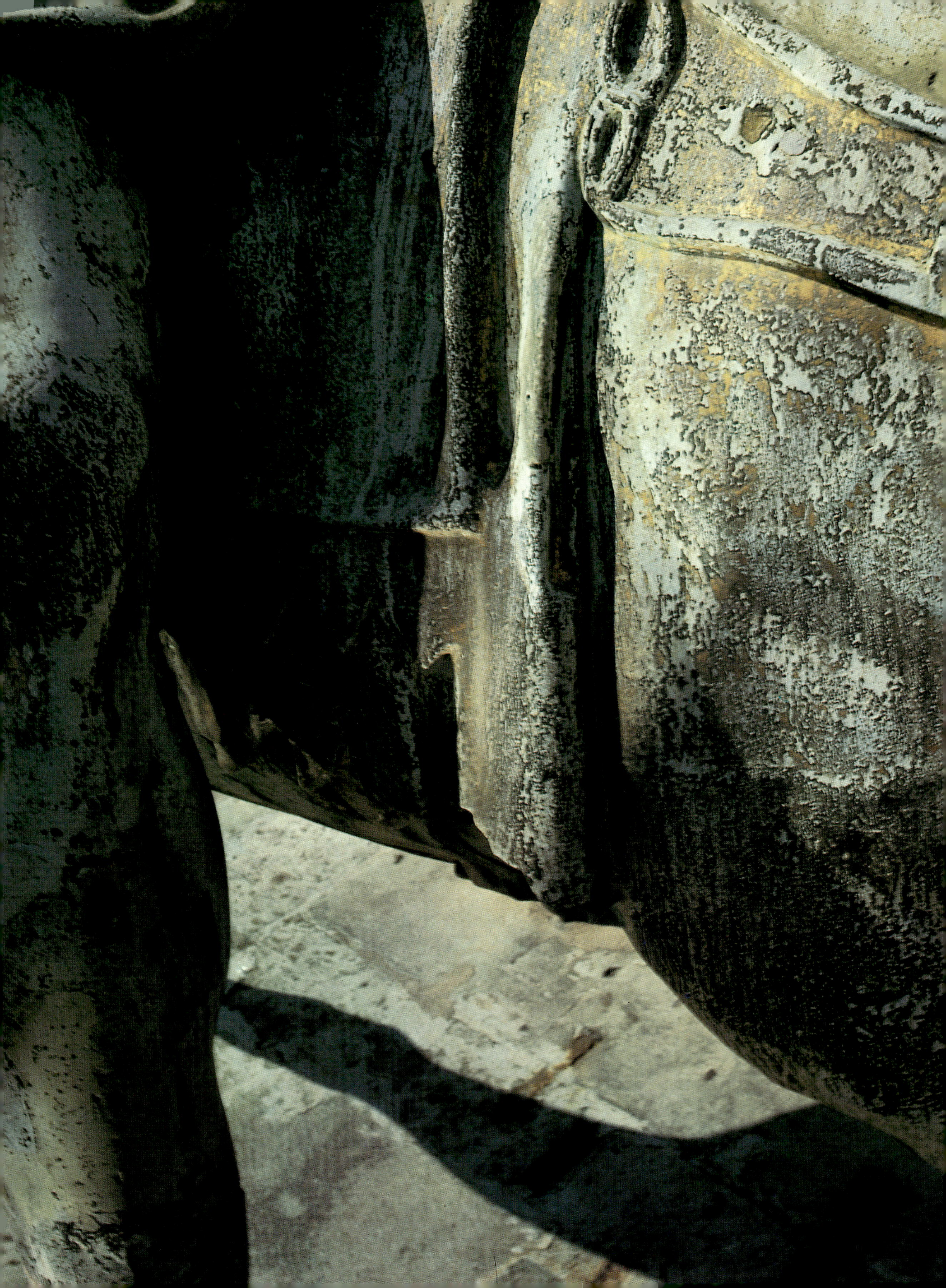

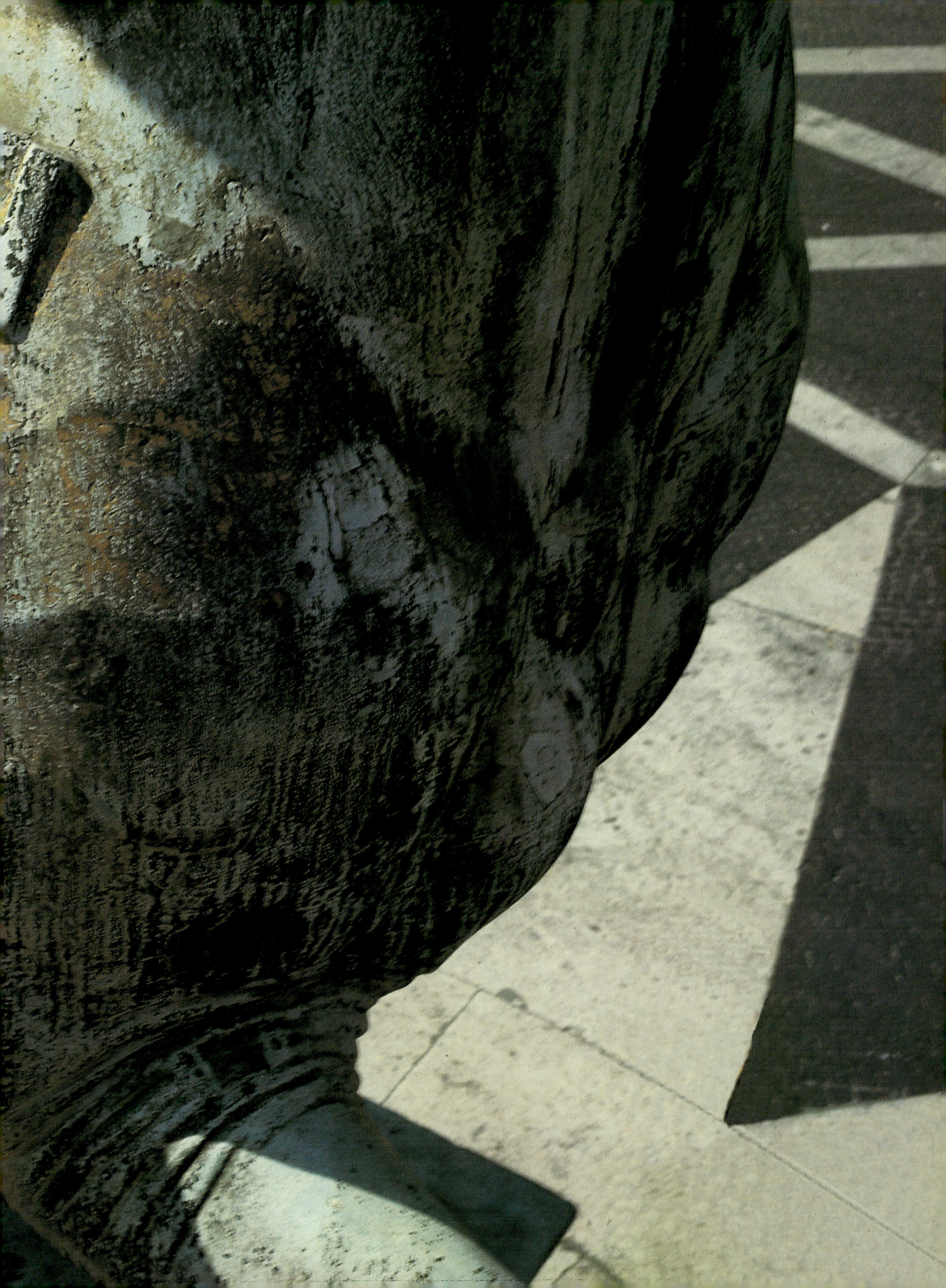

## VI

If we find the lives of Roman emperors highly absorbing, it is because we are highly self-absorbed creatures. To say the least, we regard ourselves as centers of our own universes, varying to be sure in width, but universes nonetheless, and as such having centers. The difference between an empire and a family, a network of friends, a web of romantic entanglements, a field of expertise, etc., is a difference in volume, not in structure. Also, because the caesars are so much removed from us in time, the complexity of their predicament appears to be graspable, shrunk, as it were, by the perspective of two millennia to almost a fairy-tale scale, with its wonders and its naïveté. Our address books are their empires, especially after hours. One reads Suetonius or Aelius or, for that matter, Psellus, for archetypes even if all one runs is a bike shop or a household of two. Somehow it is easier to identify with a caesar than with a consul, or praetor, or lictor, or slave, even though that is what one's actual station in the modern reality corresponds to. This has nothing to do with self-aggrandizement or aspirations but is due to the understandable attraction of king-size (so to speak), clear-cut versions of compromised virtue, vice, or self-delusion rather than their fuzzy, inarticulate originals next door or, for that matter, in the mirror. That's why, perhaps, one looks at their likenesses, at the marbles especially. For in the end, a human oval can accommodate only so much. You can't have more than two eyes or less than one mouth; surrealism wasn't yet invented and African masks were not yet in vogue. (Or maybe the Romans clung so much to Greek standards precisely because they were.) So in the end you are bound to recognize yourself in one of them. For there is no caesar without a bust, as there is no swan without a reflection. Clean-shaven, bearded, bald, or well coiffed, they all return a vacant, pupil-free marble stare, pretty much like that of a passport photo or the mug-shot of a criminal. You won't know what they have been up to; and putting these faces to their stories is what, perhaps, makes them indeed archetypal. It also moves them somewhat closer to us, since, being depicted fairly often, they, no doubt, must also have developed a degree of detachment vis-à-vis their physical reality. In any case, to them a bust or a statue was indeed what a photograph is to us, and the most "photographed" person would obviously be a caesar. There were of course others: their wives, senators, consuls, praetors, great athletes or beauties, actors and orators. On the whole, though, judging by what has survived, men were chiseled more often than women, which presumably reflects who controlled the purse as much as the society's ethos. By either standard, a caesar would be a winner. In the Capitoline Museum you can shuffle for hours through chambers filled up practically to the rafters with rows and rows of marble portraits of caesars, emperors, dictators, augusti hoarded there from all over what used to be the place they ran. The longer one stayed on the job, the more numerous would be one's "photographs." One would be depicted in one's youth, maturity, decrepitude; sometimes the distance between one's busts is no more, it would seem, than a couple of years. It appears that marble portraiture was an industry, and, with its calibrations of decay, something of a mortuary one; the rooms strike you in the end as not unlike a library housing the encyclopedia of a beheading. It is hard to "read," though, because marble is notoriously blank. In a sense, what it also has in common with photography—or, more accurately, with what photographs used to be—is that it is literally monochrome. For one thing, it renders everyone blond. Whereas in their real lives, some of the models—caesars' wives, to say the least, since many of them came from Asia Minor—were not. Yet one is almost grateful to marble for its lack of pigmentation, the way one is grateful to a black-and-white photograph, for it unleashes one's fantasy, one's intuition, so that viewing becomes an act of complicity: like reading.

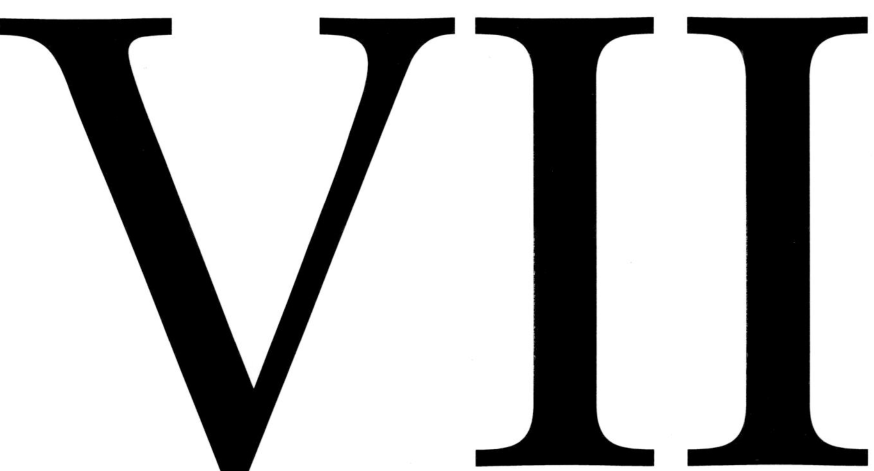

And there are ways of turning viewing into reading. When I was a boy I used to frequent a big museum in my hometown. It had a vast collection of Greek and Roman marbles, not to mention those by Canova and Thorvaldsen. I'd noticed that, depending on the time of day as well as the season, those carved features would wear different expressions, and I wondered what they would look like after hours. But the museum closed at 6 P.M., presumably because the marbles were not accustomed to electricity. I couldn't do much about that. In general, one can't do much about statues anyway. One can circle around them, squint at them from different angles; but that's that. With busts, though, one can go a bit further, as I discovered inadvertently. One day, staring at the little white face of some early Roman fanciulla, I lifted my hand, presumably to smooth my hair, and thus obstructed the single source of light coming to her from the ceiling. At once her facial expression changed. I moved my hand a bit to the side: it changed again. I began moving both of my arms rather frantically, casting each time a different shadow upon her features: the face came to life. Eventually, of course, I was interrupted by the shrieks of the guard. He ran toward me, but looking at his screaming face I thought it less animated than that of a little marble girl from B.C.

# VIII

Of all Roman emperors, Marcus Aurelius gets the best press. Historians love him, and so do philosophers. It is to the latter, though, that Marcus Aurelius owes his good standing to this day, since this discipline proved to be more durable than the Roman Empire or the aspects of one's statecraft in it. Actually, historians should be perhaps less enthusiastic about him than they are, because a couple of times he came very close to depriving them of their subject, particularly by designating his son, the really moronic Commodus, to be his heir. But historians are a sturdy lot; they've digested things much harder than Commodus's idea of renaming Rome after himself. They could live with—as well as live in—Commodiopolis and research the history of the Commodian Empire. As for philosophers, they were, and some still are, enamored of Marcus Aurelius's *Meditations* perhaps not so much for the depth of its probing as the respectability the discipline itself gained in the royal embrace. Politics is far more often the pursuit of philosophers than philosophy is the sideline of kings. Besides, for Marcus Aurelius philosophy was a lot more than a sideline: it was, as we'd say today, a therapy, or, as Boethius put it later, a consolation. He wasn't a great philosopher, nor was he a visionary; not even a sage; his *Meditations* is at once a melancholy and repetitive book. The Stoic doctrine at the time had become a doctrine indeed, and, though he did write in Greek, he is no match for Epictetus. Most likely a Roman emperor was drawn to this kind of language out of respect for the doctrine's origins, and also perhaps out of nostalgia, in order not to forget the language of civilized discourse; the language, after all, of his youth and pursuits more noble perhaps than those at hand. Add to that, if you will, possible considerations of secrecy, and the benefit of detachment: the purpose and the method of the discipline itself, enhanced here by the very means of expression. Not to mention that his reign simply happened to coincide with a substantial revival of Greek culture in Rome, the first Renaissance, if you will, owing no doubt to the long era of considerable stability historians dubbed the "Pax Romana." And historians love Marcus Aurelius precisely because he was the last guardian of that Pax. Because his reign effectively and neatly concluded a period of Roman history lasting nearly two centuries that began with Augustus and, to all intents and purposes, ended with our man. They love him because he is the end of the line, and a very coherent one at that: which, for historians, is a luxury. Marcus was a highly conscientious ruler; perhaps because he was appointed to the job, not anointed; because he was adopted into the dynasty, not born to it. And both historians and philosophers love him precisely for carrying out so well the commission for which he thought himself ill suited, and was in fact reluctant to accept. To them, his predicament presumably echoes in some fashion their own: he is as it were a model for those who have to go in this life against their calling. In any case, the Roman Empire gained a lot more from his dual loyalty to duty and philosophy than did the Stoic doctrine (which, in its own turn, comes with Marcus to the end of its own line: ethics). So much so that it's been maintained, often vigorously, that this sort of inner split is a good recipe for ruling. That it's better if one's spiritual yearnings have their own outlet and don't interfere too much with one's actions. This is what the whole philosopher-king business is all about, isn't it? When your metaphysics get short shrift. As for Marcus, however, he dreaded this prospect from the very beginning, dreaded being summoned to Hadrian's court, for all its comforts and bright perspectives. Perhaps precisely because of those; a true product of the Greek doctrine, all he aspired to was "the camp-bed and skin coverlet." Philosophy for him was a manner of dressing as much as it was a manner of discourse: the texture of existence, not just a mental pursuit. Picture him as a Buddhist monk then; you won't be much off target, since the "way of life" was the essence of Stoicism as well; emphatically so, we may add. The young Marcus must have been apprehensive of the royal adoption for more reasons than Hadrian's sexual predilections: it meant a wardrobe as different as the accompanying mental diet. That he went for it had to do, one imagines, less with royal pressure than with our man's own misgivings about his intellectual fortitude: apparently it's easier to be a king than a philosopher. Anyhow, it came to pass, and here's a monument. The good question, though, is, to whom? To a philosopher? Or to a king? To both? Perhaps to neither.

# IX

A monument is by and large a vertical affair, a symbolic departure from the general horizontality of existence, an antithesis to spatial monotony. A monument never actually departs from this horizontality—well, nothing does—but rather rests upon it, punctuating it at the same time like an exclamation mark. In principle, a monument is a contradiction. In this way, it resembles its most frequent subject: a human being, equally endowed with vertical and horizontal properties, but eventually settling for the latter. The durability of the material a monument is usually made of—marble, bronze, increasingly cast-iron, and now even concrete—highlights the contradictory nature of the undertaking even further, especially if a monument's subject is a great battle, a revolution, or a natural disaster—i.e., an event that took a great toll and was momentary. Yet even if the subject is an abstract ideal or the consequences of a momentous event, there is a detectable clash of time-frames and notions of viability, not to mention textures. Perhaps given the material's aspiration for permanence, the best subject for a monument is indeed destruction. Zadkin's statue of bombed-out Rotterdam immediately comes to mind: its verticality is functional, since it points at the catastrophe's very source. Also, what could be more horizontal than the Netherlands? And it occurs to one that the monument owes its genealogy to great planes, to the idea of something being seen from afar—whether in a spatial or a temporal sense. That it is of nomadic origin, for at least in a temporal sense we are all nomads. A man as aware of the futility of all human endeavor as our philosopher-king would of course be the first to object to being turned into a public statue. On the other hand, twenty years of what appears to have been practically nonstop frontier combat, taking him all over the place, effectively turned him into a nomad. Besides, here's his horse.

# X

The Eternal City is a city of hills, though. Of seven of them, actually. Some are natural, some artificial, but negotiating them is an ordeal in any case, especially on foot and especially in summer, although the adjacent seasons' temperatures don't fall too far behind. Add to that the emperor's rather precarious health; add to that its not getting any better with age. Hence, a horse. The monument sitting at the top of the Capitoline actually fills up the vacuum left by Marcus's mounted figure, which, some two thousand years ago, occupied that space quite frequently, not to say routinely. On the way to the Forum, as the saying goes. Actually, on his way from it. Were it not for Michelangelo's pedestal, the monument would be a footprint. Better yet a hoof print. The Romans, superstitious like all Italians, maintain that when the bronze Marcus hits the ground, the end of the world will occur. Whatever the origin of this superstition, it stands to reason if one bears in mind that Marcus's motto was Equanimity. The word suggests balance, composure under pressure, evenness of mental disposition; literally: equation of the animus, i.e., keeping the soul—and thus the world—in check. Give this formula of the Stoic posture a possible misspelling, and you'll get the monument's definition: Equinimity. The horseman tilts, though, somewhat, as if leaning toward his subjects, and his hand is stretched out in a gesture that is a cross between a greeting and a blessing. So much so that for a while some insisted that this was not Marcus Aurelius but Constantine, who converted Rome to Christianity. For that, however, the horseman's face is too serene, too free of zeal or ardor, too uninvolved. It is the face of detachment, not of love—and detachment is precisely what Christianity never could manage. No, this is no Constantine, and no Christian. The face is devoid of any sentiment; it is a postscript to passions, and the lowered corners of the mouth bespeak the lack of illusion. Had there been a smile, you could think perhaps of the Buddha; but the Stoics knew too much about physics to toy with the finality of human existence in any fashion. The face shines with the bronze's original gold but the hair and the beard have oxidized and turned green, the way one turns gray. All thought aspires to the condition of metal; and the bronze denies you any entry, including interpretation or touch. What you've got here, then, is detachment per se. And out of this detachment the emperor leans toward you slightly, extending his right hand either to greet you or to bless you—which is to say acknowledge your presence. For where he is, there is no you, and vice versa. The left hand theoretically holds the reins, which are either missing now or were never there in the first place: a horse would obey this rider no matter what. Especially if it represented Nature. For he represents Reason. The face is clearly of the Antonine dynasty, though he wasn't born into it but adopted. The hair, the beard, the somewhat bulging eyes and slightly apoplectic posture are those of his stepfather turned father-in-law and his very own son. Small wonder that it is so hard to tell the three of them apart among the Ostia marbles. But, as we know nowadays, a period's fashion may easily beat the genes. Remember the Beatles. Besides, he revered Antoninus Pius enough to emulate him in a variety of ways; his appearance could be simply that attitude's spin-off. Also the sculptor, being a contemporary, might have wished to convey the sense of continuum perceived by the historians of the step-father's and the step-son's reigns: a sense that Marcus himself, needless to say, sought to create. Or else the sculptor just tried to produce a generic portrait of the era, of the perfect ruler, and what we've got here is the fusion of the two best emperors the realm had had since the murder of Domitian—the way he did the horse, whose identity we don't ponder. In all probability, however, this is the author of the *Meditations* himself: the face and the torso slightly tilted toward his subjects fit extremely well the text of that melancholy book, which itself leans somewhat toward the reality of human existence, in the attitude not so much of a judge as of an umpire. In this sense this monument is a statue to a statue: it's hard to picture a Stoic in motion.

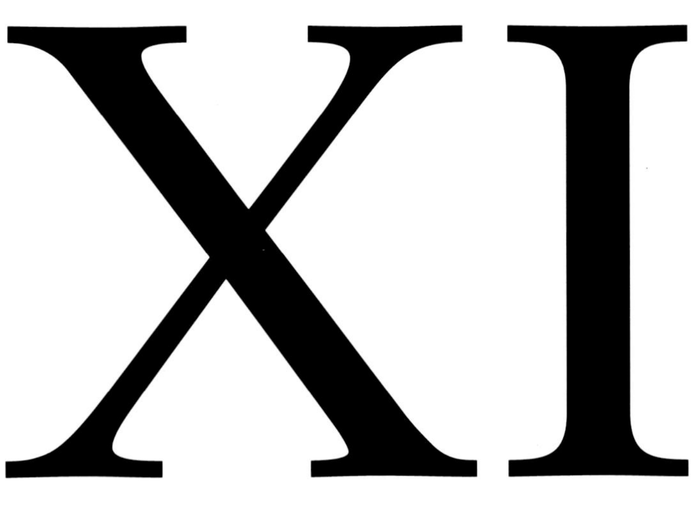


The Eternal City resembles a gigantic old brain that long ago gave up any interest in the world—it being too graspable a proposition—and settled for its own crevasses and folds. Negotiating their narrows, where even a thought about yourself is too cumbersome, or their expanses, where the concept of the universe itself appears puny, you feel like a worn-out needle shuffling the grooves of a vast record—to the center and back—extracting with your soles the tune that the days of yore hum to the present. This is the real His Master's Voice for you, and it turns your heart into a dog. History is not a discipline but something that is not yours—which is the main definition of beauty. Hence the sentiment, for it is not going to love you back. It is a one-way affair, and you recognize its Platonic nature in this city instantly. The closer you get to the object of your desire, the more marble or bronze it gets, as the natives' fabled profiles scatter around like animated coins escaped from some broken terra-cotta jar. It is as though here time puts, between bedsheets and mattress, its own carbon paper—since time mints as much as it types. The moment you leave the Bolivar or the equally smelly yet cheaper Nerva, you hit Foro Trajano with its triumphant column tightly wrapped in conquered Dacians and soaring like a mast above the marble ice floe of broken pillars, capitols, and cornices. Now this is the domain of stray cats, reduced lions in this city of reduced Christians. The huge white slabs and blocks are too unwieldy and random to arrange them in a semblance of order or drag them away. They are left here to absorb the sun, or to represent "antiquity." In a sense they do; their ill-matching shapes are a democracy, this place is still a Forum. And on his way from it, just across the road, beyond pines and cypresses, atop the Capitoline Hill, stands the man who made the fusion of republic and imperial rule probable. He has no company: virtue, like a malady, alienates. For a split second, it is still A.D. 176 or thereabouts, and the brain ponders the world.

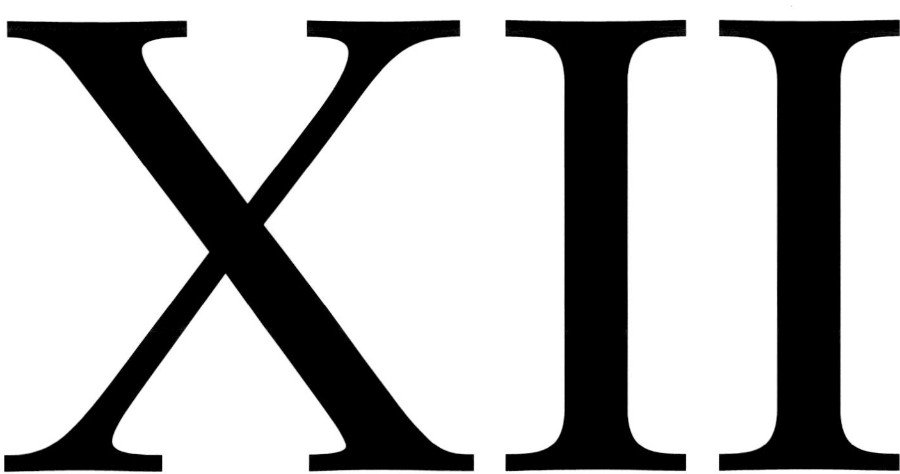

Marcus was a good ruler and a lonely man. In his line of work, loneliness of course comes with the territory; but he was lonelier than most. *Meditations* gives you a greater taste of that than his correspondence; yet it is just a taste. The meal had many courses and was pretty heavy. To begin with, he knew that his life had been subverted. For the ancients, philosophy wasn't a by-product of life but the other way around, and Stoicism was particularly exacting. Perhaps we should momentarily dispense here with the very word philosophy, for Stoicism, its Roman version especially, shouldn't be characterized as love for knowledge. It was rather a lifelong experiment in endurance, and a

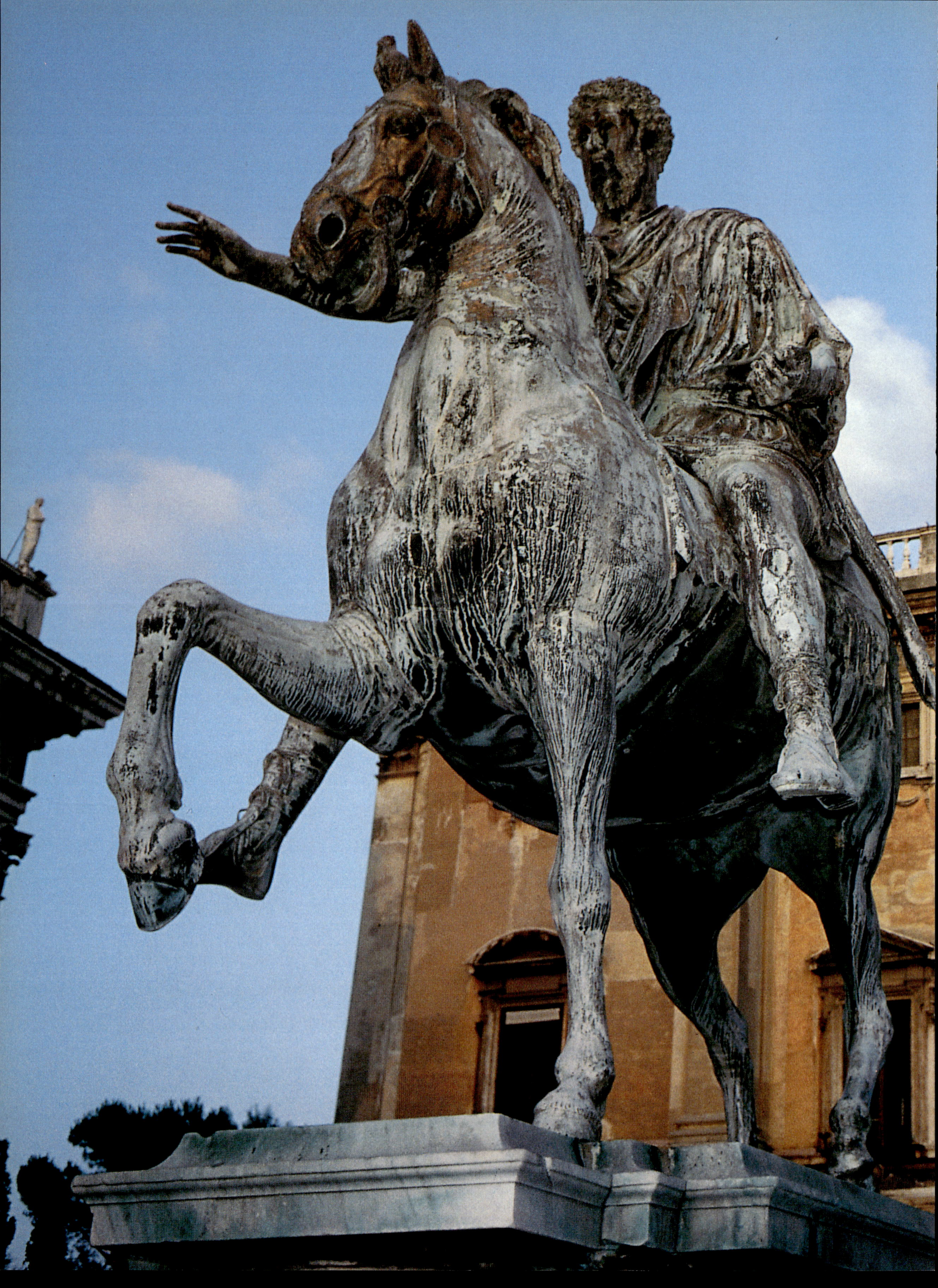

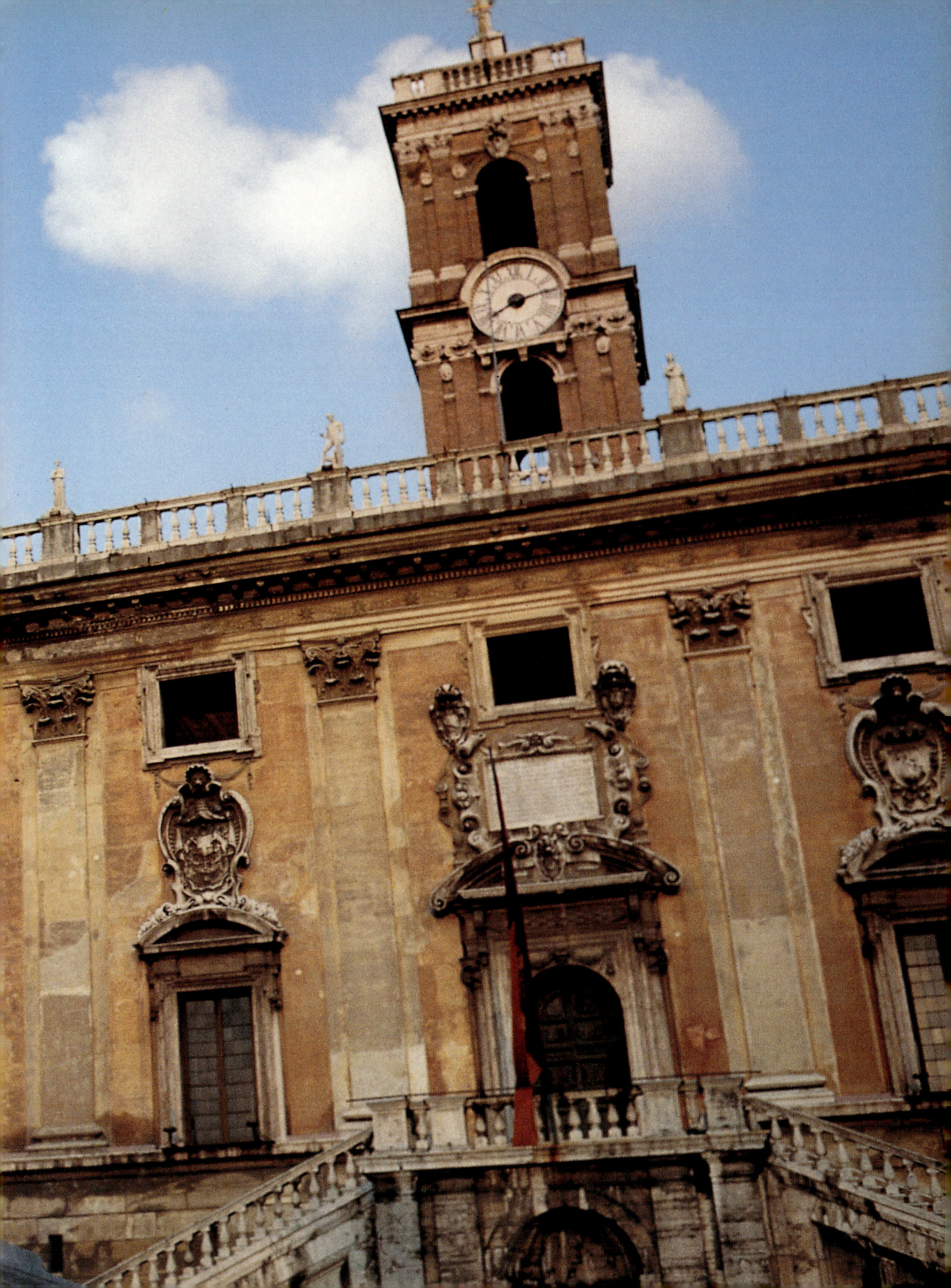

man was his own guinea pig: he was not a probing instrument, he was an answering instrument. By the time of Marcus, the doctrine's knowledge was to be lived rather than loved. Its materialist monism, its cosmogony, its logic, and its criterion of truth (the perception that irresistibly compels the subject to assent to it as true) were already in place, and for a philosopher, life's purpose was to prove the validity of this knowledge by applying it to reality till the end of his days. In other words, a Stoic's life was a study in ethics, since ethics buys nothing except osmosis. And Marcus knew that his experiment was interrupted, or qualified, to a degree he himself wouldn't be able to comprehend; worse still, that his findings—provided there were any—could have no application. He believed Plato, but not to this extent. At any rate, he would be the first to square the common good with individual unhappiness, and that's what *Meditations* is perhaps all about: a postscript to *The Republic*. He knew that as a philosopher he was finished: that concentration was out, that all he could hope for was some time for sporadic contemplation. That the best that his life would amount to would be a few glimpses of eternity, a true surmise now and then. He accepted that, for the sake of the common good no doubt, but hence *Meditations'* overriding melancholy or, if you will, pessimism—all the more deep because the man definitely suspected that there was rather more to the story. *Meditations* is a patchy book, nurtured by interference. It is a disjointed, rambling internal monologue, with occasional flashes of pedantry as well as of genius. It shows you what he might have been rather than what he was: his vector, rather than an attained destination. It appears to have been jotted down amidst the hubbub and babel of this or that military campaign, successful as they might have been—by the campfire, indeed, and the soldier's cloak played the Stoic philosopher's body coverlet. In other words, it was done in spite of—or, if you will, against—history, of which his destiny was trying to make him a part. A pessimist he perhaps was, but certainly not a determinist. That's why he was a good ruler, why the mixture of republic and imperial rule under him didn't look like a sham. (One may even argue that the larger democracies of the modern world show an increasing preference for his formula. Good examples are contagious, too; but virtue, as we said, alienates. Not to mention that time, wasting its carbon paper on subjects, seems to have very little left for rulers.) To say the least, he was a good caretaker: he didn't lose what he inherited; and if the Empire under him didn't expand, it was just as well;

as Augustus said, "enough is enough." For somebody in charge of an entity so vast and for so long (practically thirty-three years, from A.D. 147, when his father-in-law conferred upon him the powers of emperorship, to his death in A.D. 181 near the would-be Vienna), he has surprisingly little blood on his hands. He would rather pardon than punish those who rebelled against him; those who fought him, he would rather subdue than destroy. The laws he made benefited the most powerless: widows, slaves, juniors, although it must be said that he was the first to introduce the double standard in prosecuting criminal offenses by members of the Senate (the office of special prosecutor was his invention). He used the state's purse sparingly and, being abstemious himself, tried to encourage this in others. On several occasions, when the Empire needed money, he sold imperial jewels rather than hit his subjects up for new taxes. Nor did he build anything extravagant, no Pantheon or Coliseum. In the first place, because those already existed; secondly, because his sojourn in Egypt was quite brief and he didn't go beyond Alexandria, unlike Agrippa and unlike Titus and Hadrian, to have his mind fired up by the gigantic, desert-fitting scale of Egyptian edifices. Besides, he didn't like circenze that much and when he had to attend a show, he is reported to have read or written or been briefed during the performance. It was he, however, who introduced to the Roman Circus the safety net for acrobats.

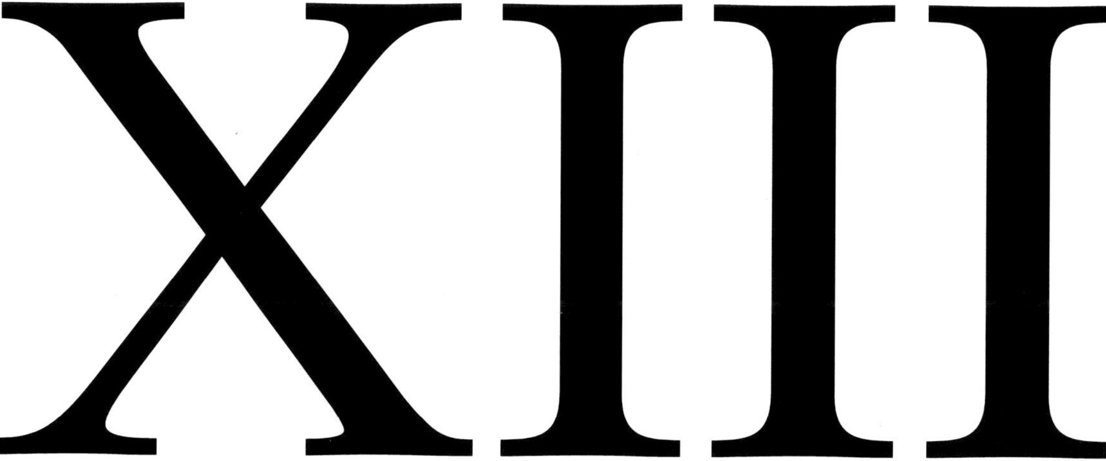

Antiquity is above all a visual concept, generated by objects whose age escapes definition. The Latin "anticum" is essentially a more drastic term for "old," deriving from the equally Latin "ante," which means "before," and used to be applied presumably to things Greek. "Beforishness," then. As for the Greeks themselves, their "arche" denotes beginning or genesis, the moment when something occurs for the first time. "Firstness," then? Herein in any case lies a substantial distinction between the Romans and the Greeks—a distinction owing its existence partly to the Greeks having fewer objects at their disposal to fathom the provenance of, partly to their general predilection for dwelling on origins. The former, in fact, may very well be an explanation for the latter, since next to archaeology there is only geology. As for our own version of antiquity, it eagerly swallows both the Greeks and the Romans, yet, if worse comes to worst, might cite the Latin precedent in its defense. Antiquity to us is a vast chronological jumble, filled with historical, mythical, and divine beings, interrelated among themselves by marble and also because a high percentage of the depicted mortals claim divine descendence or were deified. This last aspect, resulting in the practically identical scant attire of those marbles and in the confusion on our part of attributing fragments (did this splintered arm belong to a mortal or to a deity?), is worth noticing. The blurring of distinctions between mortals and deities was habitual with the ancients, with the Roman caesars in particular. While the Greeks on the whole were interested in lineage, the Romans were after promotion. The target, however, was the same: Celestial Mansions, yet vanity or boosting the ruler's authority played a rather small part in this. The whole point of identifying with the gods lies not so much in the notion of their omniscience as in the sense that their extreme carnality is fully matched by the extremes of their detachment. To begin with, a ruler's own margin of detachment would make him identify with a god (carnality, of course, would be Nero or Caligula's short cut). By acquiring a statue, he'd boost that margin considerably, and it's best if it's done in the course of one's lifetime, since marble reduces both the expectations of the subjects and the model's own willingness to deviate from manifest perfection. It sets one free, as it were, and freedom is the province of deities. Putting it very broadly, the marble and mental vista that we call antiquity is a great repository of shed and shredded skins, a landscape after the departure, if you will; a mask of freedom, a jumble of discarded boosters.

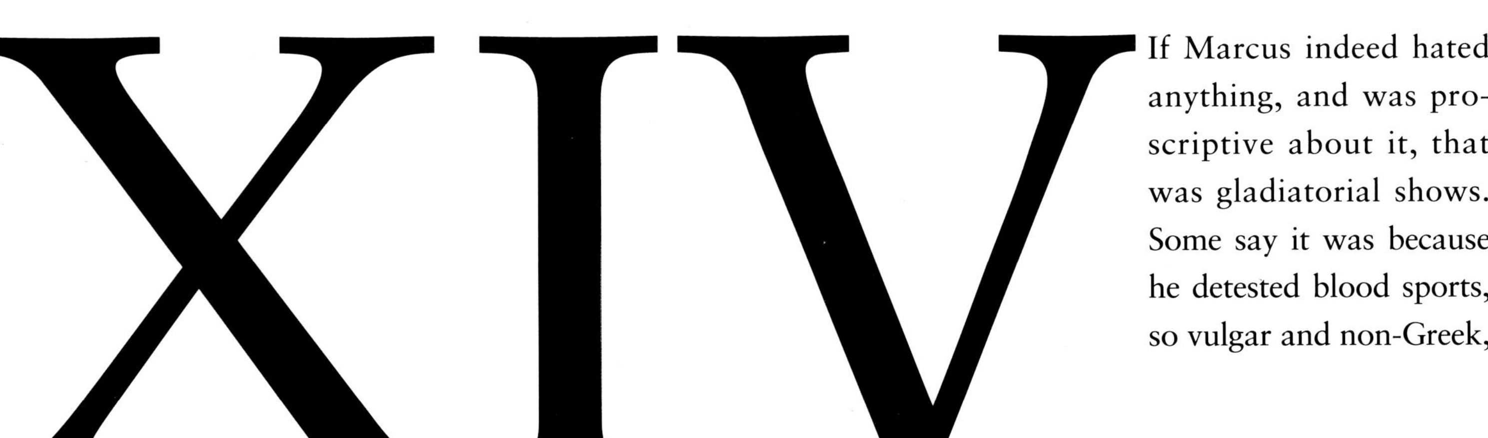

# XIV

If Marcus indeed hated anything, and was proscriptive about it, that was gladiatorial shows. Some say it was because he detested blood sports, so vulgar and non-Greek, because siding with a team would, for him, be the beginning of partiality. Others insist that it had to do with his wife, Faustina, who, for all her thirteen children—only six survived—was remarkably promiscuous for an empress. Among her numerous affairs, these others single out a particular gladiator who, they claim, was the real father of Commodus. But Nature works in mysterious ways; an apple often rolls far from the tree, especially if that tree grows on a slope. Commodus was both a rotten apple and its slope. Actually, as far as the imperial fortunes were concerned, he was a precipice. And perhaps an inability to grasp Nature's mysterious ways was the source of Faustina's reputation (though if Marcus had it against the gladiators because of Faustina, he should have proscribed also against sailors, pantomime actors, generals, and so forth). Marcus himself would make light of this. Once, approached with these rumors and the suggestion that he get rid of her, he retorted: "If we send our wife away, we must give back her dowry, too." The dowry here was the Empire itself, since Faustina was the daughter of Antoninus Pius. On the whole, he stood by her unswervingly, and judging by the honors he bestowed upon her when she died perhaps even loved her. She was, it appears, one of those heavy main courses whose taste you barely sample in the *Meditations*. In general, Caesar's wife is beyond reproach and suspicion. And perhaps precisely in order to uphold this attitude as well as to save Faustina's reputation Marcus departed from the nearly two-century-old tradition of selecting an heir to the throne and passed the crown to what he thus asserted to be his own flesh and blood. At any rate, it was Faustina's. His reverence for his father-in-law was enormous and he simply couldn't believe that someone in whose veins ran the blood of the Antonines could be all that bad. Perhaps he regarded Faustina as a force of Nature; and Nature for a Stoic philosopher was the ultimate authority. If anything, Nature taught him indifference and a sense of proportion; otherwise his life would have been pure hell; *Meditations* strings out solipsism like glacial debris. Toward the wrong and atrocious, Marcus was not so much forgiving as dismissive. Which is to say that he was impartial rather than just and that his impartiality was not the product of his mind's fairness but of his mind's appetite for the infinite; in particular, for impartiality's own limits. This would stun his subjects no less than it does his historians, for history is the domain of the partial. And as his subjects chided Marcus for his attitude toward gladiatorial shows, historians jumped on him for his persecution of Christians. It is unclear of course how much Marcus was informed about the Christian creed, but it is easy to imagine him finding its metaphysics myopic and its ethics detestable. From a Stoic point of view, a god with whom you trade in virtue to obtain eternal favors wouldn't be worth a prayer. For somebody like Marcus, virtue's value lay precisely in its being a gamble, not an investment. Intellectually, to say the least, he had very little reason to favor the Christians; still less could he do so as a ruler, faced at the time with wars, plague, uprisings—and a disobedient minority. Besides, he didn't introduce new laws against the Christians; those of Hadrian, and those of Trajan before him, were quite enough. It is obvious that, following his beloved Epictetus, Marcus regarded a philosopher, i.e., himself, as the missionary of Divine Providence to mankind, i.e., to his own subjects. You are welcome to quibble with his notion of it; one thing is quite clear, though: it was far more open-ended than the Christian version. Blessed are the partial, for they shall inherit the earth.

# XV

Take white, ochre, and blue; add to that a bit of green and a lot of geometry. You'll get the formula time has picked for its backdrop in these parts, since it is not without vanity, especially once it assumes the shape of history or of an individual. It does so out of its prurient interest in finality, in its reductive ability, if you will, for which it has numerous guises, including the human brain, or the human eye. So you shouldn't be surprised, especially if you were born here, to find yourself one day surrounded by the white-cum-ochre, trapezoid square with the white-cum-blue trapeze overhead. The former is human-made (actually, by Michelangelo), the latter is heaven-made, and you may recognize it more readily. However, neither is of use to you since you are green: the shade of oxidized bronze. And if the cumulus white in the oxygen blue overhead is still preferable to the balustrade's marble calves and well-tanned tiburtine chests below, it is because clouds remind you of your native antiquity: because they are the future of any architecture. Well, you've been around for nearly two thousand years, and you ought to know. Perhaps they, the clouds, are indeed the only true antiquity there is, if only because among them you are not a bronze.

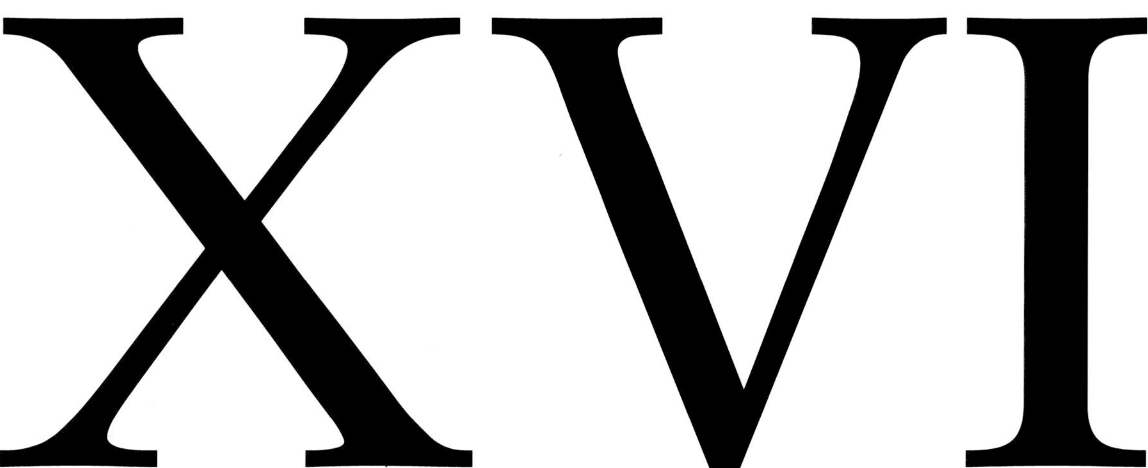

Ave, Caesar. How do you feel now, among barbarians? For we are barbarians to you, if only because we speak neither Greek nor Latin. We are also afraid of death far more than you ever were, and our herd-instinct is stronger than the one for self-preservation. Sound familiar? Maybe it's our numbers, Caesar, or maybe it's the number of our goods. We sure feel that by dying we stand to lose far more than you ever had, empire or no empire. To you, if I remember correctly, birth was an entrance, death an exit, life a little island in the ocean of particles. To us, you see, it's all a bit more melodramatic. What spooks us, I guess, is that an entrance is always guarded, whereas an exit isn't. We can't conceive of dwindling into particles again: after hoarding so many goods, that's unpalatable. Status's inertia, I guess, or fear of the elemental freedom. Be that as it may, Caesar, you are among barbarians. We are your true Parthians, Marcomanni, and Quadi, because nobody came in your stead, and we inhabit the earth. Some of us go even further, barging into your antiquity, supplying you with definitions. You can't respond, can't bless, can't greet or quell us with your outstretched right hand—the hand whose fingers still remember scribbling your *Meditations*. If that book hasn't civilized us, what will? Perhaps they billed you as the philosopher-king precisely to dodge its spell by underscoring your uniqueness. For theoretically what's unique isn't valid, Caesar, and you were unique. Still, you were no philosopher-king—you'd be the first to wince at this label. You were what the mixture of power and inquiry made you: a postscript to both, a uniquely autonomous entity, almost to the point of pathology. Hence your emphasis on ethics, for supreme power exempts one from the moral norm practically by definition, and so does supreme knowledge. You got both for the price of one, Caesar; that's why you had to be so bloody ethical. You wrote an entire book to keep your soul in check, to steel yourself for daily conduct. But was it really ethics that you were after, Caesar? Wasn't it your extraordinary appetite for the infinite that drove you to the most minute self-scrutiny, since you considered yourself a fragment, no matter how tiny, of the Whole, of the Universe—and the Universe, you maintained, changes constantly. So whom were you checking, Marcus? Whose morality did you try and, for all I know, manage to prove? Small wonder, then, that you are not surprised to find yourself now among the barbarians; small wonder that you always were far less afraid of them than of yourself—since you were afraid of yourself far more than of death. "Reflect that the chief source of all evils to man," says Epictetus, "as well as of baseness and cowardice, is not death but the fear of death." But you knew also that no man owns his future—or, for that matter, his past. That all one stands to lose by dying is the day when it happens—the day's remaining part, to be precise—and in time's eye, still less. The true pupil of Zeno, weren't you? At any rate, you wouldn't allow the prospect of nonbeing to color your being, Universe or no Universe. The eventual dance of particles, you held, should have no bearing upon the animated body, not to mention upon its reason. You were an island, Caesar, or at least your ethics were, an island in the primordial and—pardon the expression—postmordial ocean of free atoms. And your statue just marks the place on the map of the species' history where this island once stood: uninhabited, before submerging. The waves of doctrine and of creed—of the Stoic doctrine and the Christian creed—have closed over your head, claiming you as their own Atlantis. The truth, though, is that you never were either's. You were simply one of the best men that ever lived, and you were obsessed with your duty because you were obsessed with virtue. Because it's harder to master than the alternative and because, if the universal design had been evil, the world would not exist. Some will point out no doubt that the doctrine and the creed came before and after you, but it's not history that defines the good. To be sure, time, conscious of its monotony, calls forth men to tell its yesterday from its tomorrow. You, Caesar, were good because you didn't.

# XVII

I saw him for the last time a few years ago, on a wet winter night, in the company of a stray Dalmatian. I was returning by taxi to my hotel after one of the most disastrous evenings in my entire life. The next morning I was leaving Rome for the States. I was drunk. The traffic moved with the speed one wishes for one's funeral. At the foot of the Capitol I asked the driver to stop, paid, and got out of the car. The hotel was not far away and I guess I intended to continue on foot; instead, I climbed the hill. It was raining, not terribly hard but enough to turn the floodlights of the square, nay! trapeze, into fizzing-off Alka-Seltzer pellets. I hid myself under the Conservatory's arcade and looked around. The square was absolutely empty and the rain was taking a crash course in geometry. Presently I discovered I was not alone: a middle-sized Dalmatian appeared out of nowhere and quietly sat down a couple of feet away. Its sudden presence was so oddly comforting that momentarily I felt like offering it one of my cigarettes. I guess this had to do with the pattern of its spots; the dog's hide was the only place in the whole piazza free of human intervention. For a while we both stared at the horseman's statue. "The universal nature out of the universal substance, as if it were wax, now moulds the figure of a horse, then melting this down uses the material for a tree, next for a man, next for something else; and each of these things subsists for a very short time. Yet it is no hardship for a box to be broken up, as it was none for it to be nailed together." This is what a boy memorized at the age of fifteen and remembered thirty-five years later. Still, this horse didn't melt down, nor did this man. Apparently, the universal nature was satisfied with this version of its substance and cast it in bronze. And suddenly—presumably because of the rain and the rhythmic pattern of Michelangelo's pilasters and arches—all got blurred, and against that blur, the shining statue, devoid of any geometry, seemed to be moving. Not at great speed, and not out of this place; but enough for the Dalmatian to leave my side and follow the bronze progress.

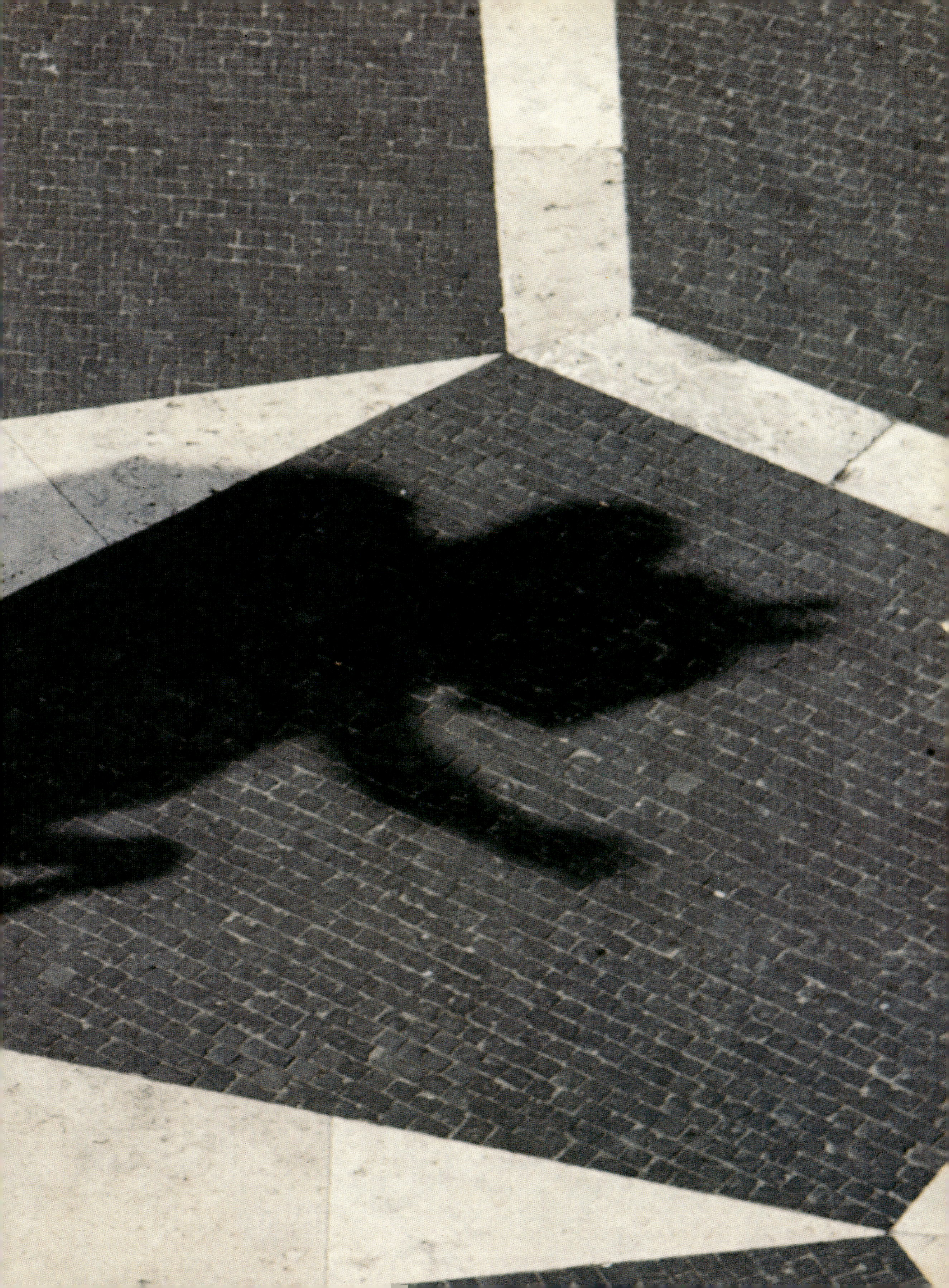

# XVIII

As absorbing as Roman antiquity appears to be, perhaps we should be a bit more careful with our retrospective proclivity. What if man-made chronology is but a self-fulfilling fallacy, a means of obscuring the backwardness of one's own intelligence? What if it's just a way of justifying the snail's pace of the species' evolution? And what if the very notion of such evolution is a lie? Ultimately, what if this good old sense of history is just the dormant majority's self-defense against the alert minority? What if our concept of antiquity, for example, is but the switching-off of an alarm clock? Let's take this horseman and his book. To begin with, *Meditations* wasn't written in the second century A.D. if only because its author wasn't going by the Christian calendar. In fact, the time of its composition is of no relevance, since its subject is precisely ethics. Unless, of course, humanity takes a special pride in having wasted fifteen centuries before Marcus's insights were reiterated by Spinoza. Maybe we are just better at counting than at thinking, or else we mistake the former for the latter? Why is it that we are always so interested in knowing when truth was uttered for the first time? Isn't this sort of archaeology in itself an indication that we are living a lie? In any case, if *Meditations* is antiquity, it is we who are the ruins. If only because we believe that ethics has the future. Well, perhaps our retrospective ability should indeed be reined in somewhat, lest it become all-consuming. For if nothing else, ethics is the criterion of the present—perhaps the only one there is, since it turns every yesterday and tomorrow into now. It is precisely that sort of arrow that at every moment of its flight is immobile. *Meditations* is no existential manual and it wasn't written for posterity. Nor should we, for that matter, be interested in the identity of its author or promote him to the rank of philosopher-king: ethics is an equalizer; thus the author here is everyman. His concept of duty cannot be attributed to his royal overdose of it, because he wasn't the only emperor around; neither can his resignation of the imperial origin, because one is able to empathize with it quite readily. Nor can we put it down to his philosophic training—and for the same reasons: there were too many philosophers apart from Marcus and, on the other hand, most of us are not Stoics. What if his sense of duty and his resignation were, in the first place, products of his individual temperament, of the melancholic disposition, if one wants to be precise; combined perhaps with the man's aging? There are after all only four known humors; so at least the melancholics among us can take this book to heart and skip the bit about the historical perspective nobody possesses anyhow. As for the sanguinics, cholerics, and phlegmatics, they too perhaps should admit that the melancholic version of ethics is accommodating enough for them to marvel at its pedigree and chronology. Perhaps short of compulsory Stoic indoctrination, the society may profit by making a detectable melancholic streak a prerequisite for anyone aspiring to rule it. To this extent, a democracy can afford what an Empire could. And on top of that, one shouldn't call the Stoic acceptance of the perceptible reality resignation. Serenity would be more apt, given the ratio between man and the subjects of his attention, or—as the case may be—vice versa. A grain of sand can't resign itself to the desert; and perhaps what's ultimately good about melancholics is that they seldom get hysterical. By and large, they are quite reasonable, and, "what is reasonable," as Marcus once said, "is consequently social." Did he say this in Greek, to fit your idea of antiquity?

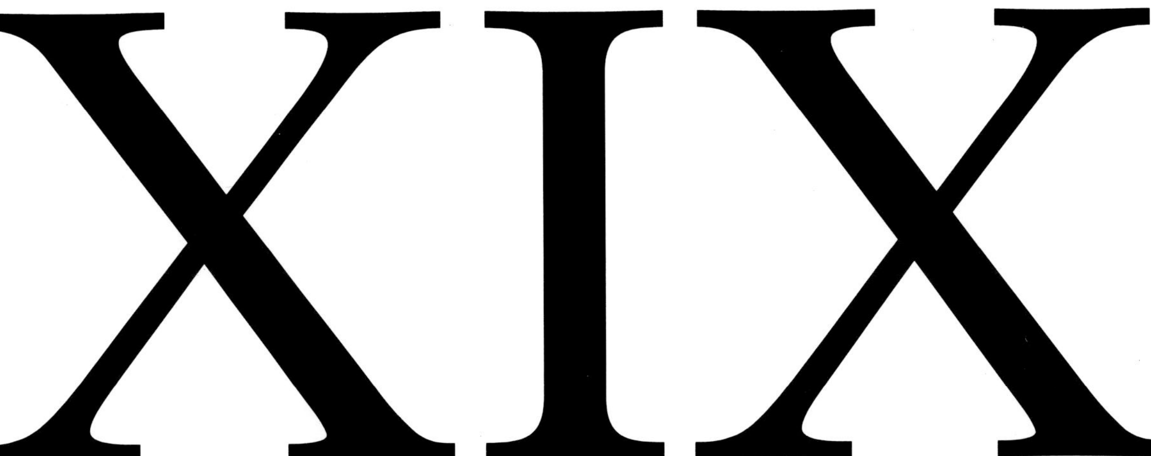

Of all Roman poets, Marcus knew best and preferred Seneca. Partly because Seneca too was of Spanish origin, sickly, and a great statesman; mainly, of course, because he was a Stoic. As for Catullus, Marcus would find him no doubt too hot and choleric. Ovid for him would be licentious and excessively ingenious, Virgil too heavy-handed and perhaps even servile, Propertius too obsessive and passionate. Horace? Horace would seem to be the most congenial author for Marcus, what with his equipoise and attachment to the Greek monody. Yet perhaps our emperor thought him too quirky, or too diverse and unsteady as well: in short, too much of a poet. In any case, there is almost no trace of Horace in *Meditations,* nor for that matter of the greatest among the Latins, Lucretius—another you would think a natural choice for Marcus. But then perhaps a Stoic didn't want to be depressed by an Epicurean. On the whole, Marcus seems to have been far more fluent in Greek literature, preferring dramatists and philosophers to poets of course, though snatches from Homer, Agathon, and Menander crop up in his book quite frequently. Come to think of it, if anything makes antiquity a coherent concept, it is the volume of its literature. The library of someone like Marcus would contain a hundred or so authors; another hundred perhaps would be hearsay, a rumor. Those were the good old days indeed: antiquity or no antiquity. And even that rumored writing would be limited to two languages: Greek and Latin. If you were he, if you were a Roman emperor, would you in the evening, to take your mind off your cares, read a Latin author if you had a choice? Even if he was Horace? No; too close for comfort. You'd pick up a Greek—because that's what you'll never be. Because a Greek, especially a philosopher, is in your eyes a more genuine item than yourself, since he knew no Latin. If only because of that he was less a relativist than you, who consider yourself practically a mongrel. So if he were a Stoic, you must take heed. You even may go so far as to take up a stylus yourself. Otherwise you might not fit into someone's notion of antiquity.

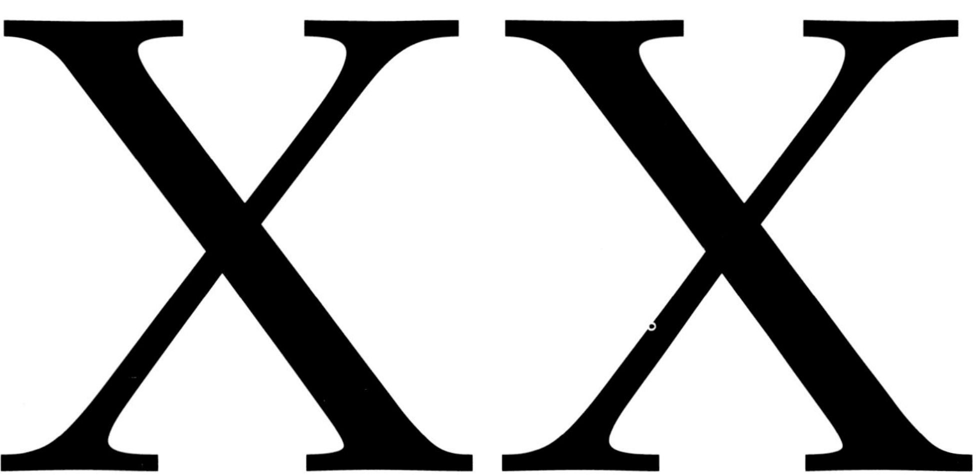

A stray Dalmatian trotting behind the bronze horseman hears something strange, sounding somewhat familiar but muffled by rain. He accelerates slightly, and, having overtaken the statue, lifts up his muzzle, hoping to grasp what's coming out of the horseman's mouth. In theory it should be easy for him, since his Dalmatia was the birthplace of so many caesars. He recognizes the language but fails to make out the accent:

*Take heed not to be transformed into Caesar, not to be dipped in purple dye; for it does happen. Keep yourself therefore simple, go pure, grave, unaffected, the friend of justice, religious, kind, affectionate, strong for your proper work. Wrestle to continue to be the man that Philosophy wished to make you. Reverence the gods, save men...*

*Let not the future trouble you, for you will come to it, if come you must, bearing with you the same reason which you are using now to meet the present.*

*All things are the same: familiar in experience, transient in time, sordid in their material; all now such as in the days of those whom we have buried.*

*To leave the company of men is nothing to fear, if gods exist; for they would not involve you in ill...*

*To turn against anything that comes to pass is a separation from Nature.*

*Men have come into the world for the sake of one another. Either instruct them then or bear with them.*

*The Universe is change, life is opinion.*

*Run always the short road, and Nature's road is short.*

*As are your repeated imaginations so will your mind be, for the soul is dyed by its imaginations.*

*Love that to which you go back, and don't return to Philosophy as to a schoolmaster, but as a man to the sponge and slave, as another to a poultice, another to fomentation...*

*The mind of the Whole is social.*

*The noblest kind of retribution is not to become like your enemy.*

*What doesn't benefit the hive is no benefit to the bee.*

*On Pain: what we cannot bear removes us from life; what lasts can be borne. The understanding, too, preserves its own tranquility by abstraction, and the governing self does not grow worse; but it is for the parts which are injured by pain, if they can, to declare it.*

*There are three relations. One is to what surrounds you. One to the divine cause from which all things come to pass for all. One to those who live at the same time with you.*

*Accept without pride, relinquish without struggle.*

And then there was nothing else, save the sound of rain crashing on Michelangelo's flagstones. The Dalmatian darted across the square like a piece of unearthed marble. He was heading no doubt for antiquity, and carried in his ears his master's—the statue's—voice:

*To acquaint yourself with these things for a hundred years, or for three, is the same.*

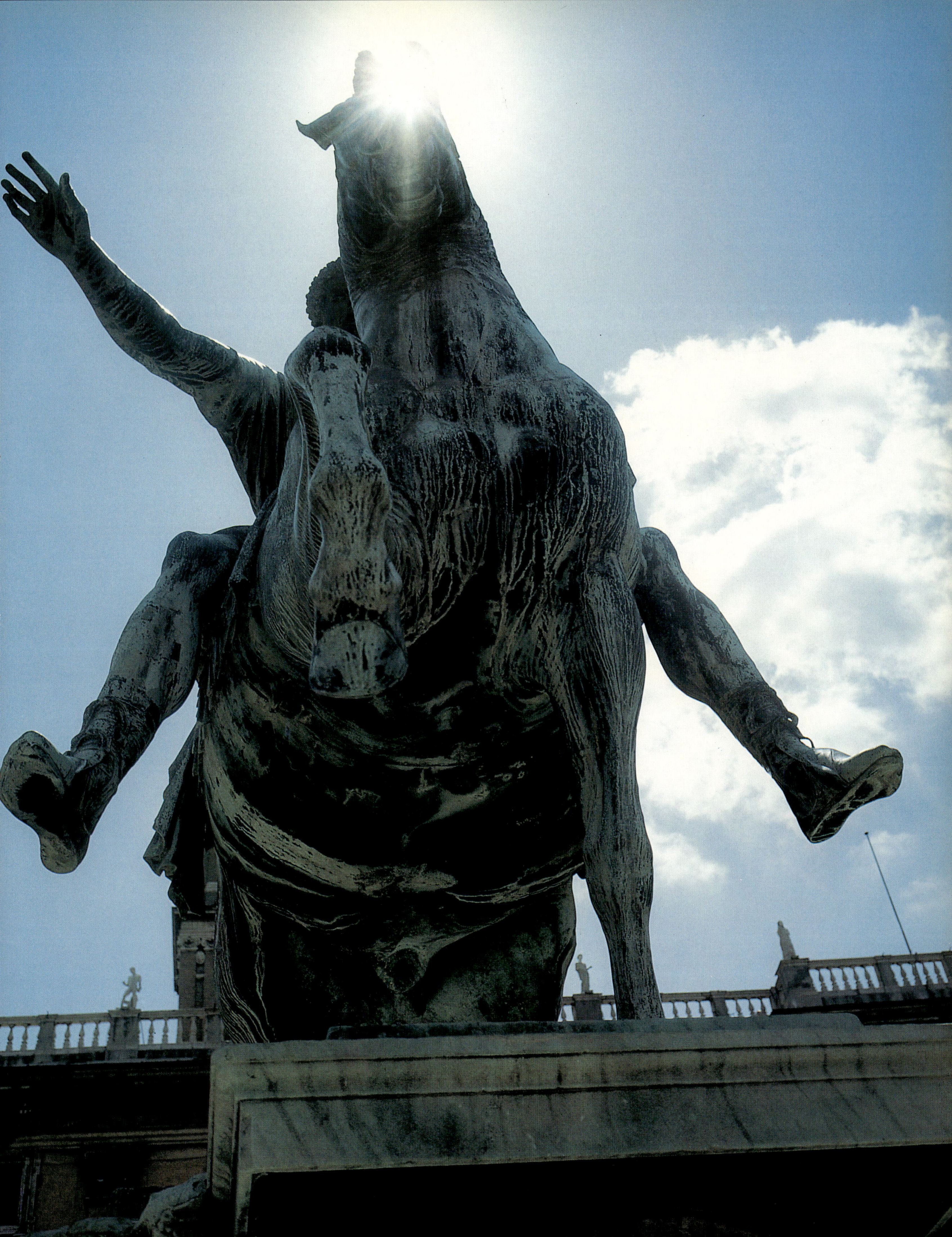

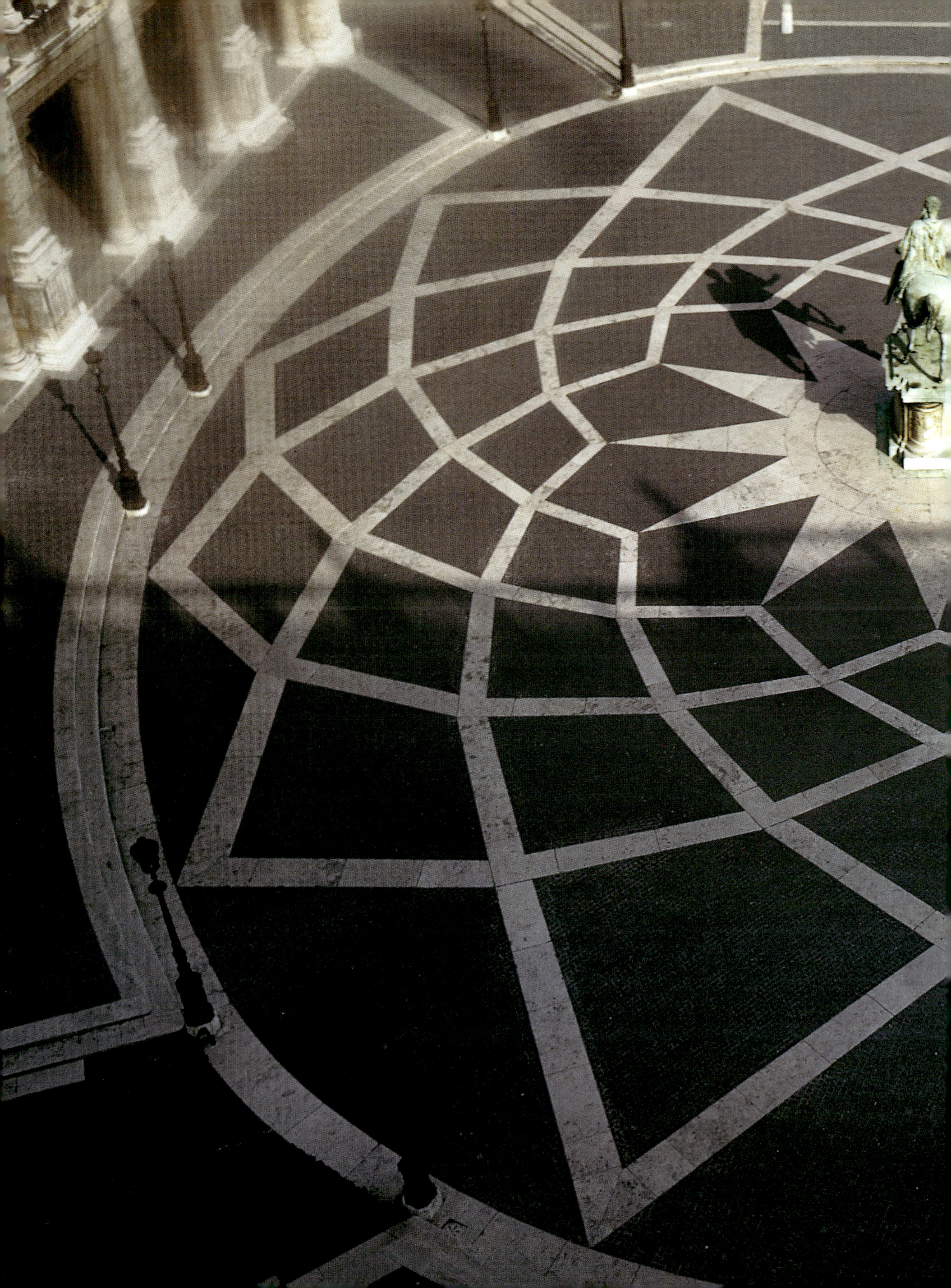

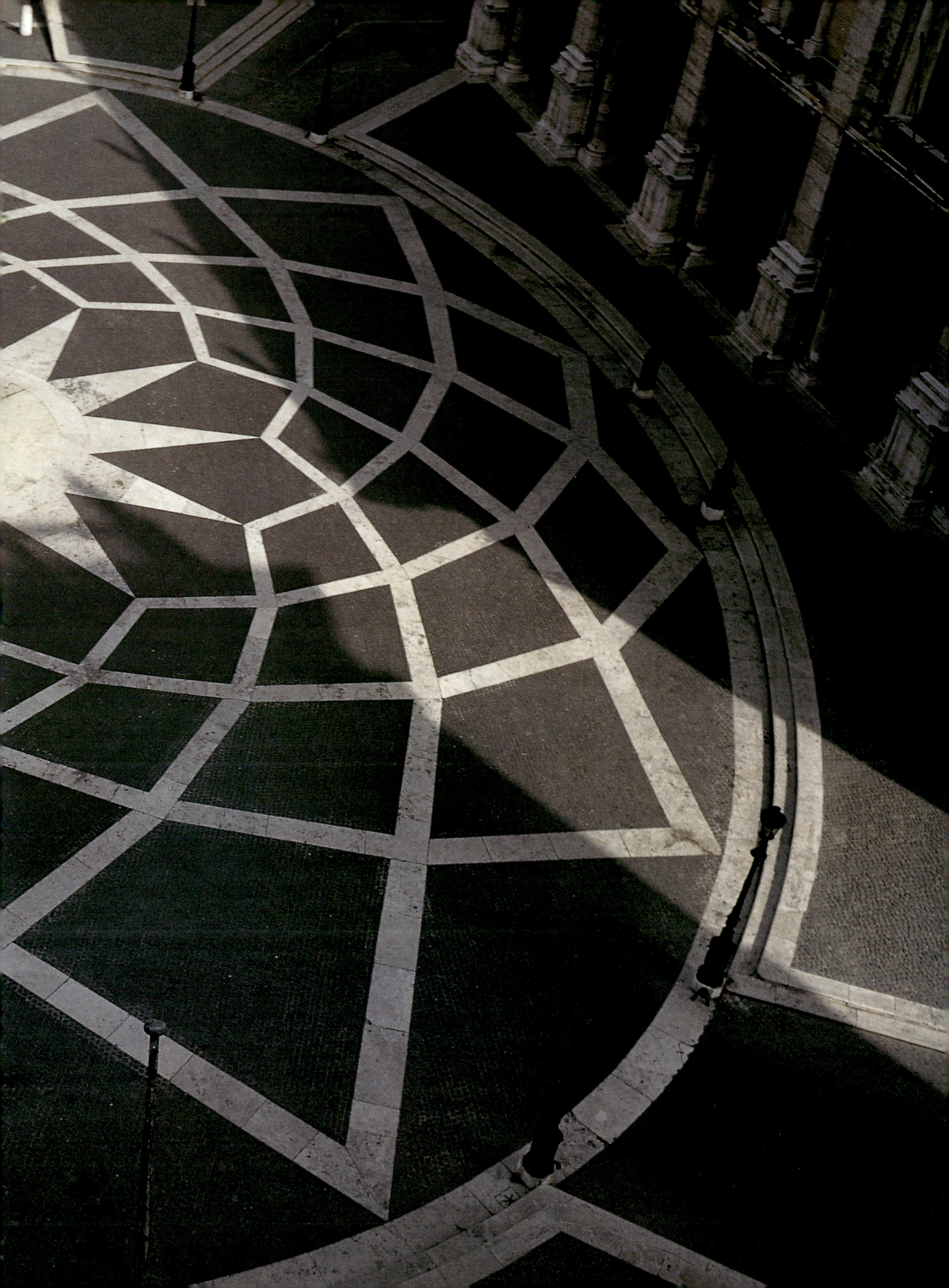

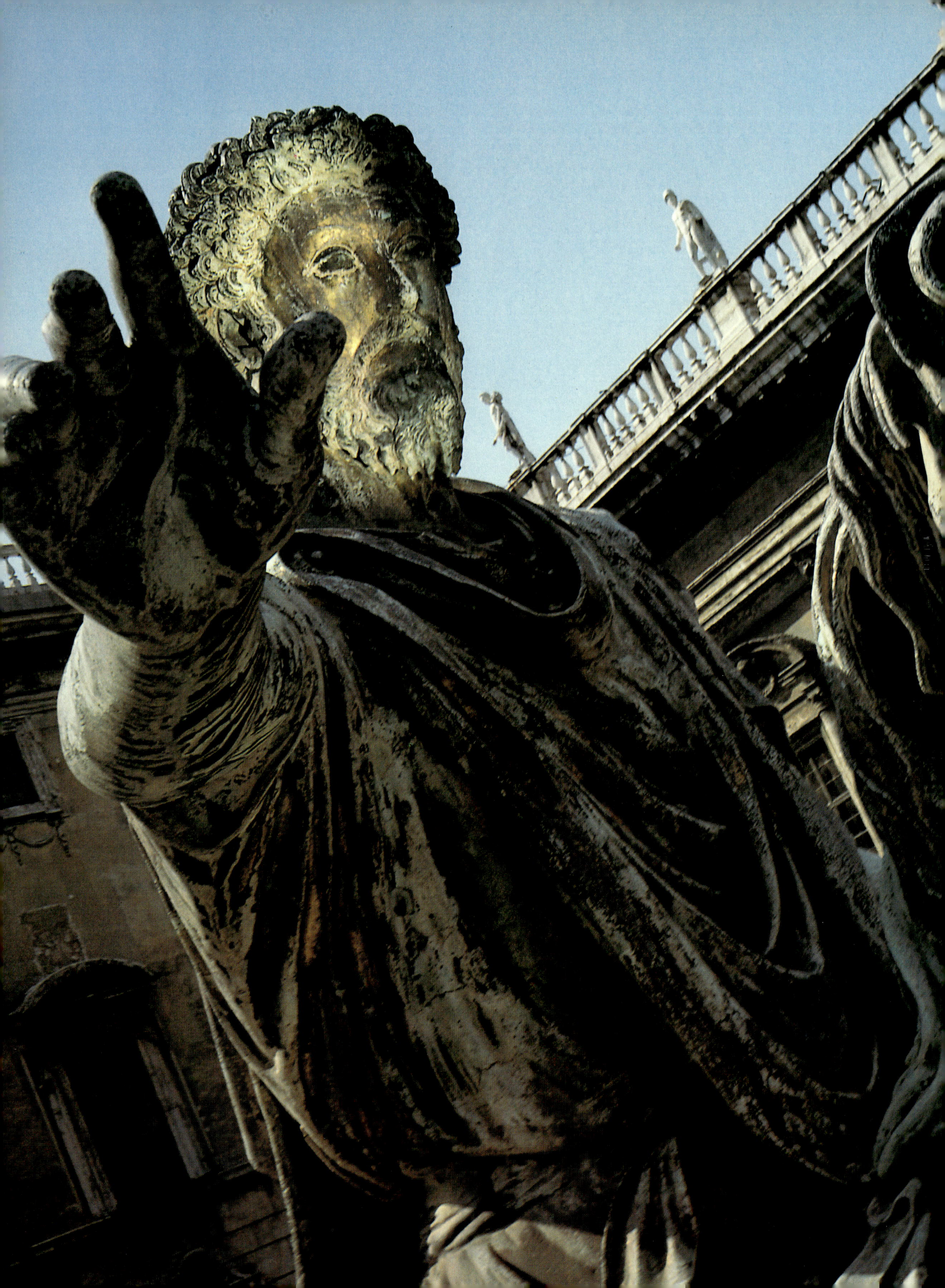

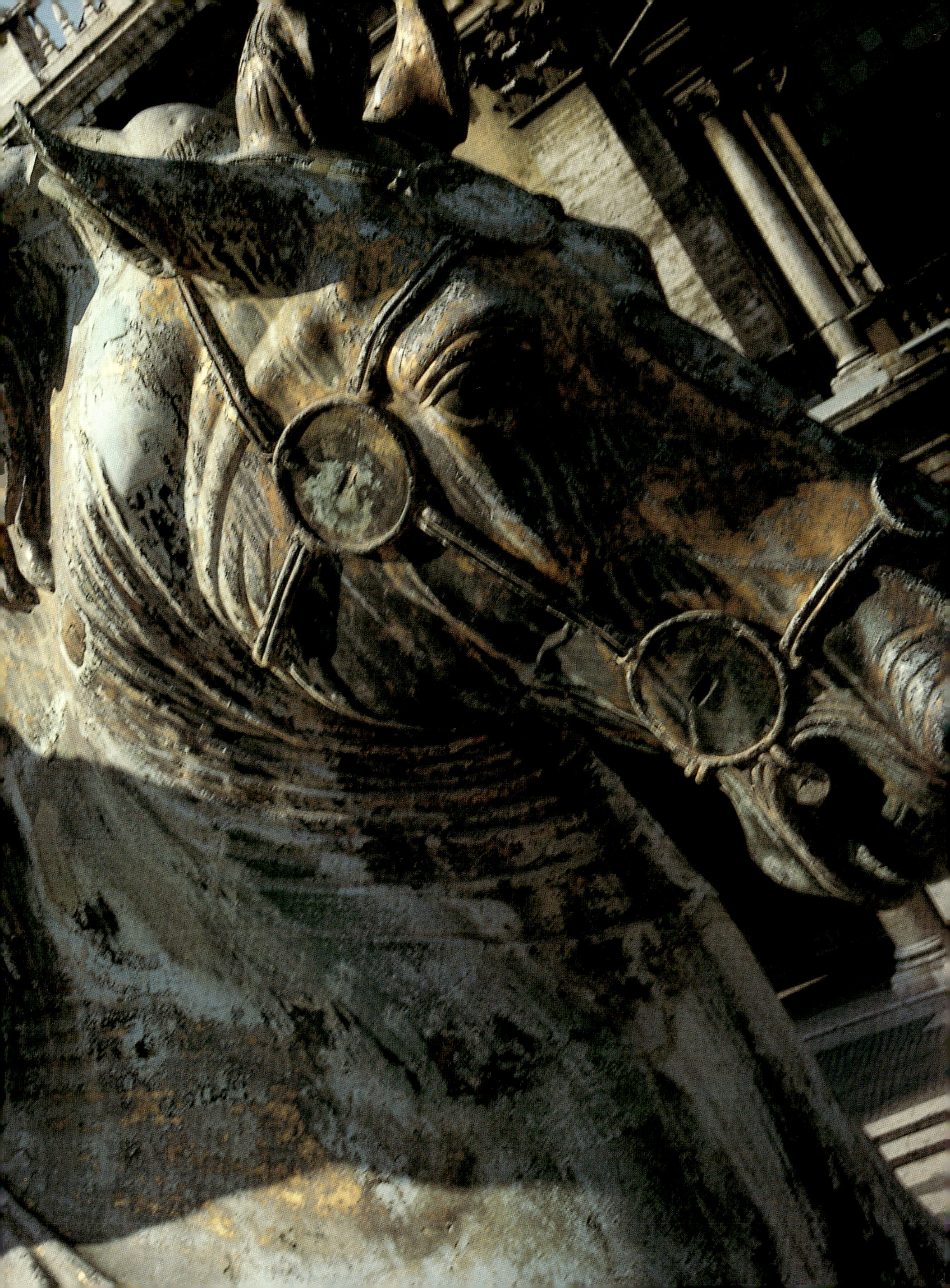

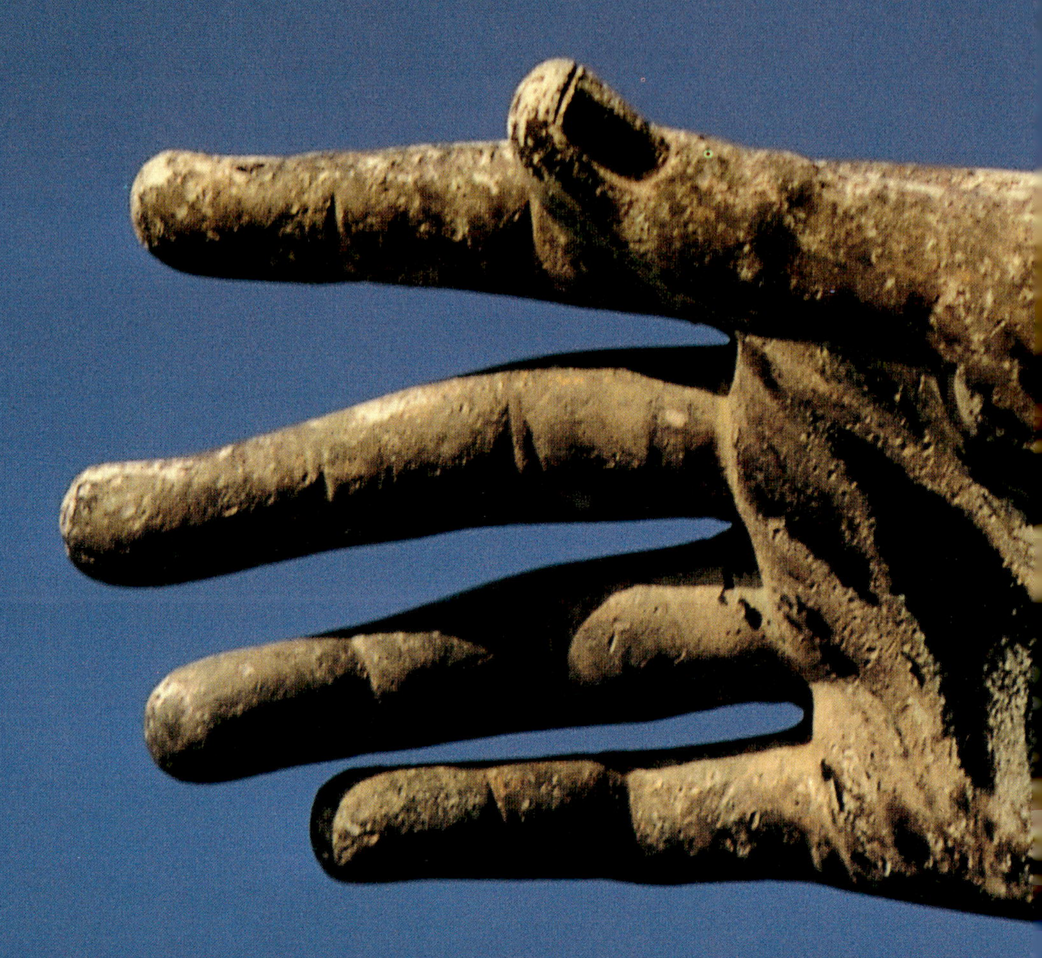

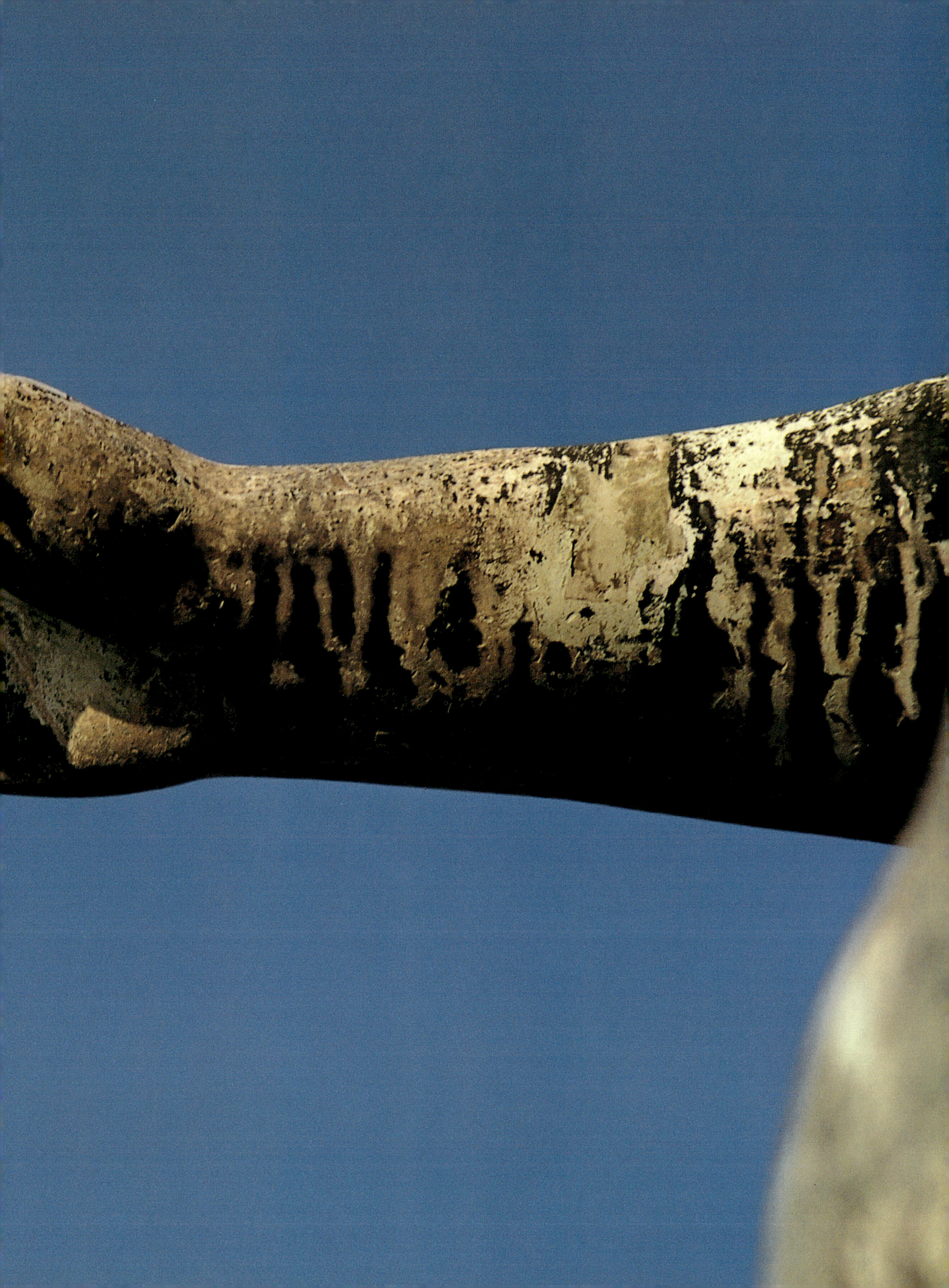

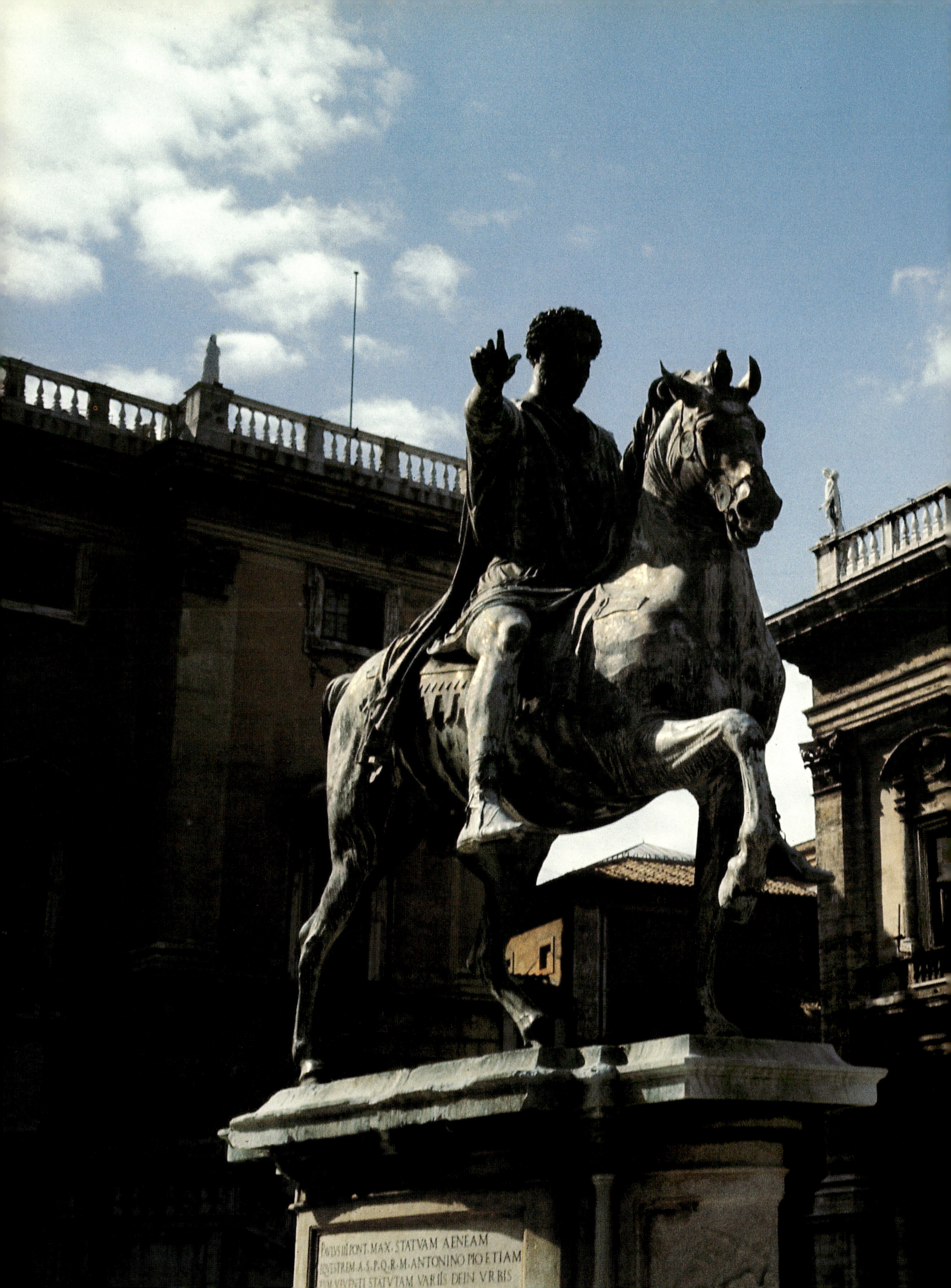
PONT. MAX. STATVAM AENEAM
A. S. P. Q. R. M. ANTONINO PIO ETIAM
STATVTAM VARIIS DEIN VRBIS

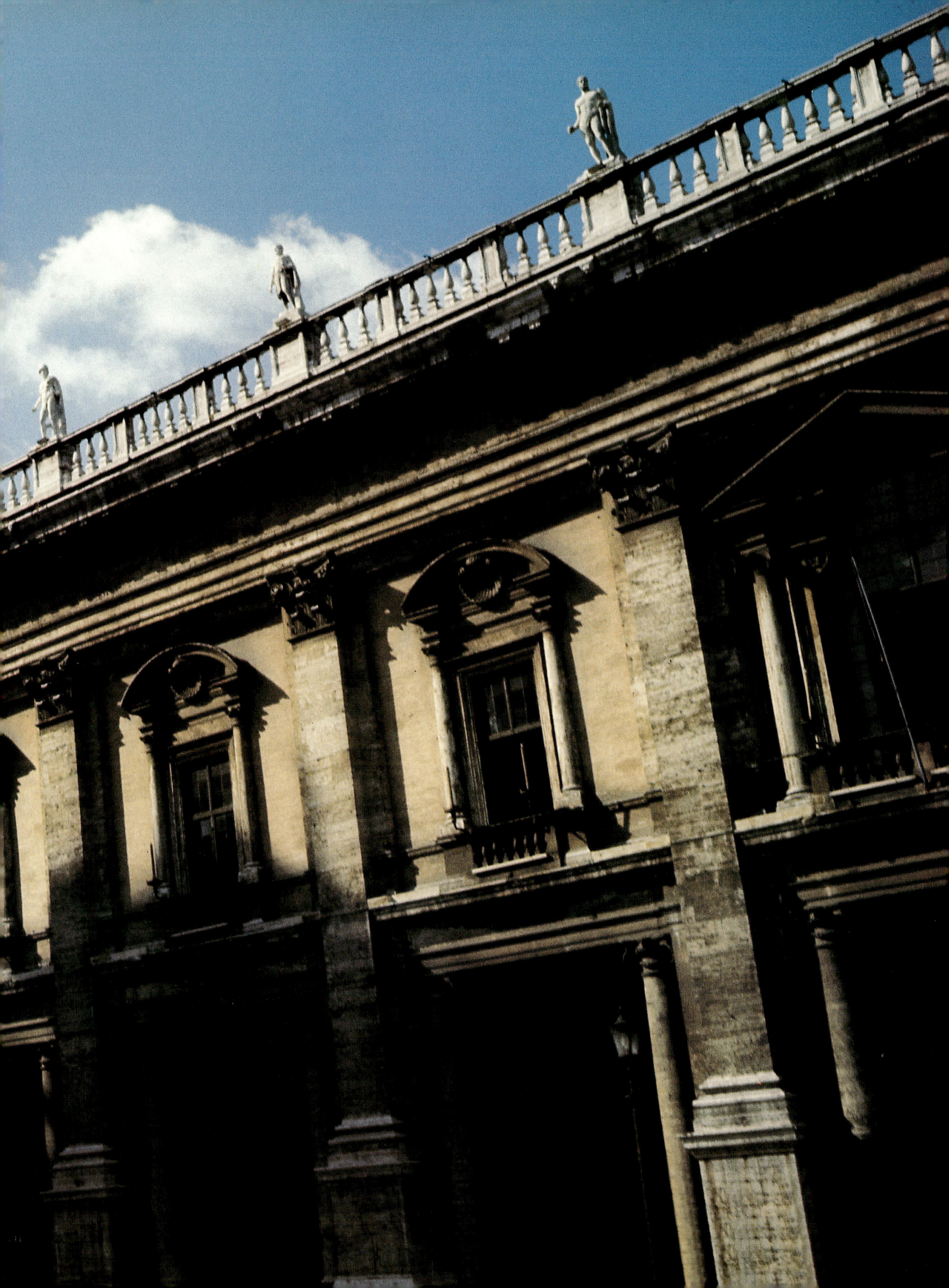

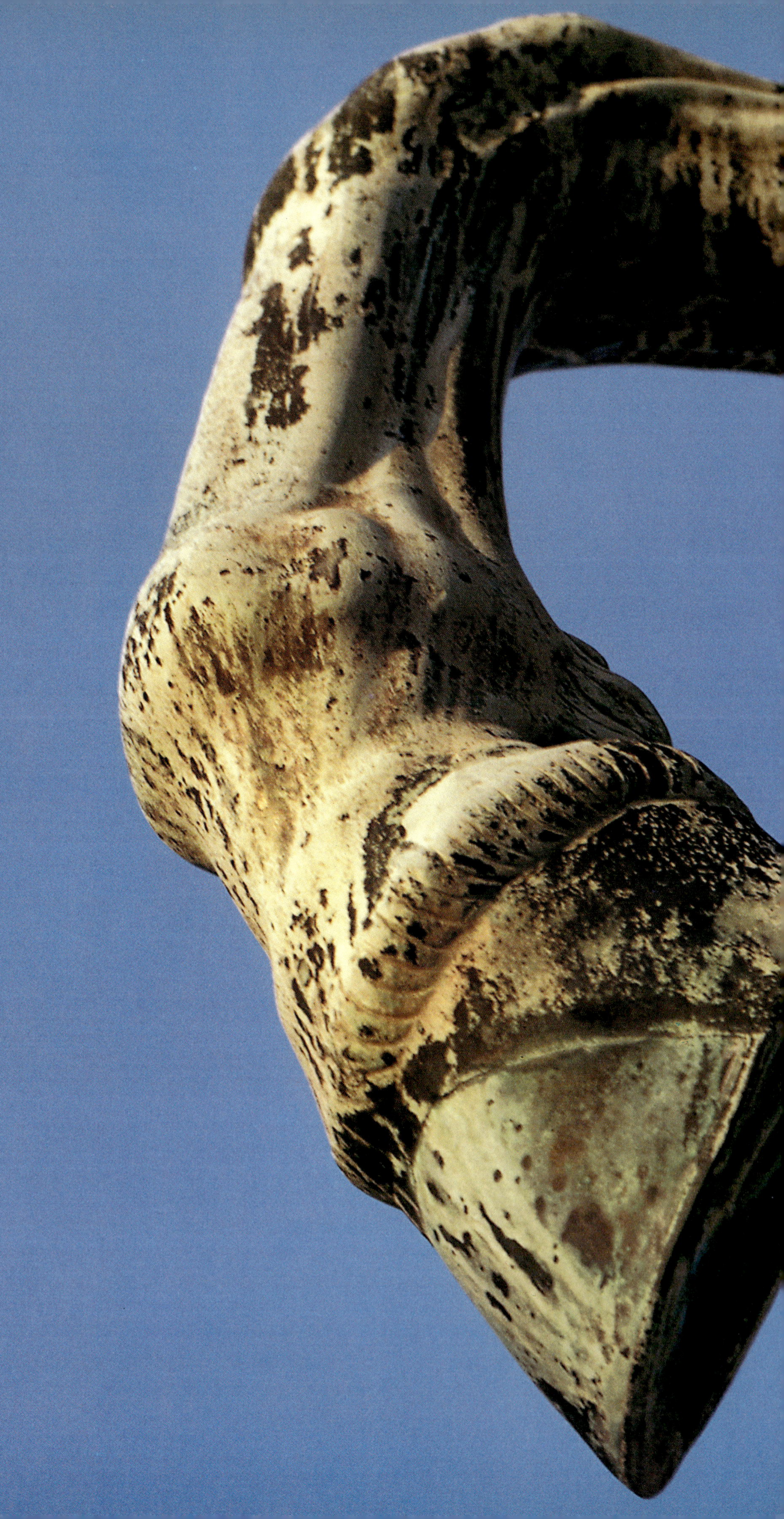

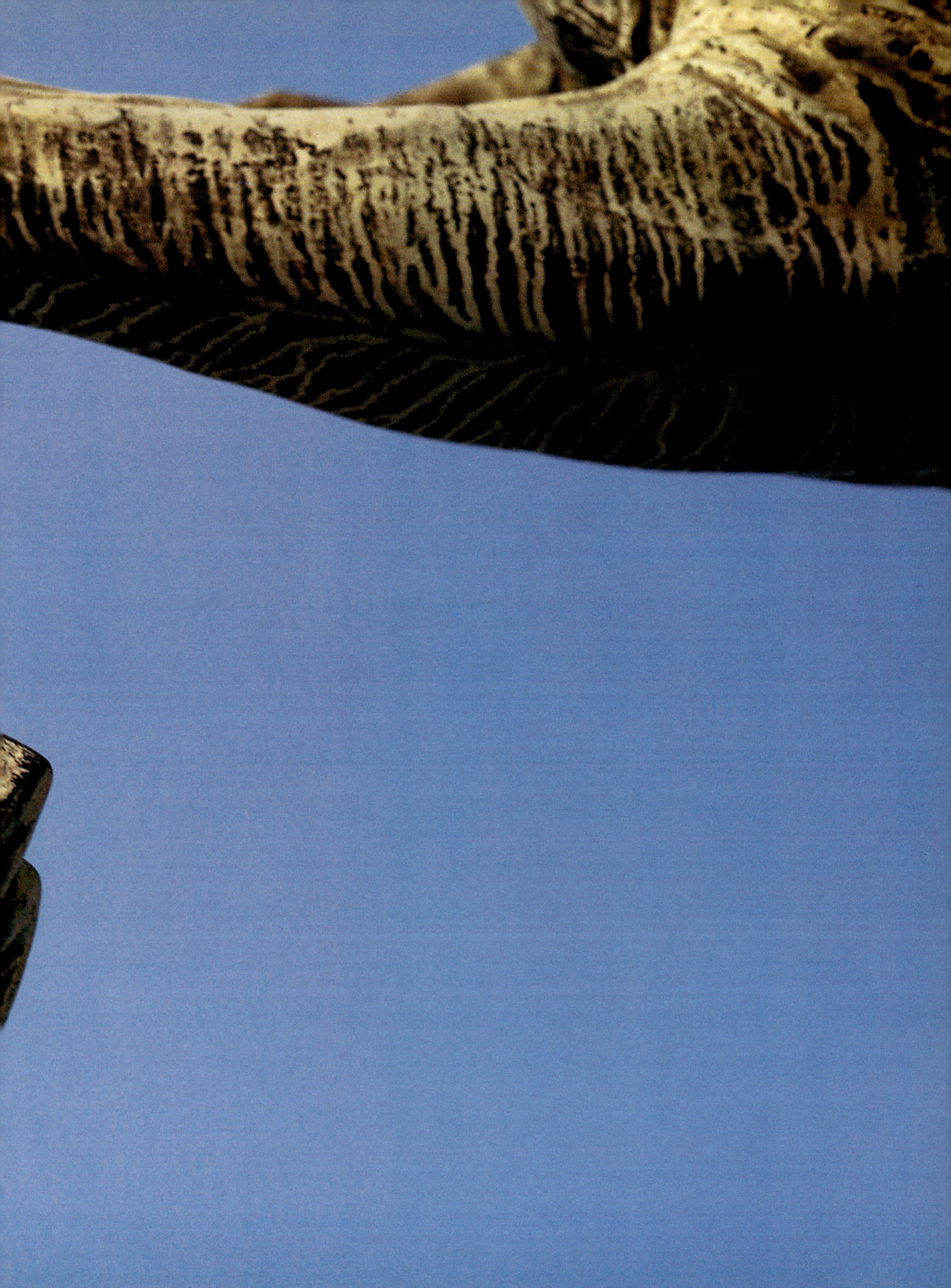

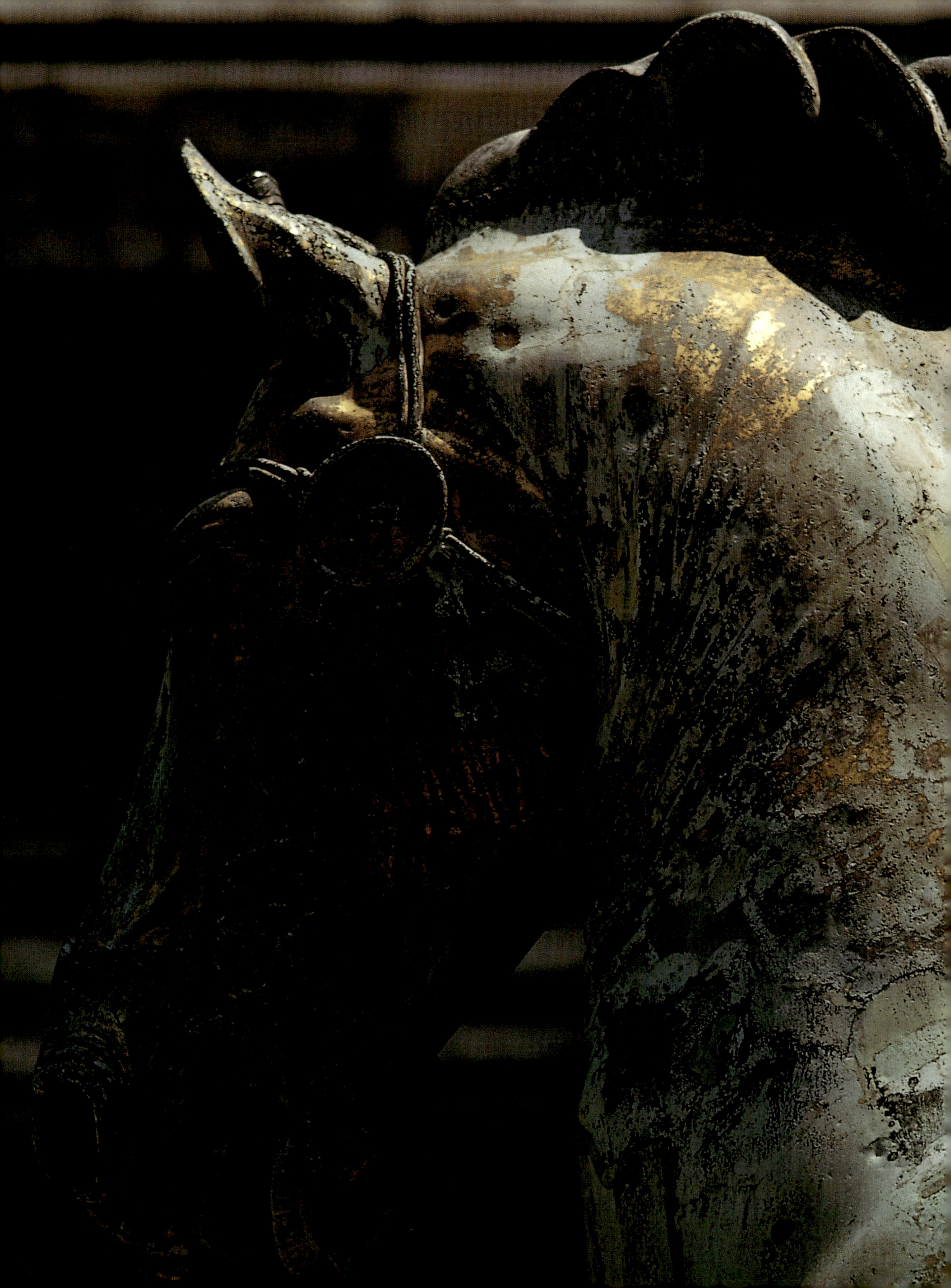

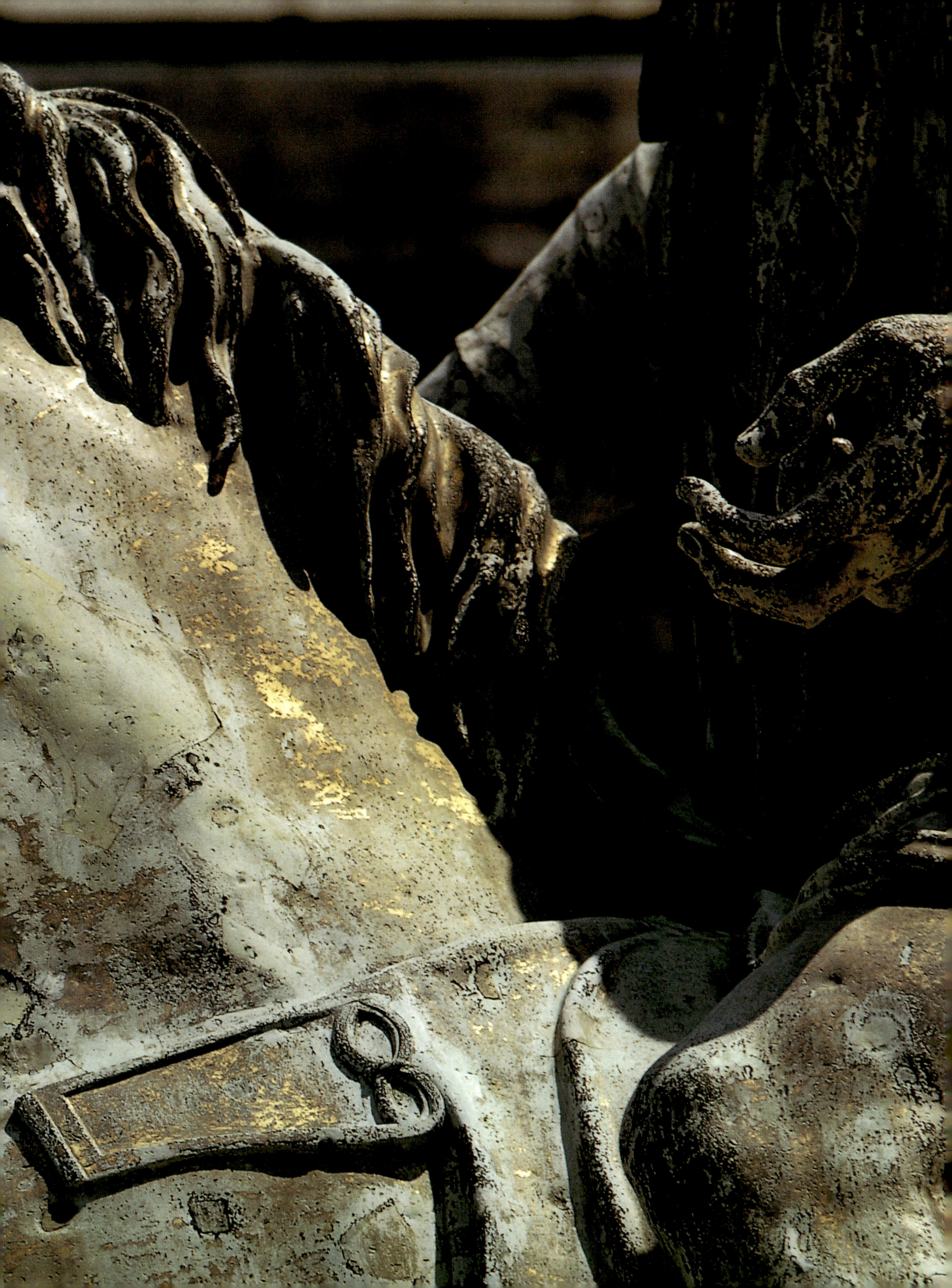

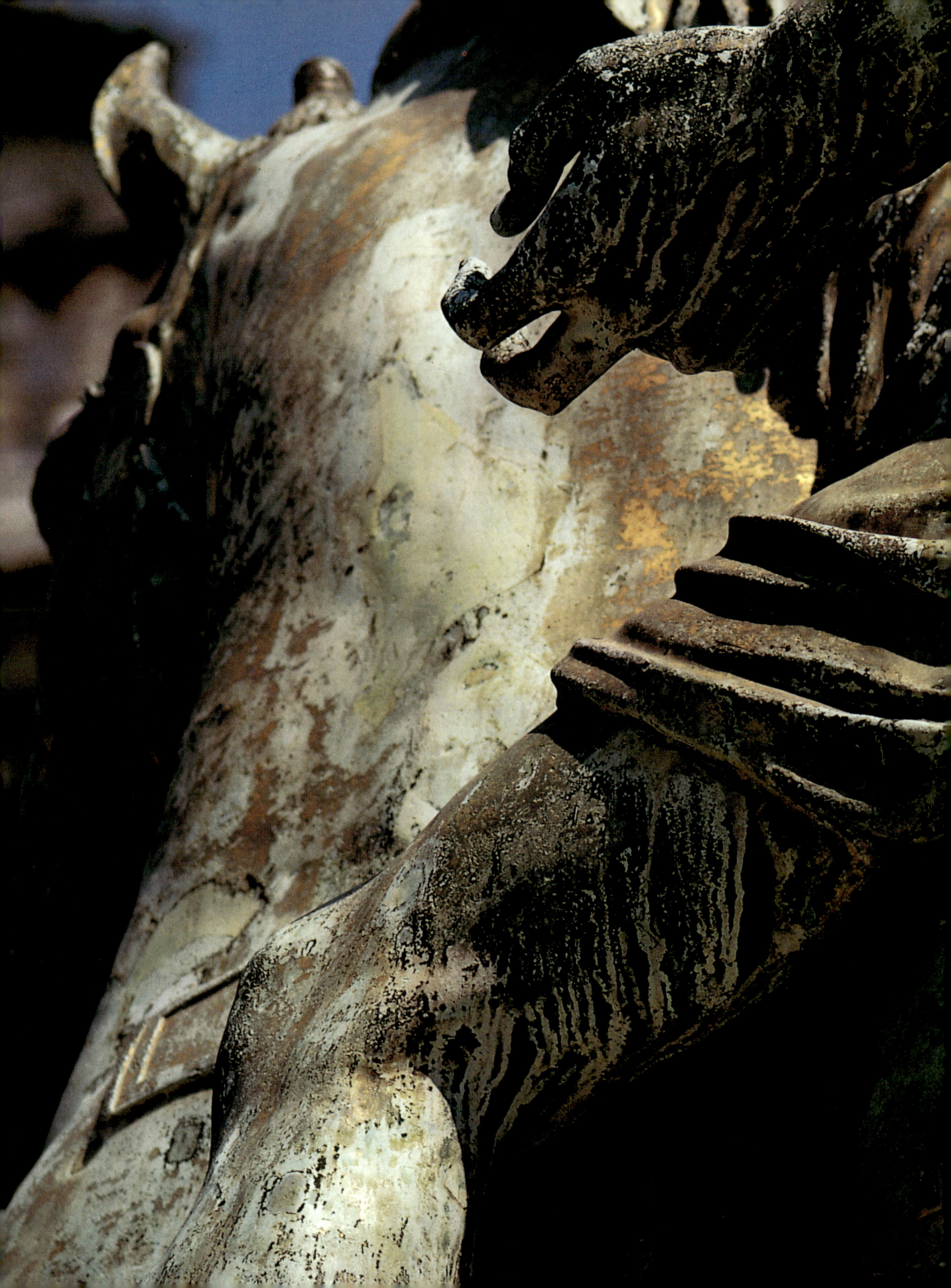

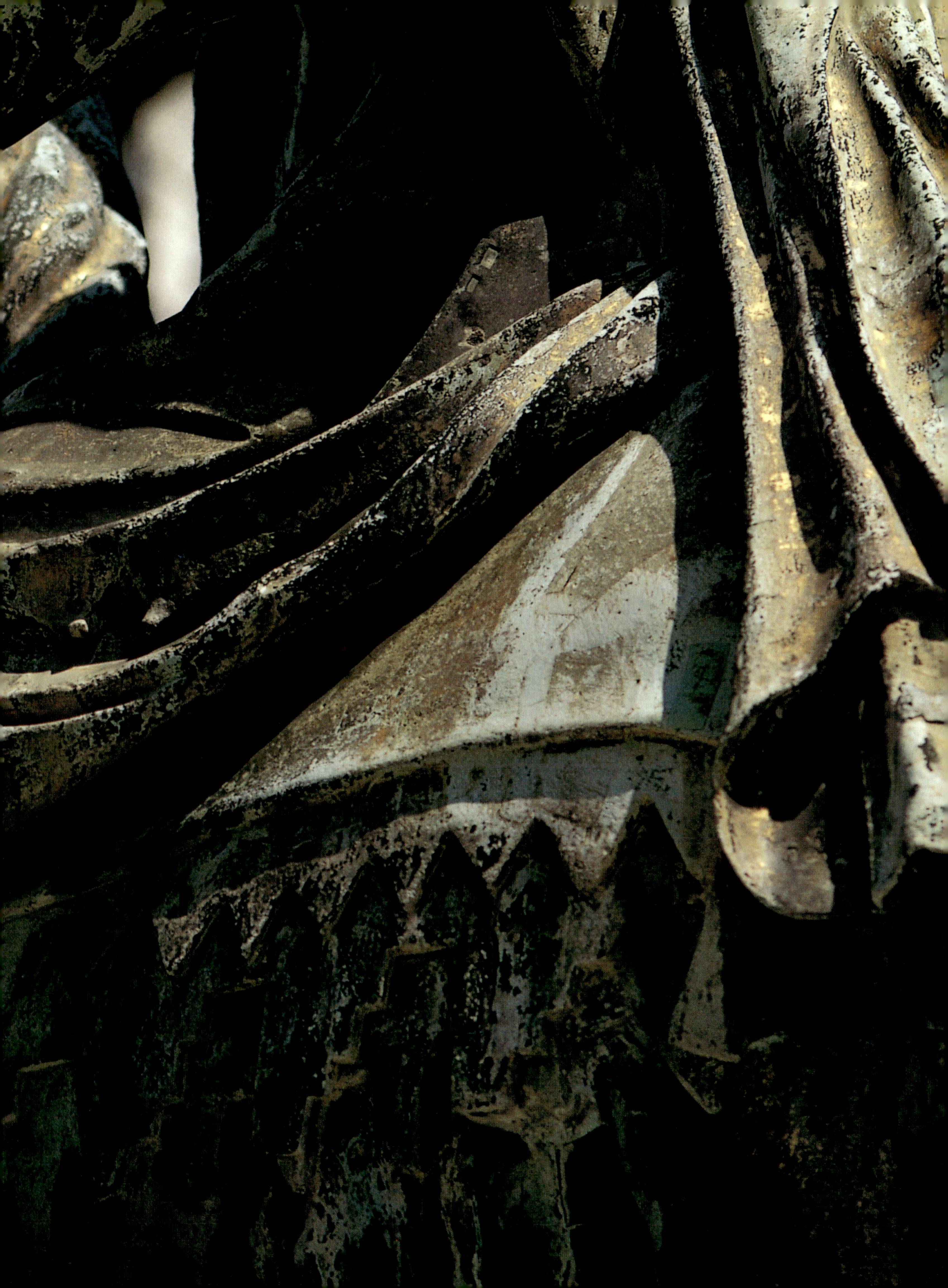

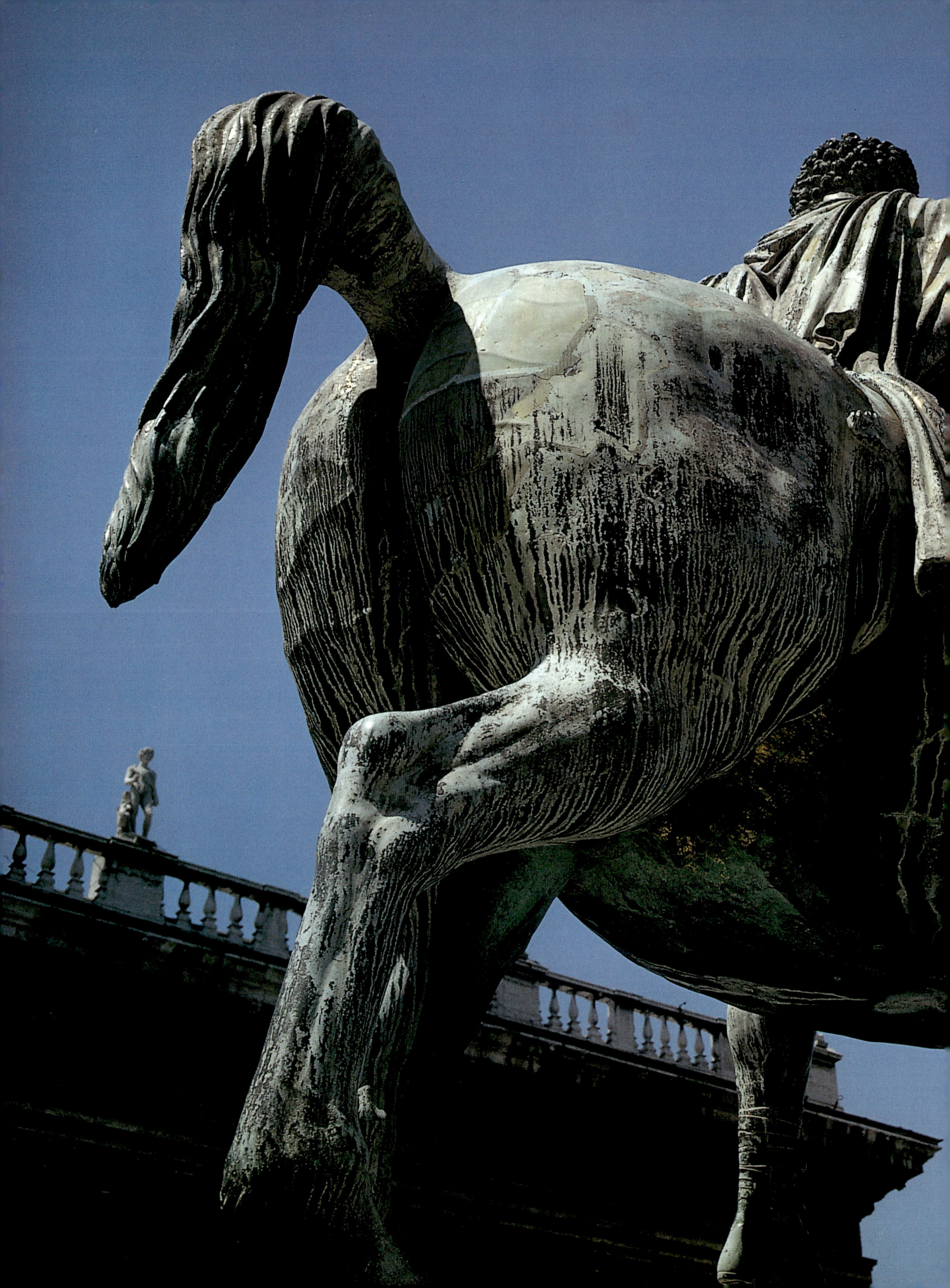

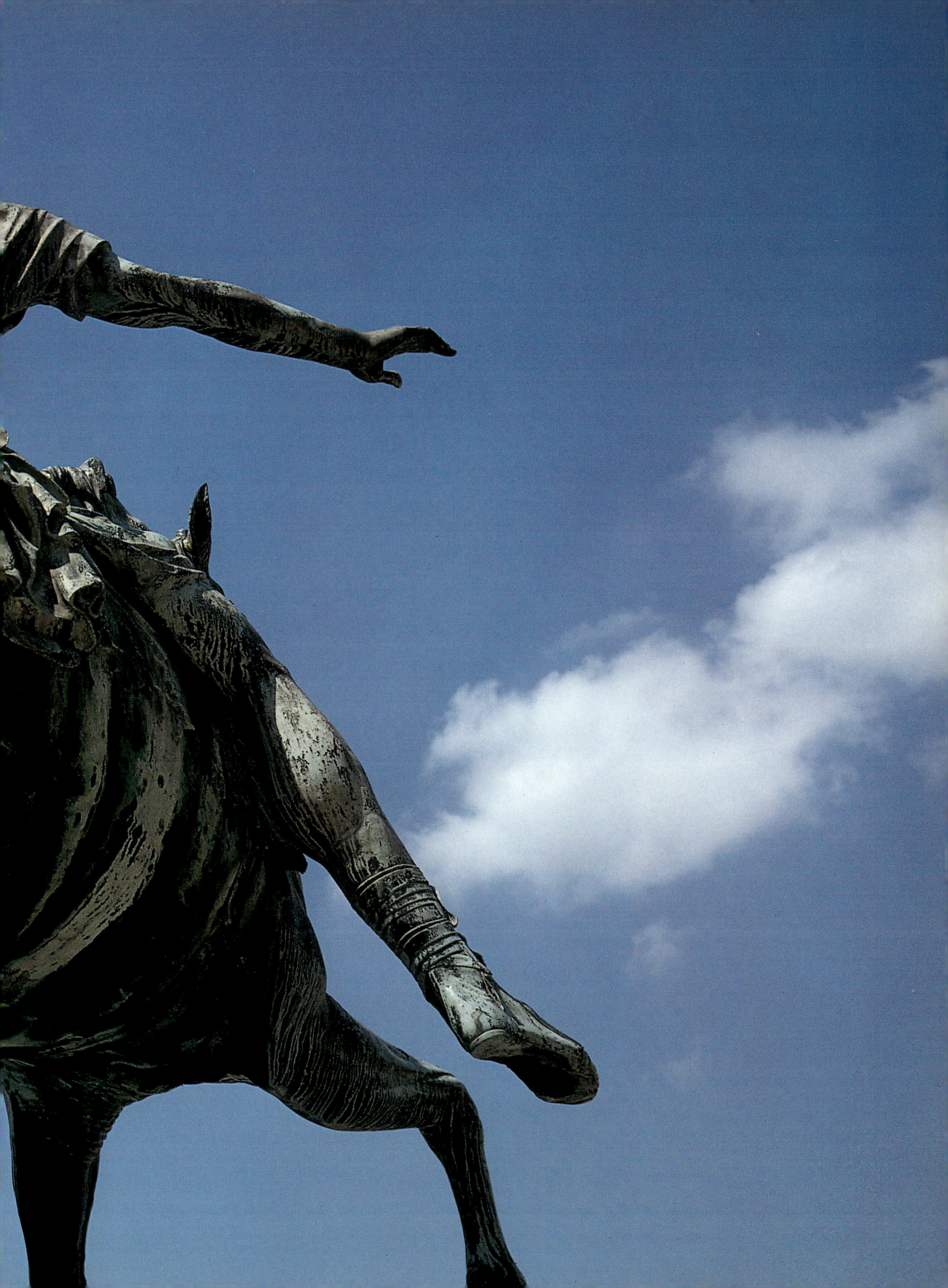

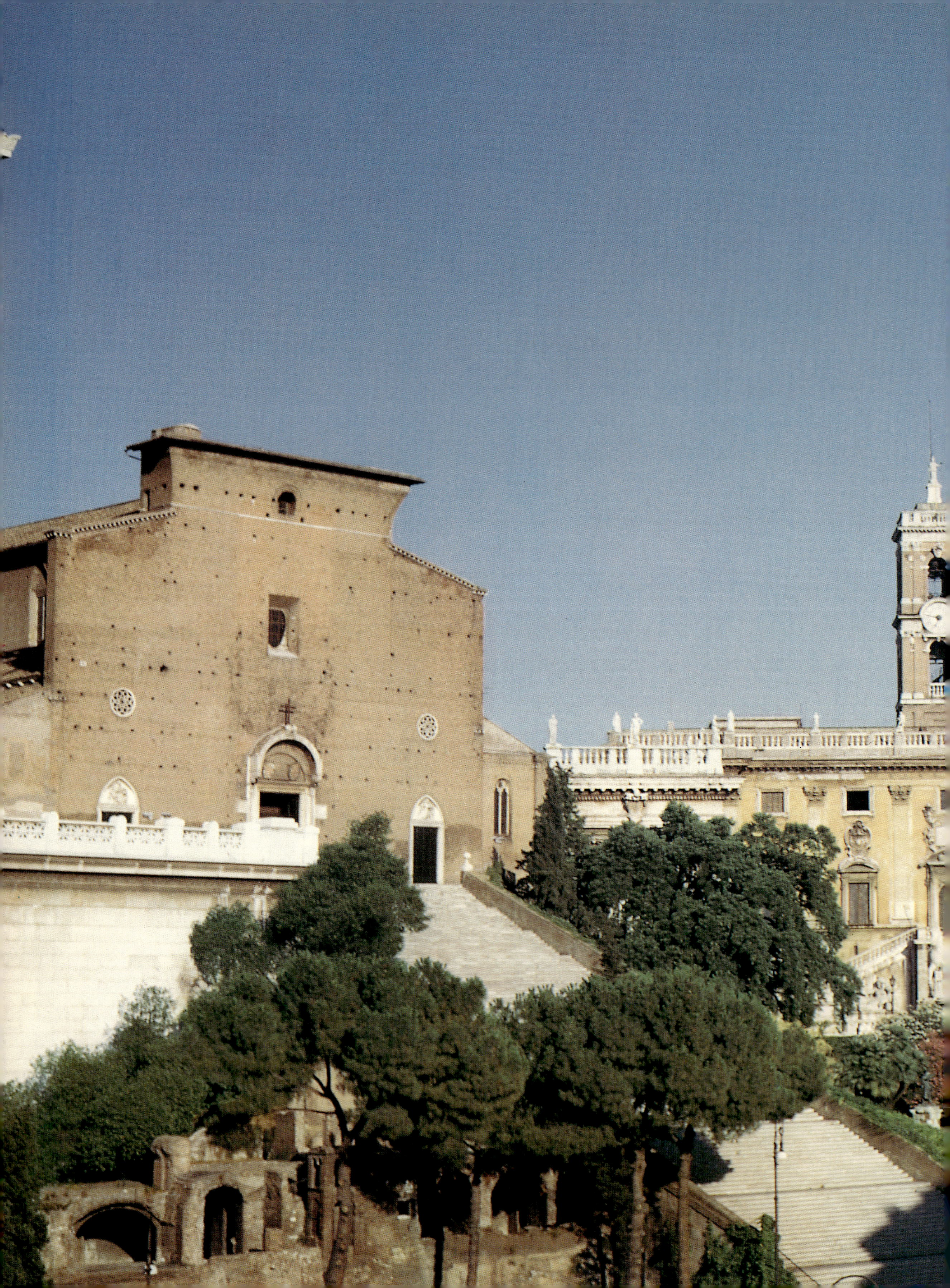

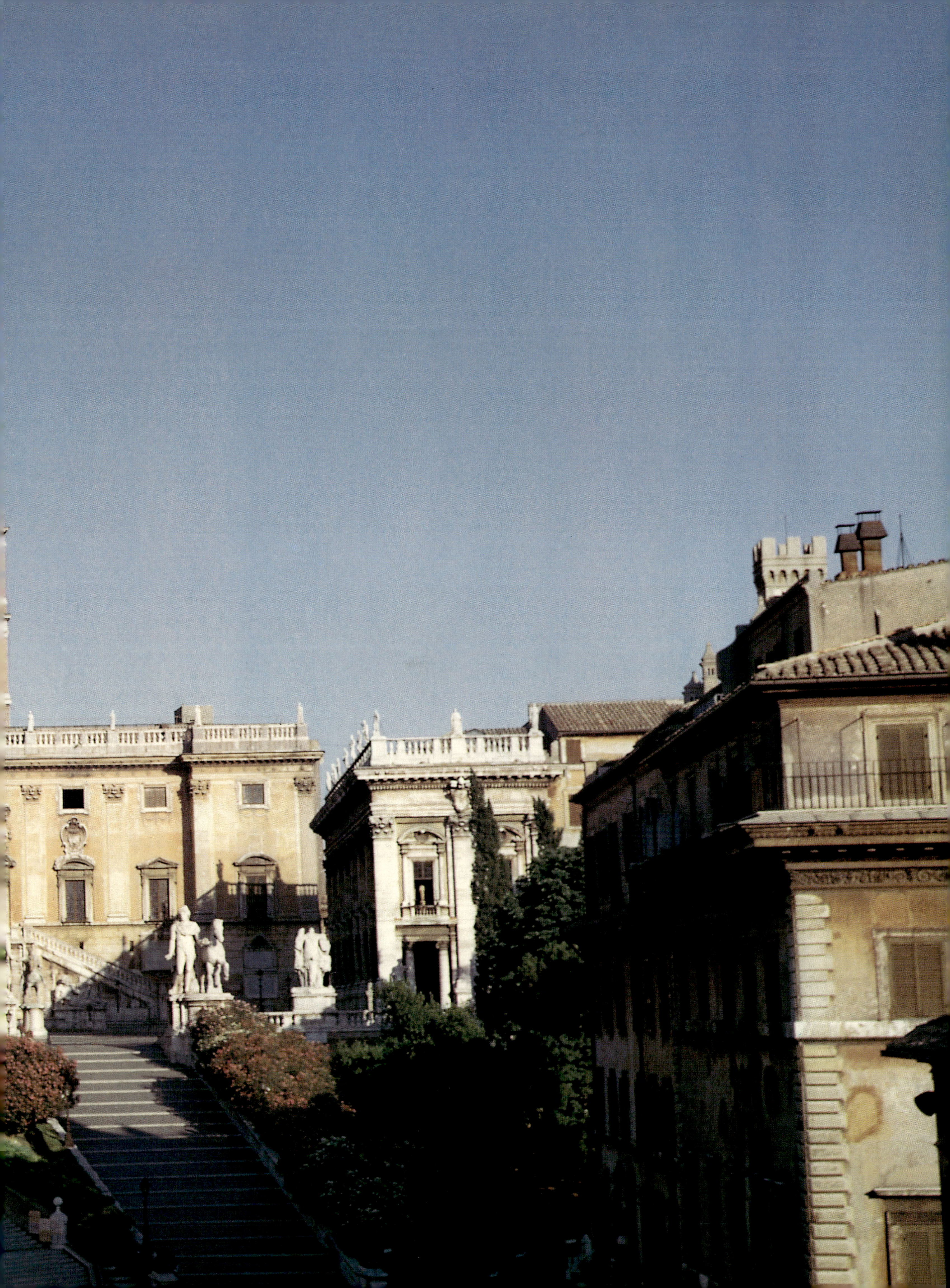

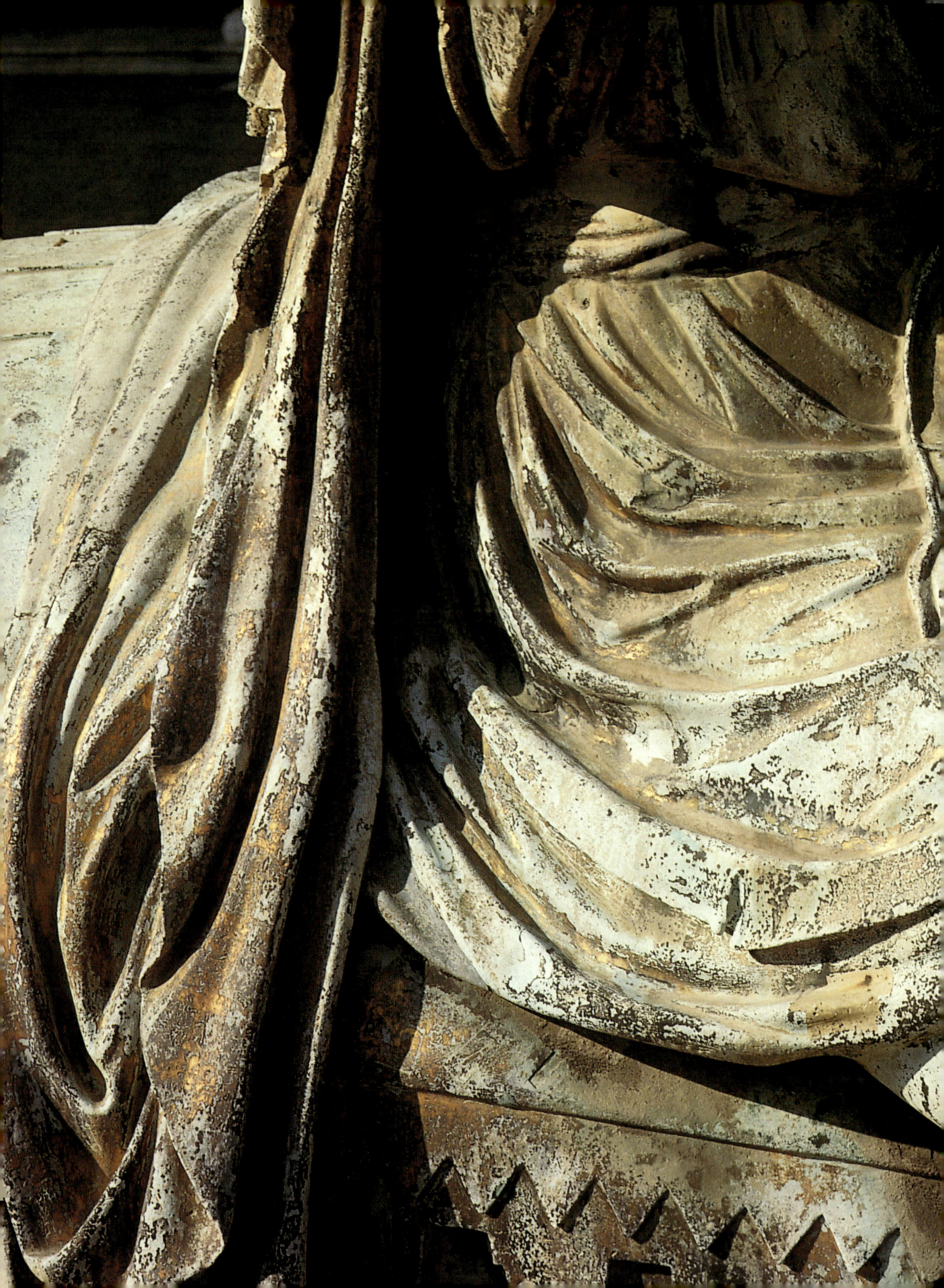

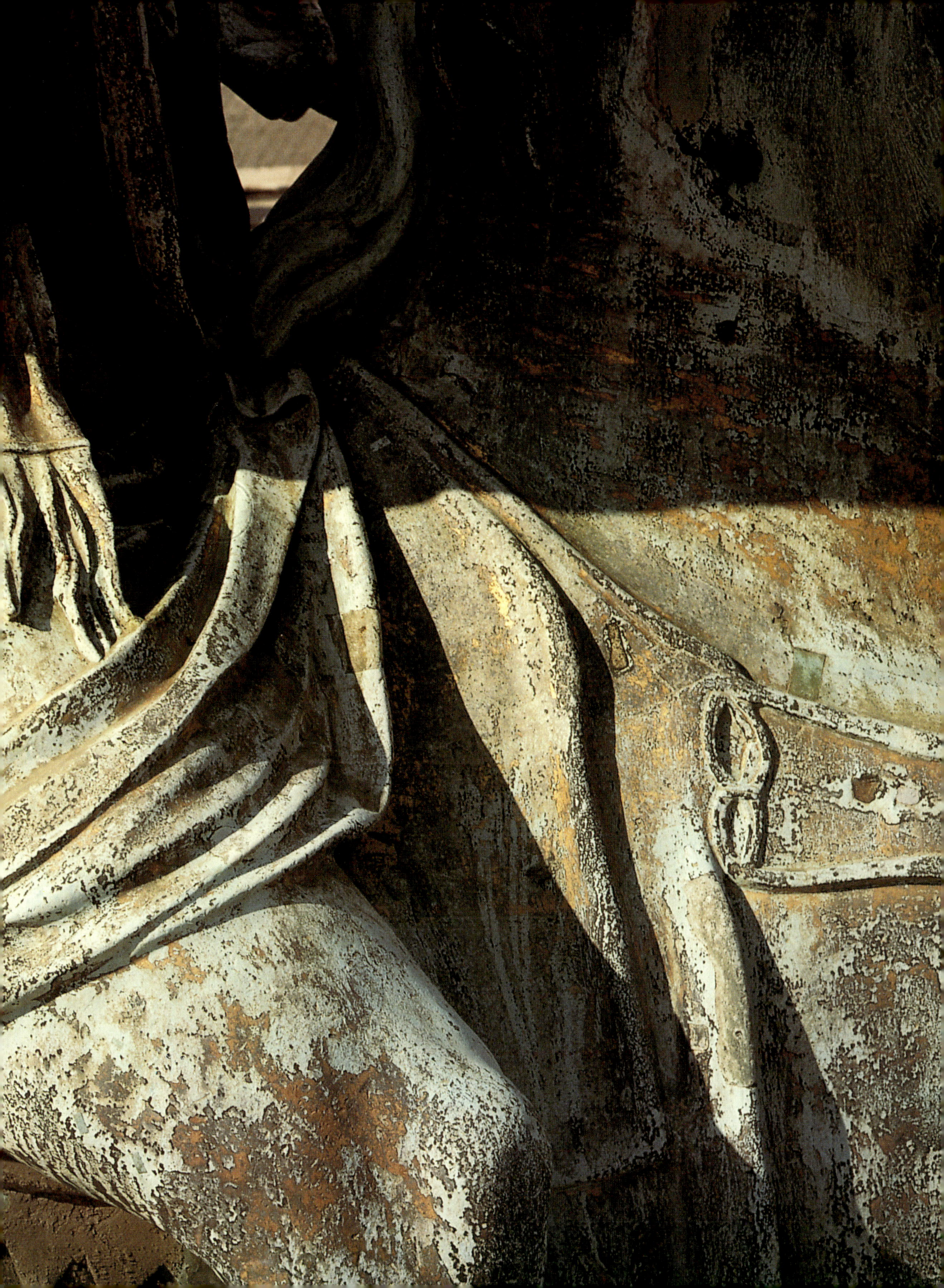

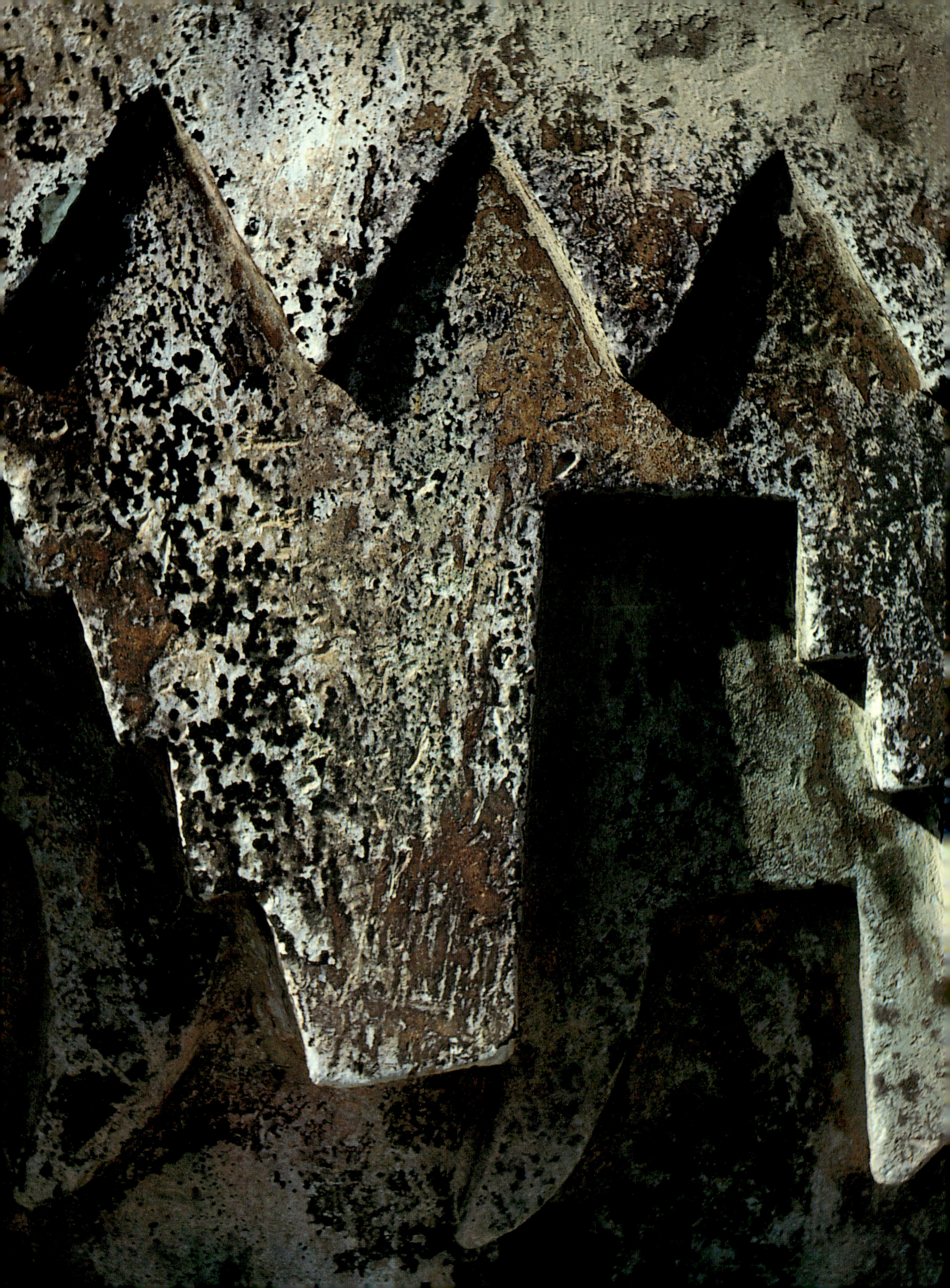

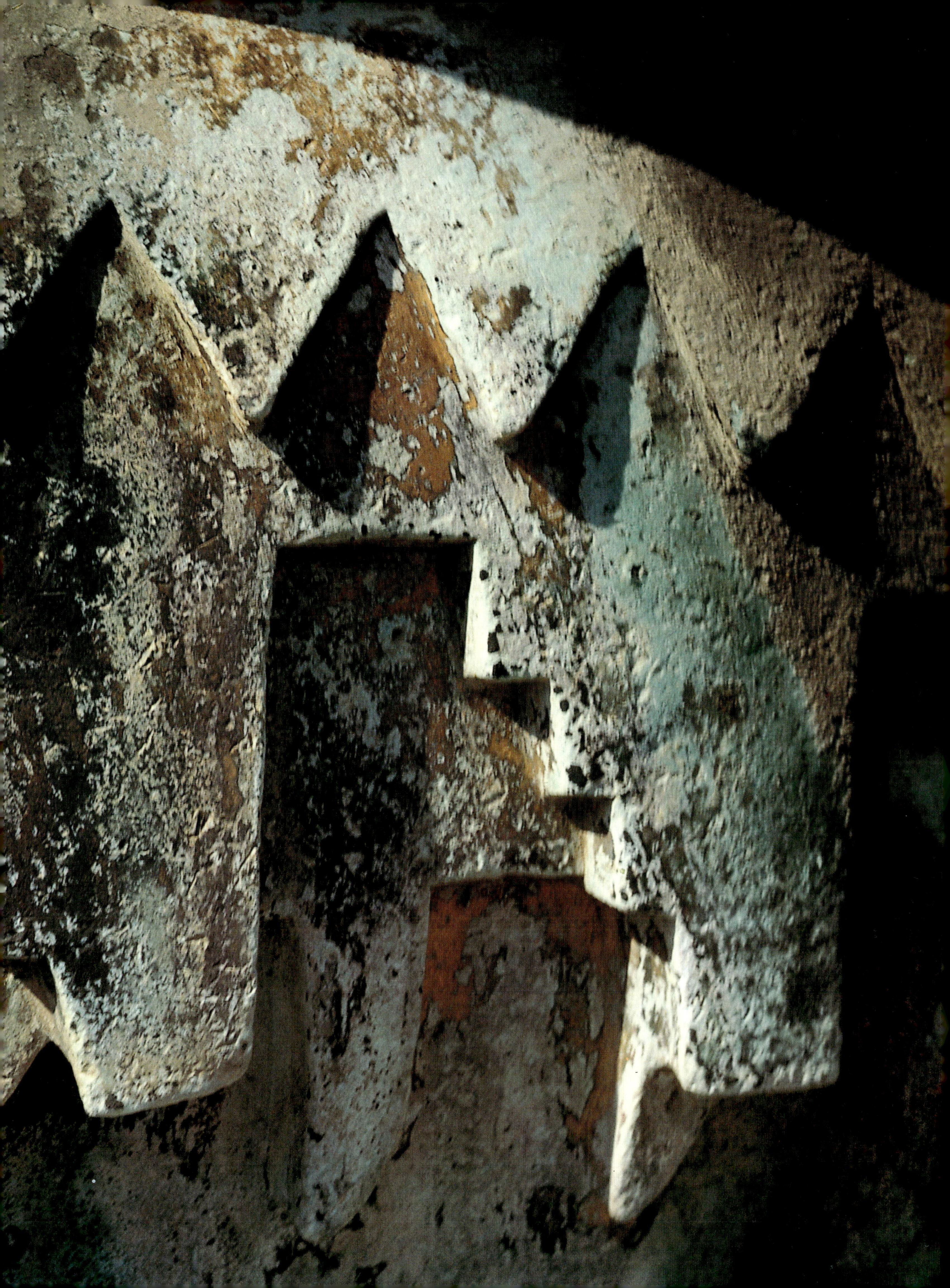

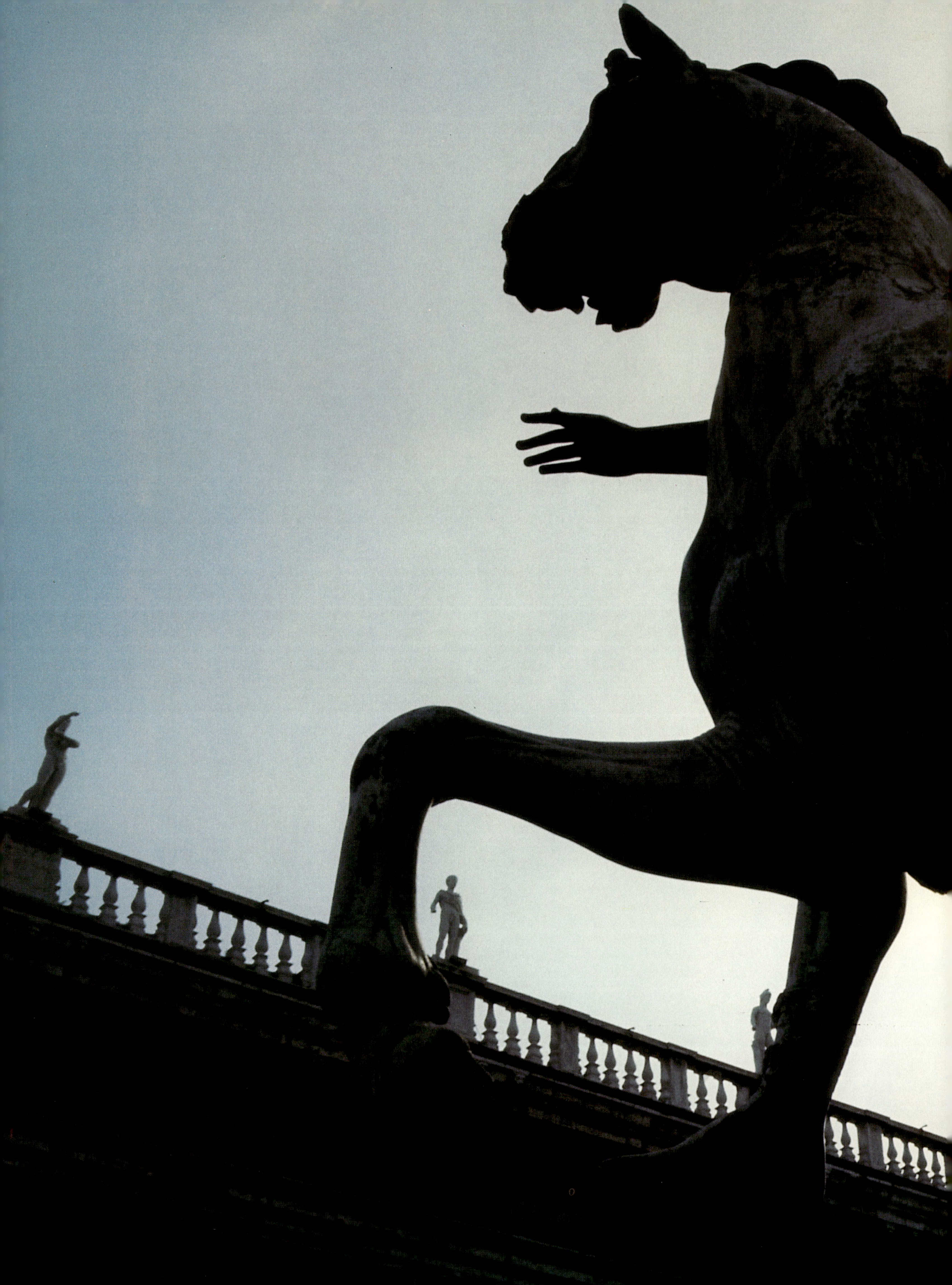

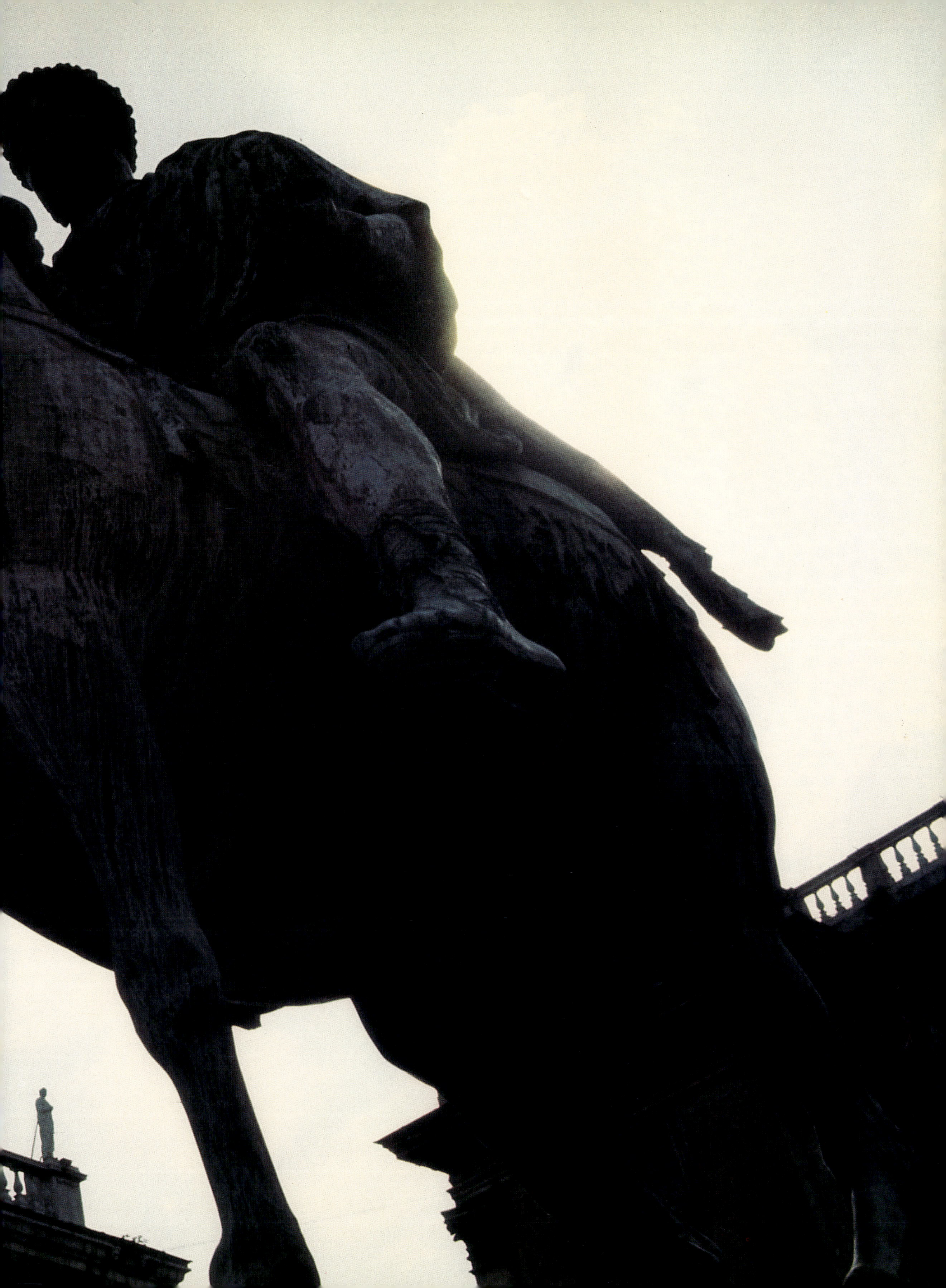

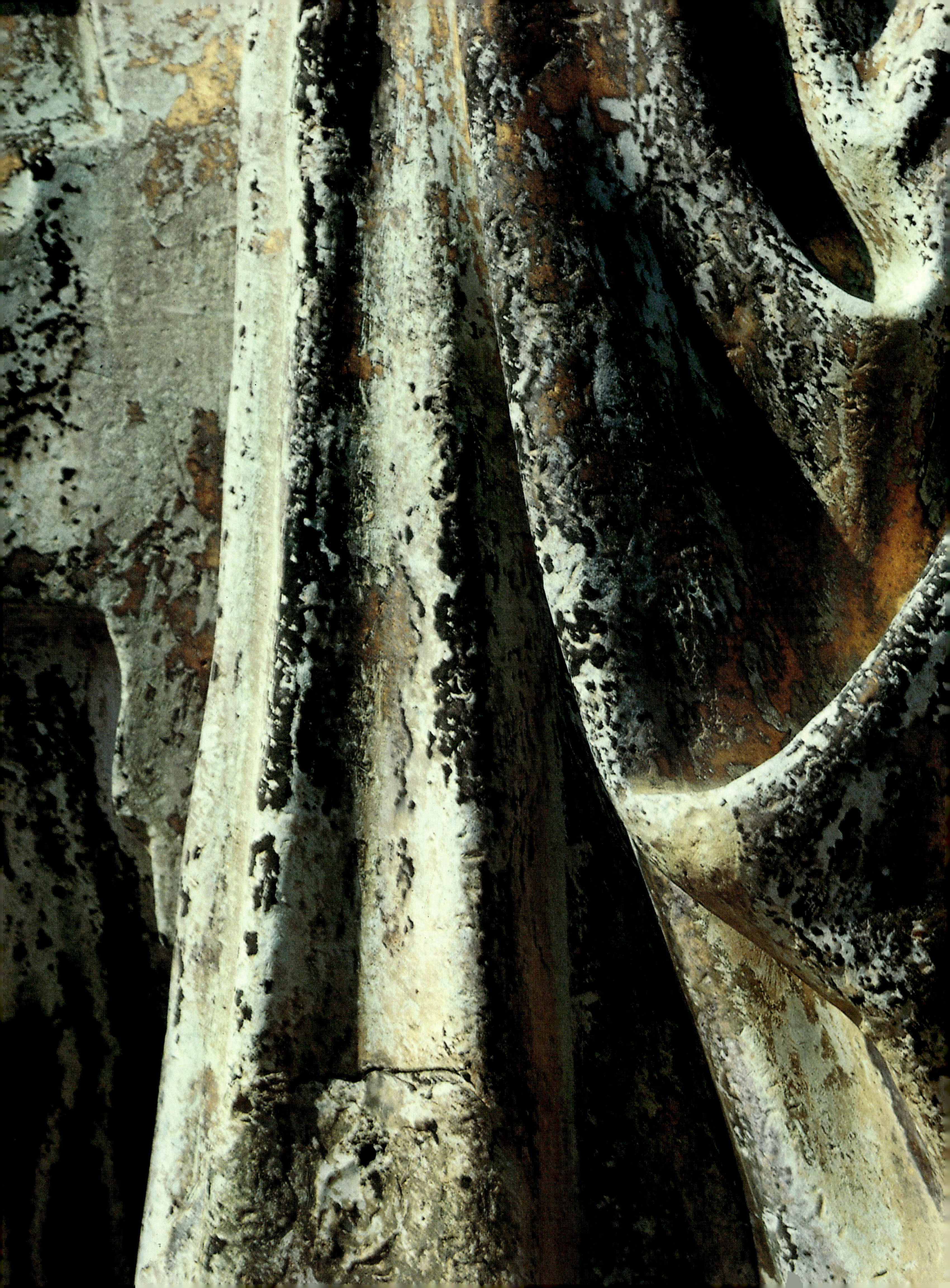

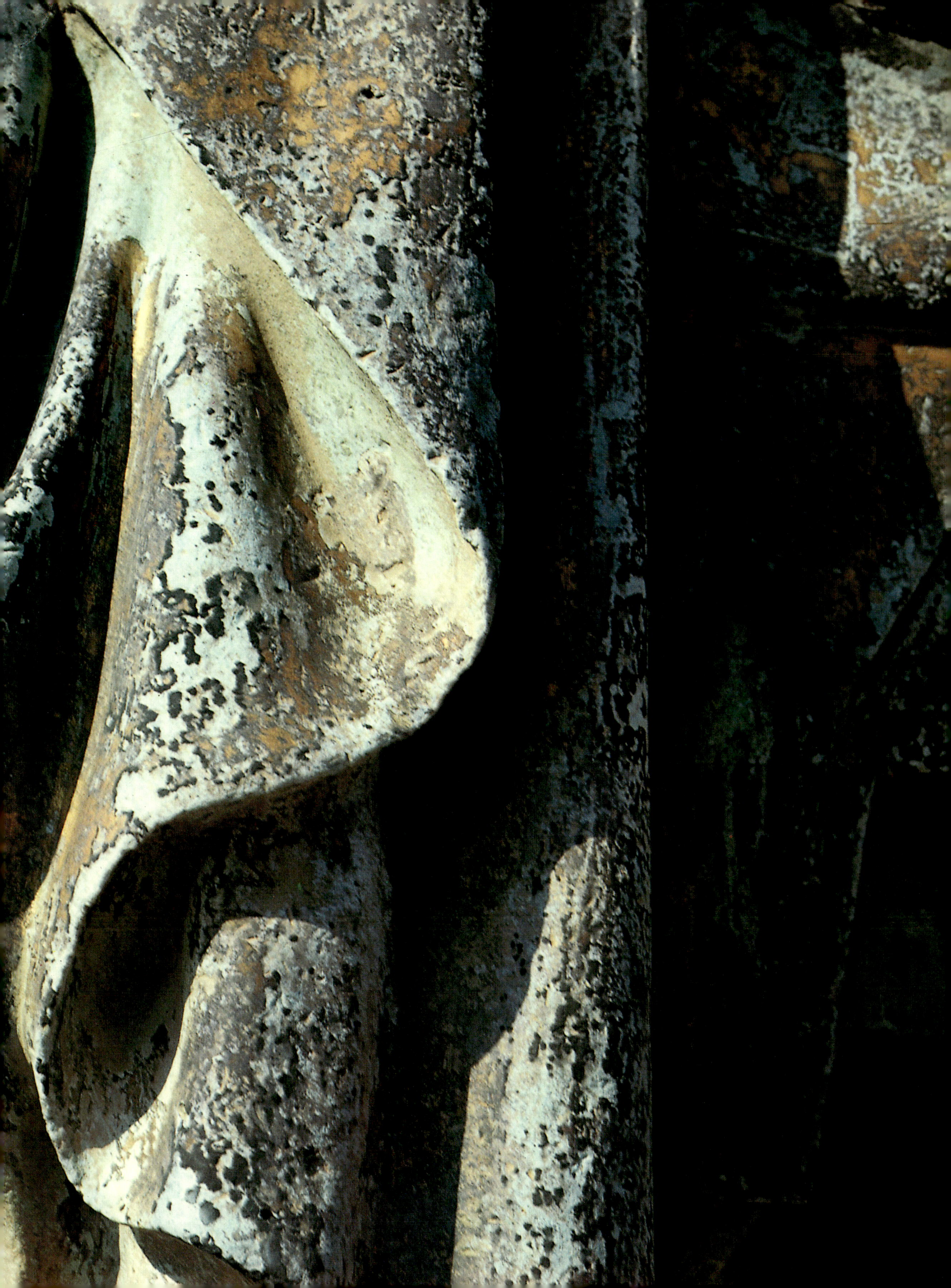

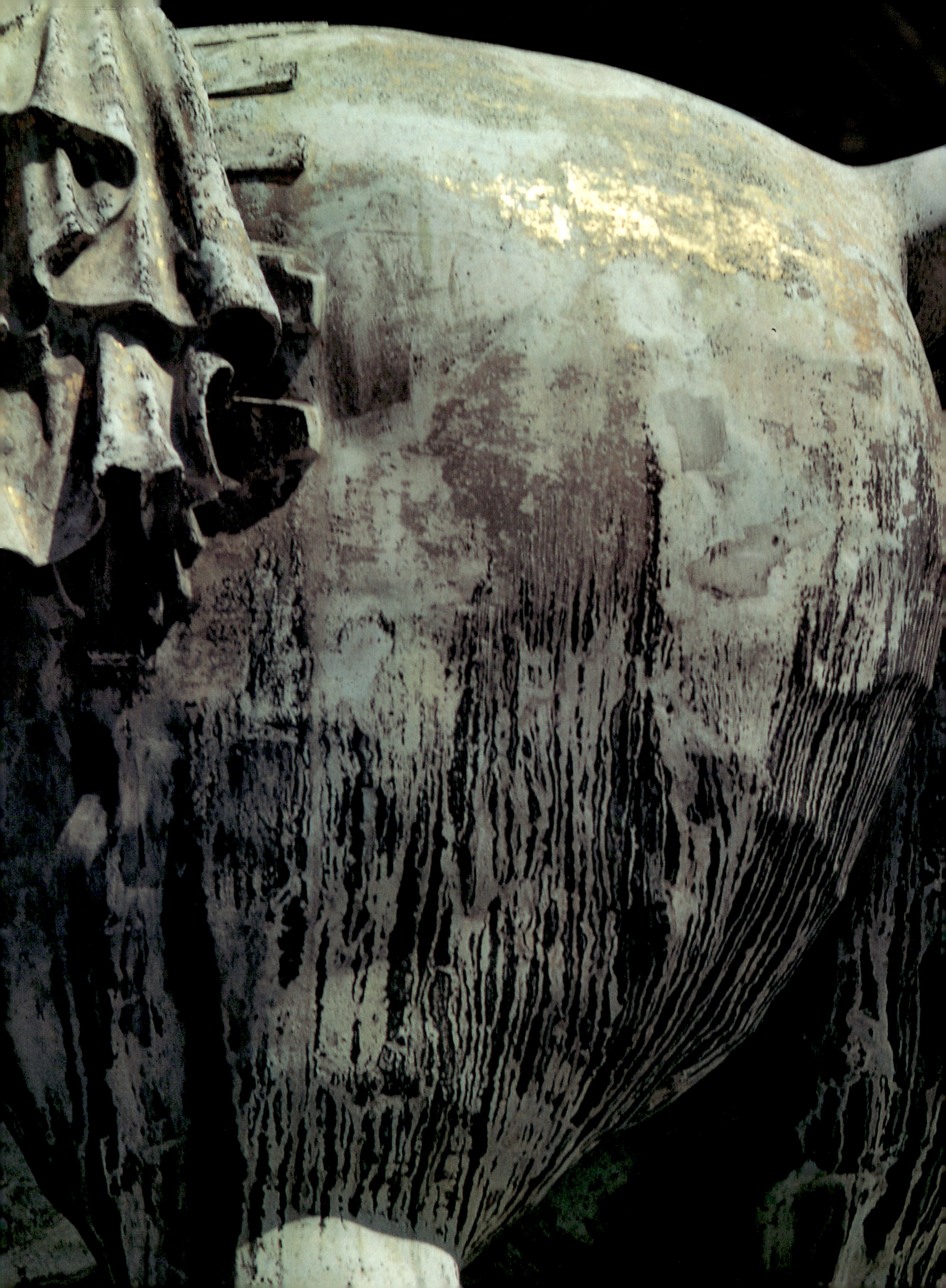

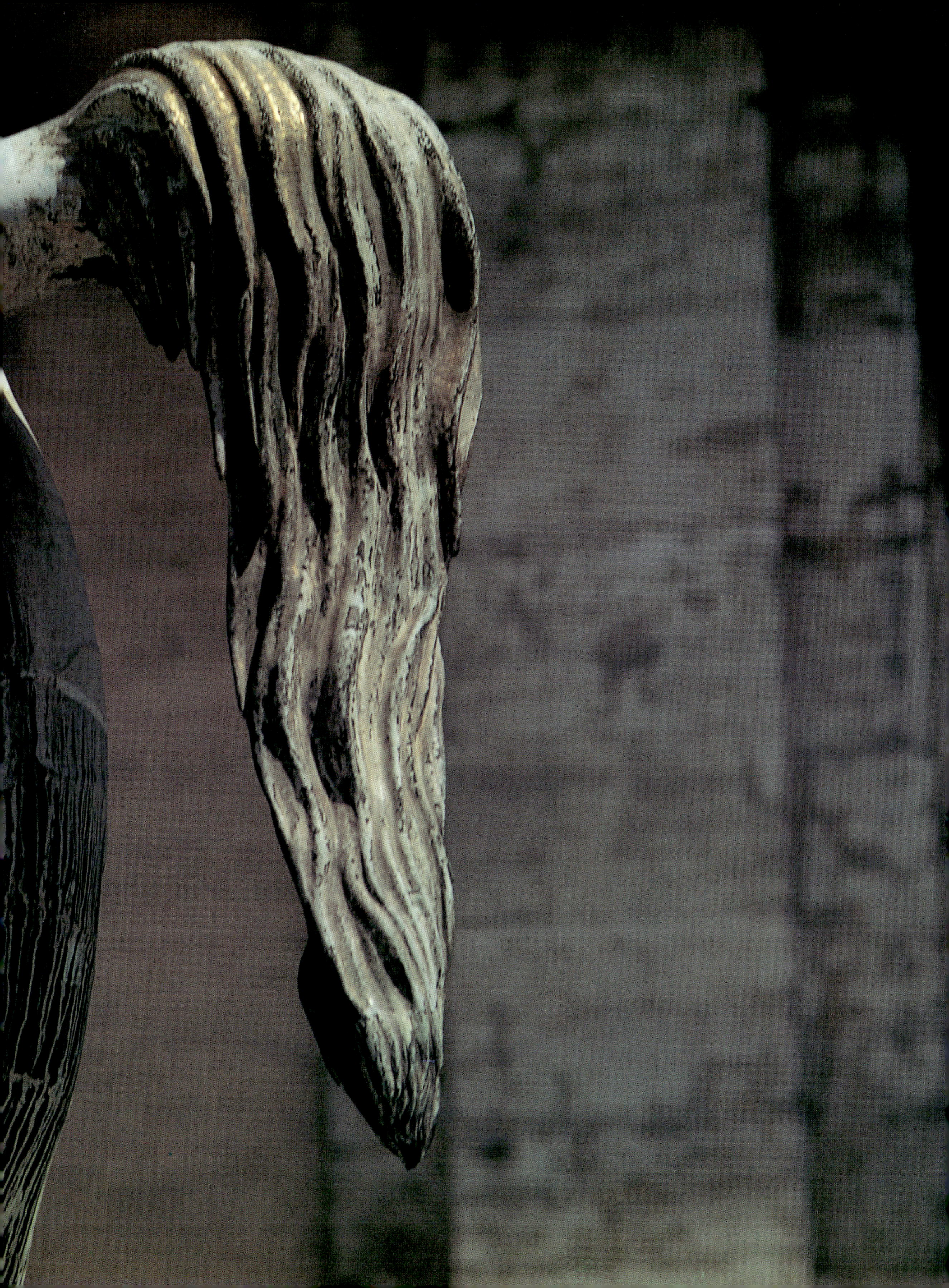

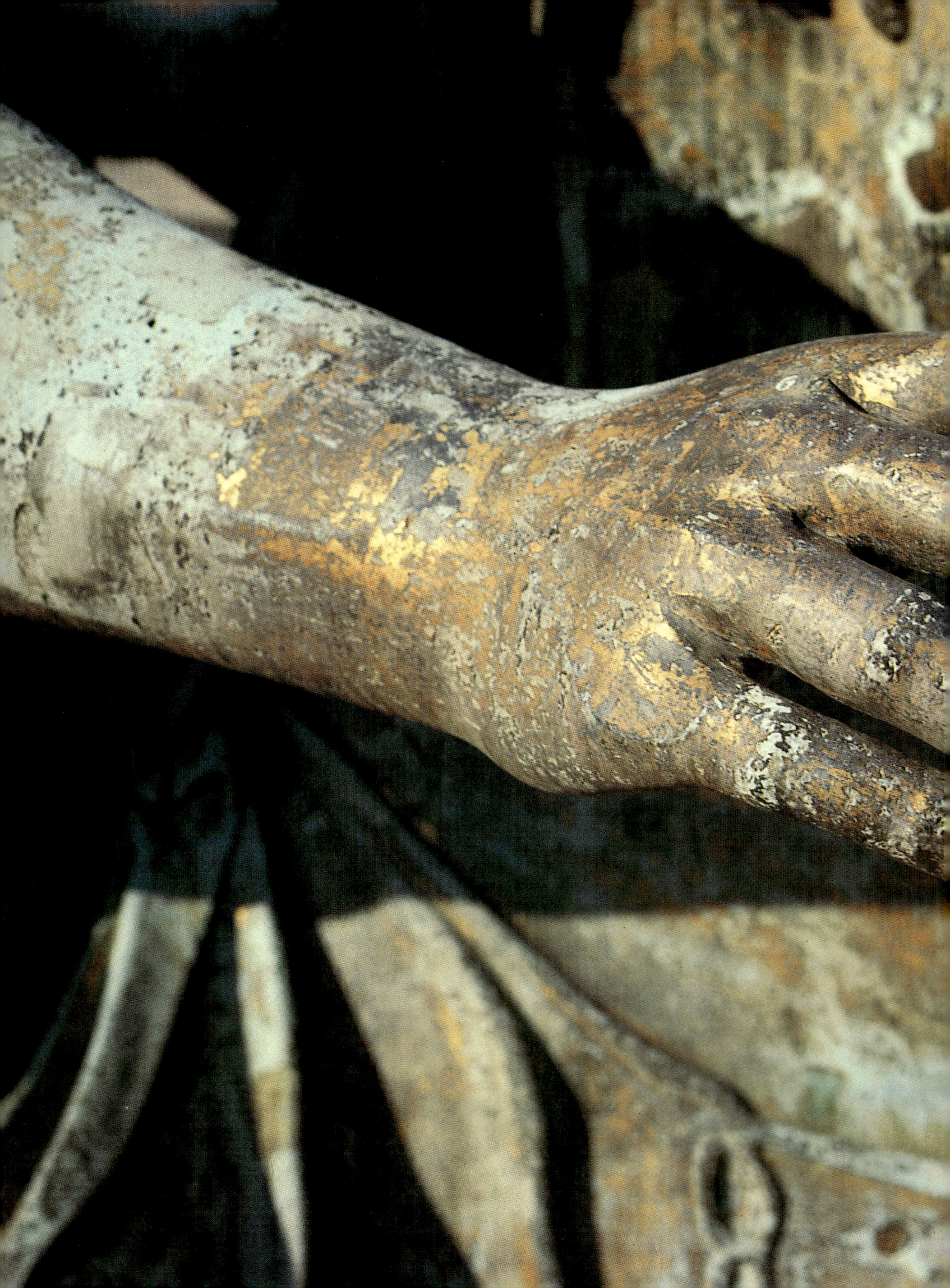

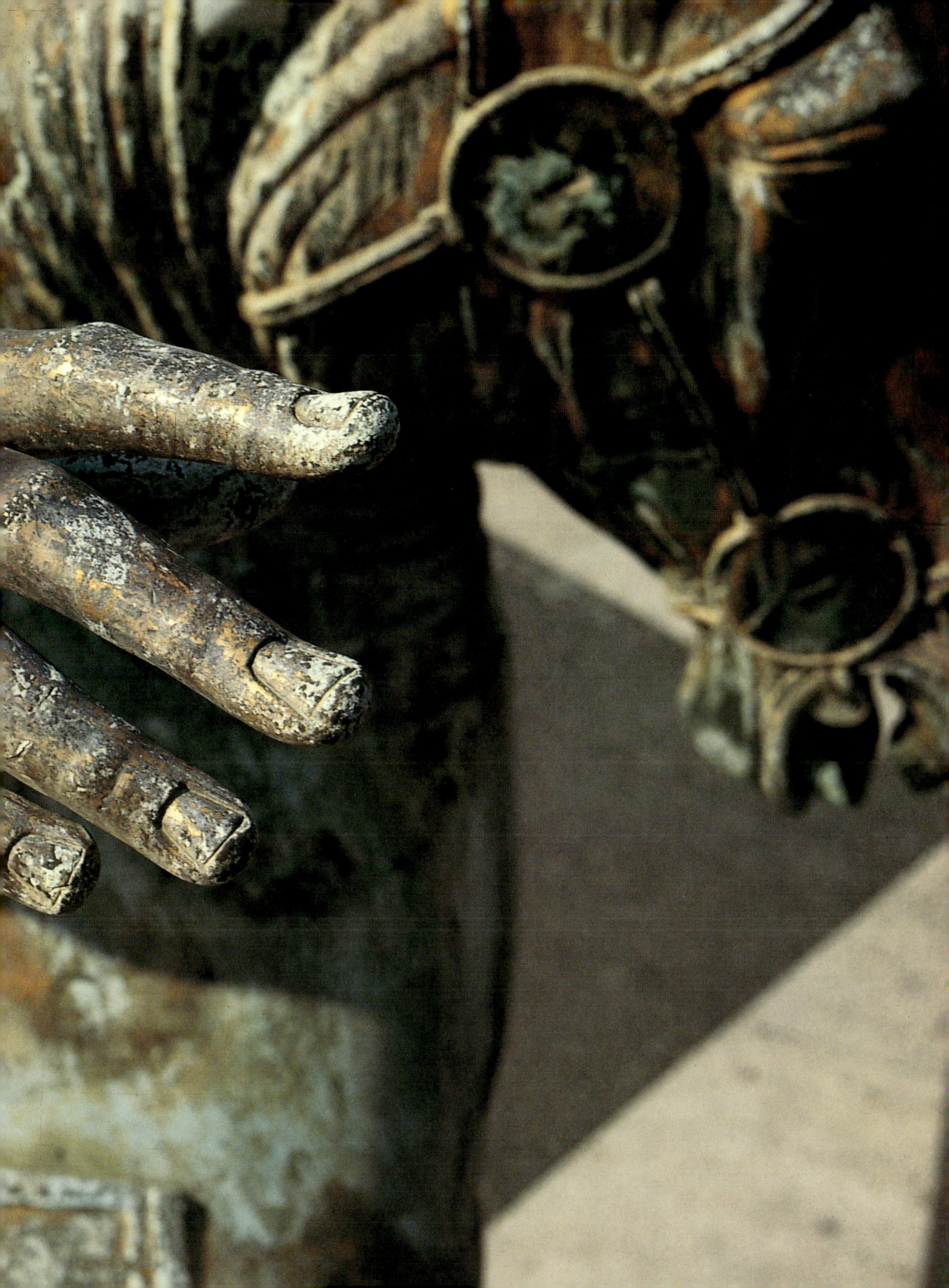

**“An angry look on the face is wholly against nature. If it be assumed frequently, beauty begins to perish, and in the end is quenched beyond rekindling.”**

—MARCUS AURELIUS

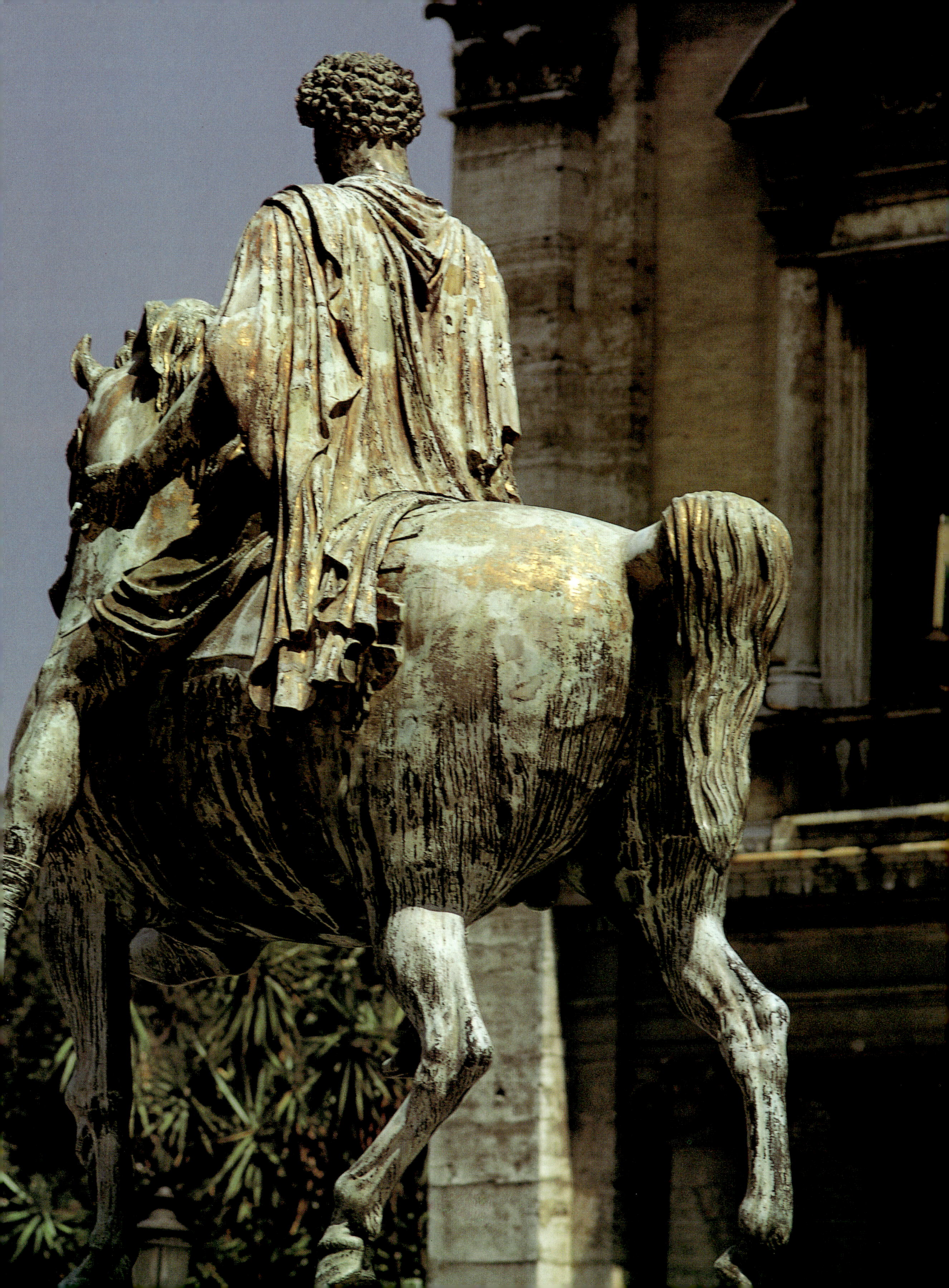

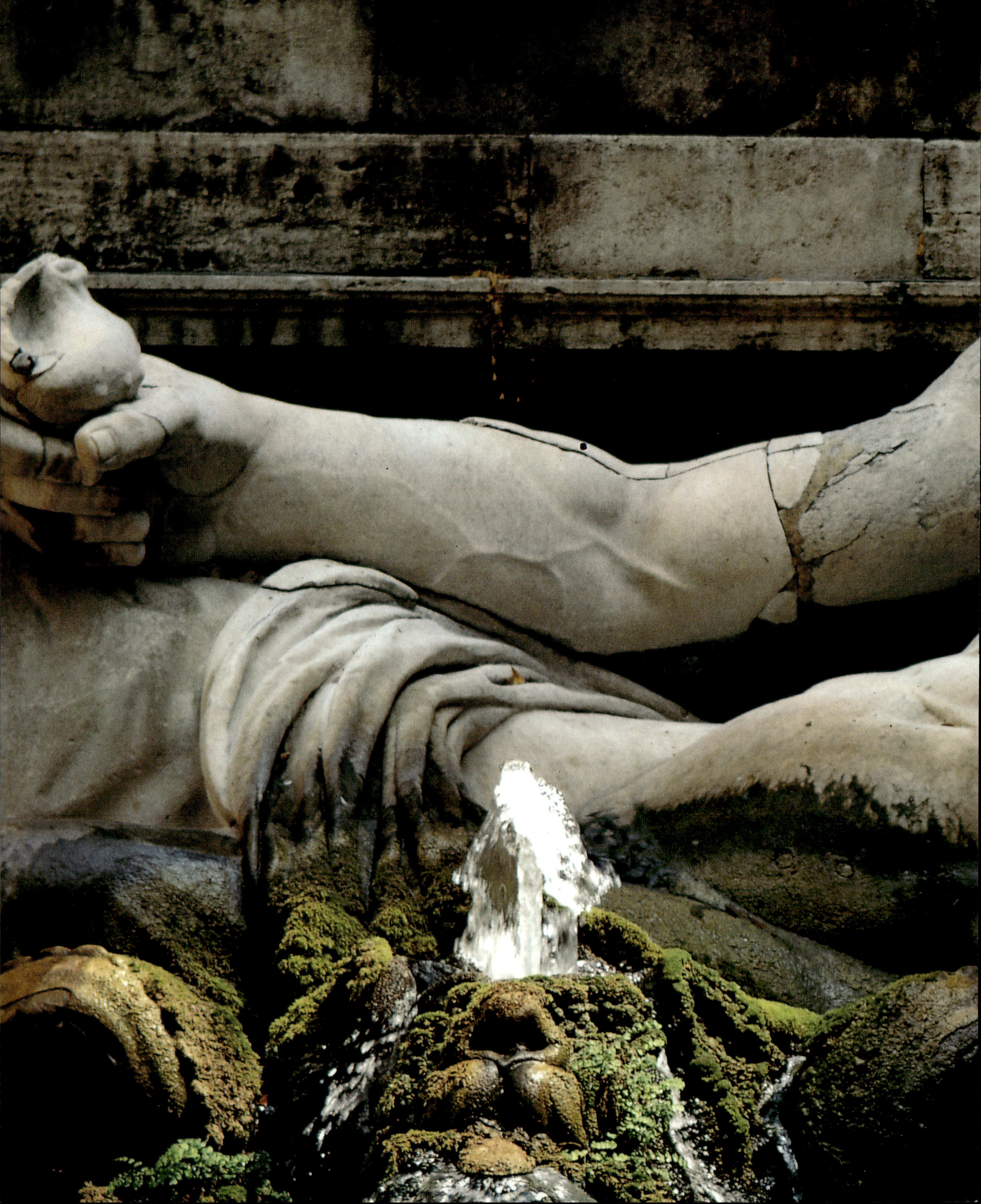

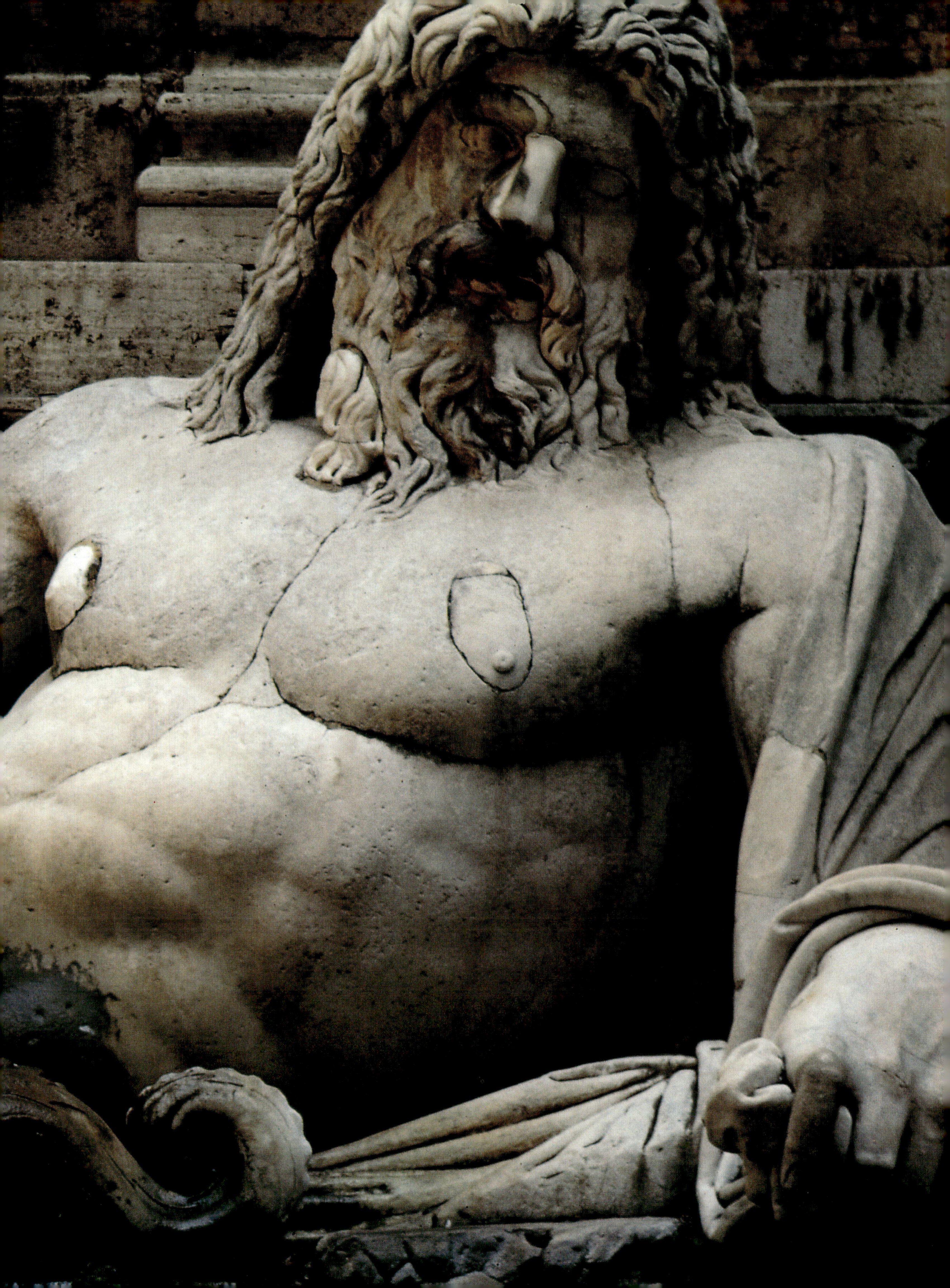

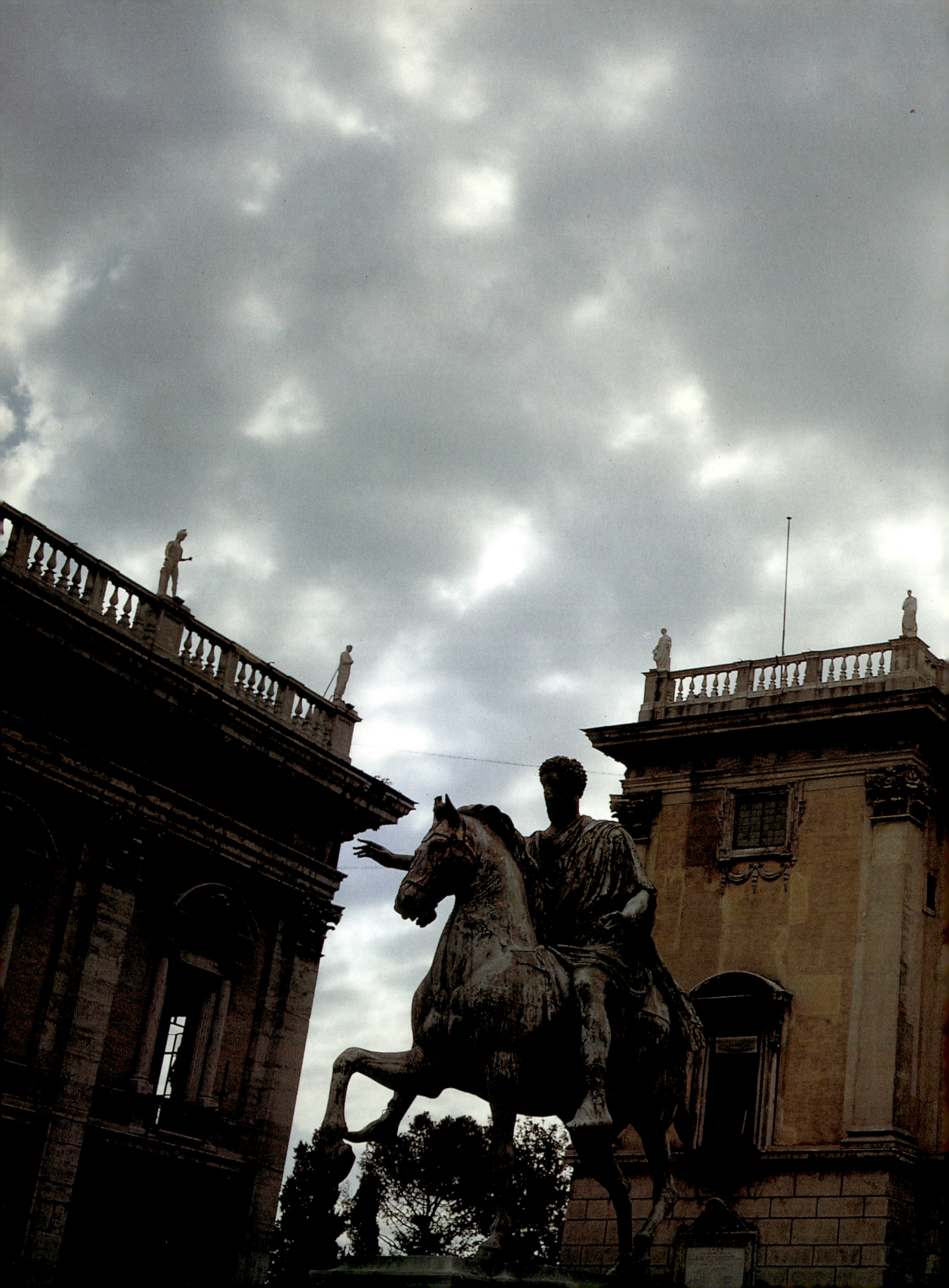

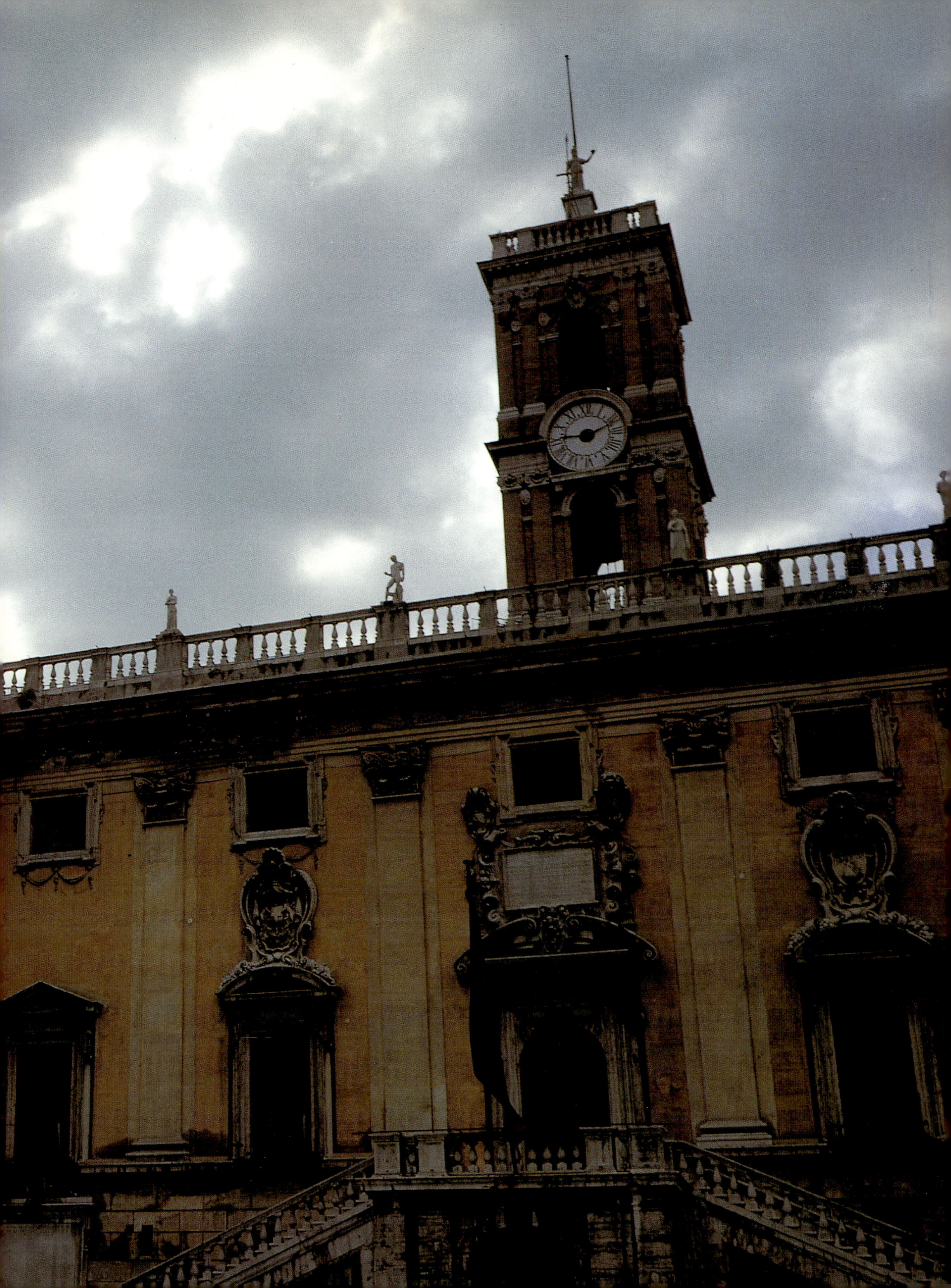

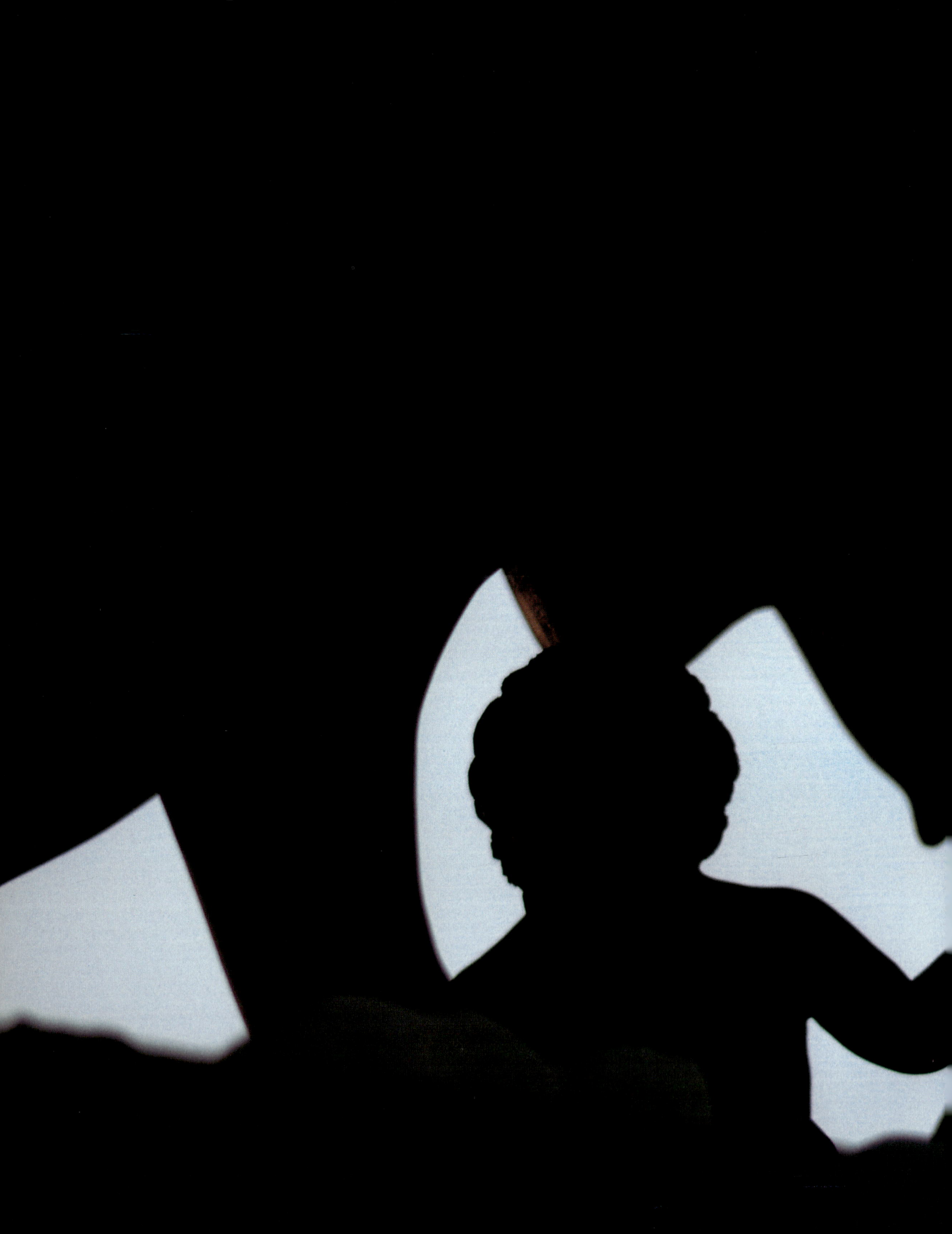

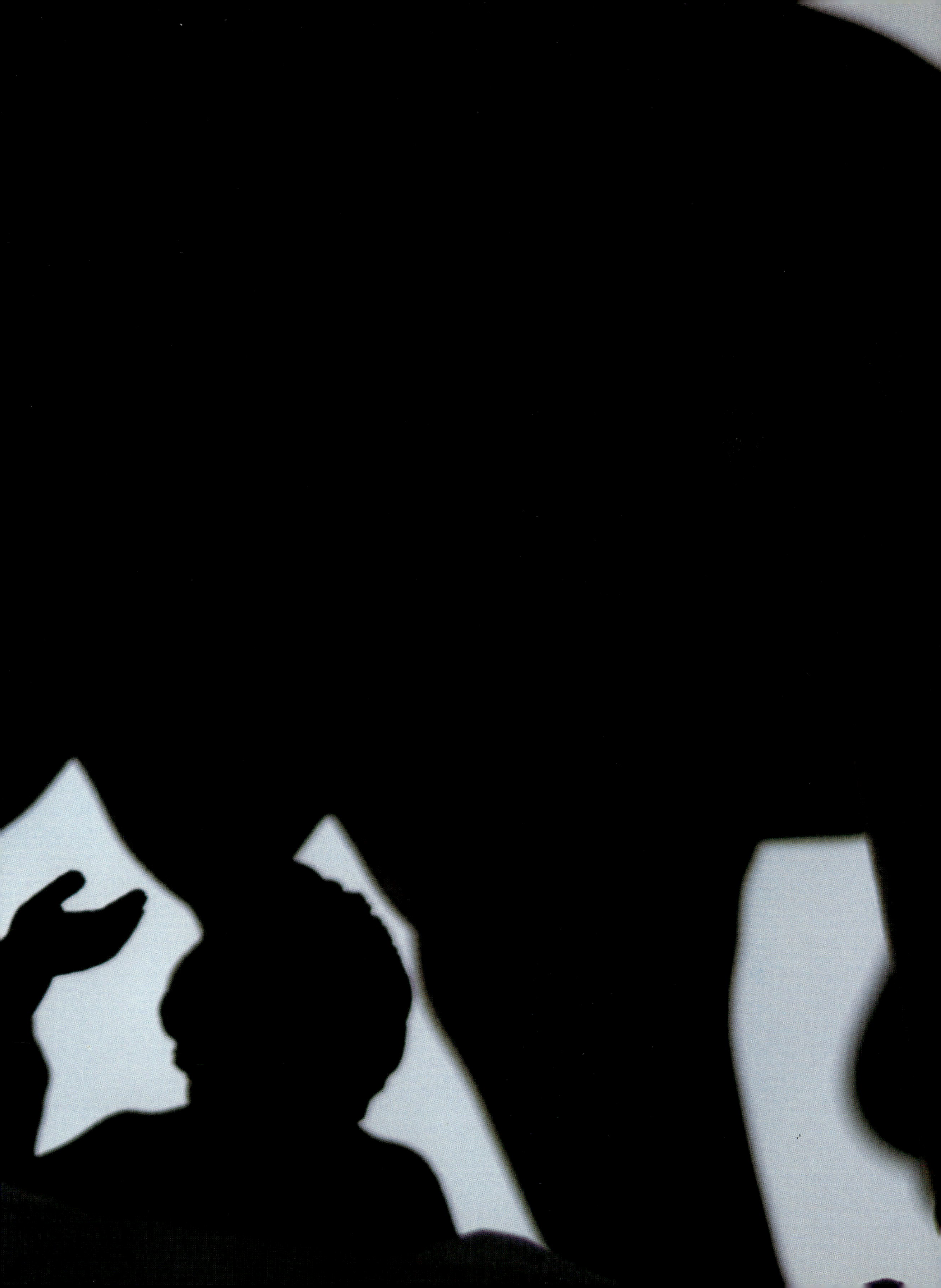

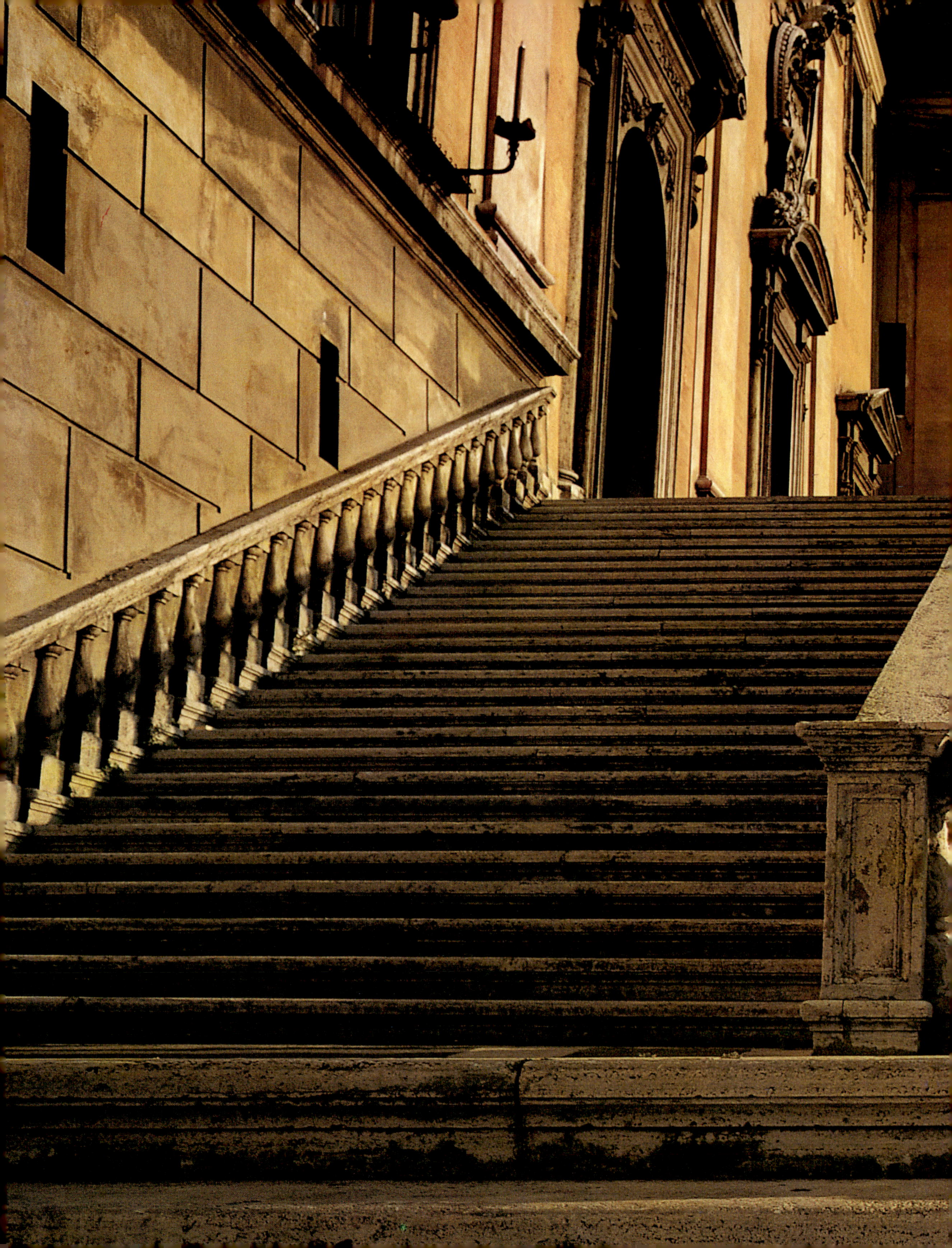

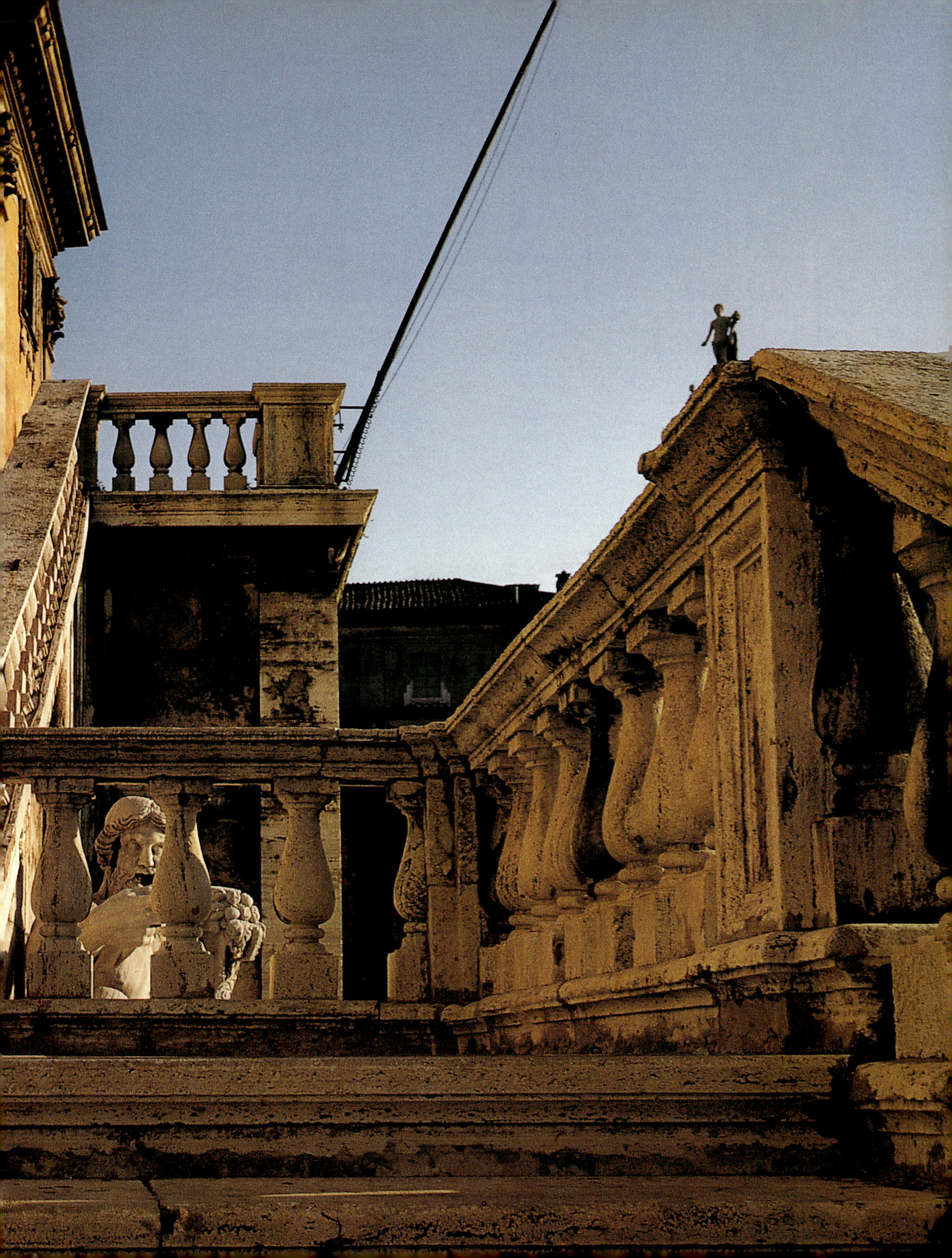

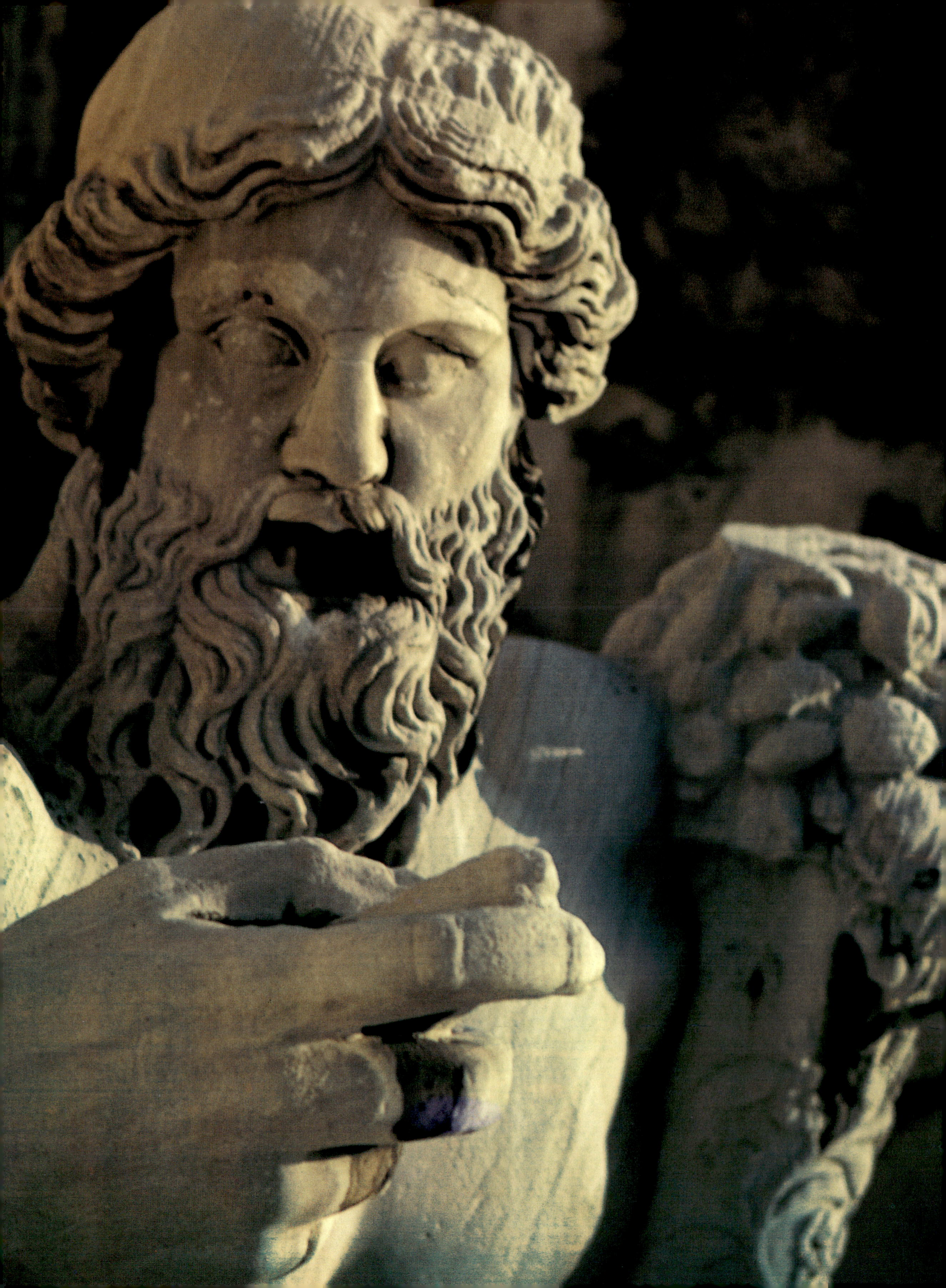

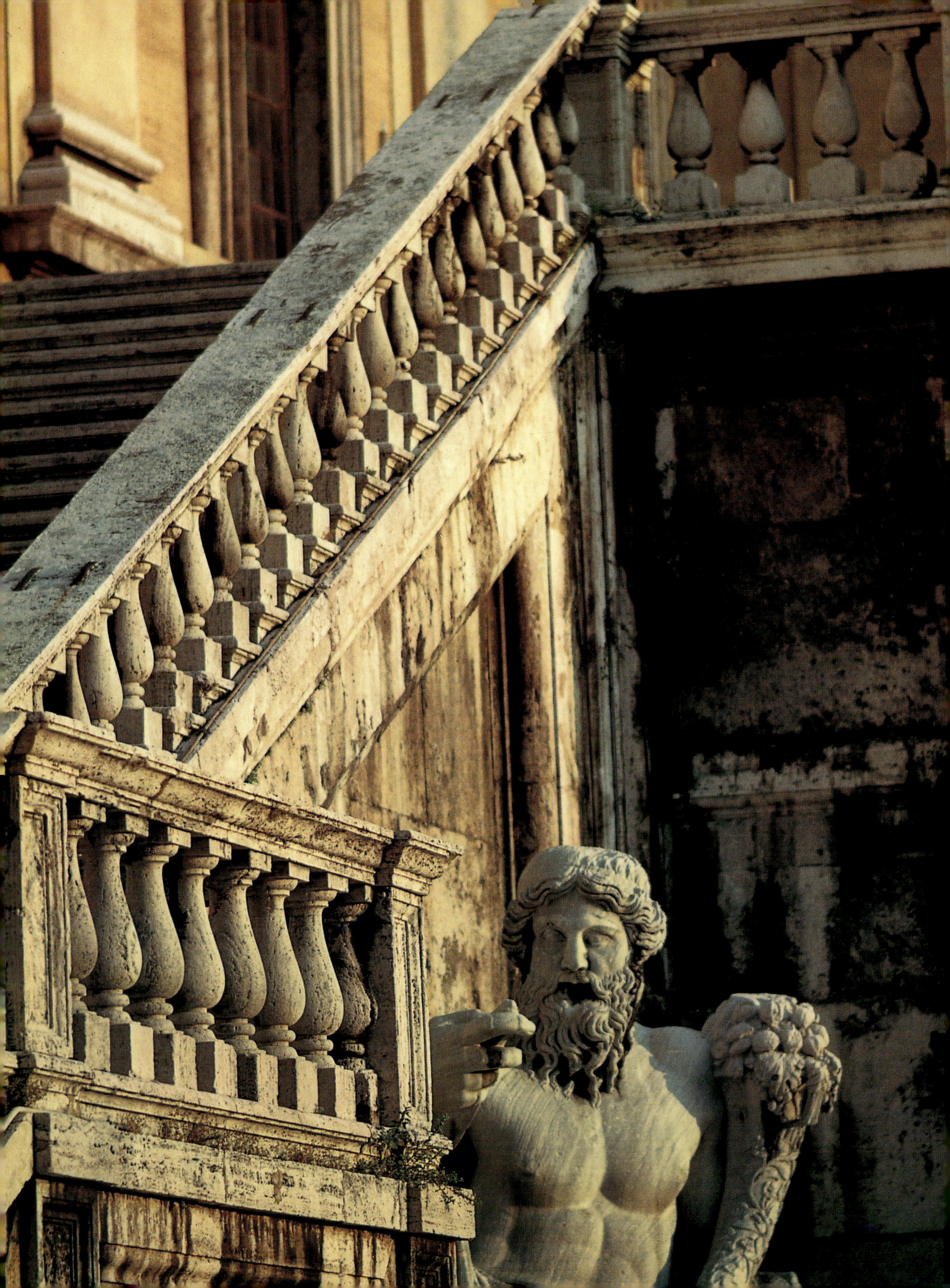

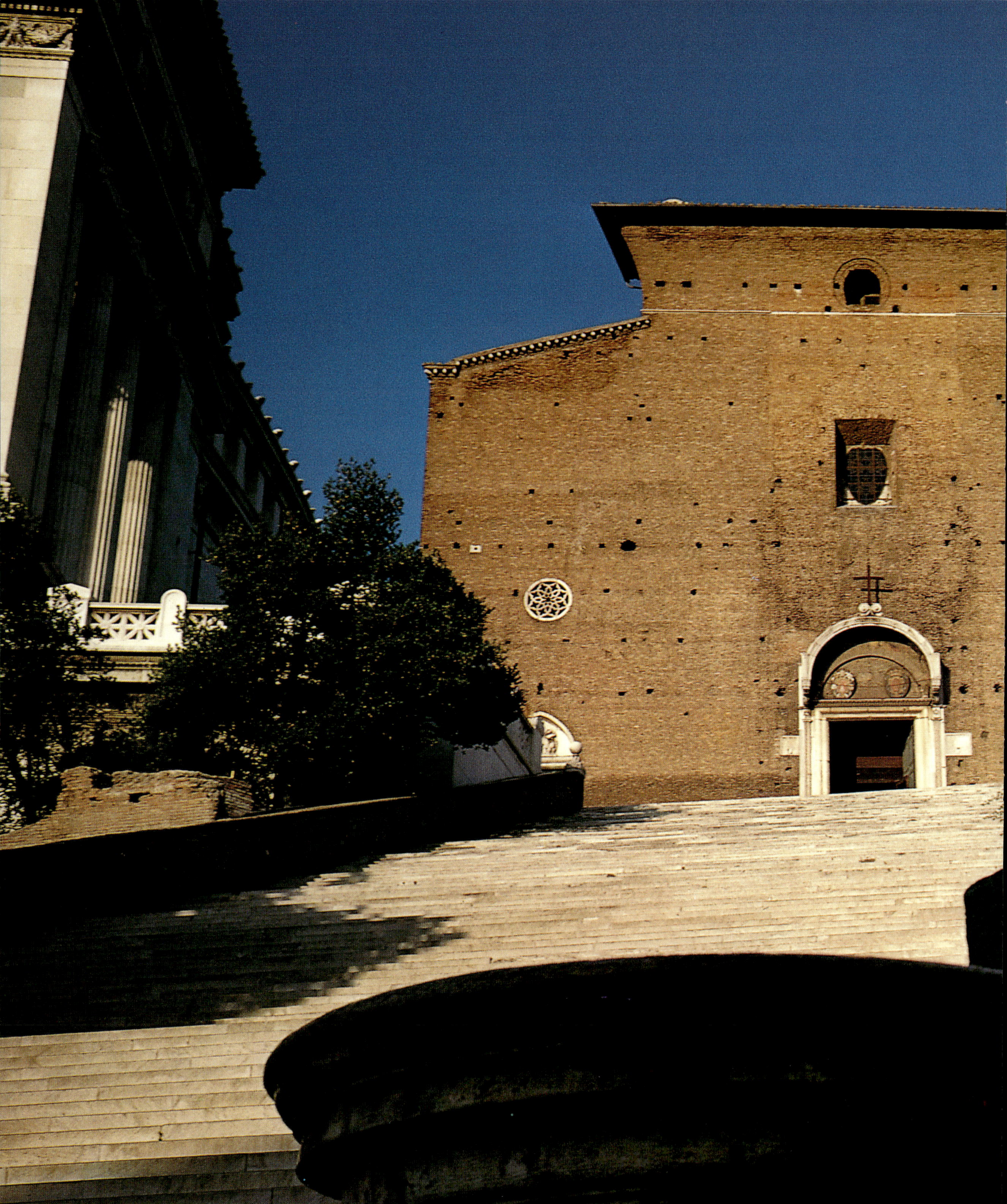

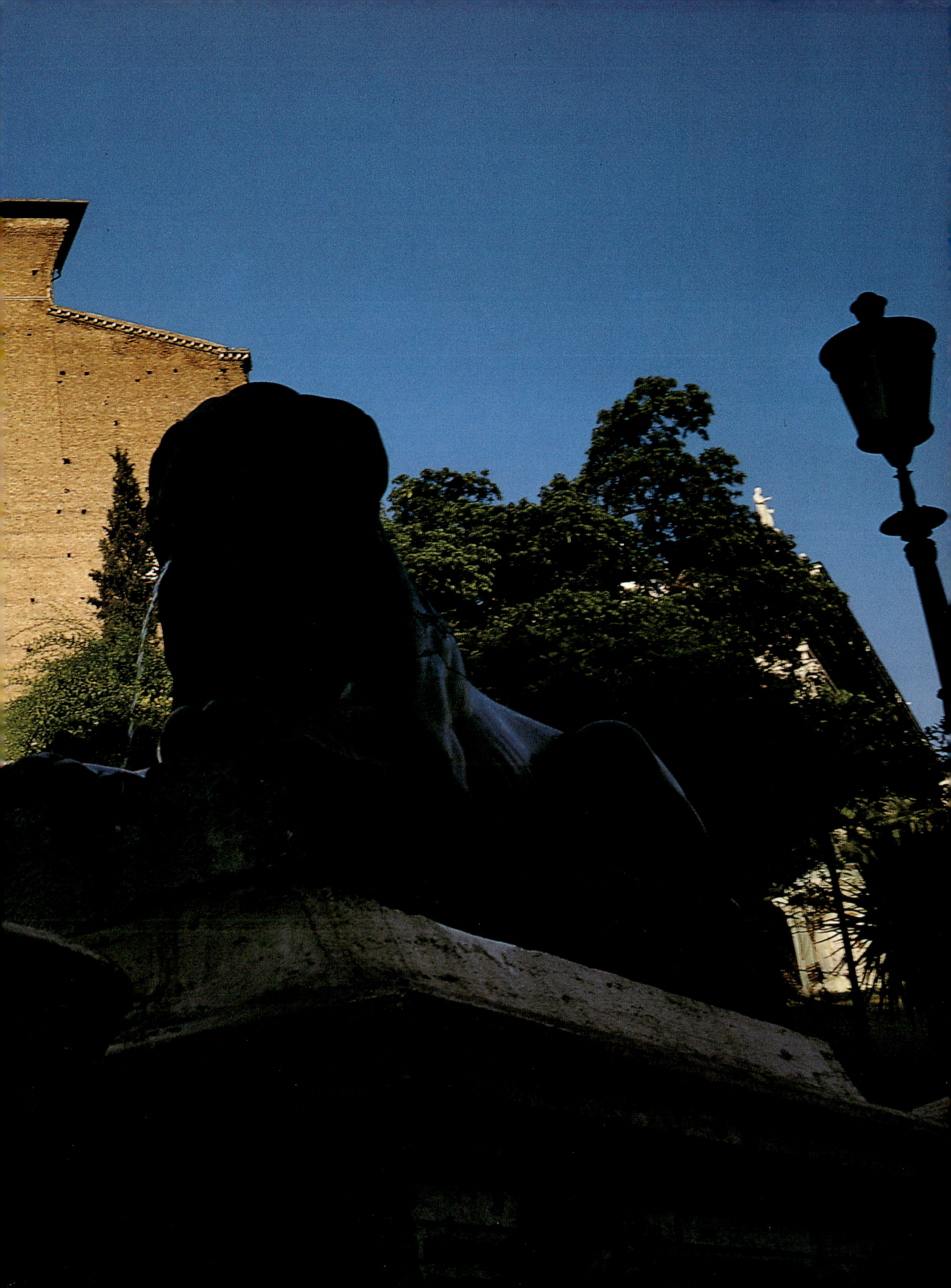

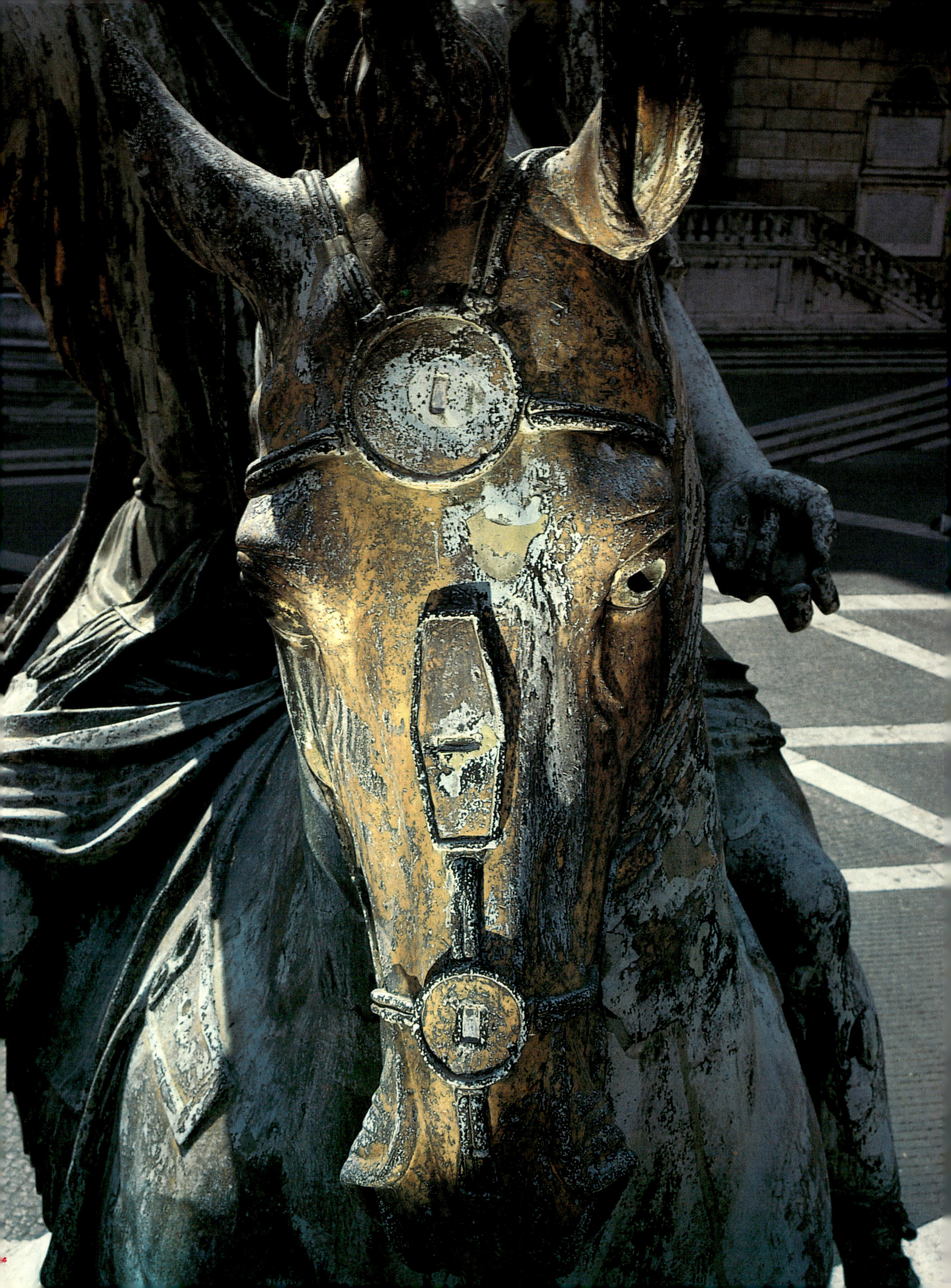

**“Always think of the universe as one living organism, with a single substance and a single soul.... Remark the intricacy of the skein, the complexity of the web.”**

—MARCUS AURELIUS

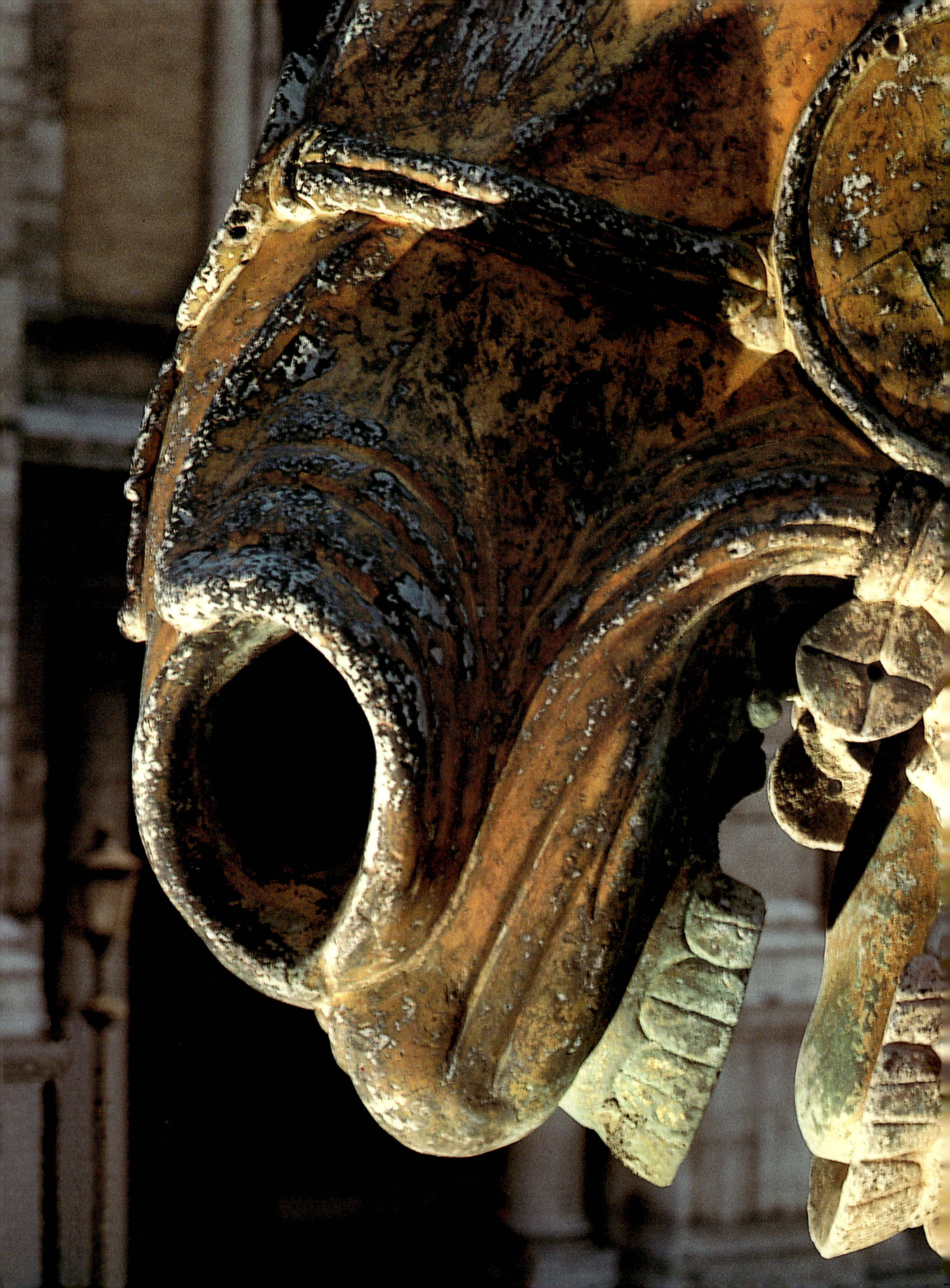

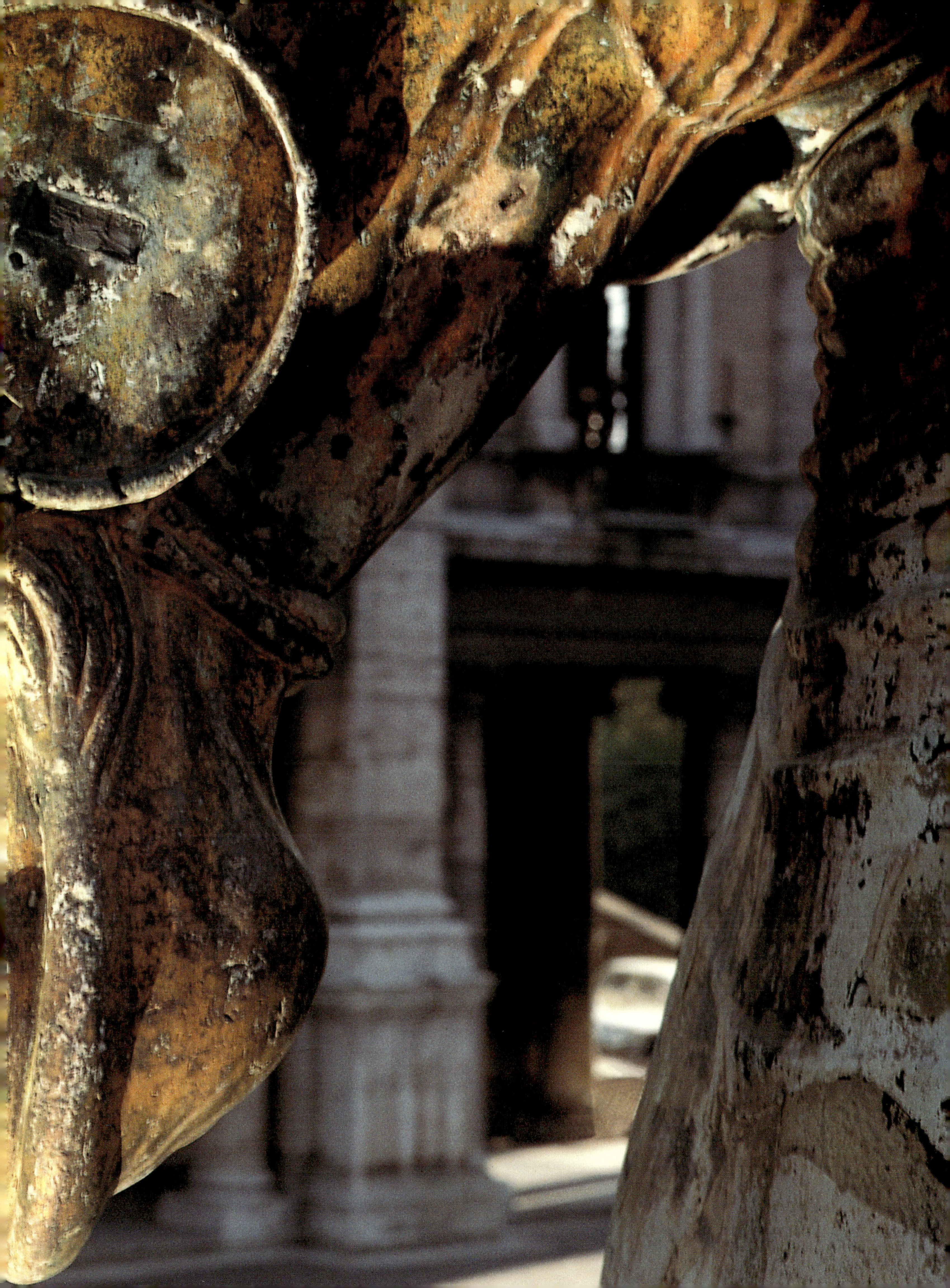

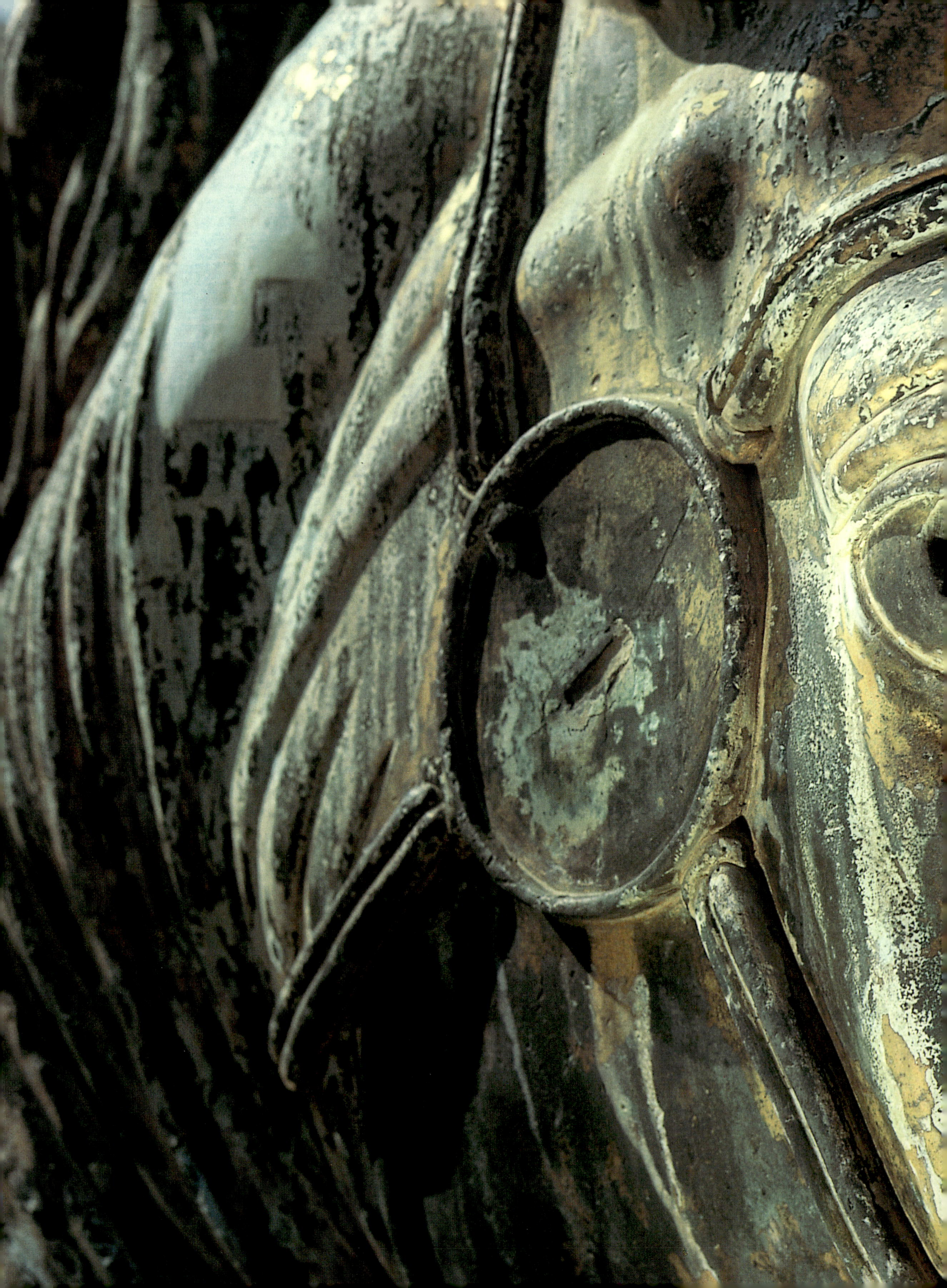

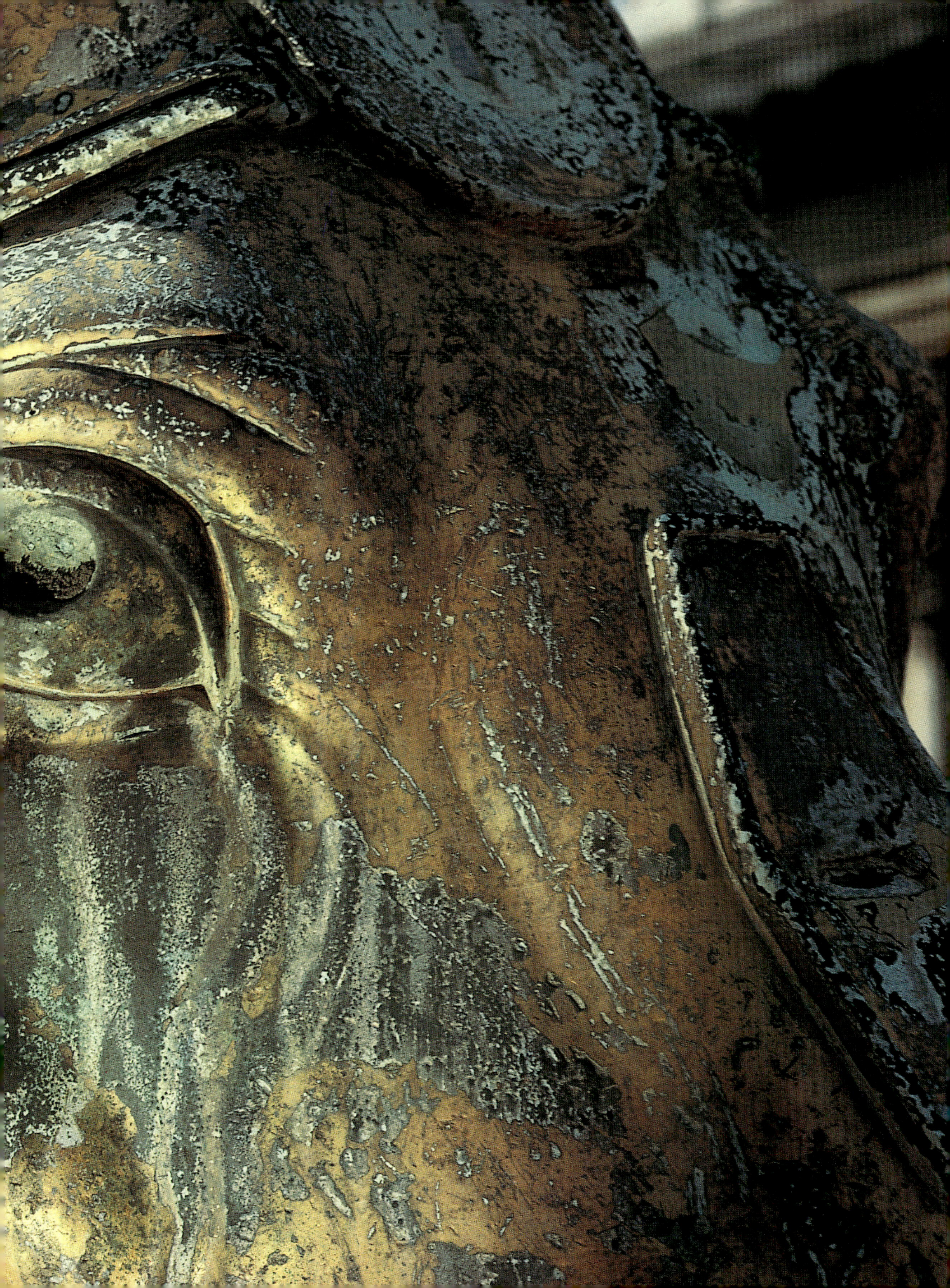

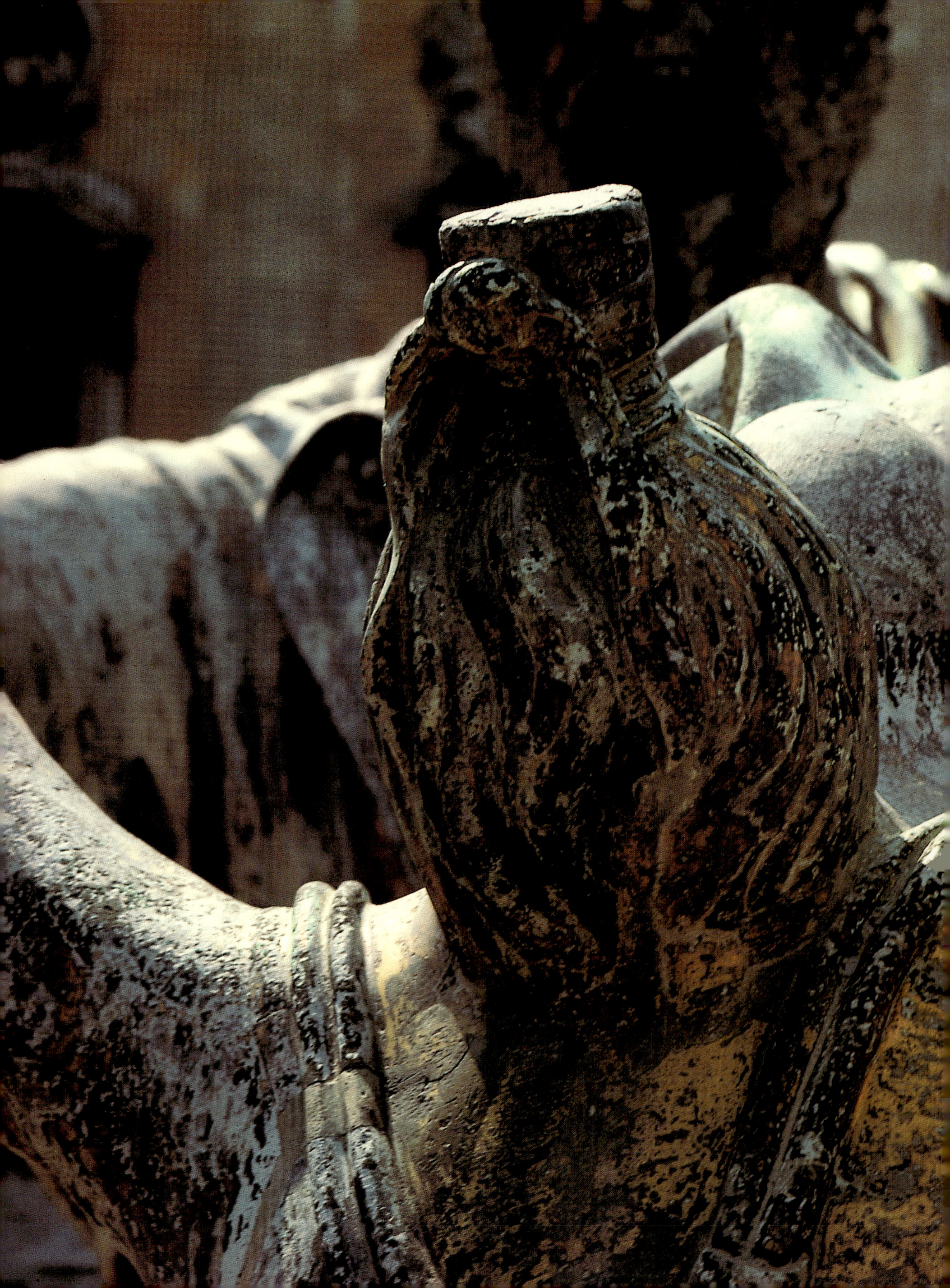

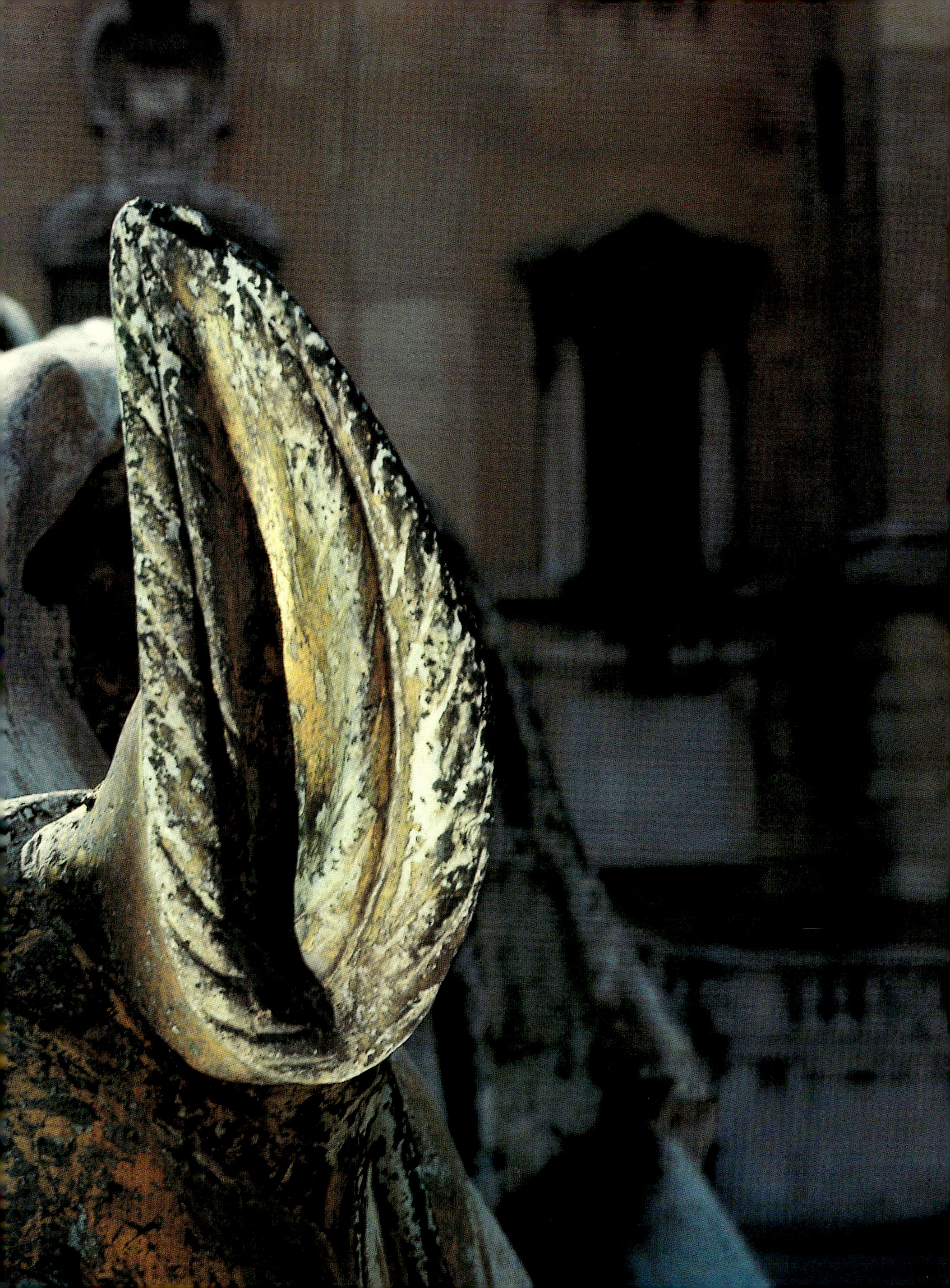

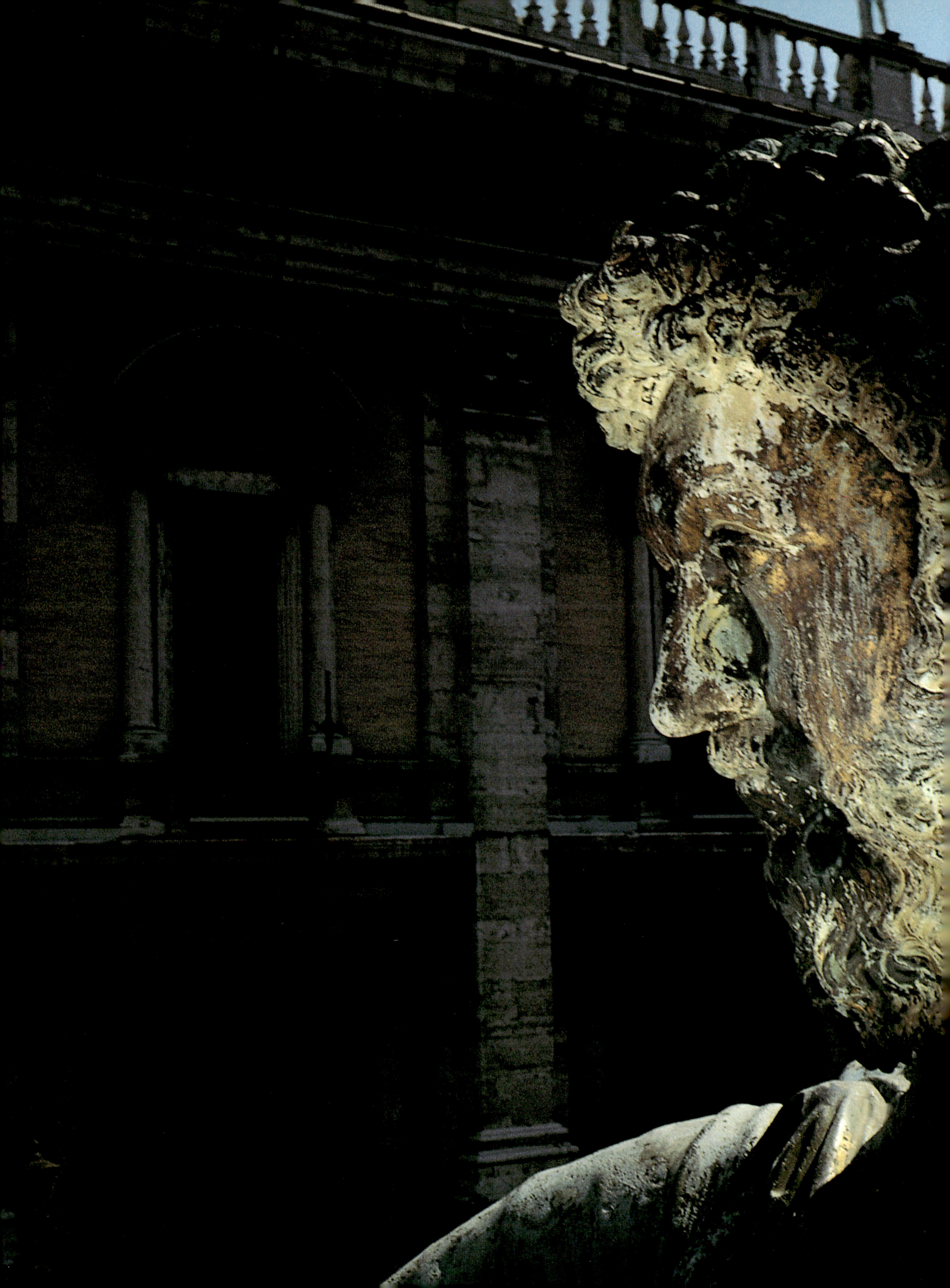

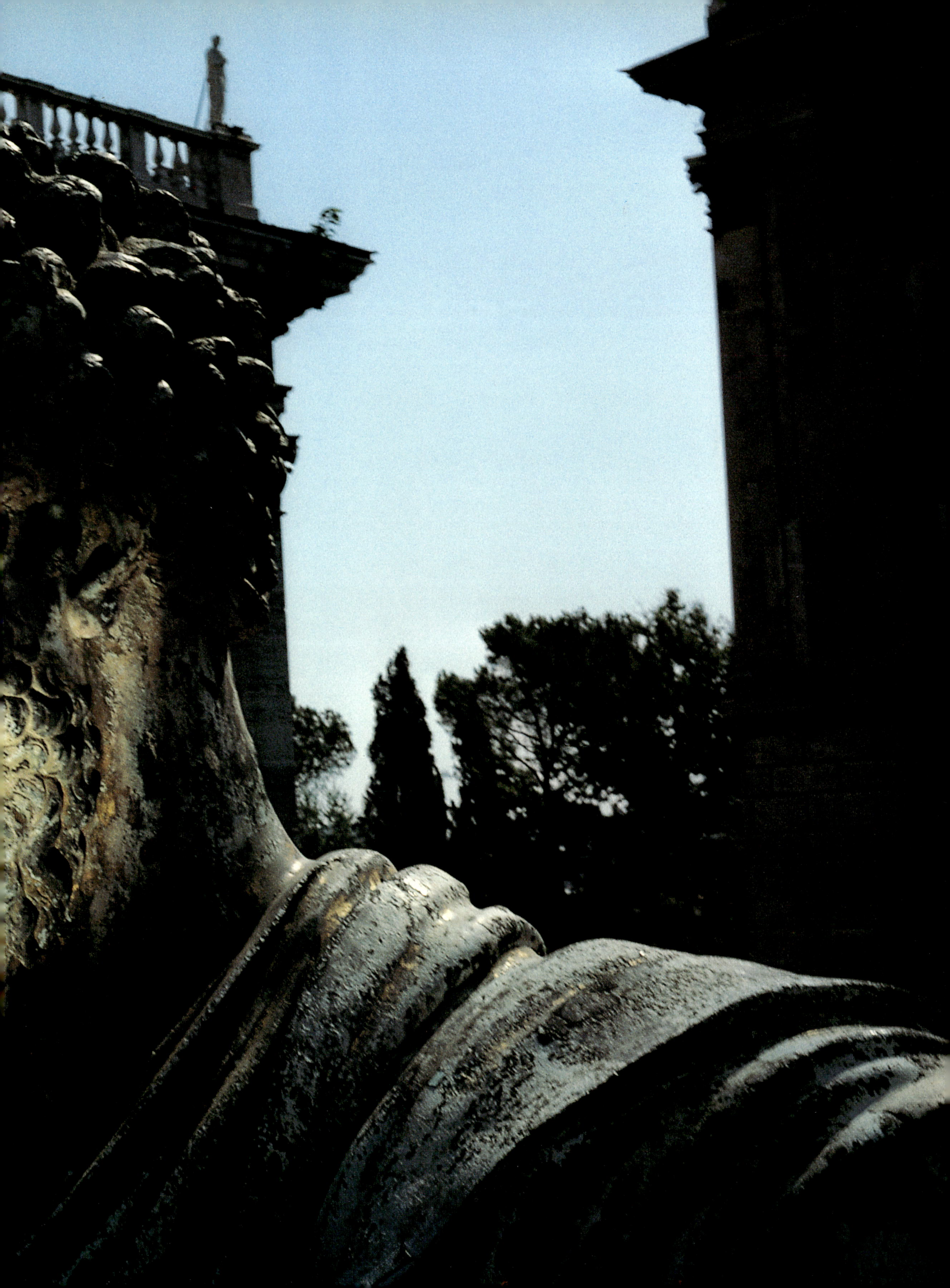

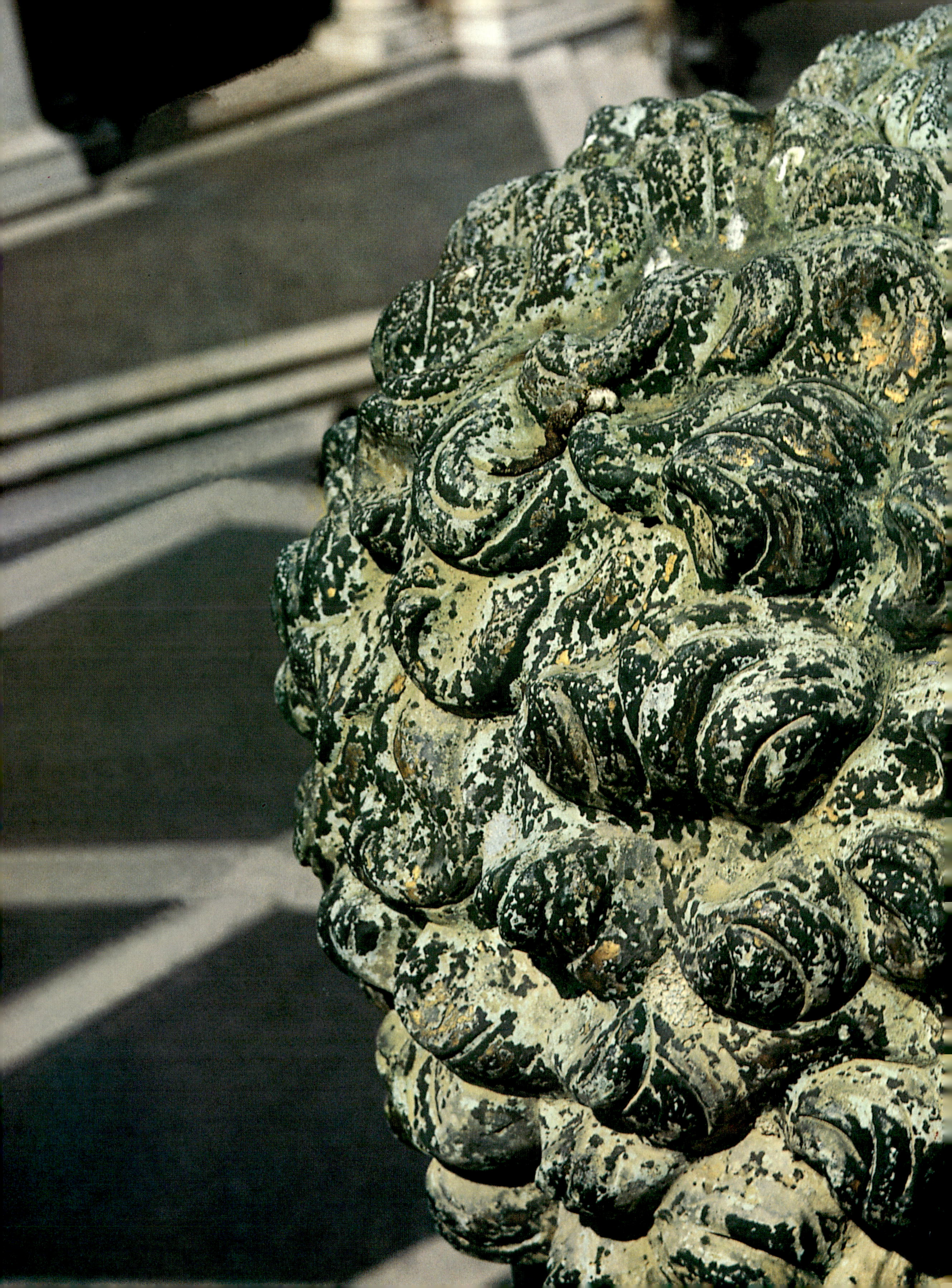

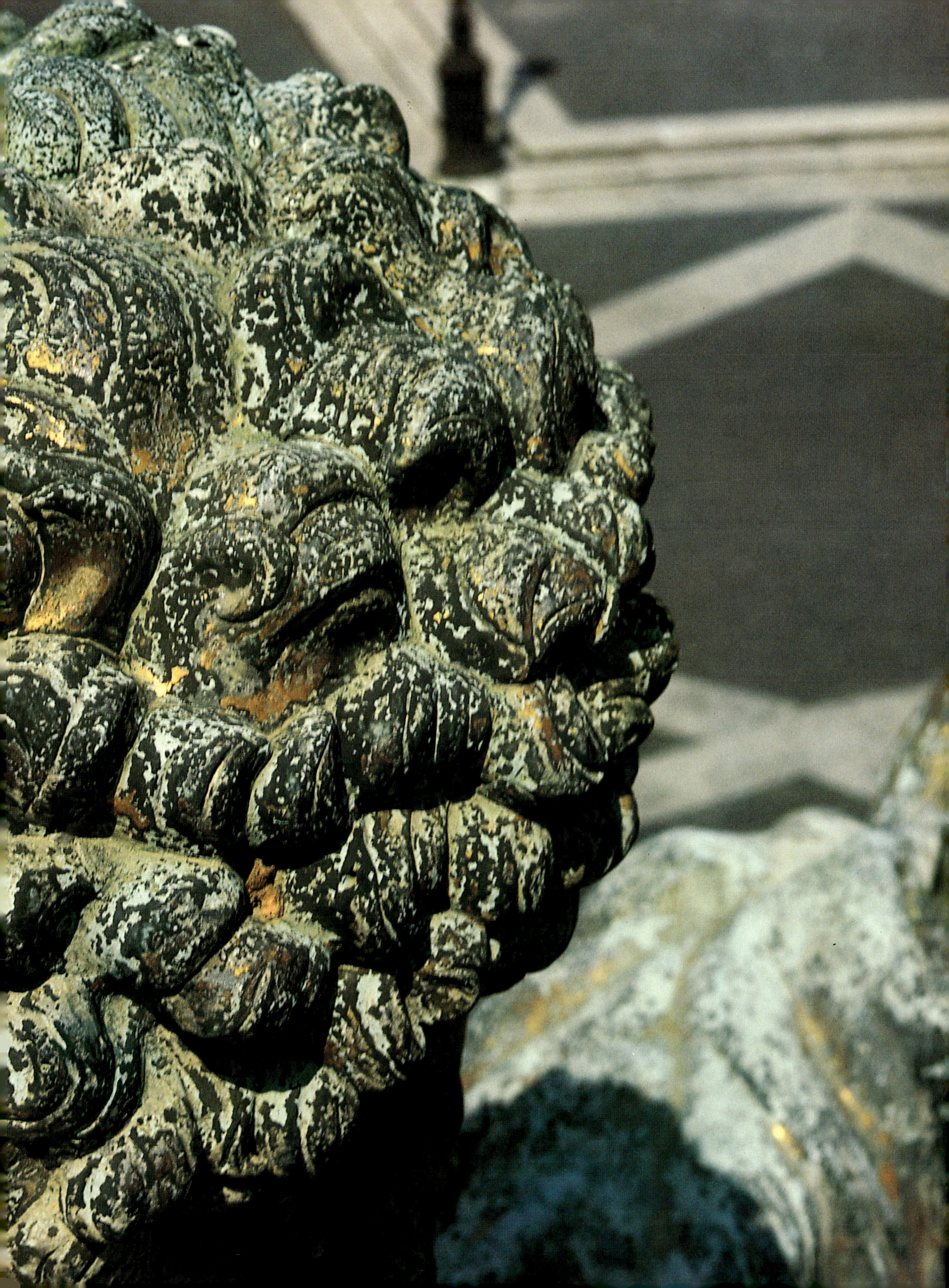

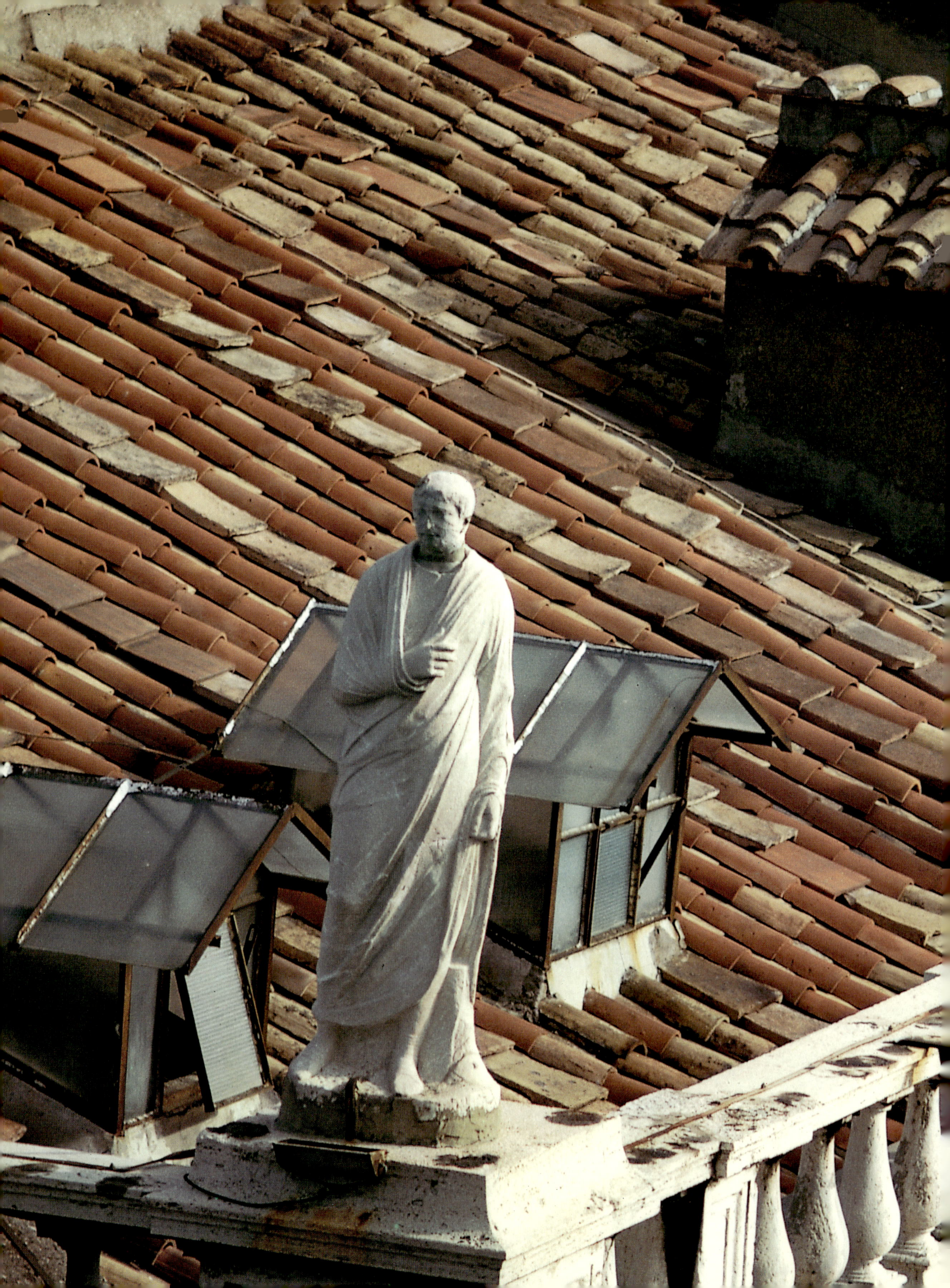

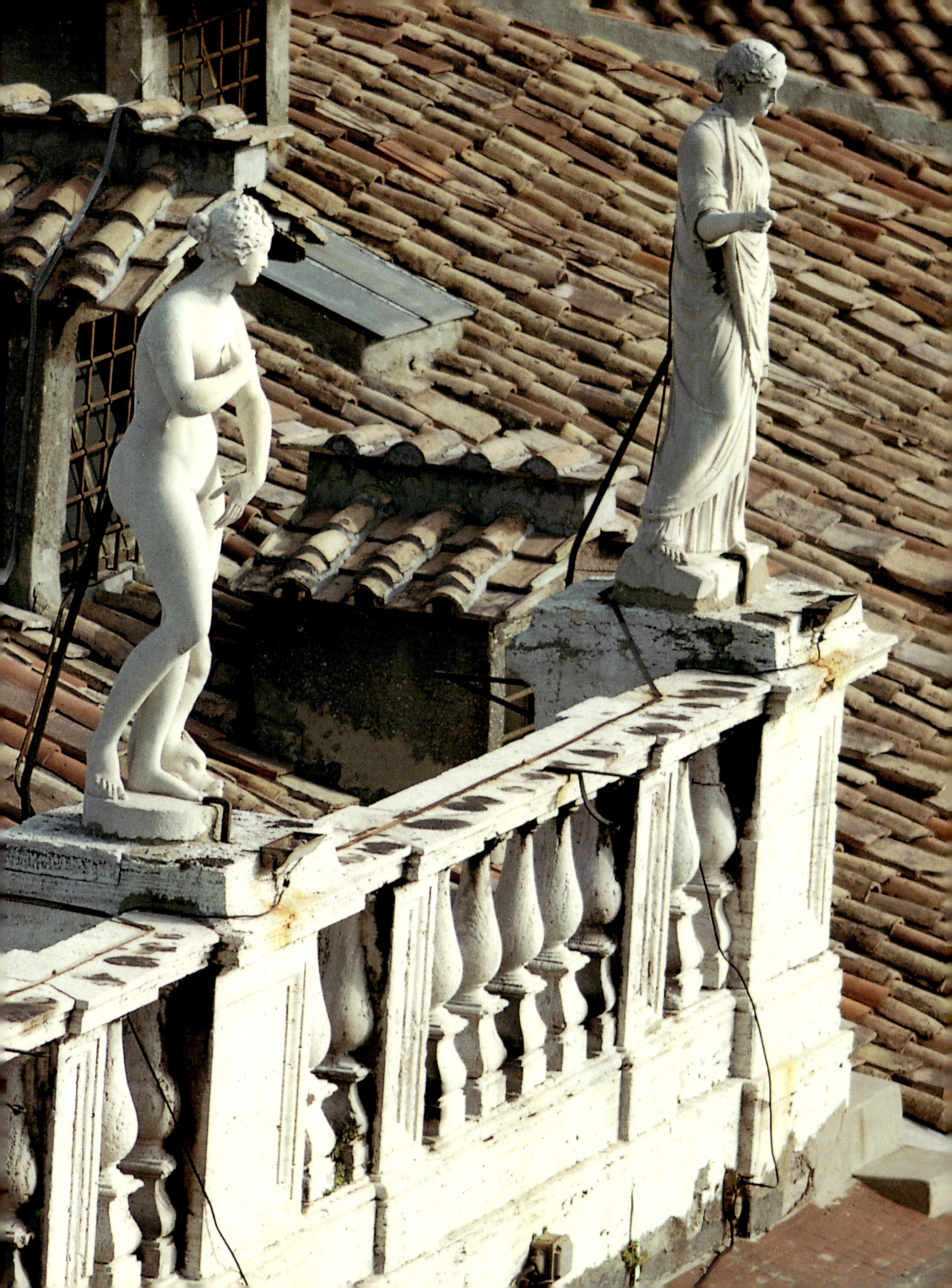

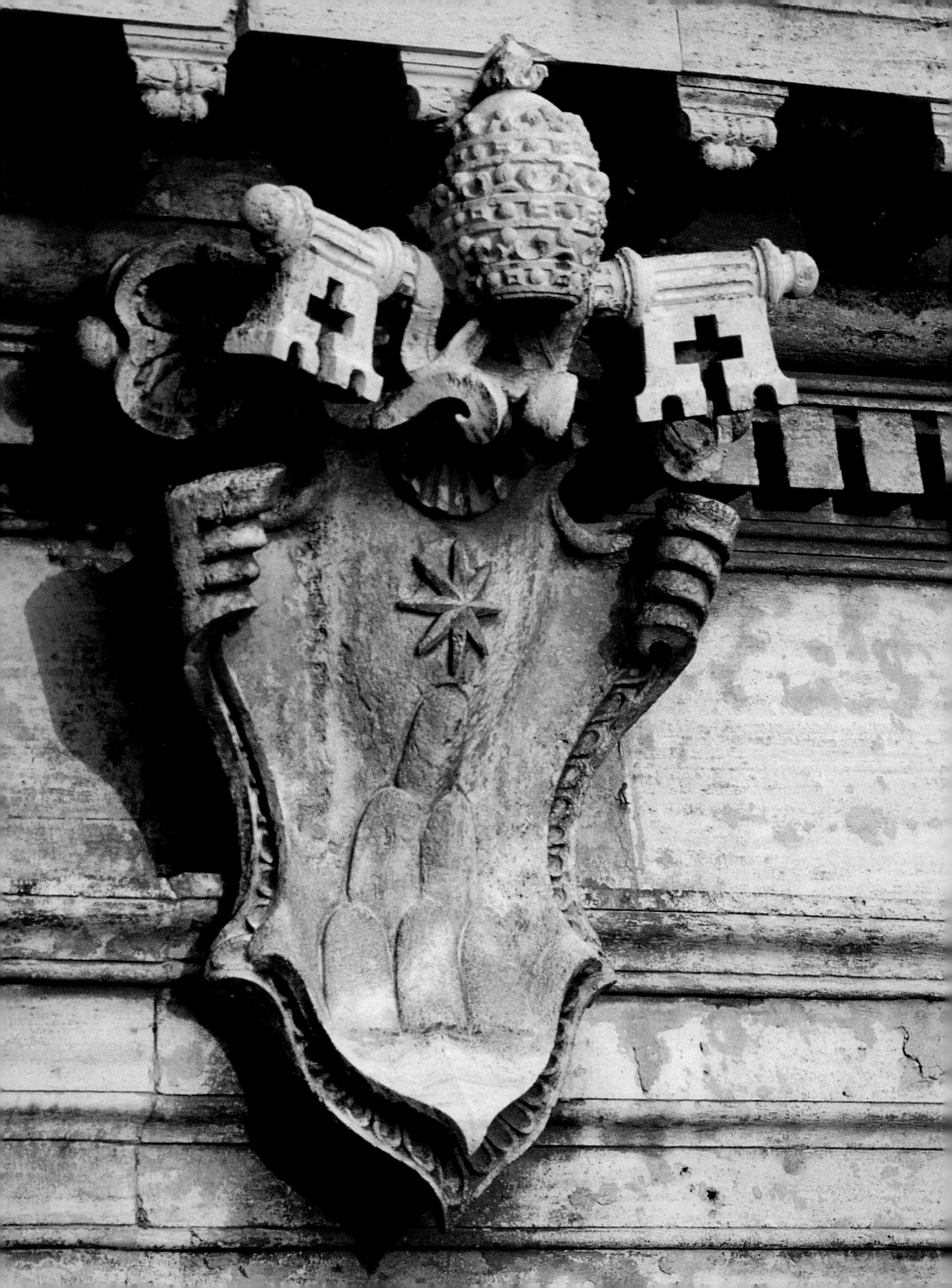

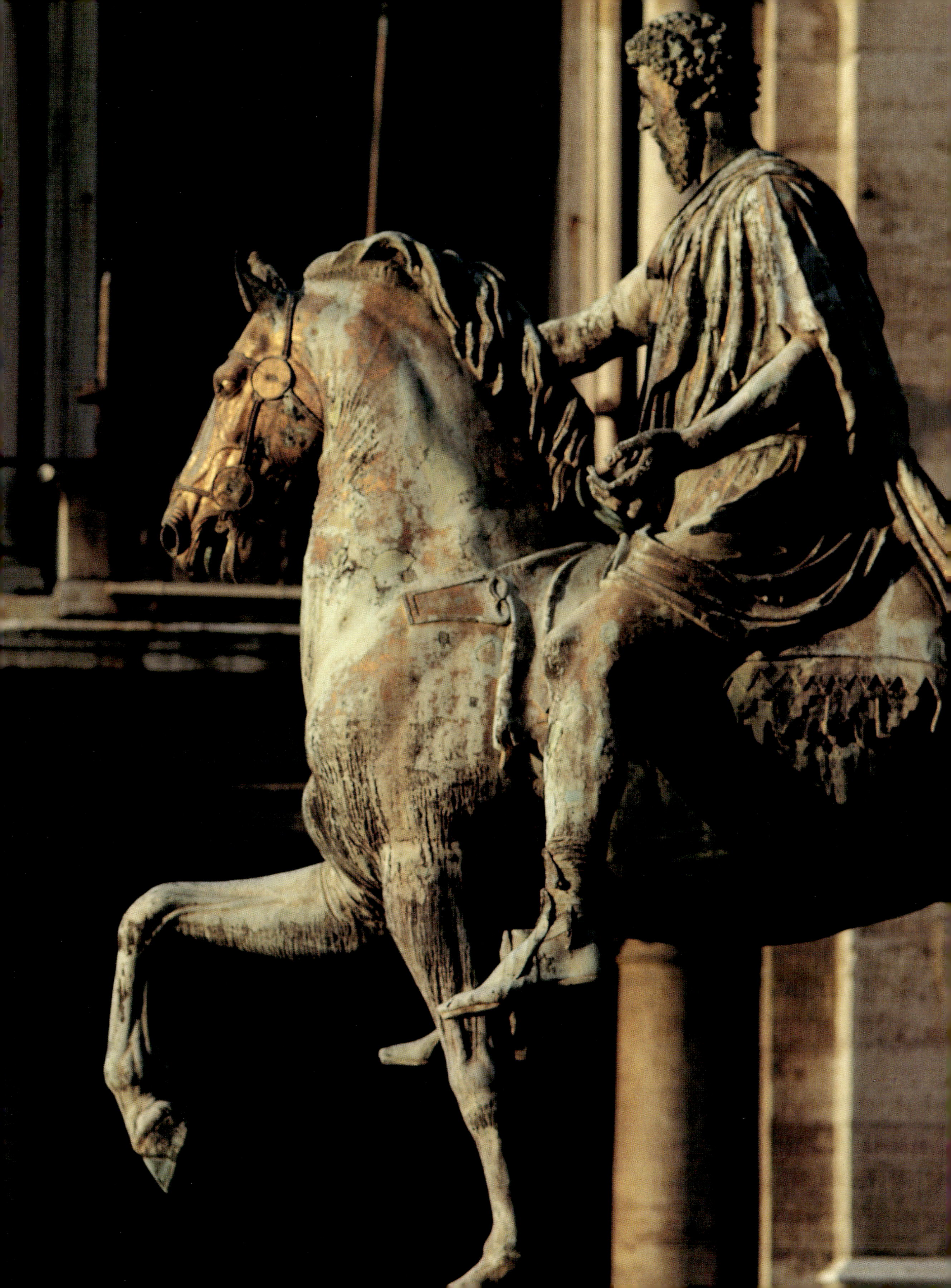

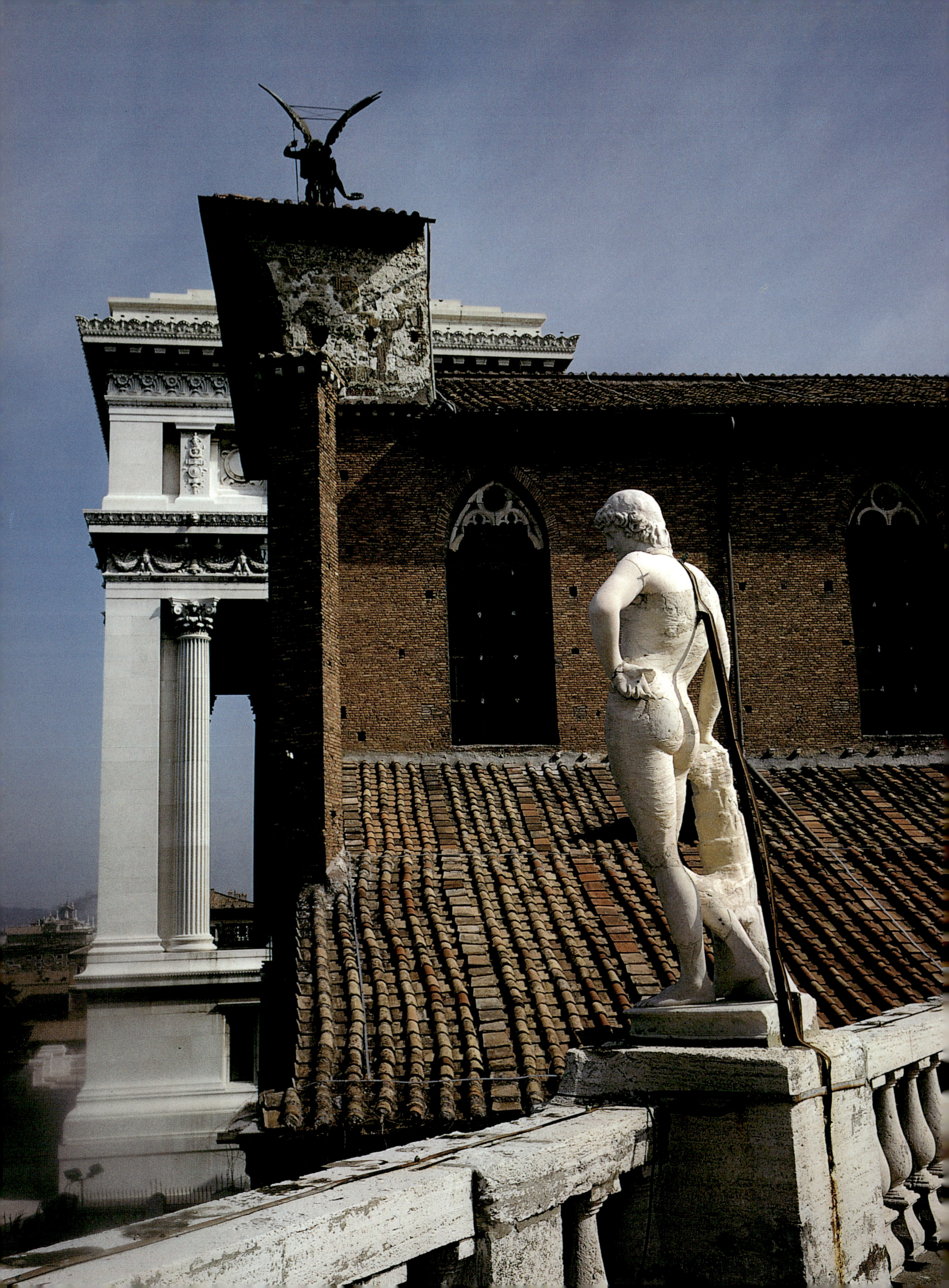

"Meditate upon what you ought to be in body and soul when death overtakes you; meditate upon the brevity of life, and the measureless gulfs of eternity behind it and before, and upon the frailty of everything material."

—MARCUS AURELIUS

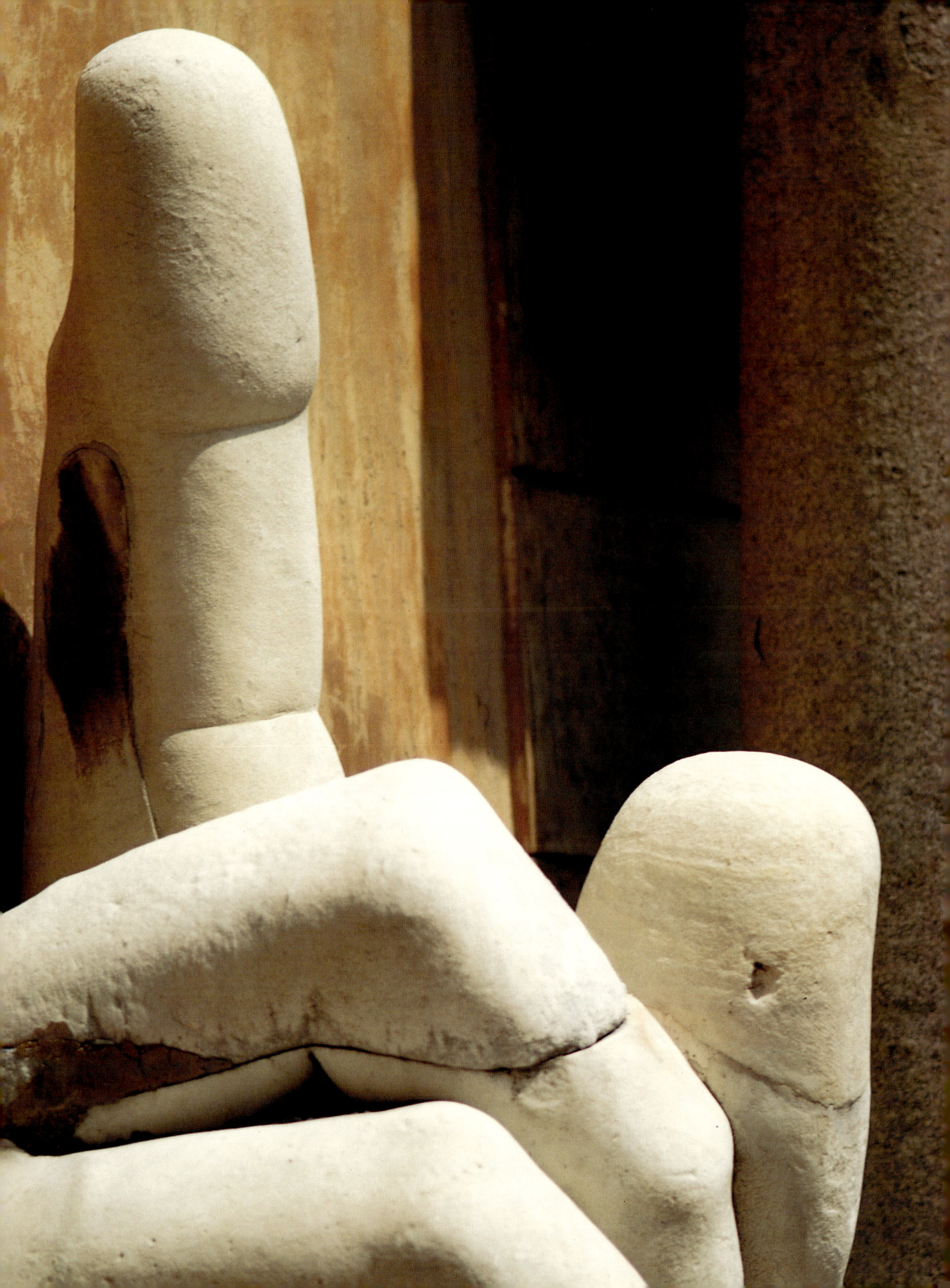

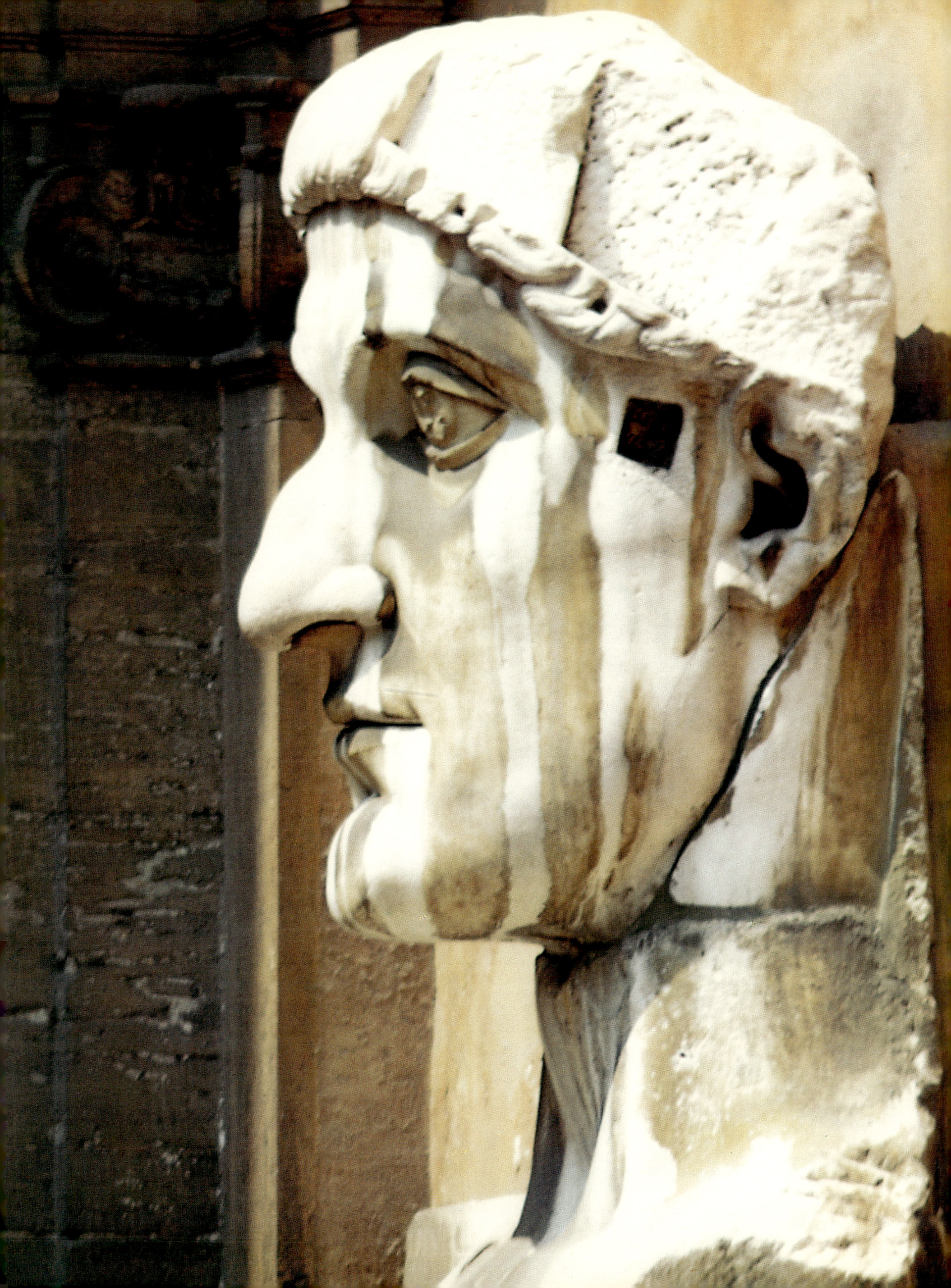

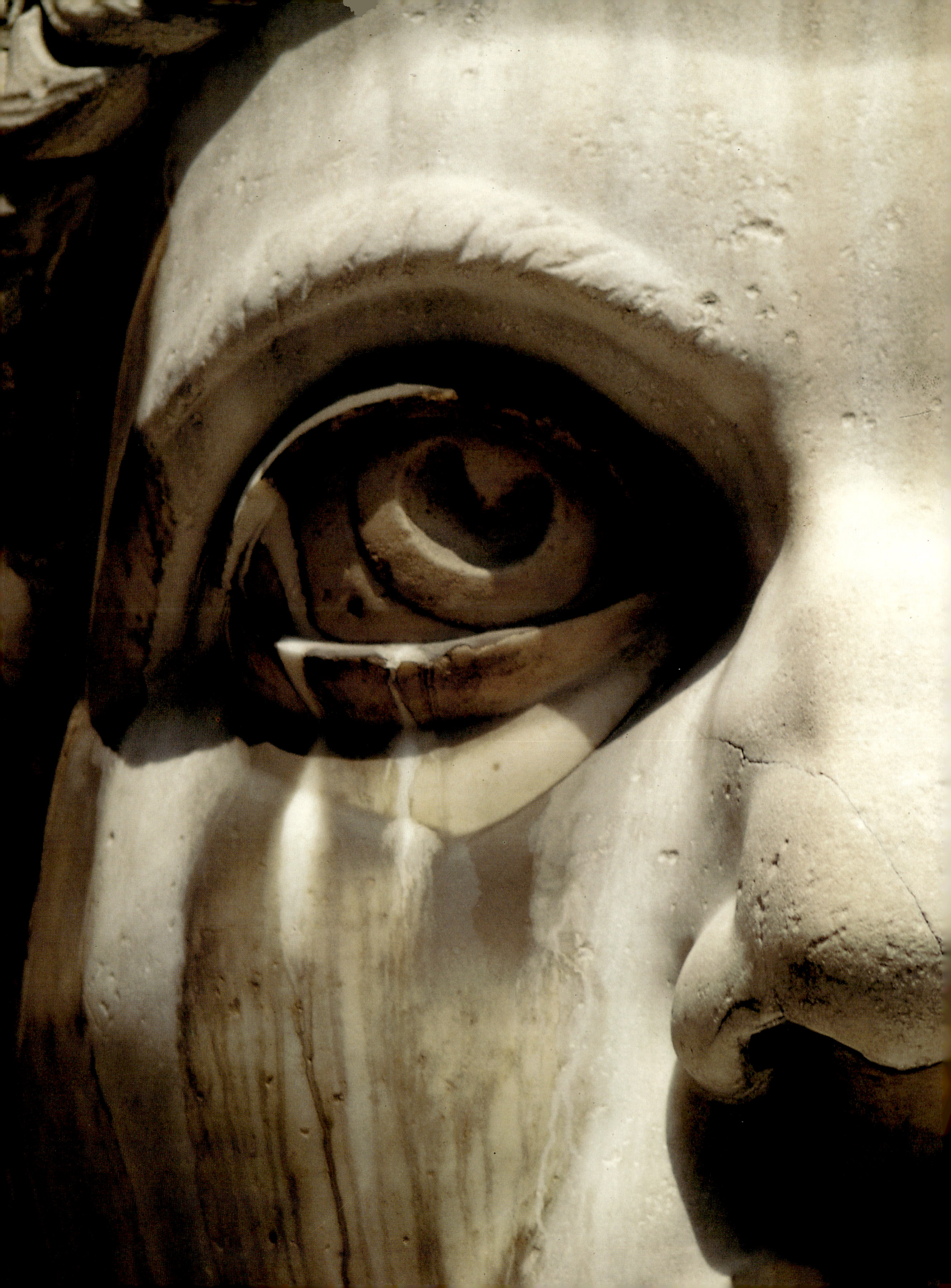

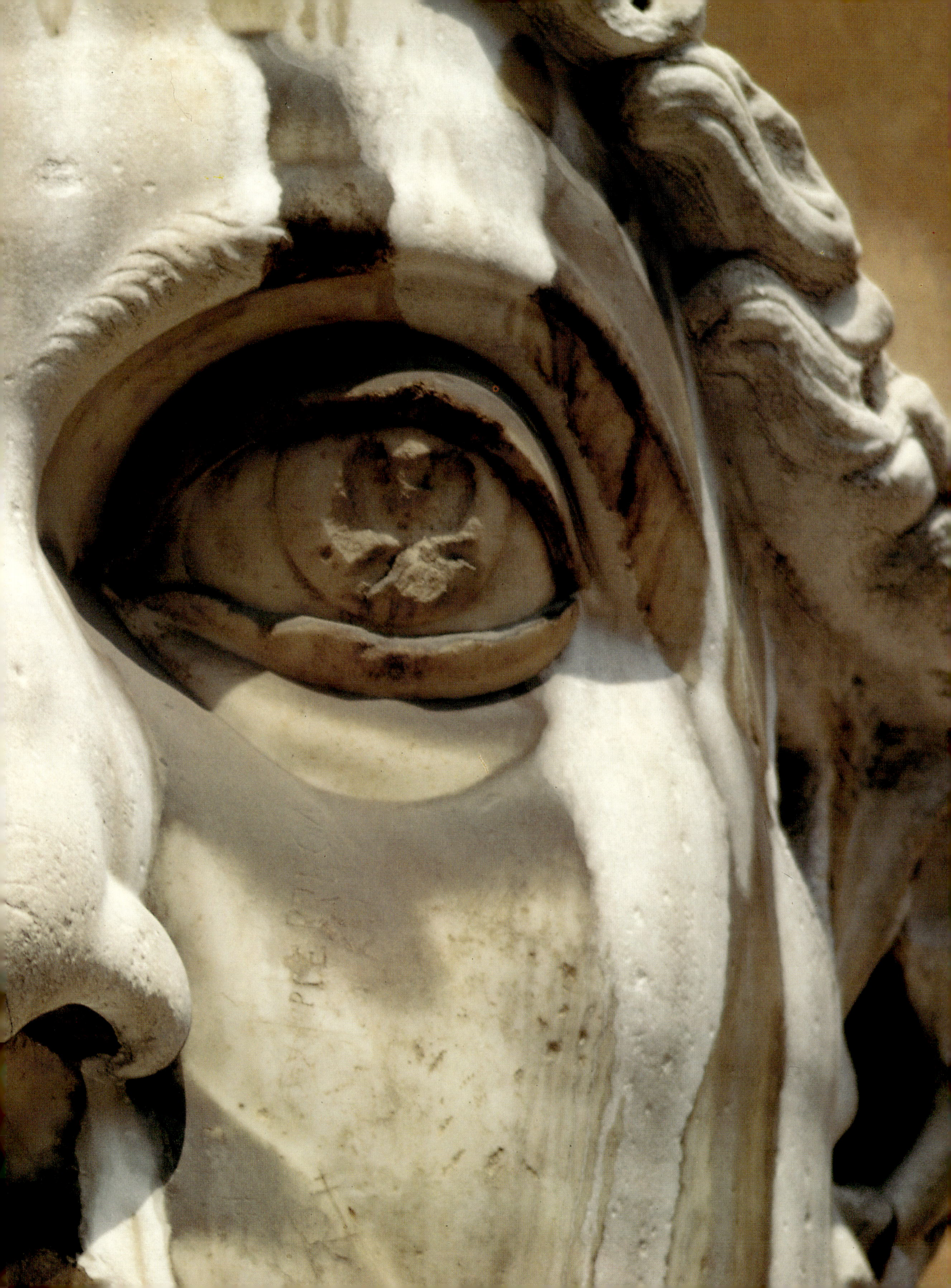

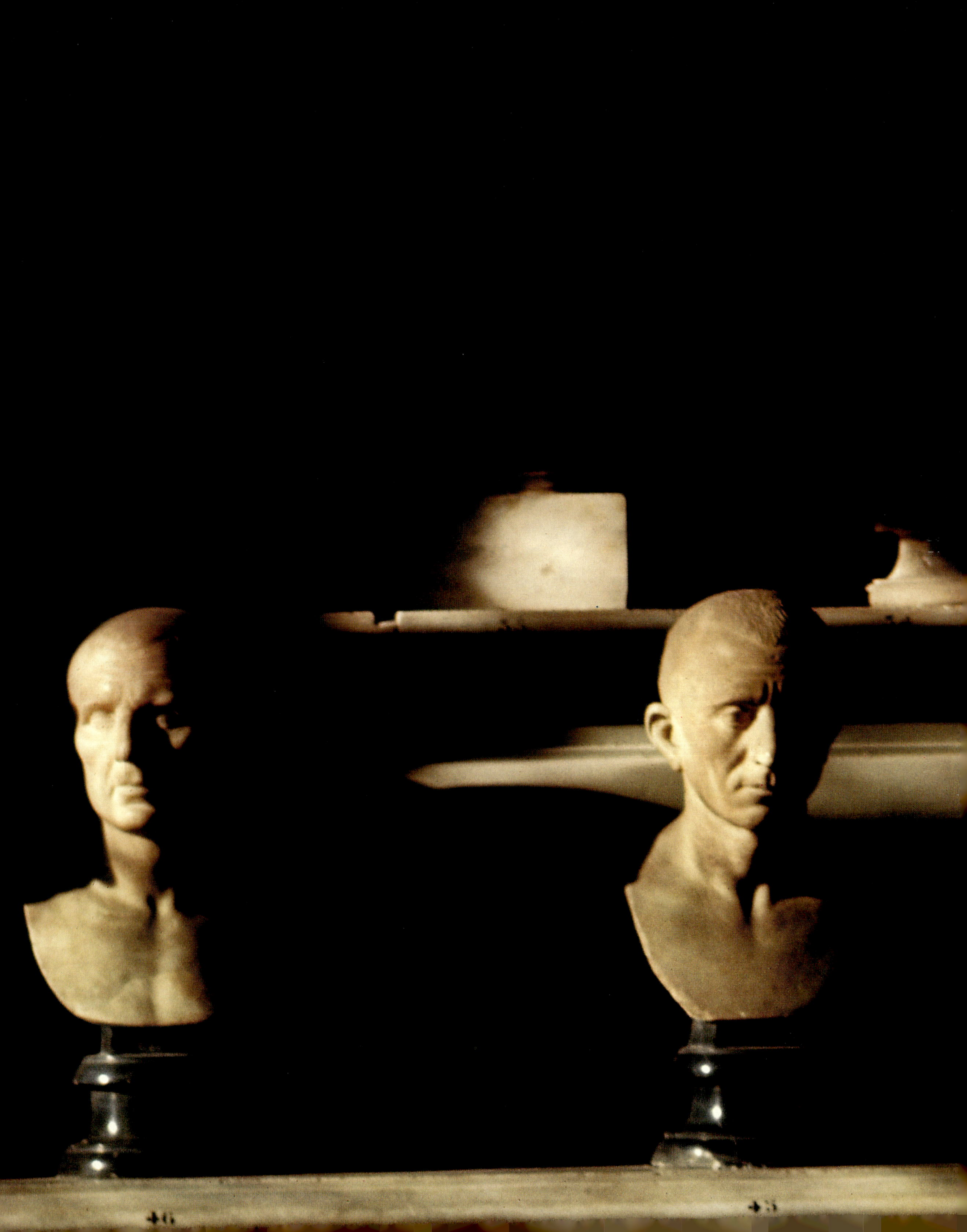

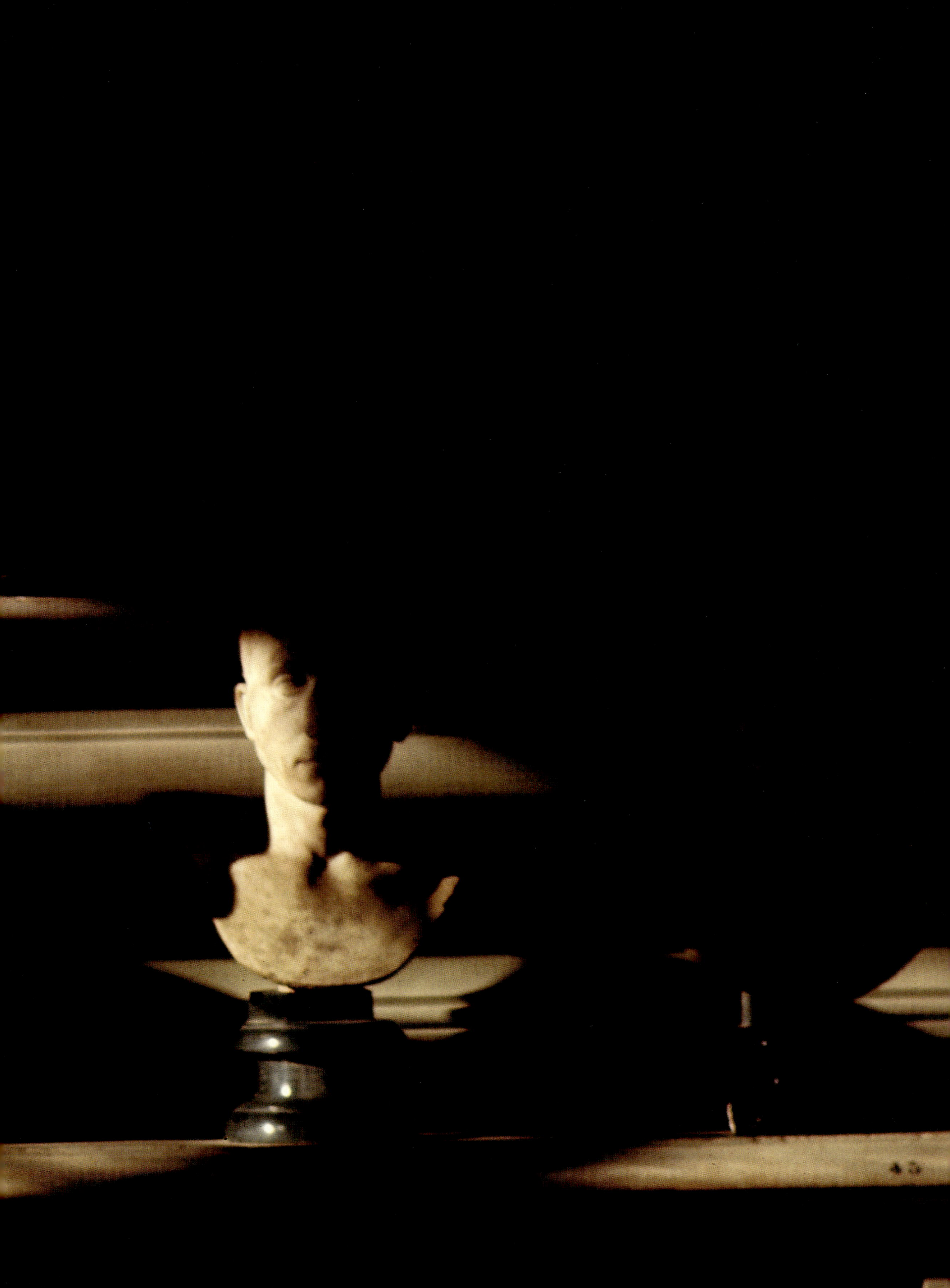

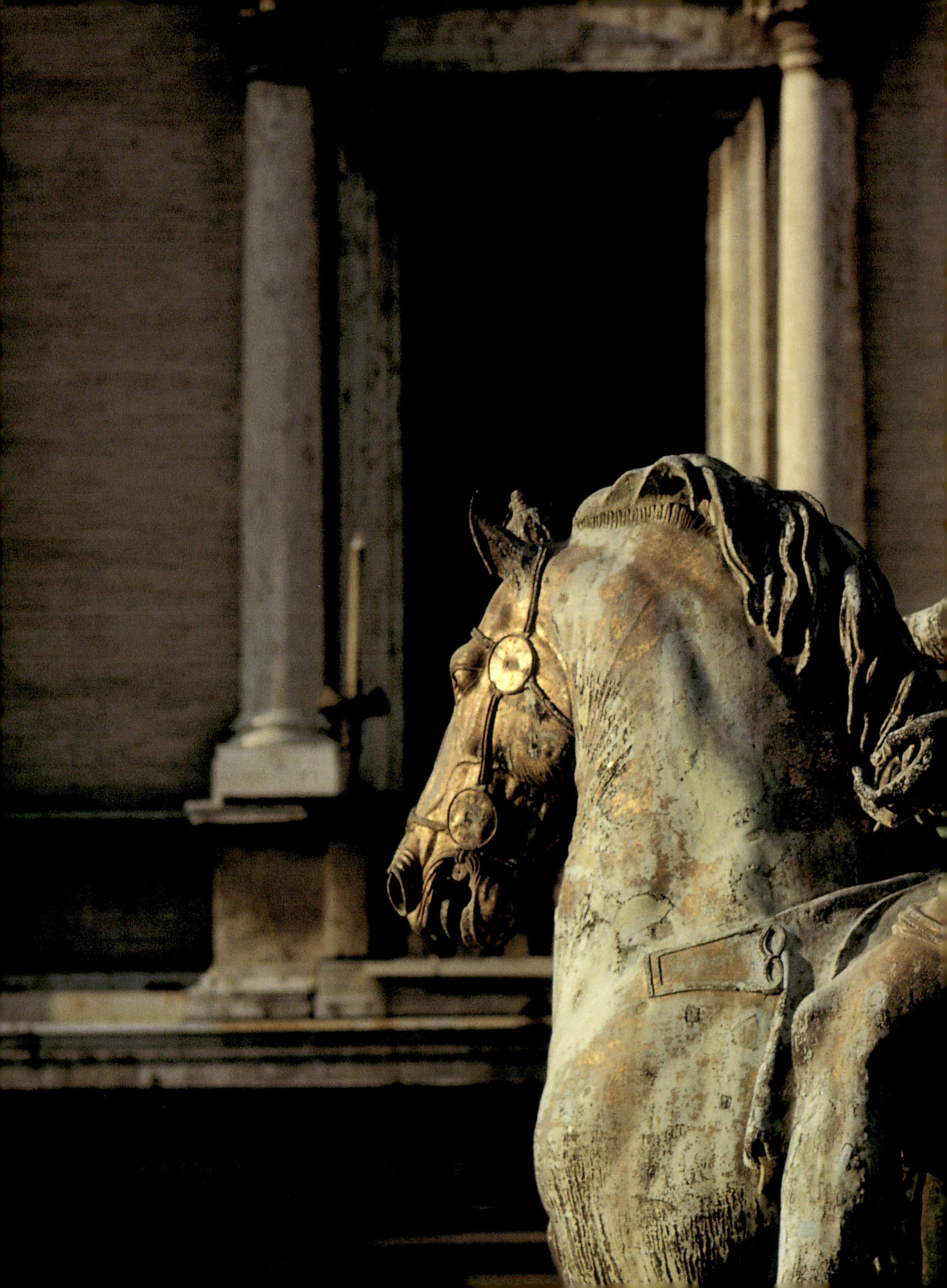

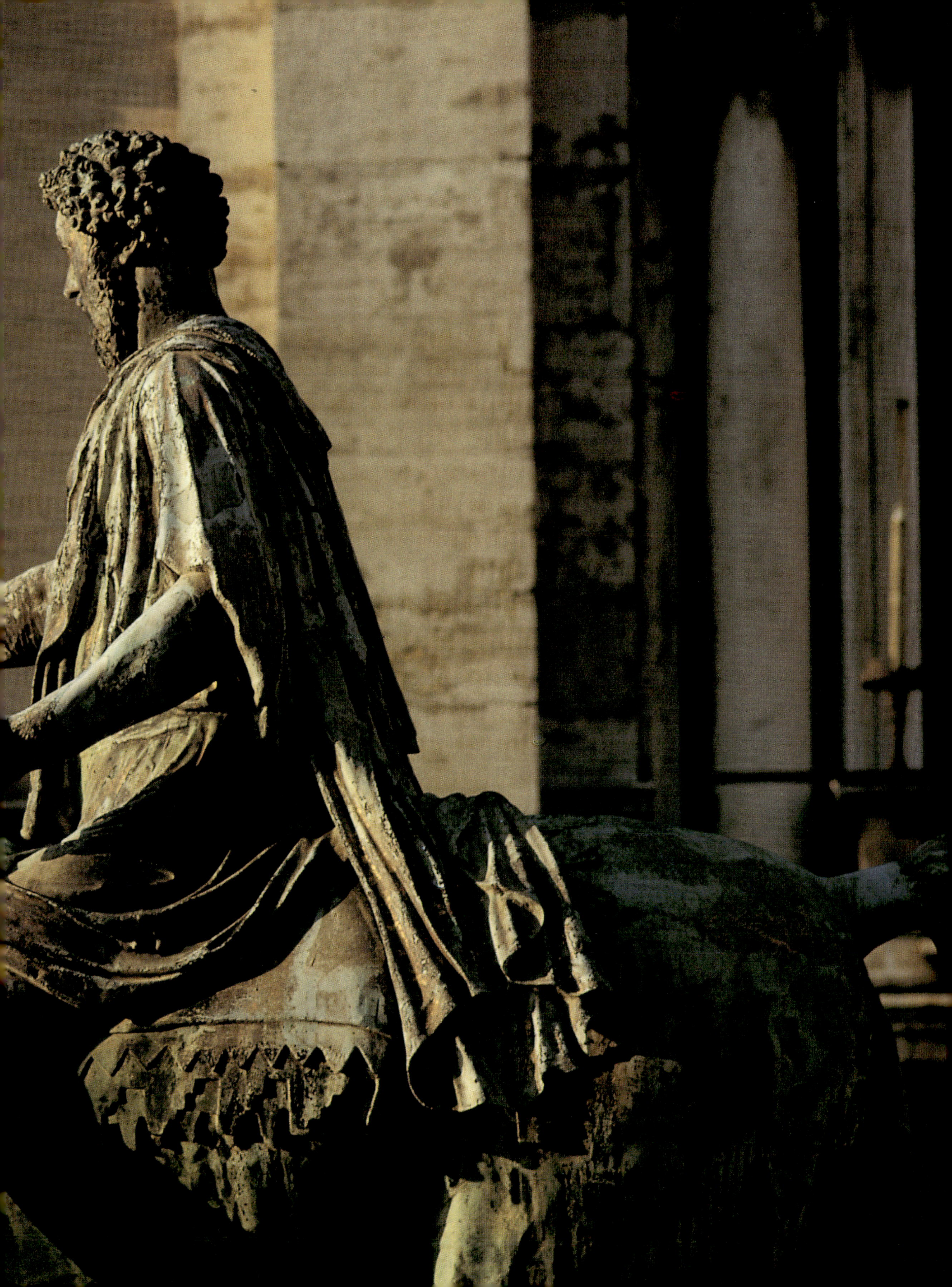

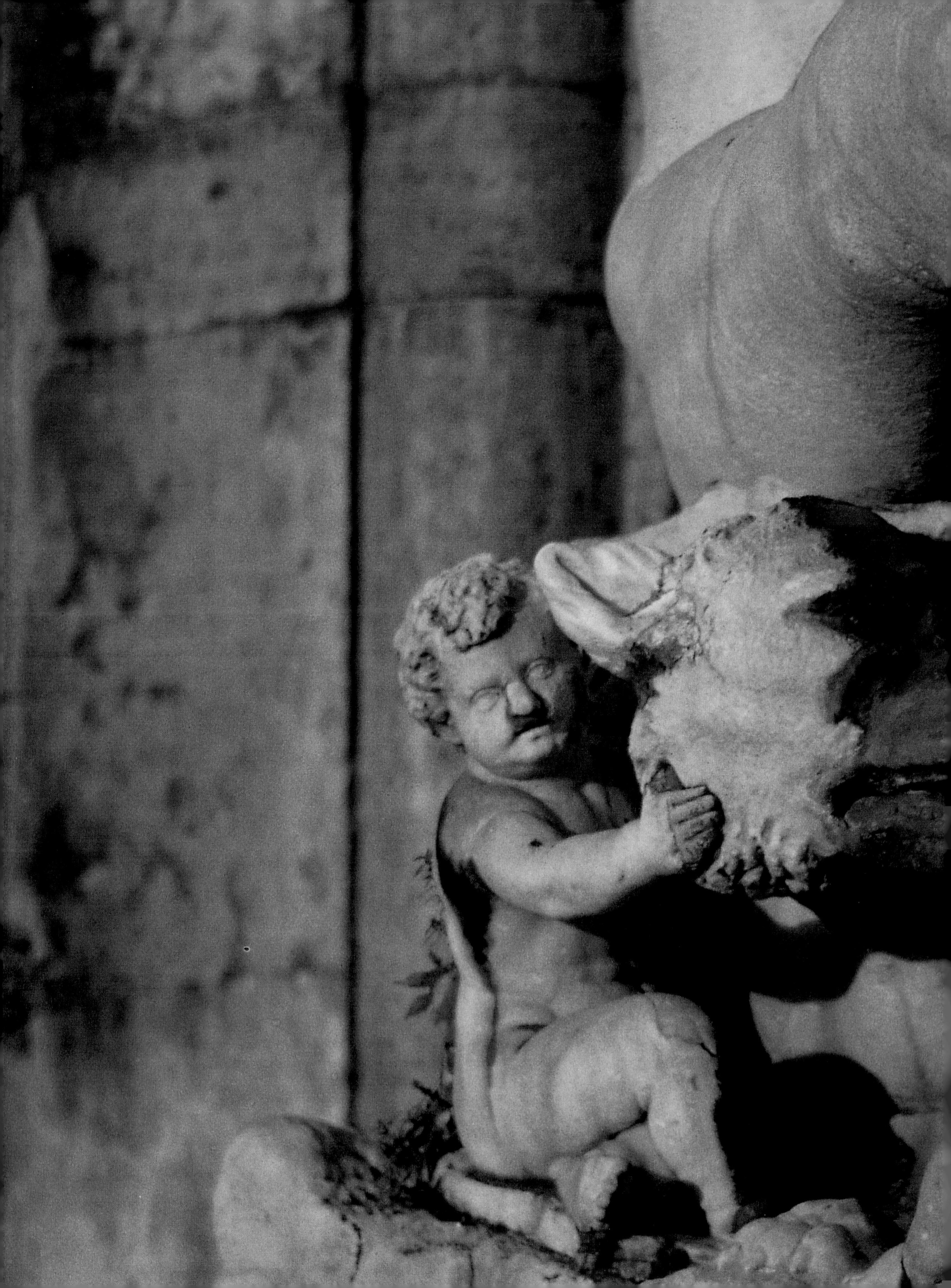

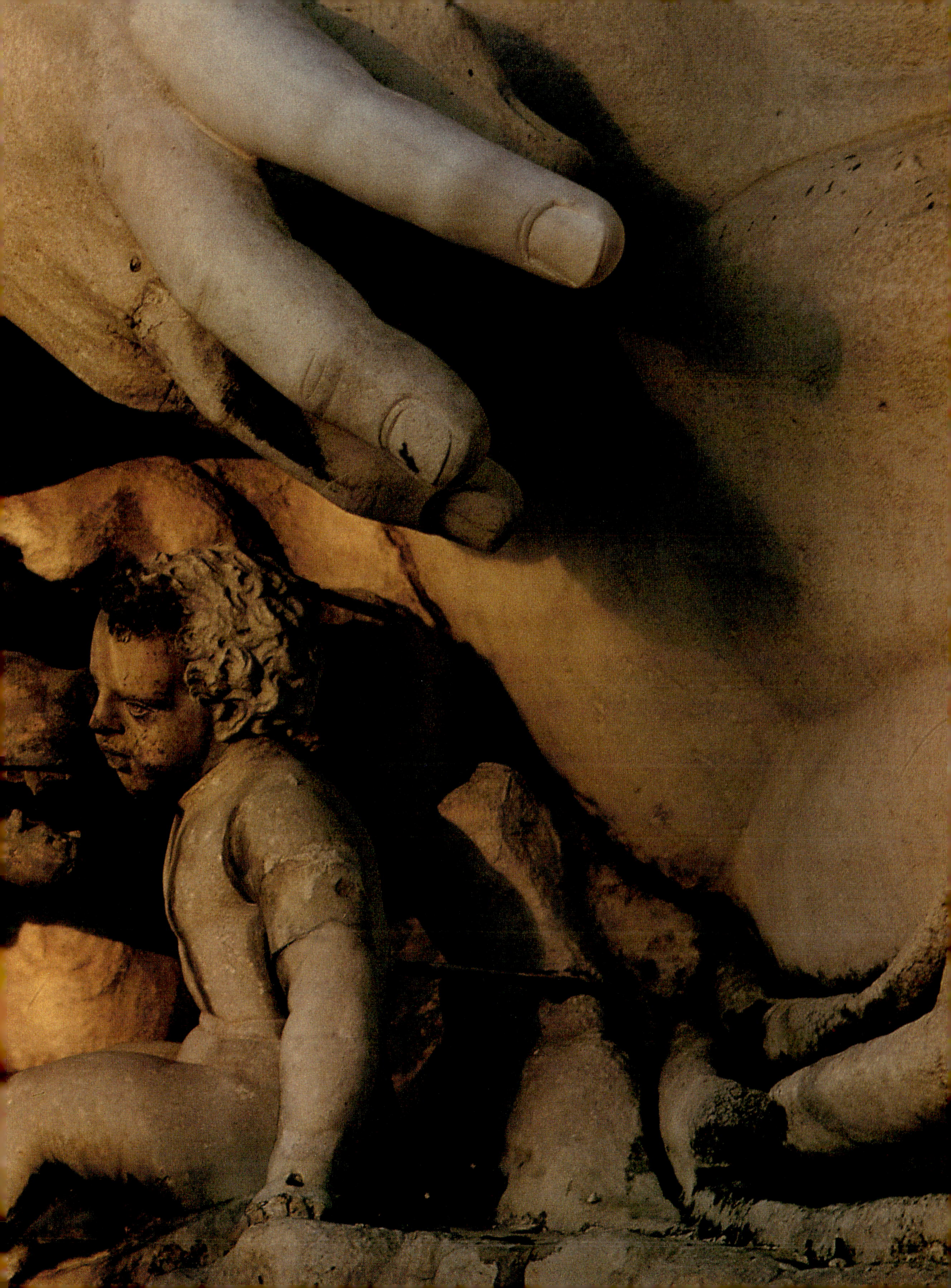

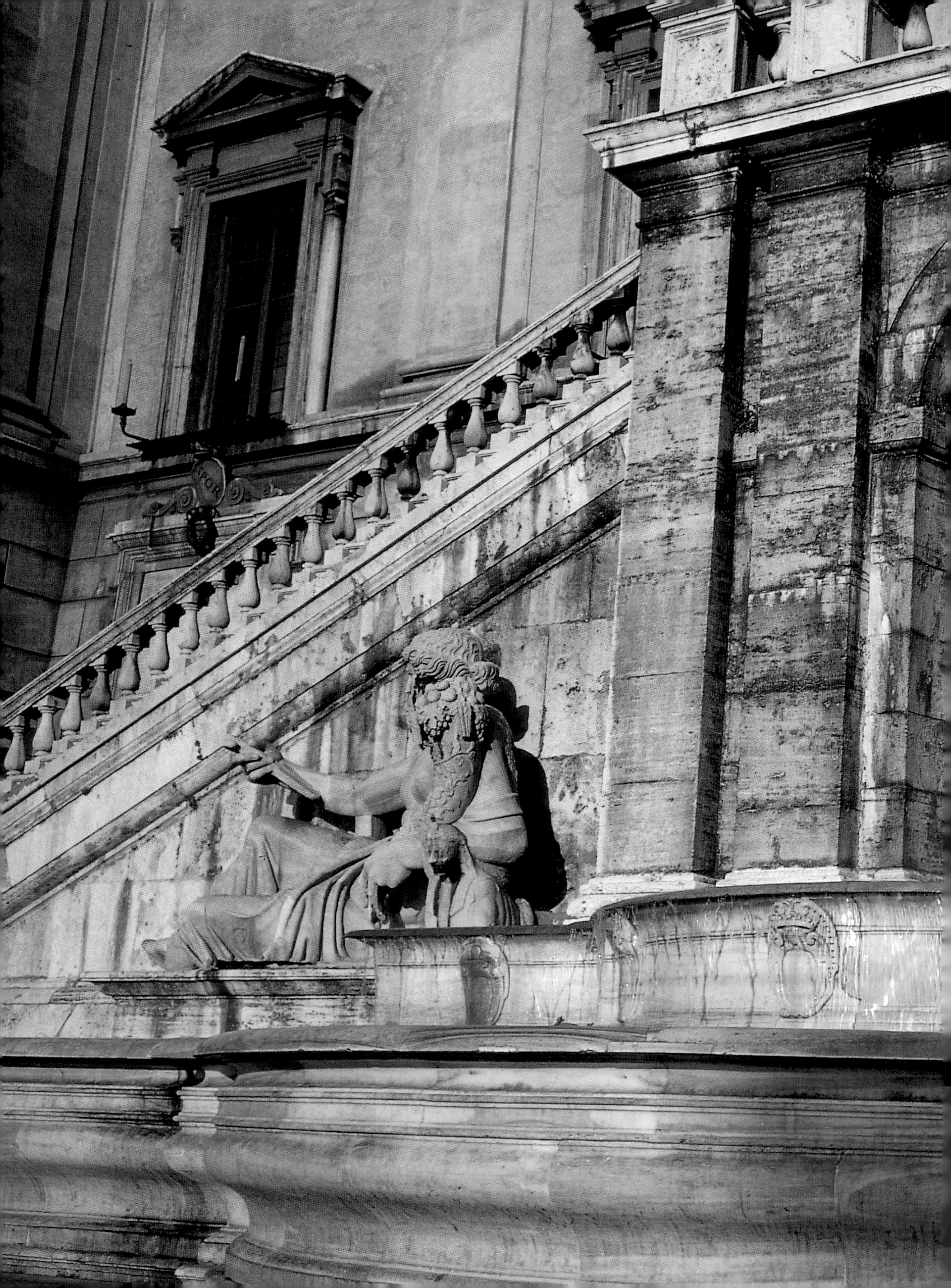

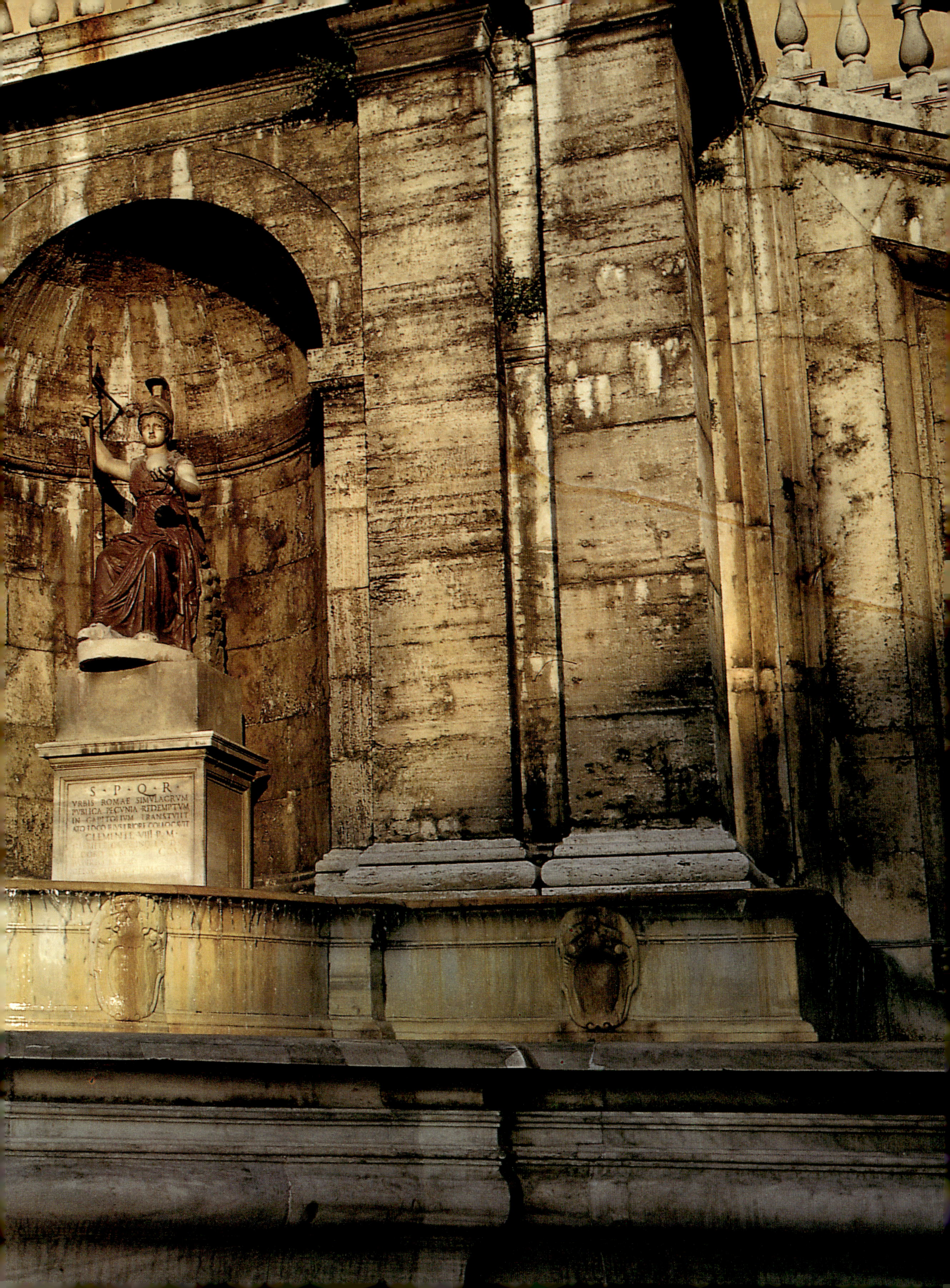
S·P·Q·R
VRBIS ROMAE SIMVLACRVM
PVBLICA PECVNIA REDEMPTVM
IN CAPITOLIVM TRANSTVLIT

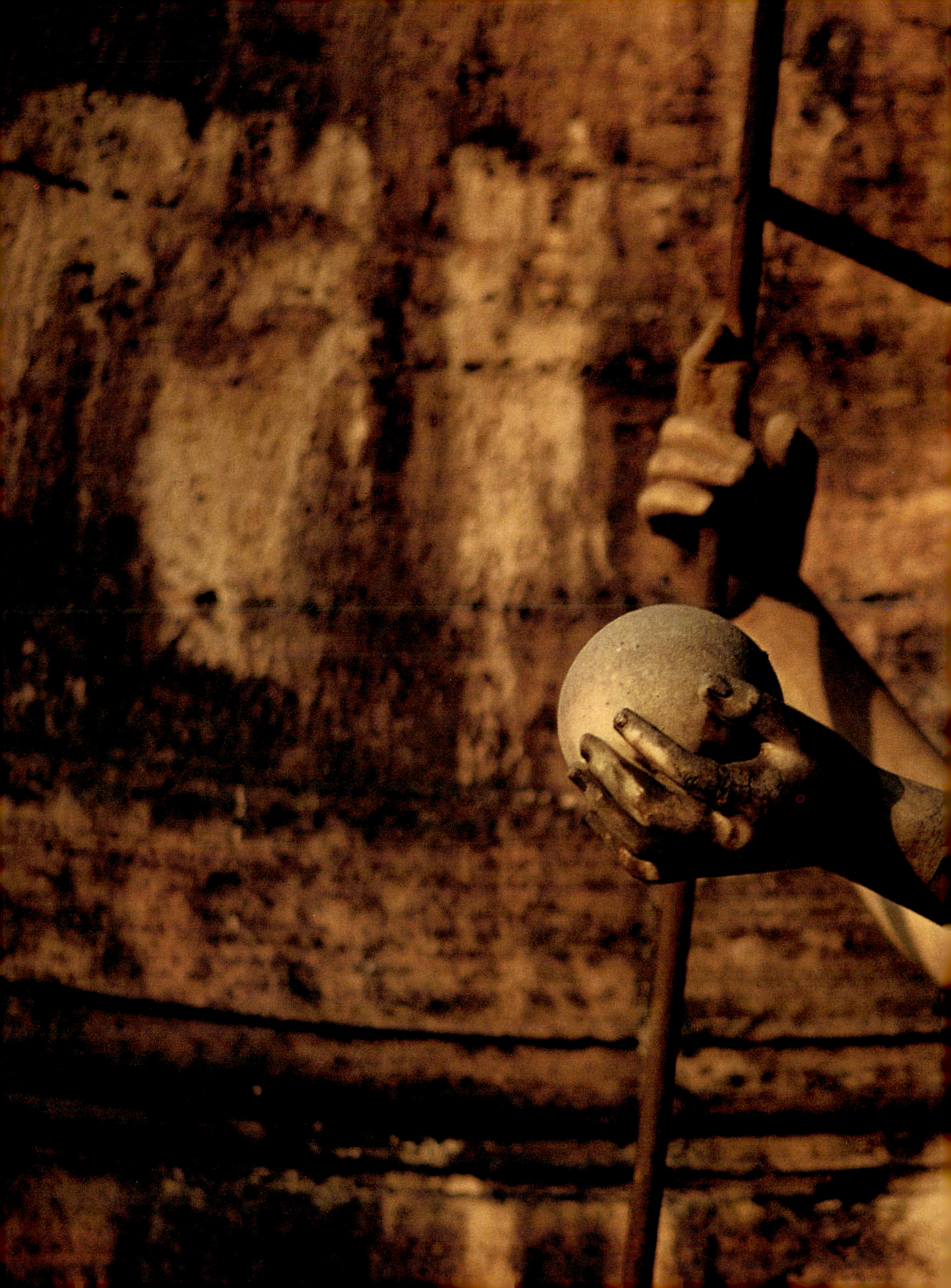

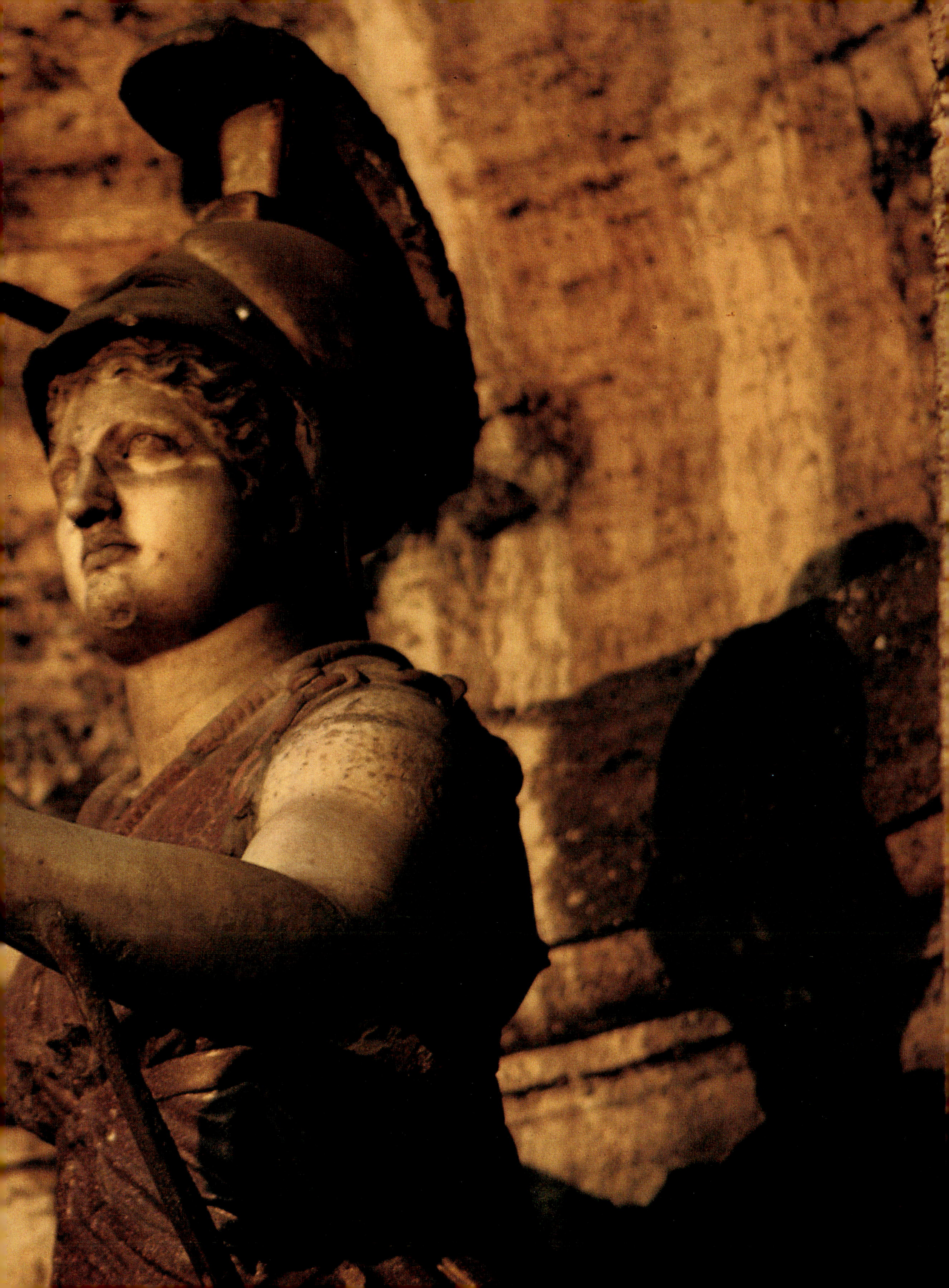

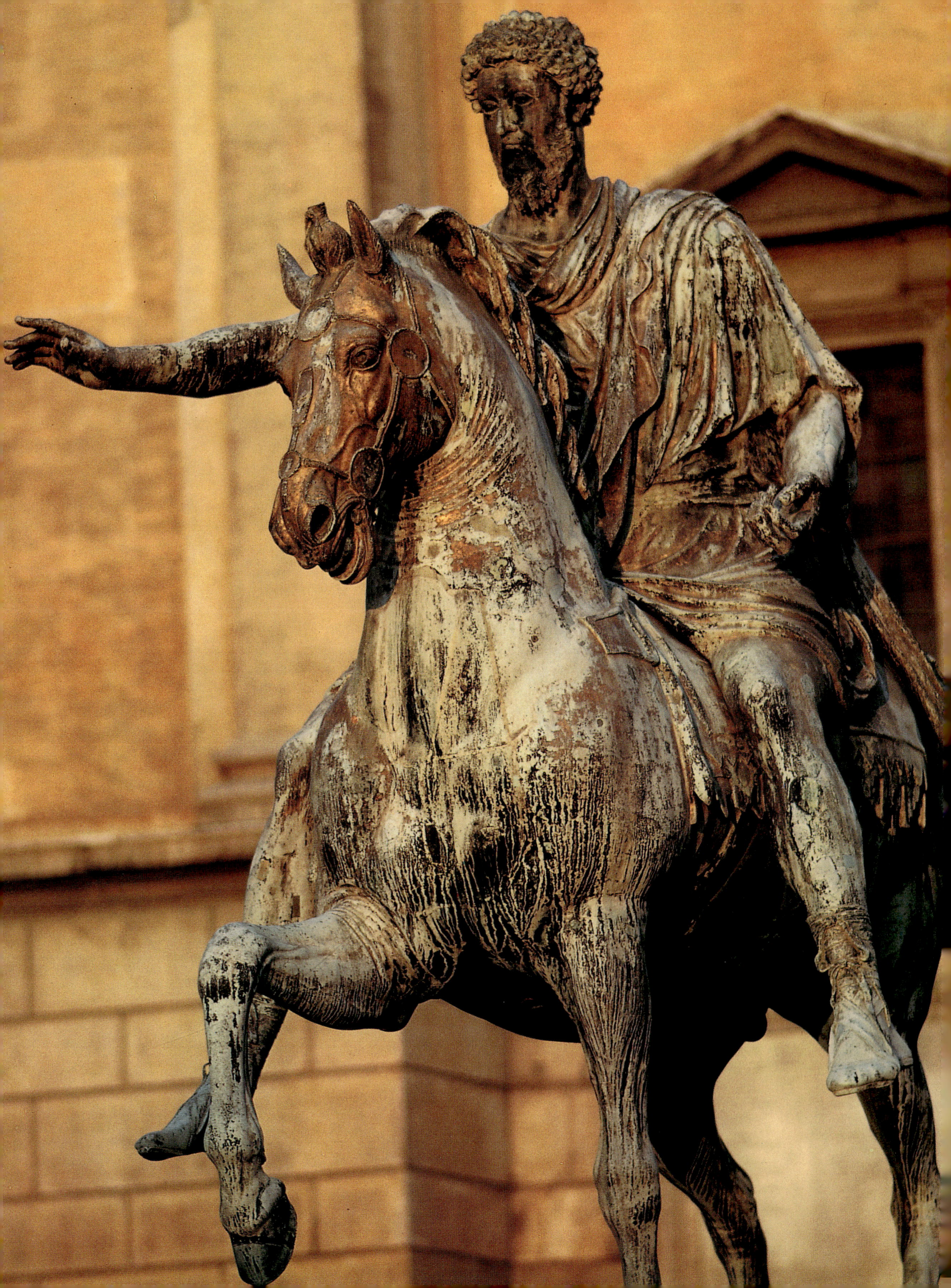

**“Reflect how speedily in this life the things of today are buried under those of tomorrow, even as one layer of drifting sand is quickly covered by the next.”**

—MARCUS AURELIUS

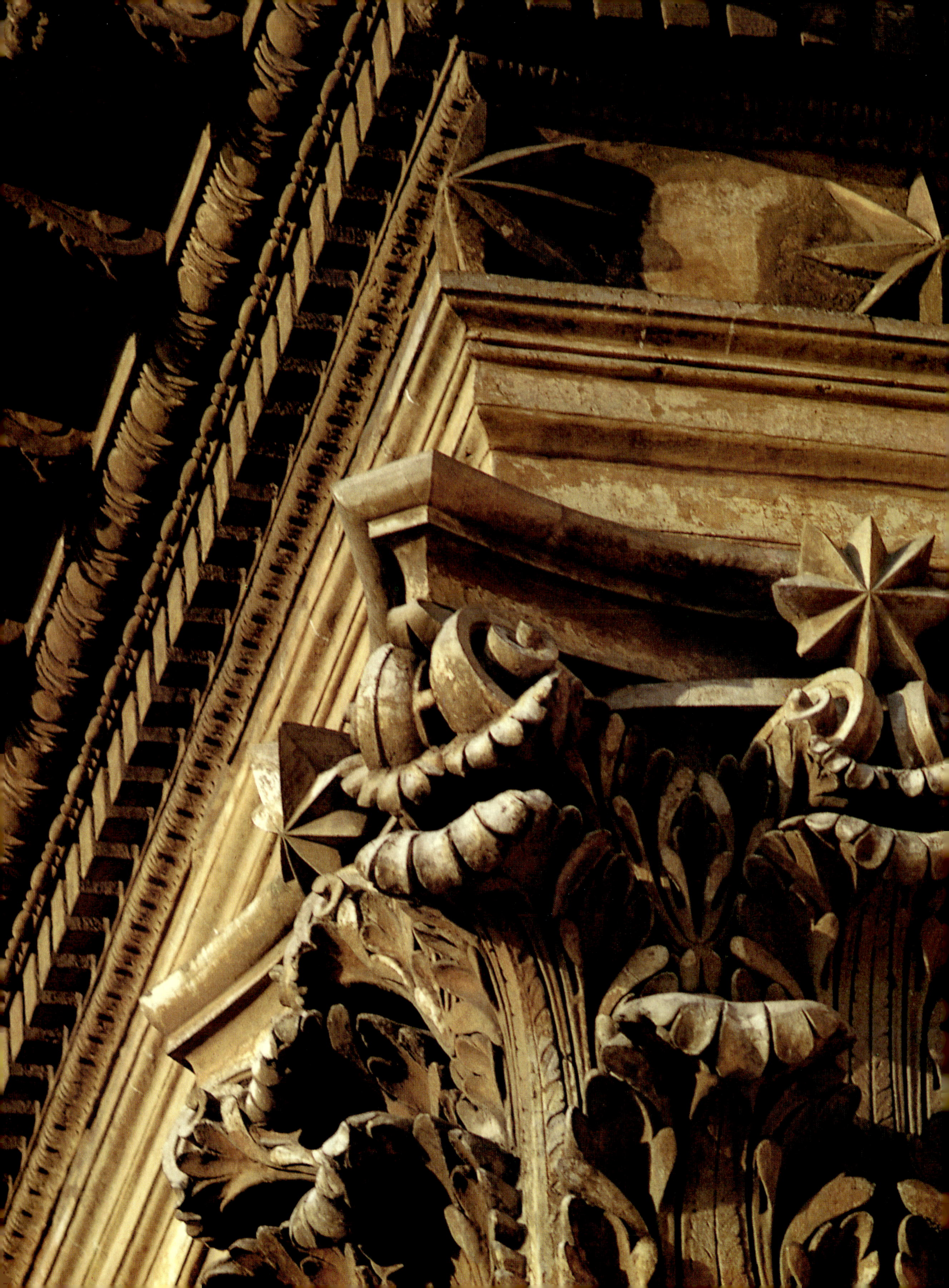

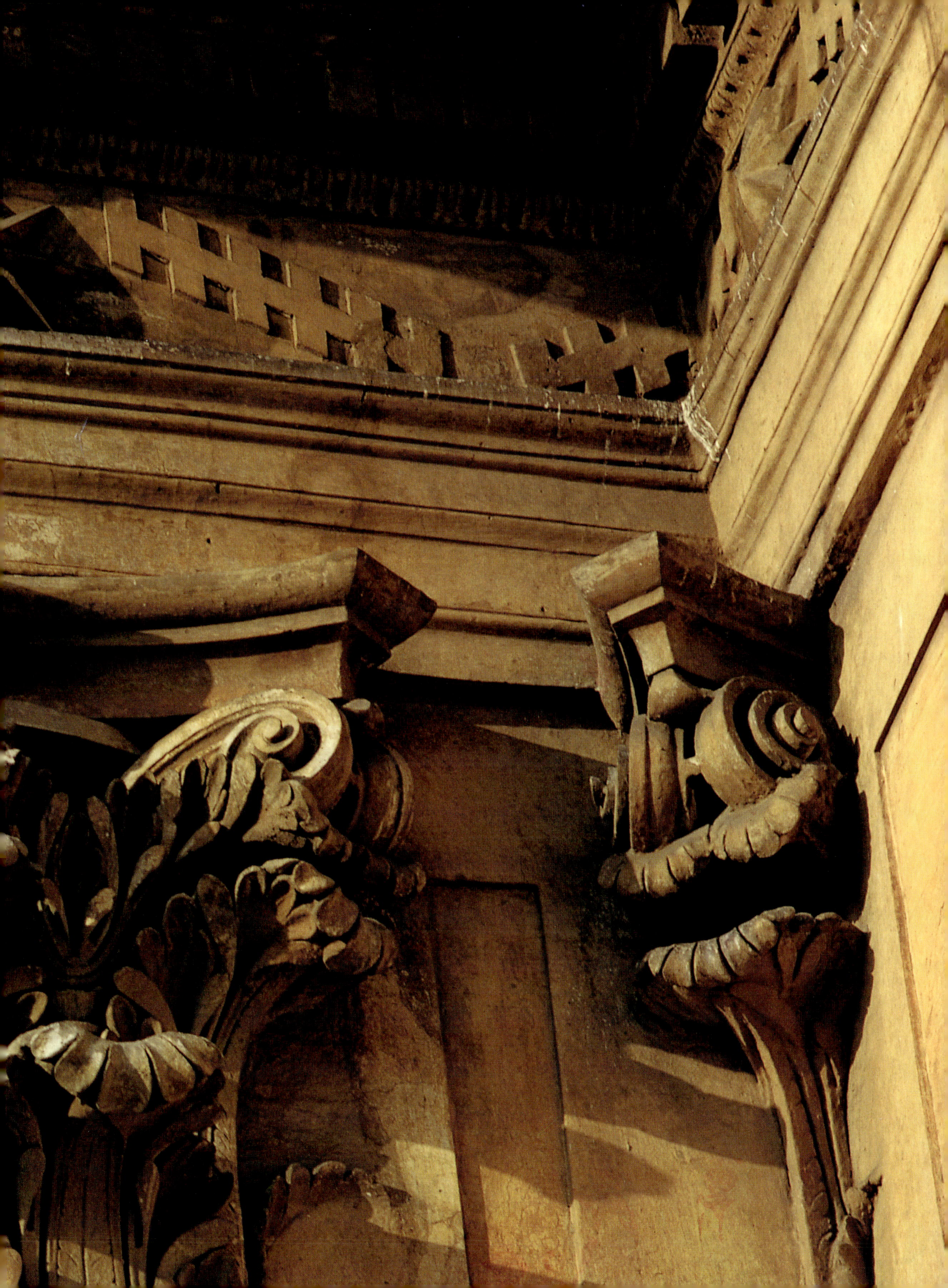

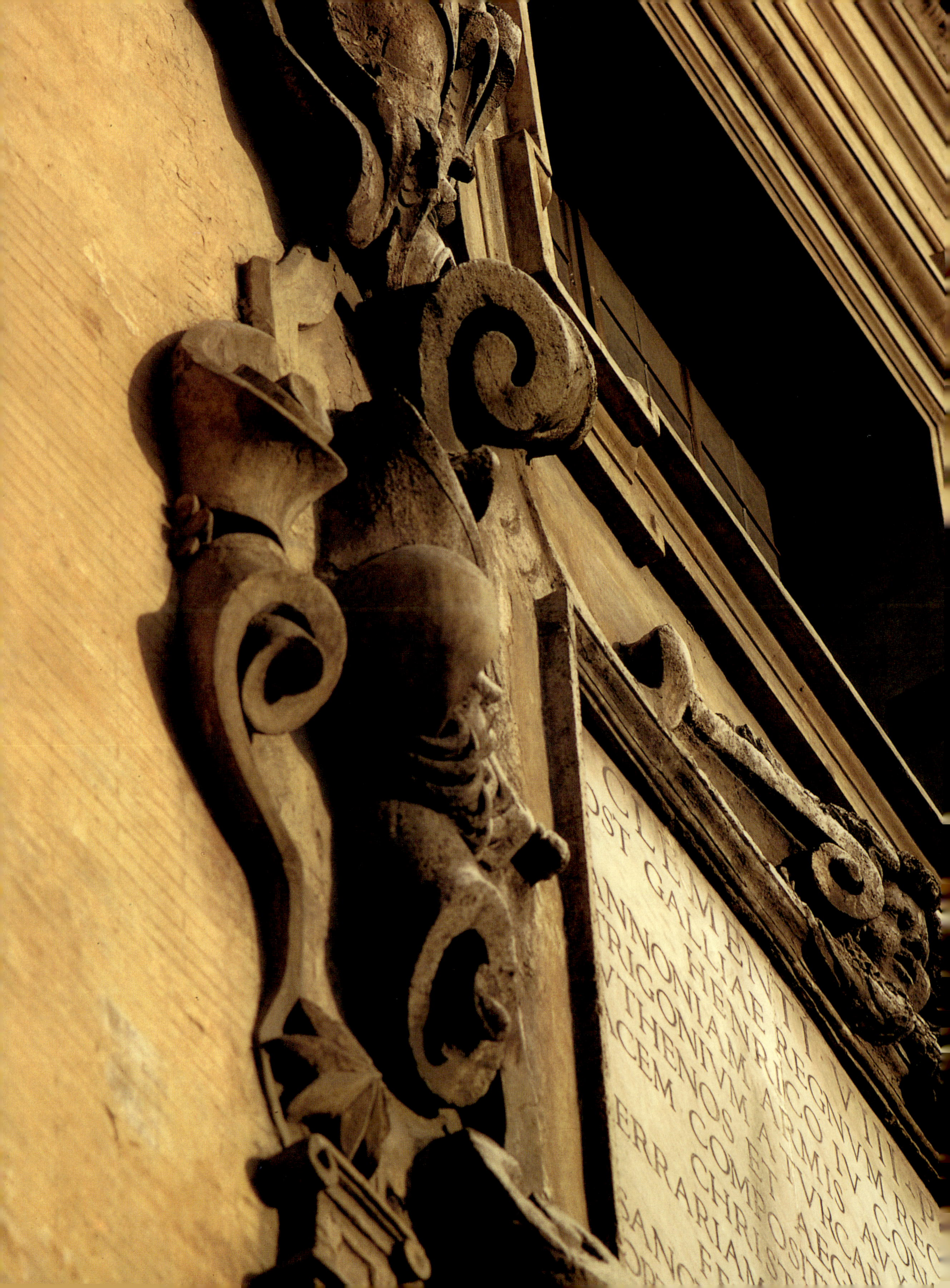
CLEMENTI VIII
POST GALLIAE REGNVM

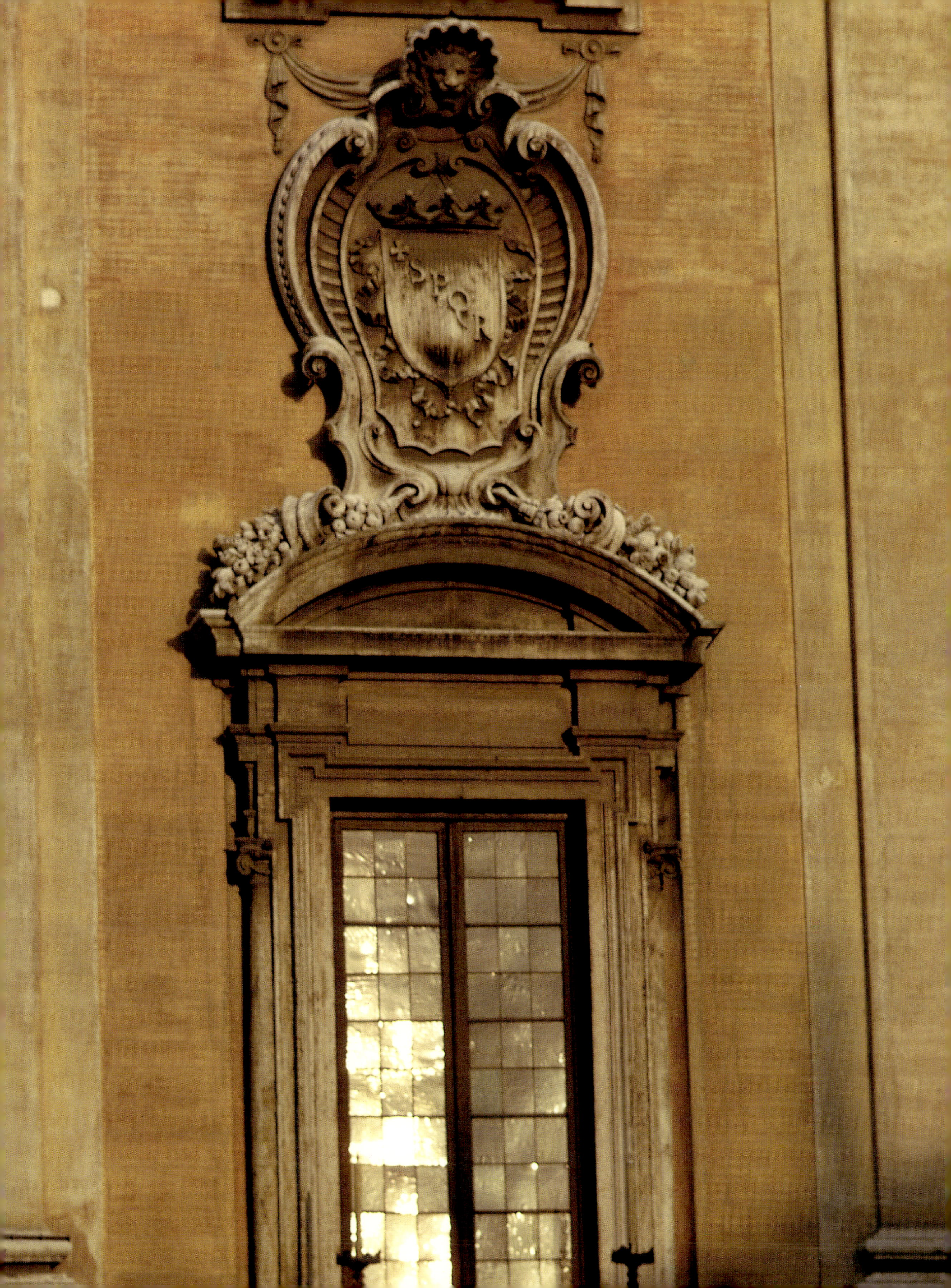
SPQR

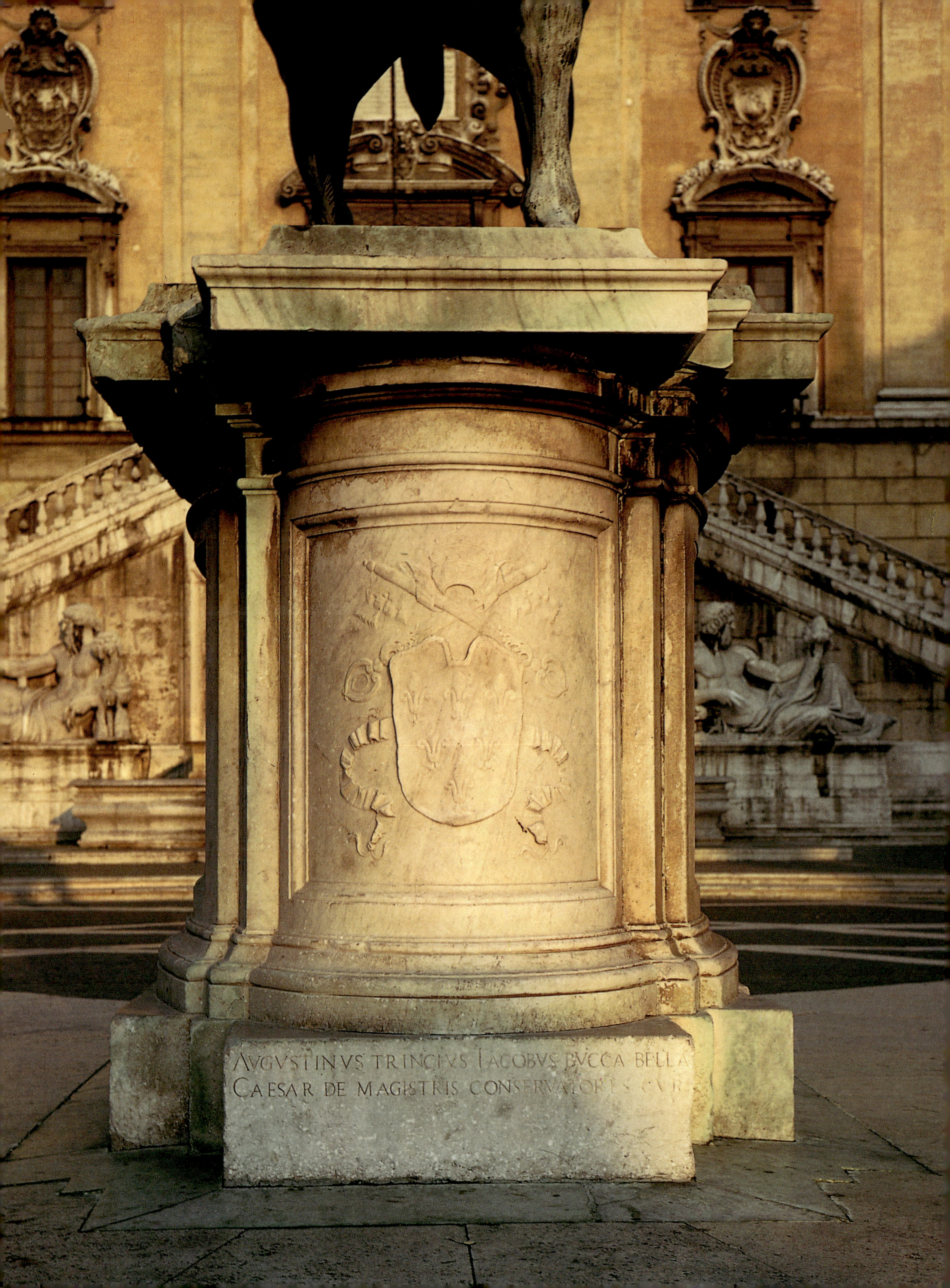
AVGVSTINVS TRINCIVS IACOBVS BVCCA BELLA
CAESAR DE MAGISTRIS CONSERVATORES

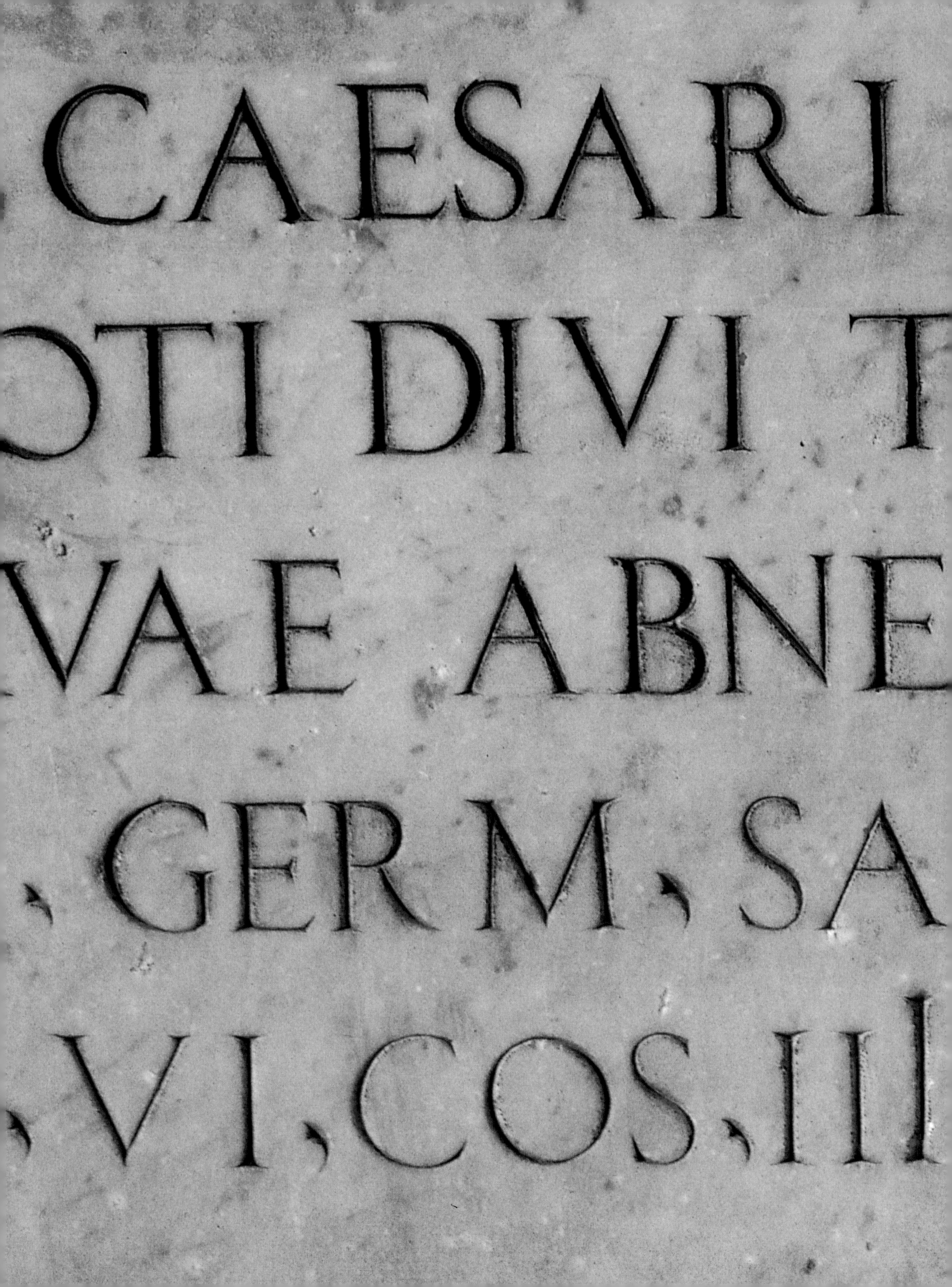

CAESARI

OTI DIVI T

VAE ABNE

· GERM · SA

· VI · COS · II

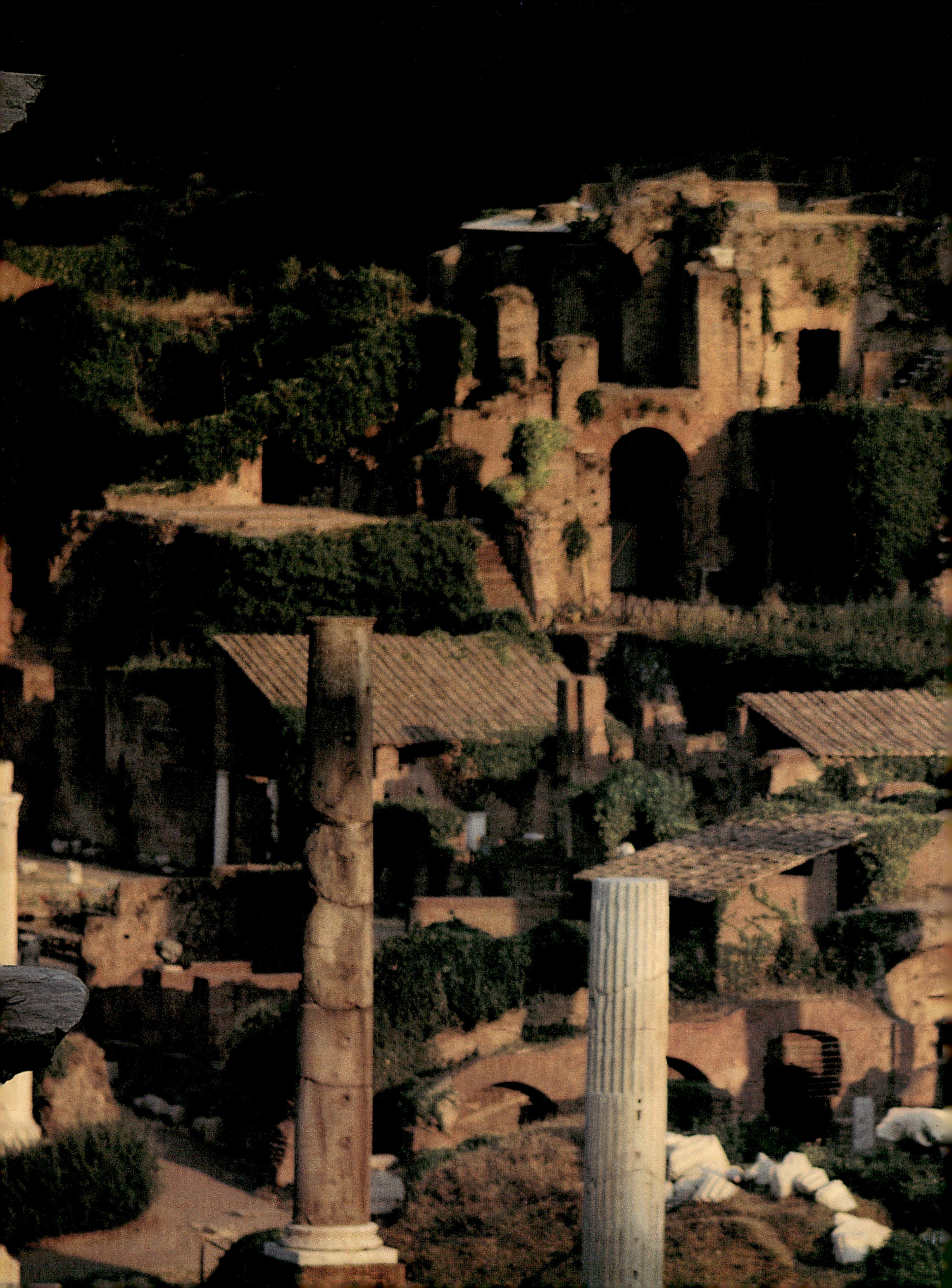

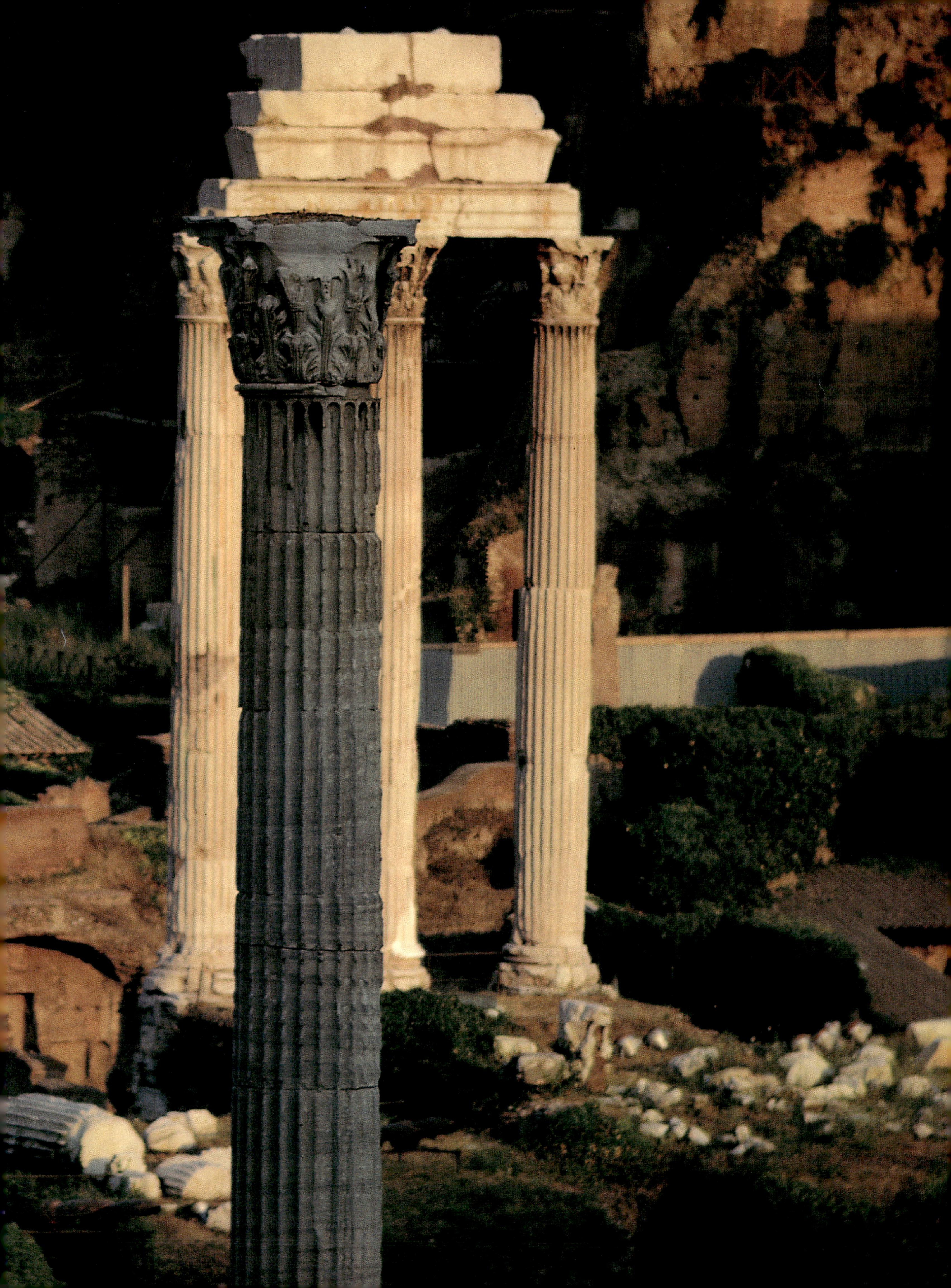

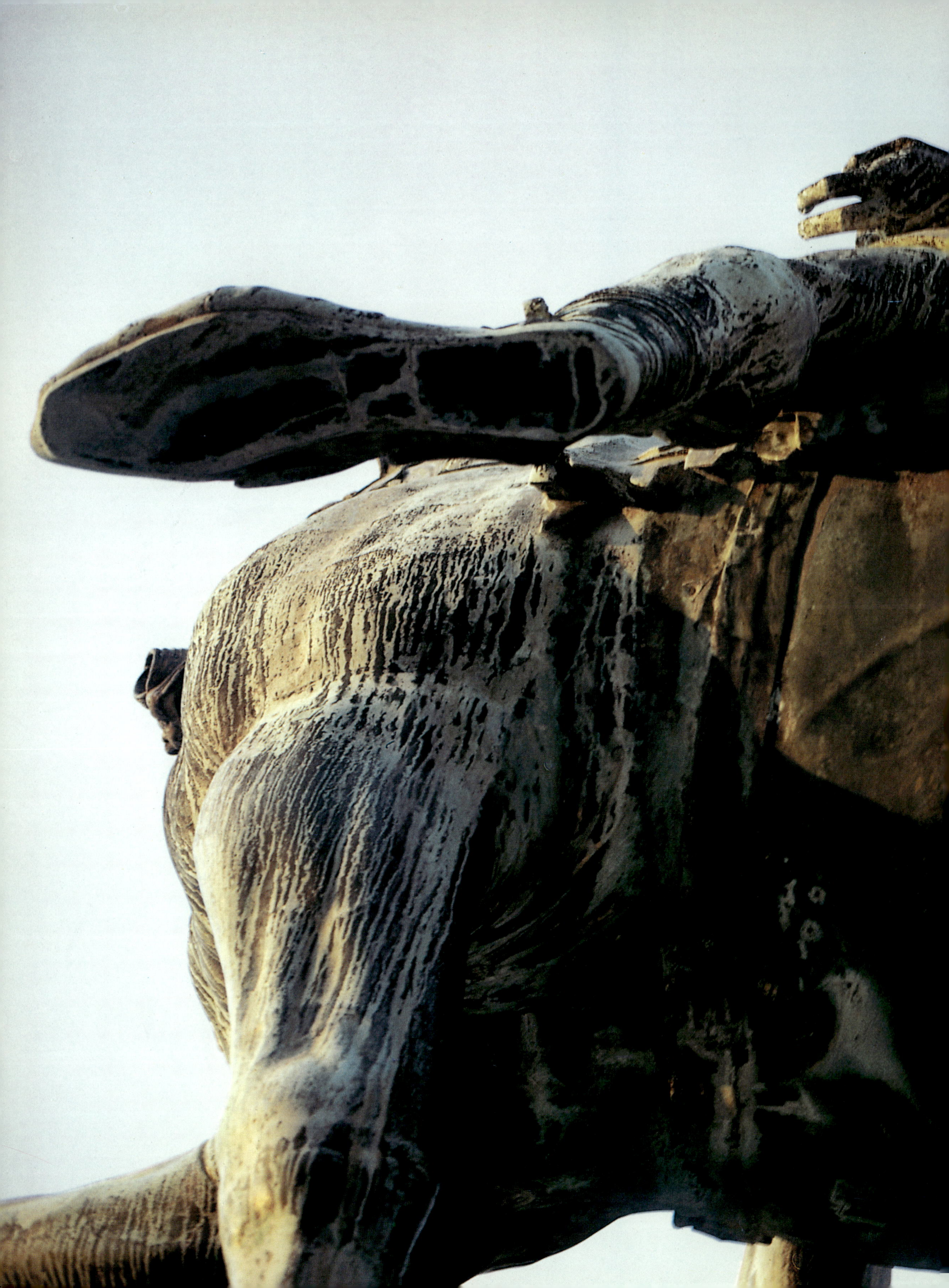

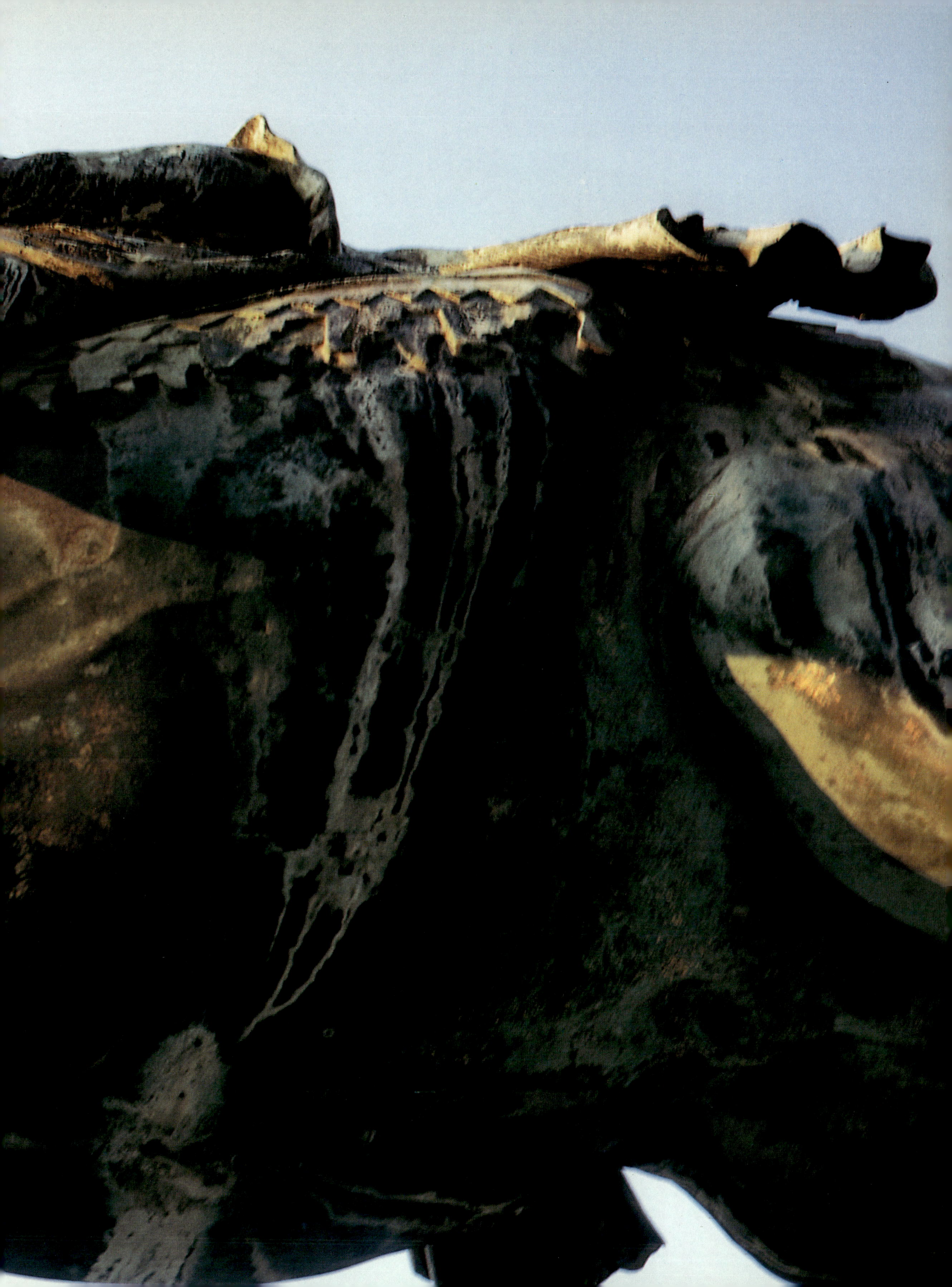

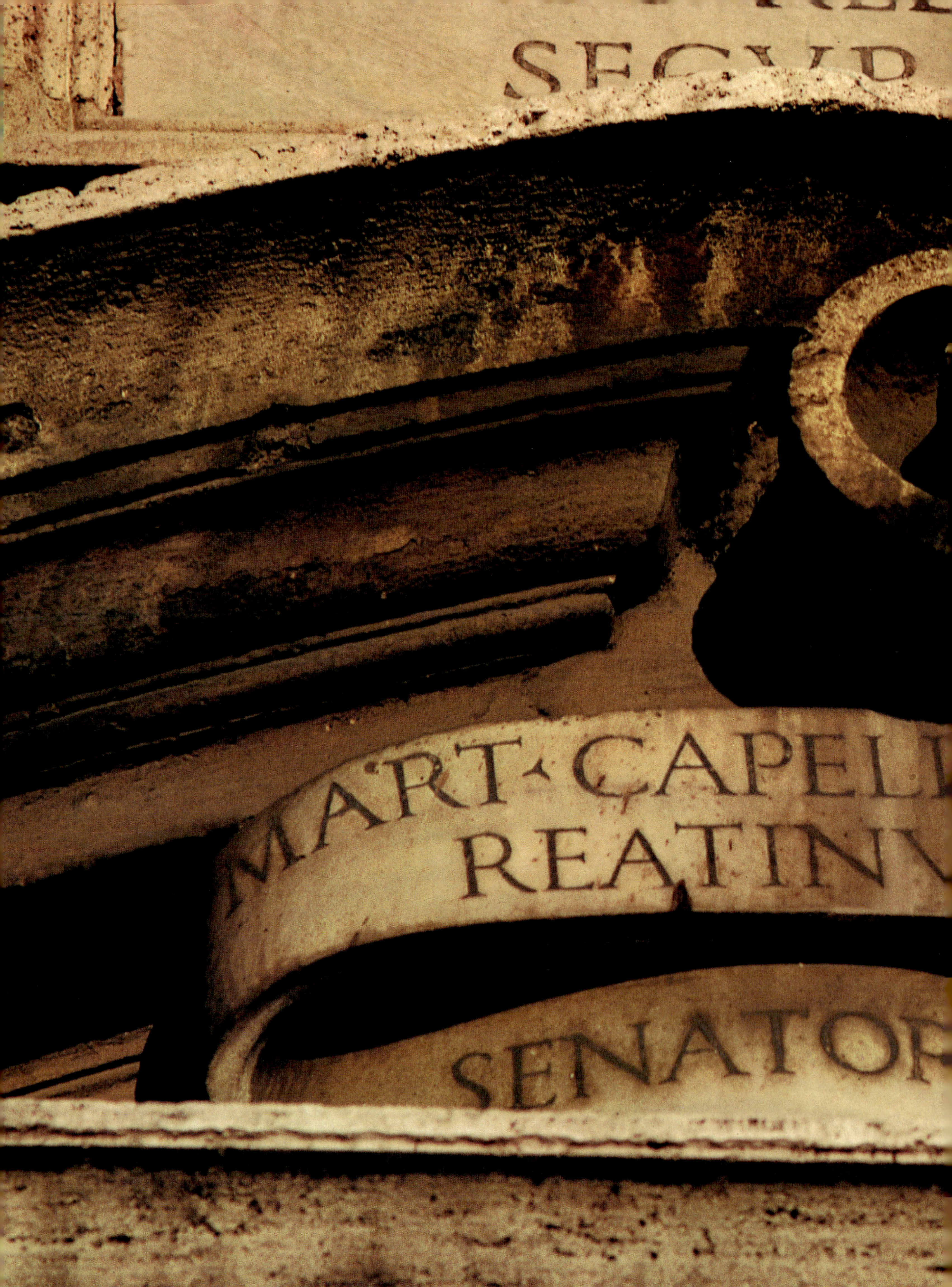
MART·CAPEL
REATIN
SENATO

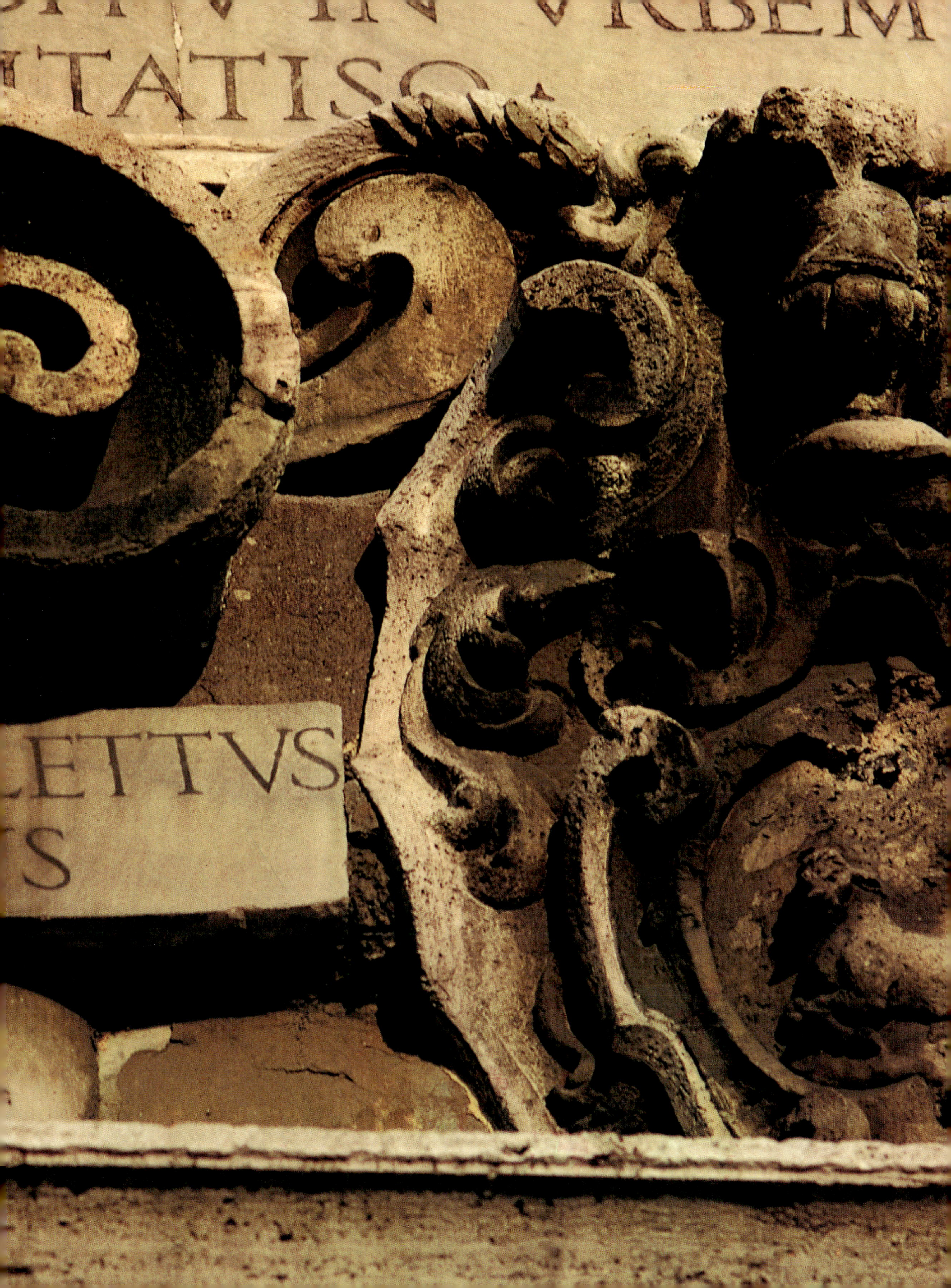
ITATIS
LETTVS
S

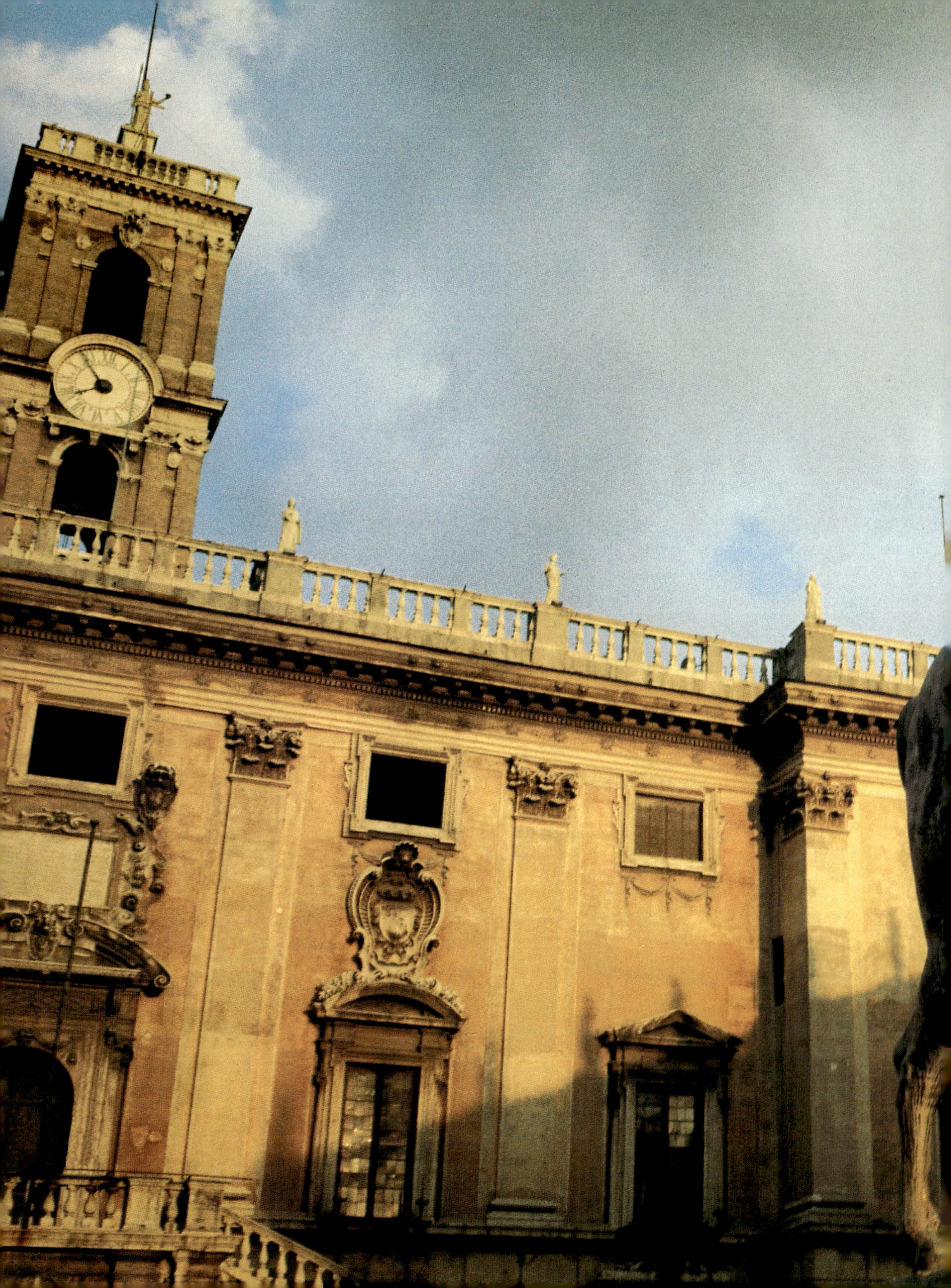

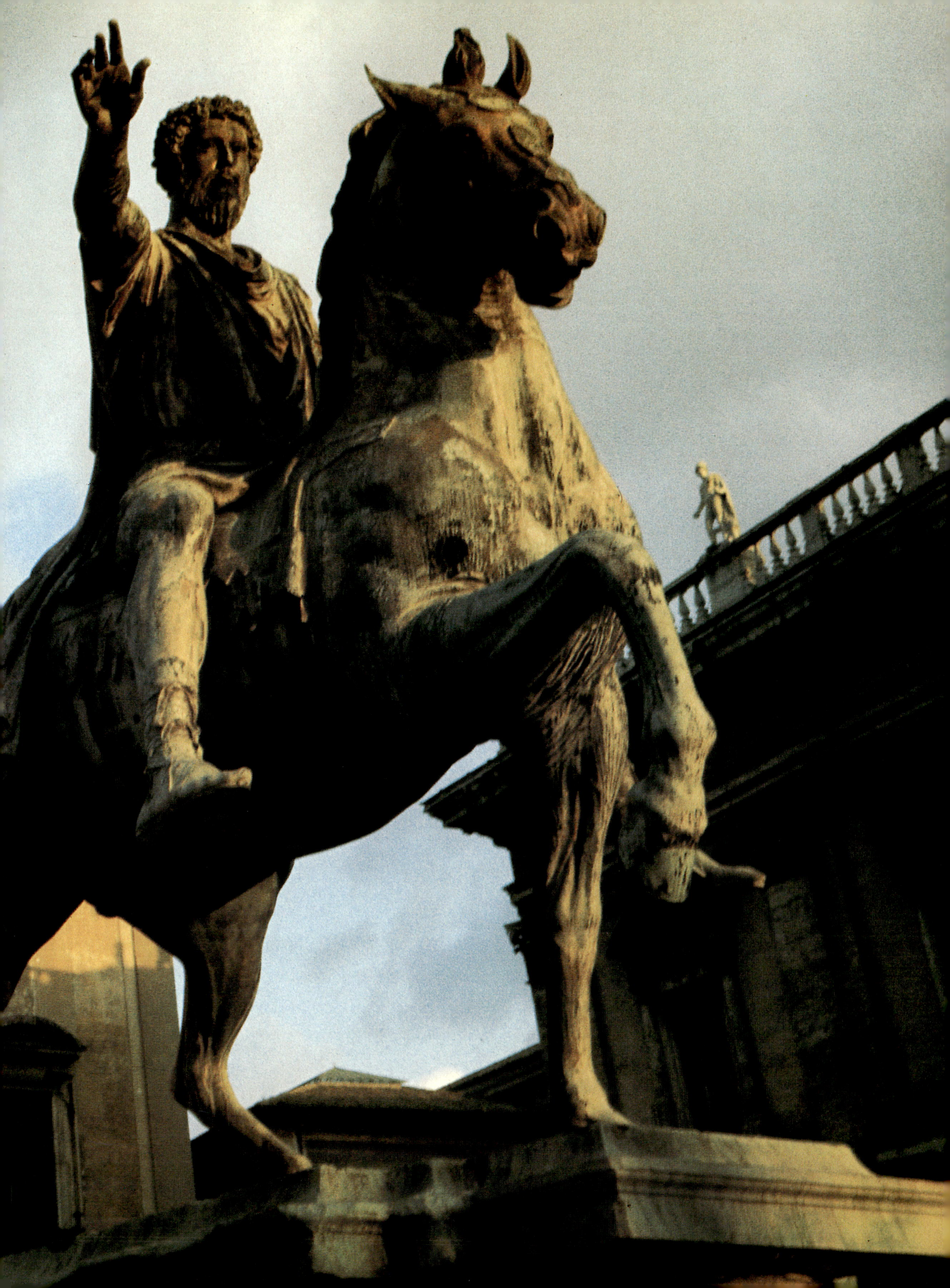

**“Let no emotions of the flesh, be they of pain or pleasure, affect the supreme and sovereign portion of the soul.”**

—MARCUS AURELIUS

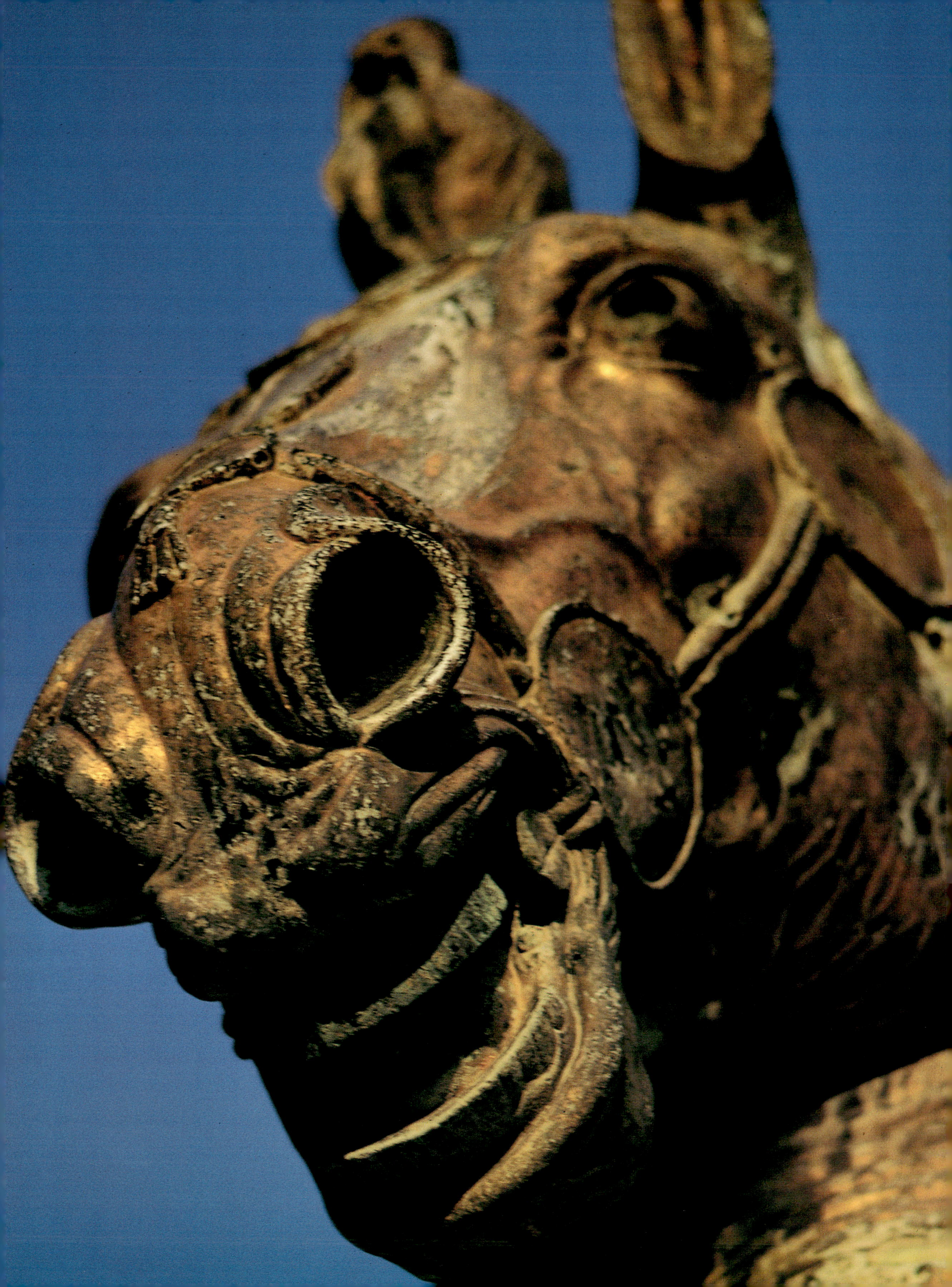

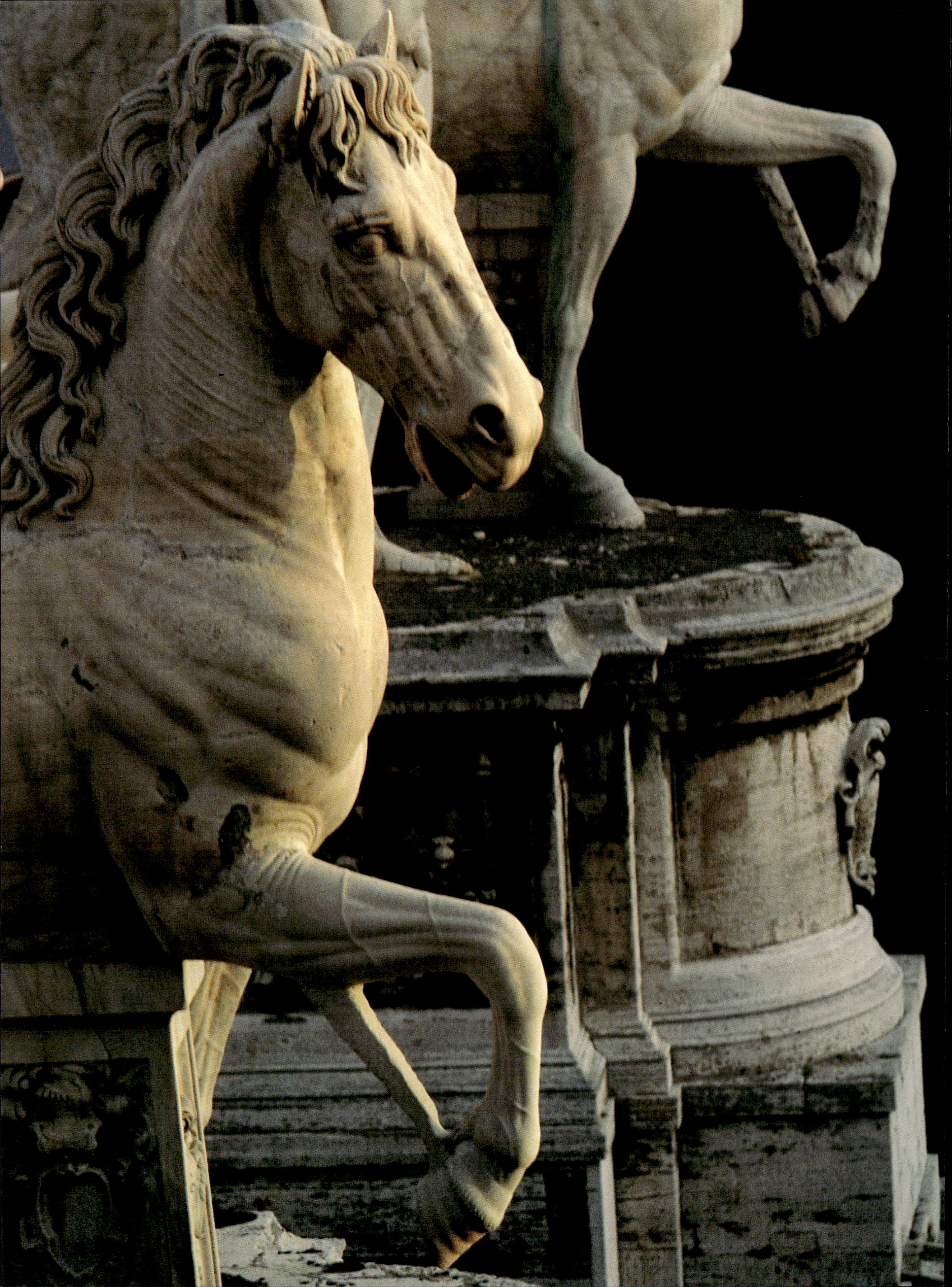

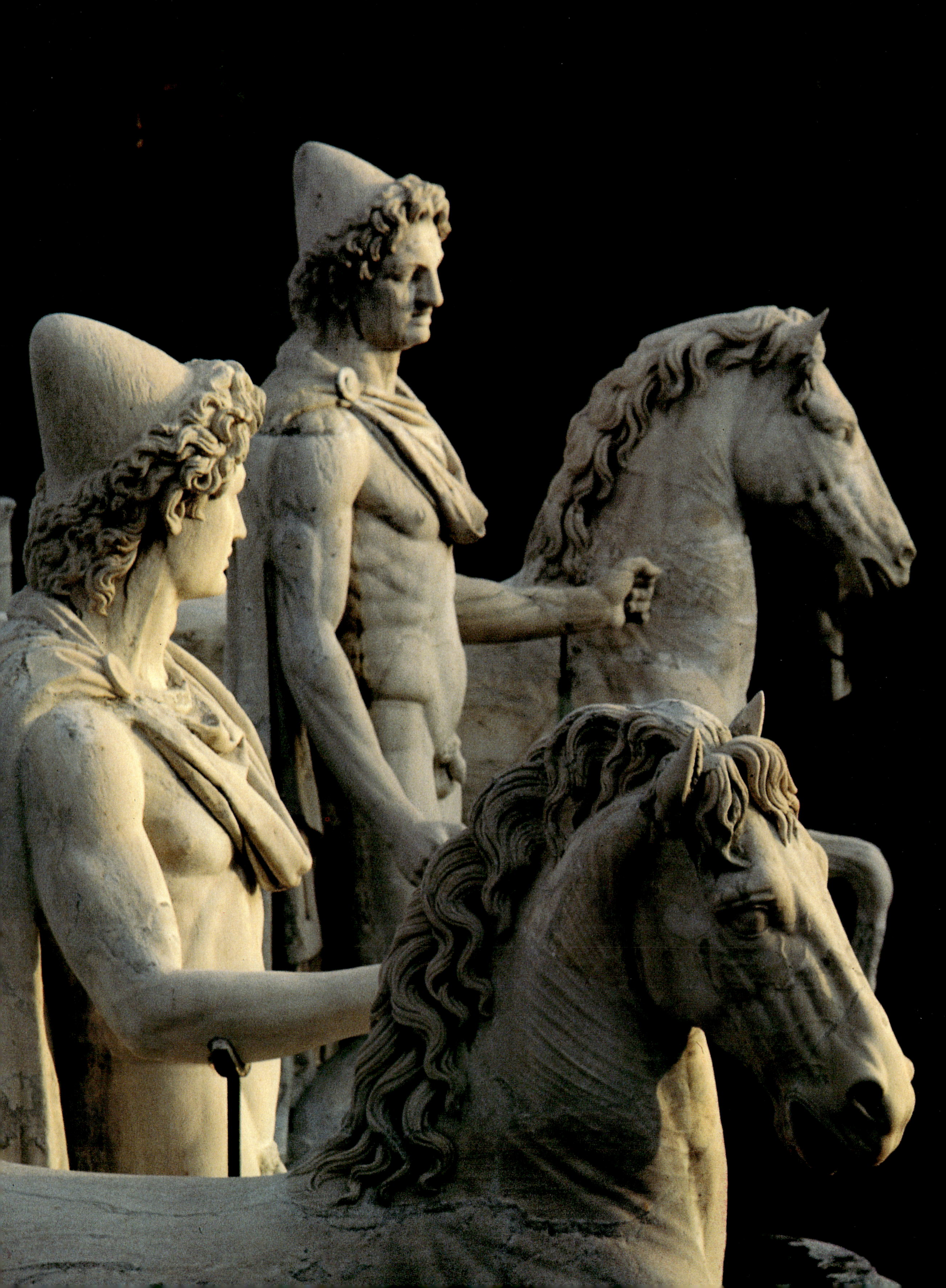

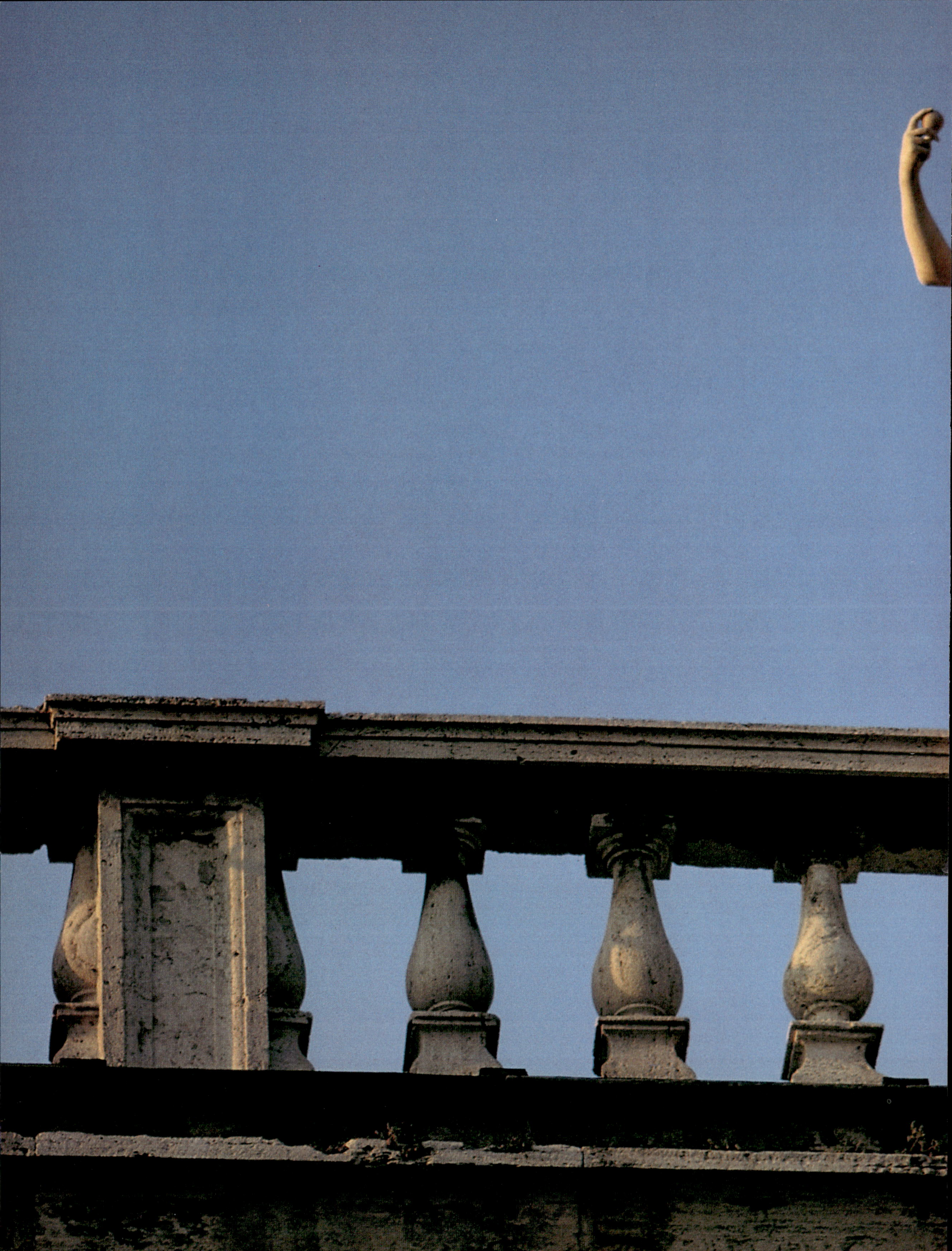

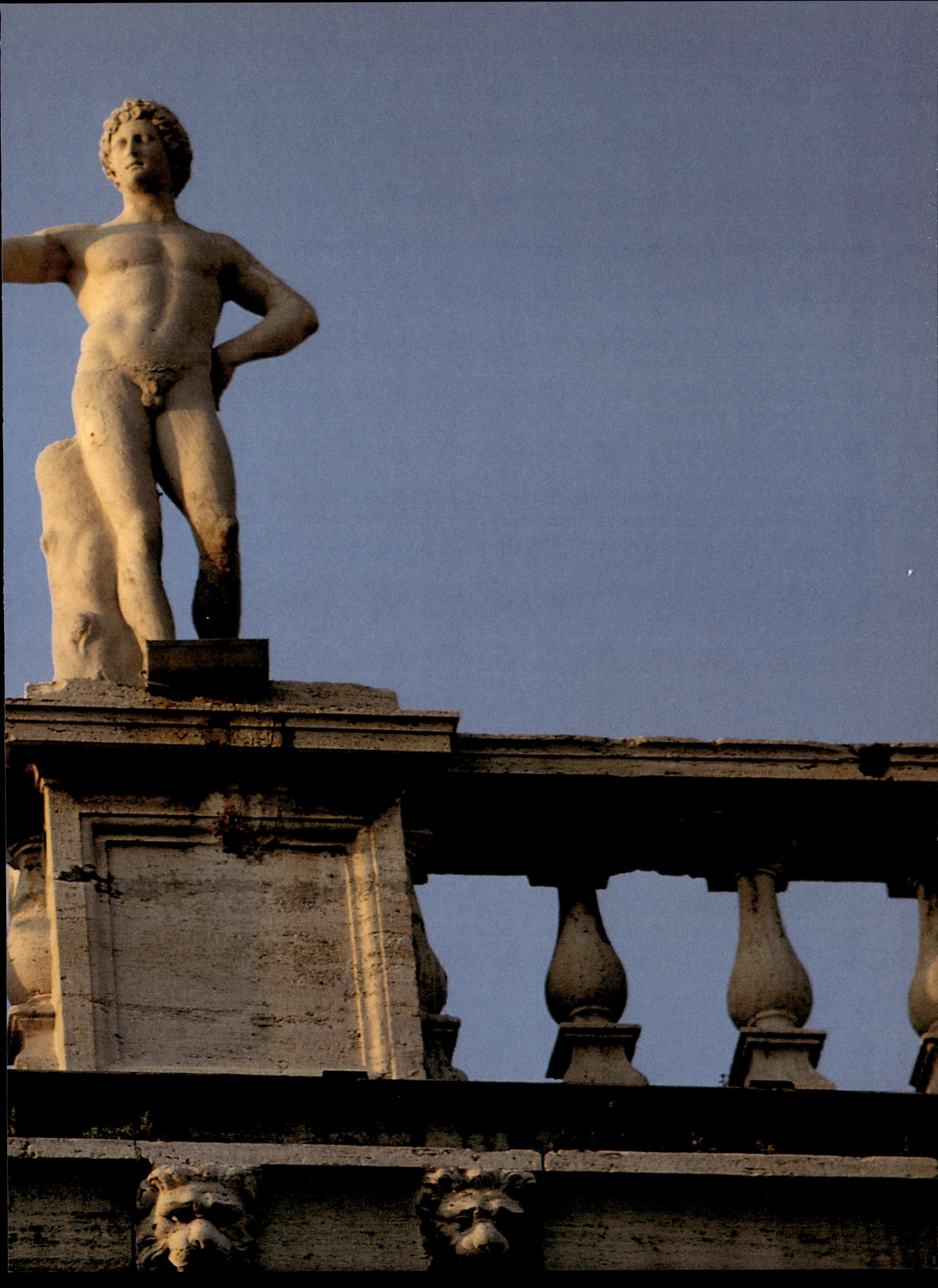

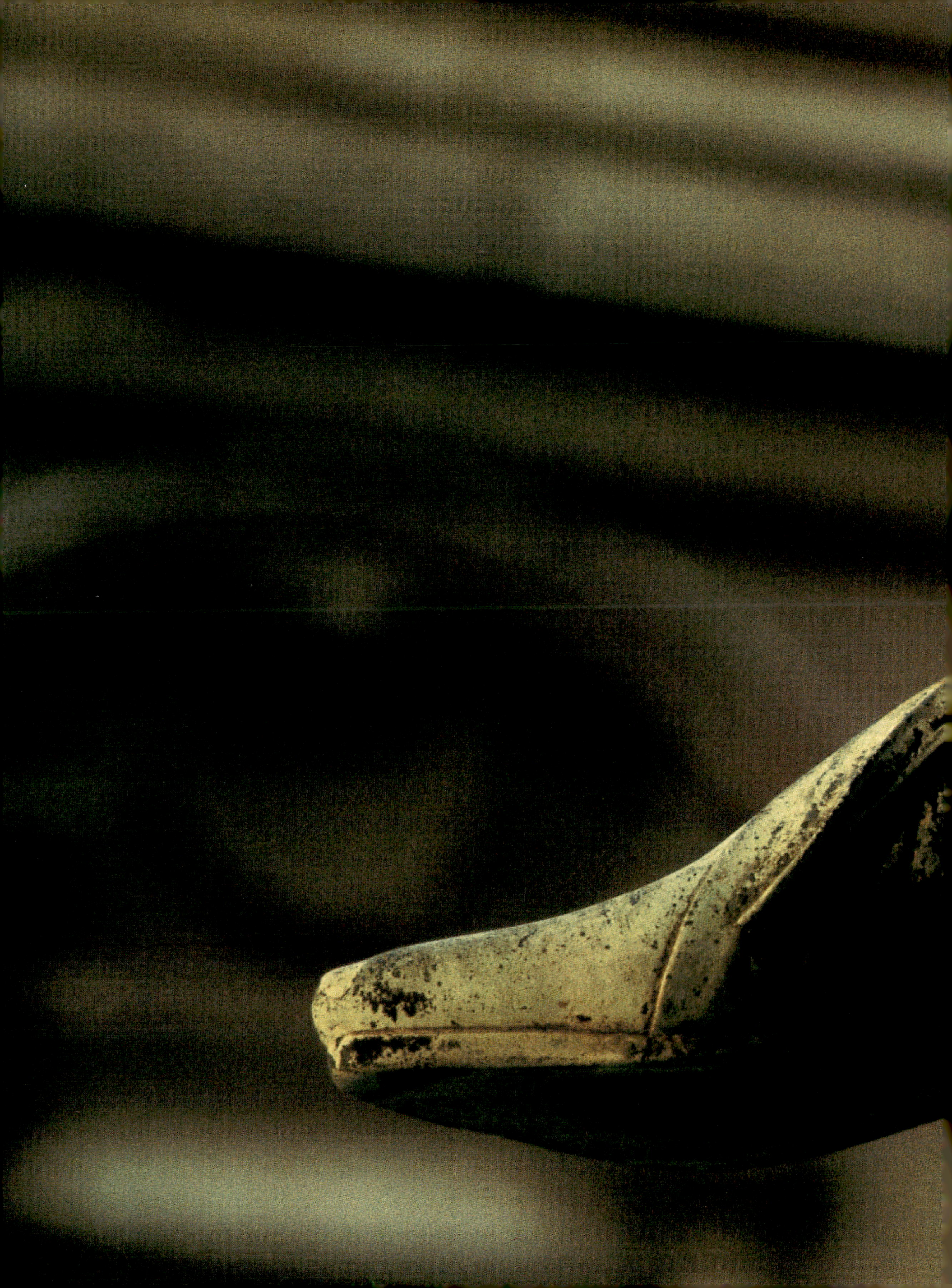

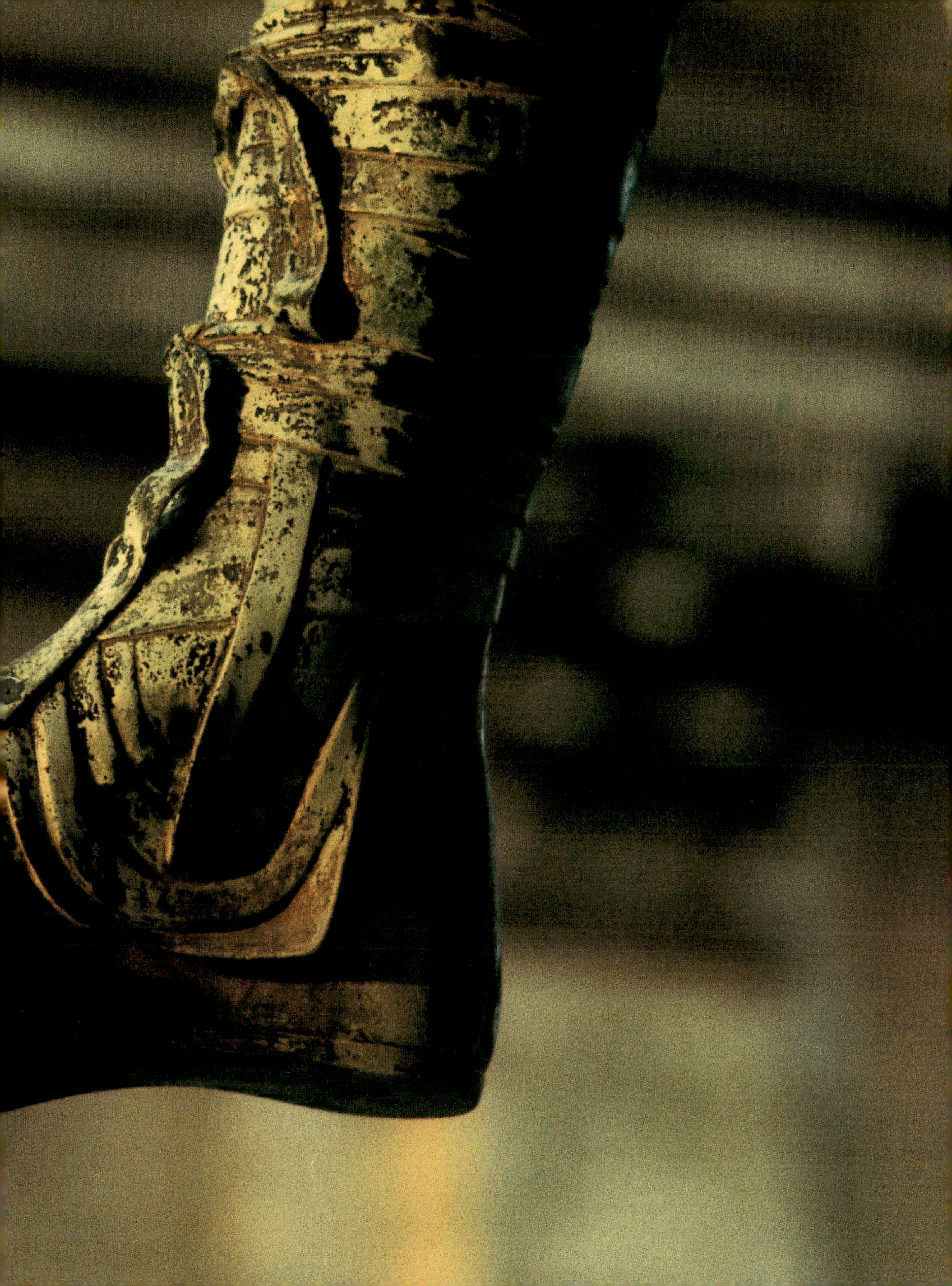

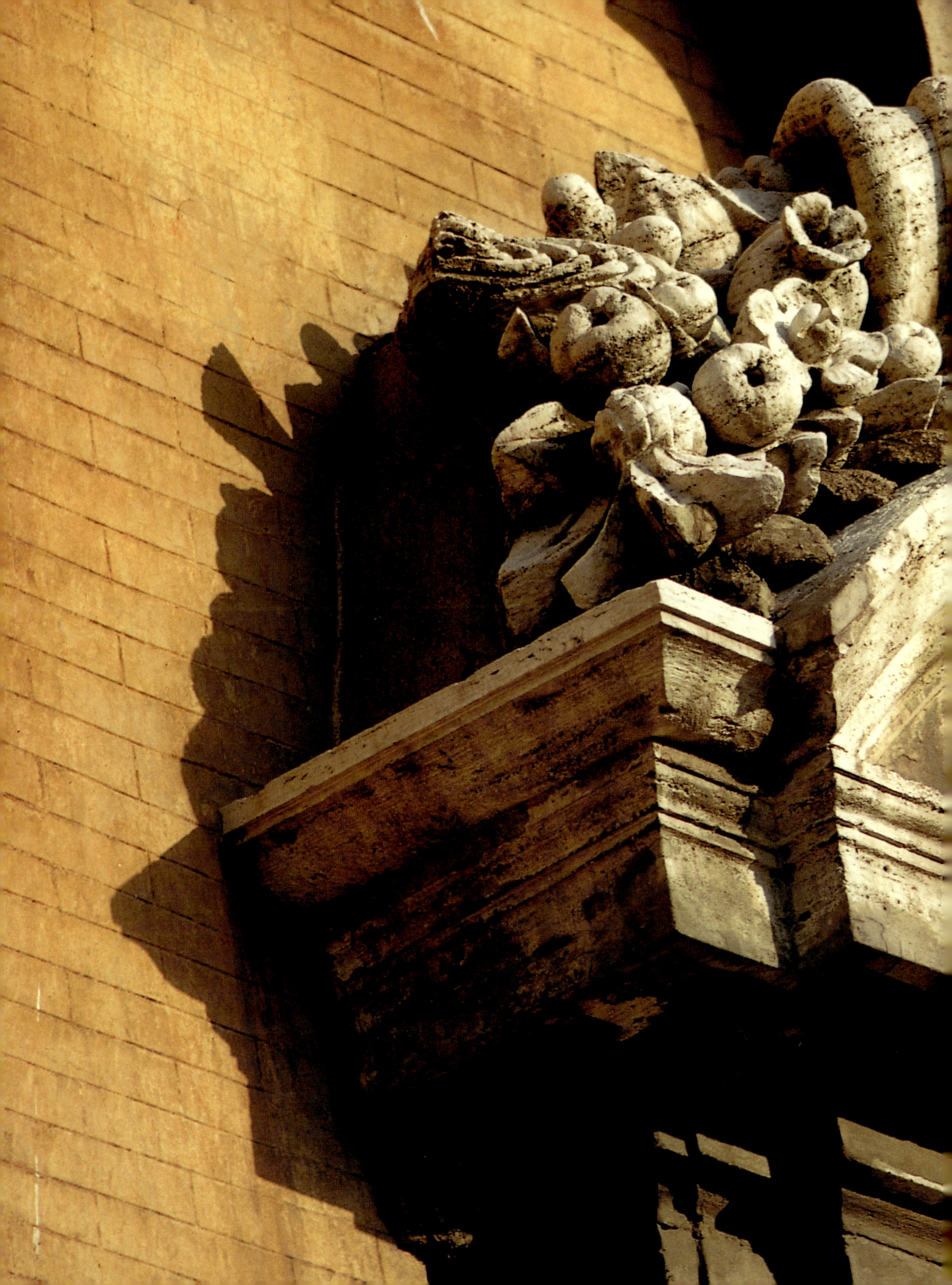

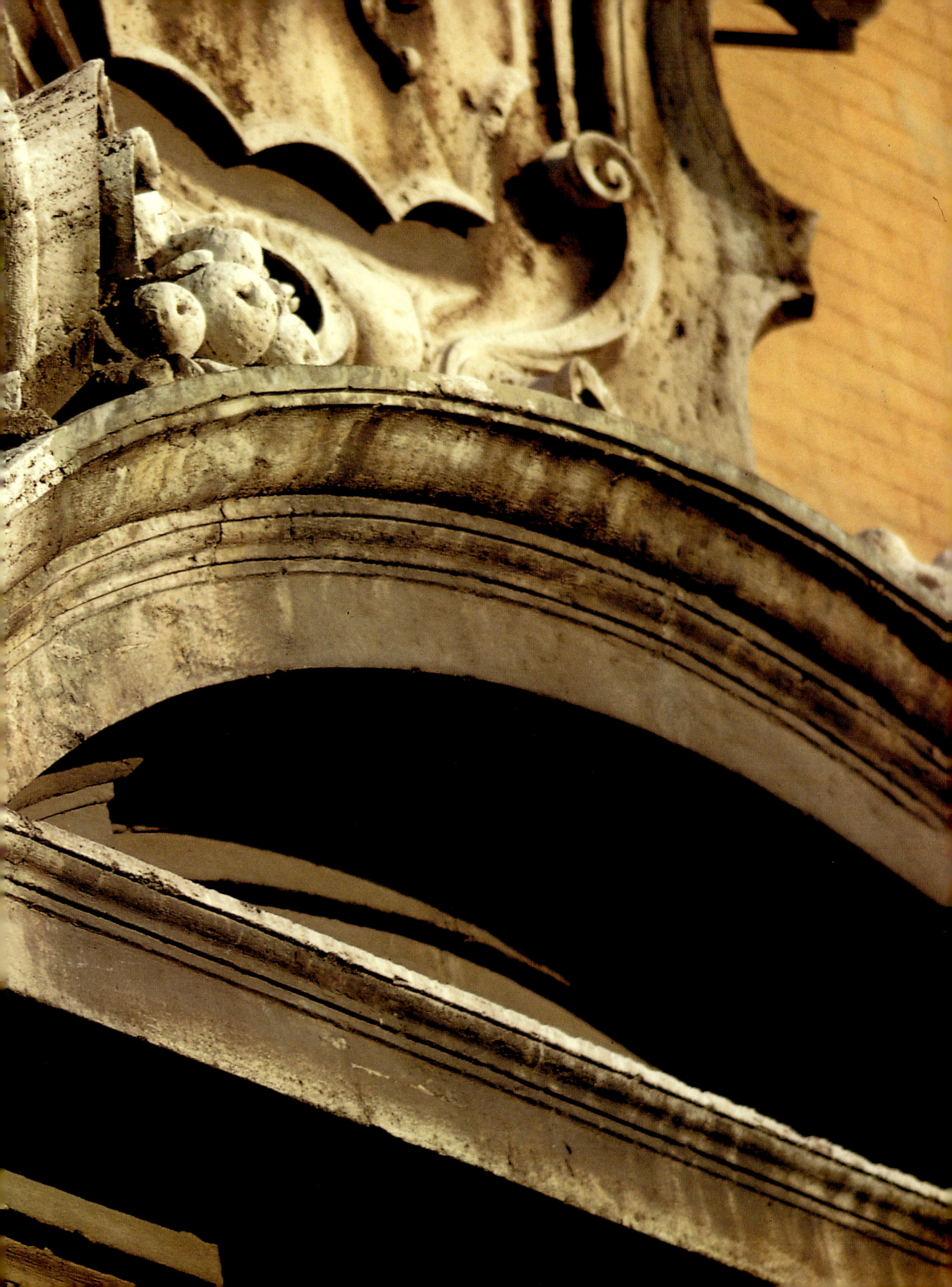

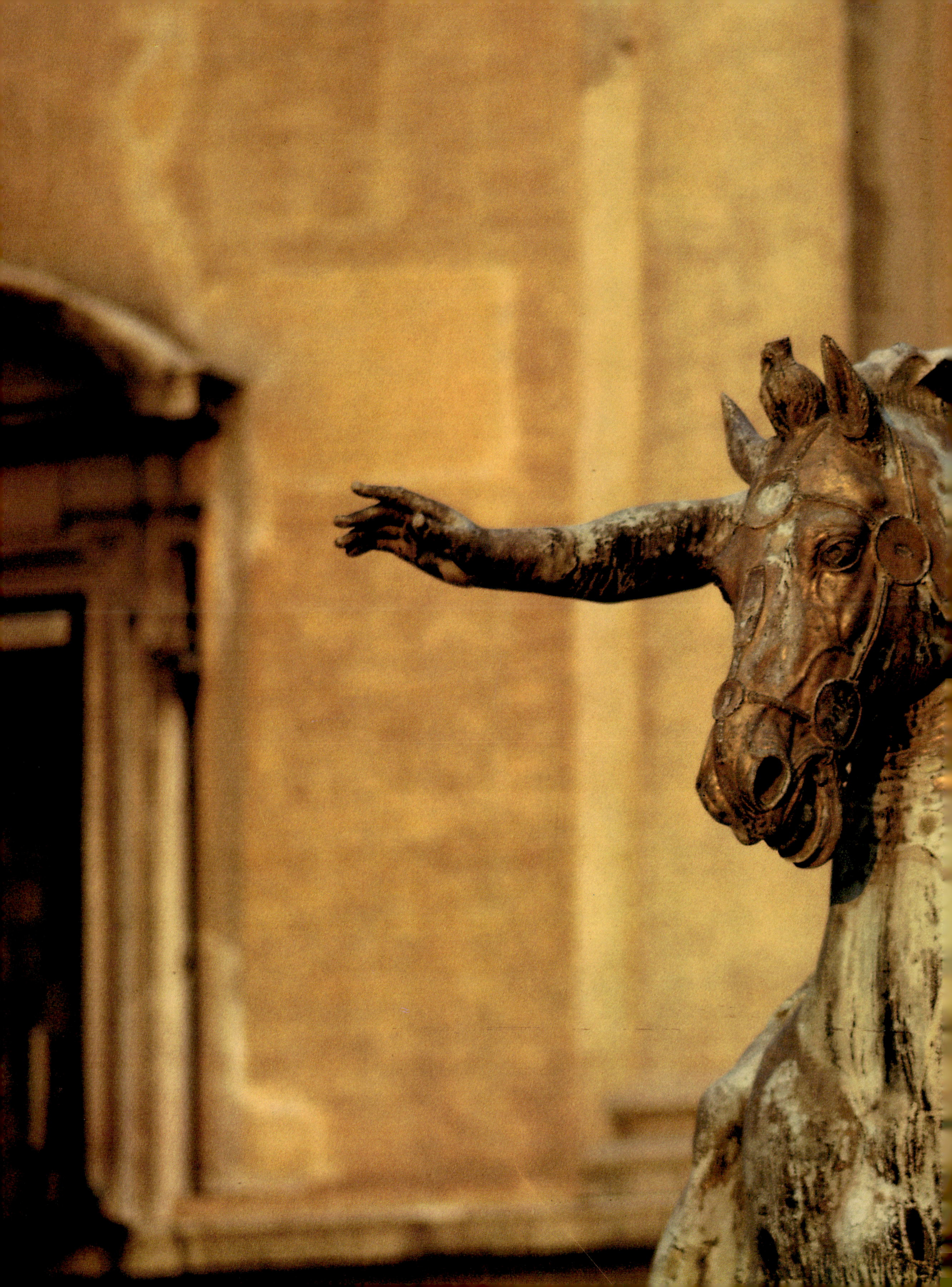

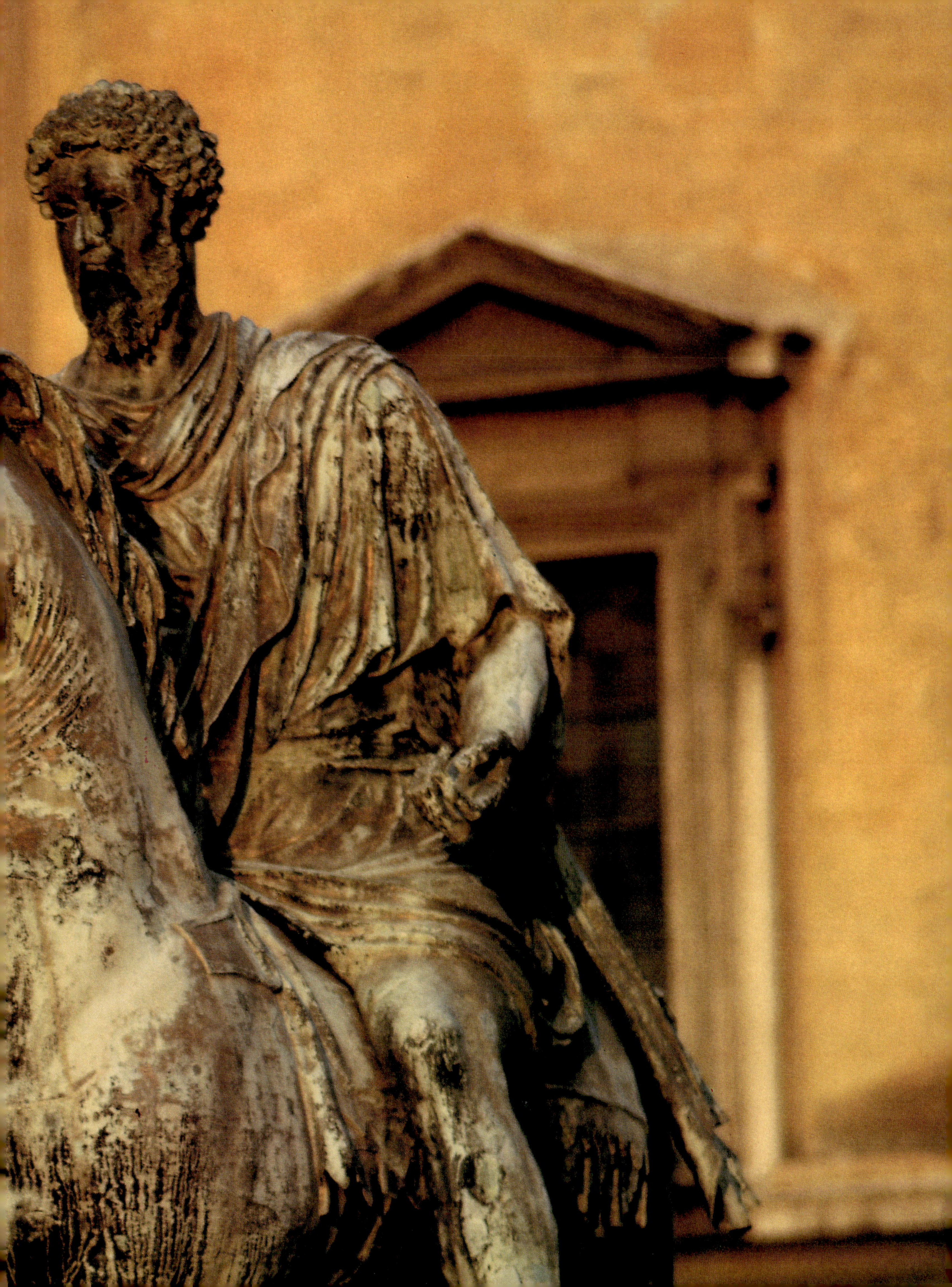

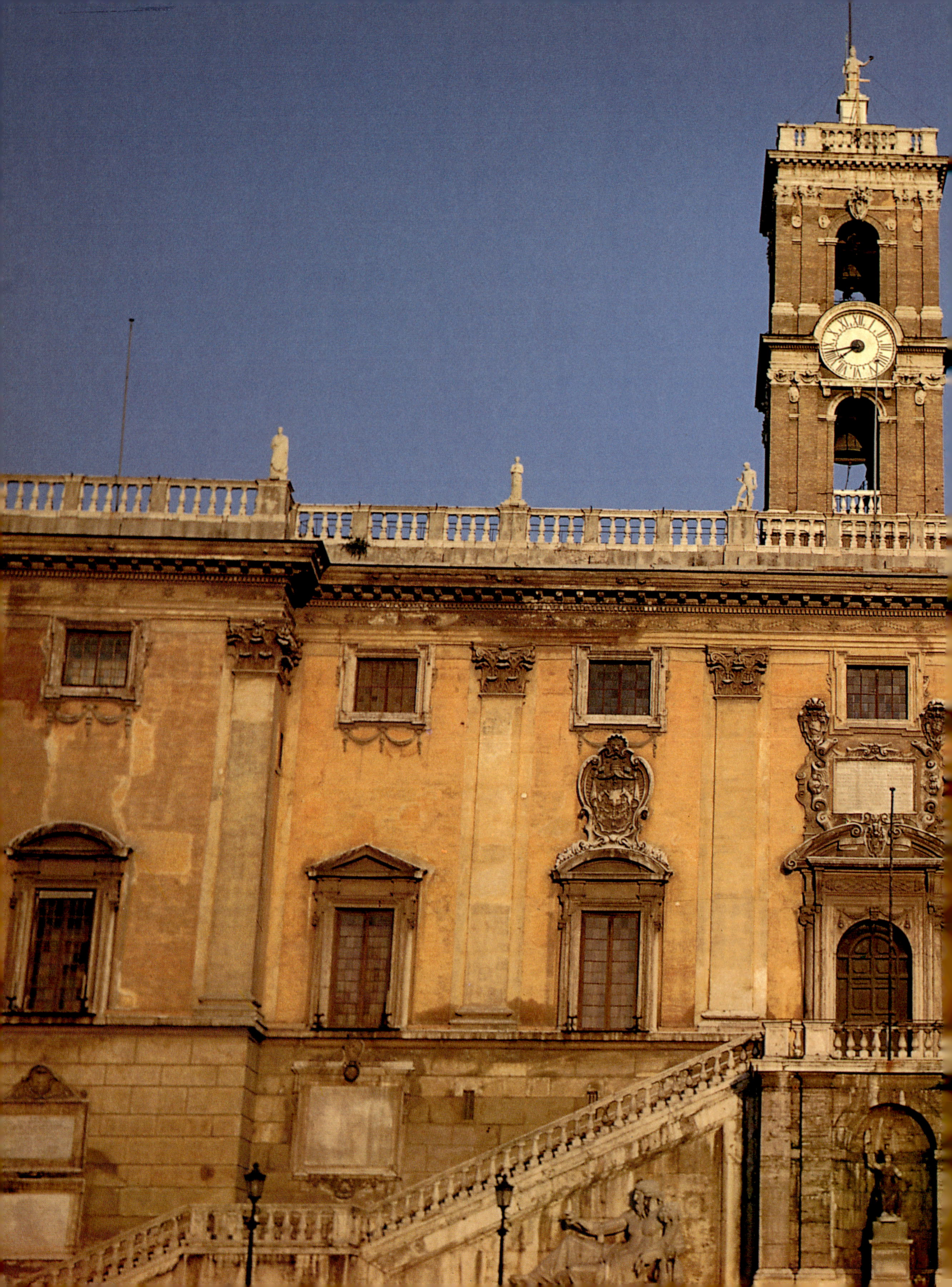

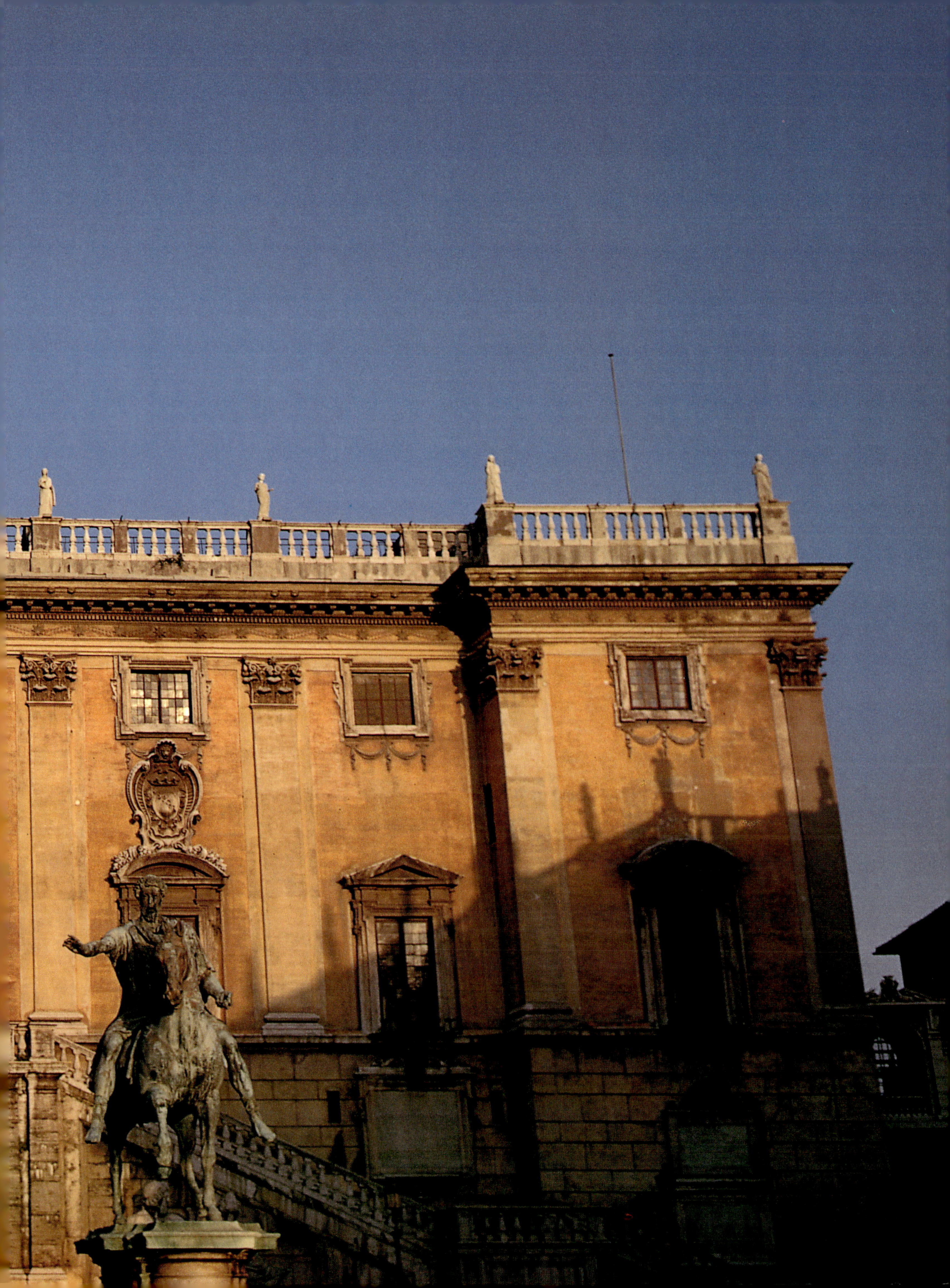

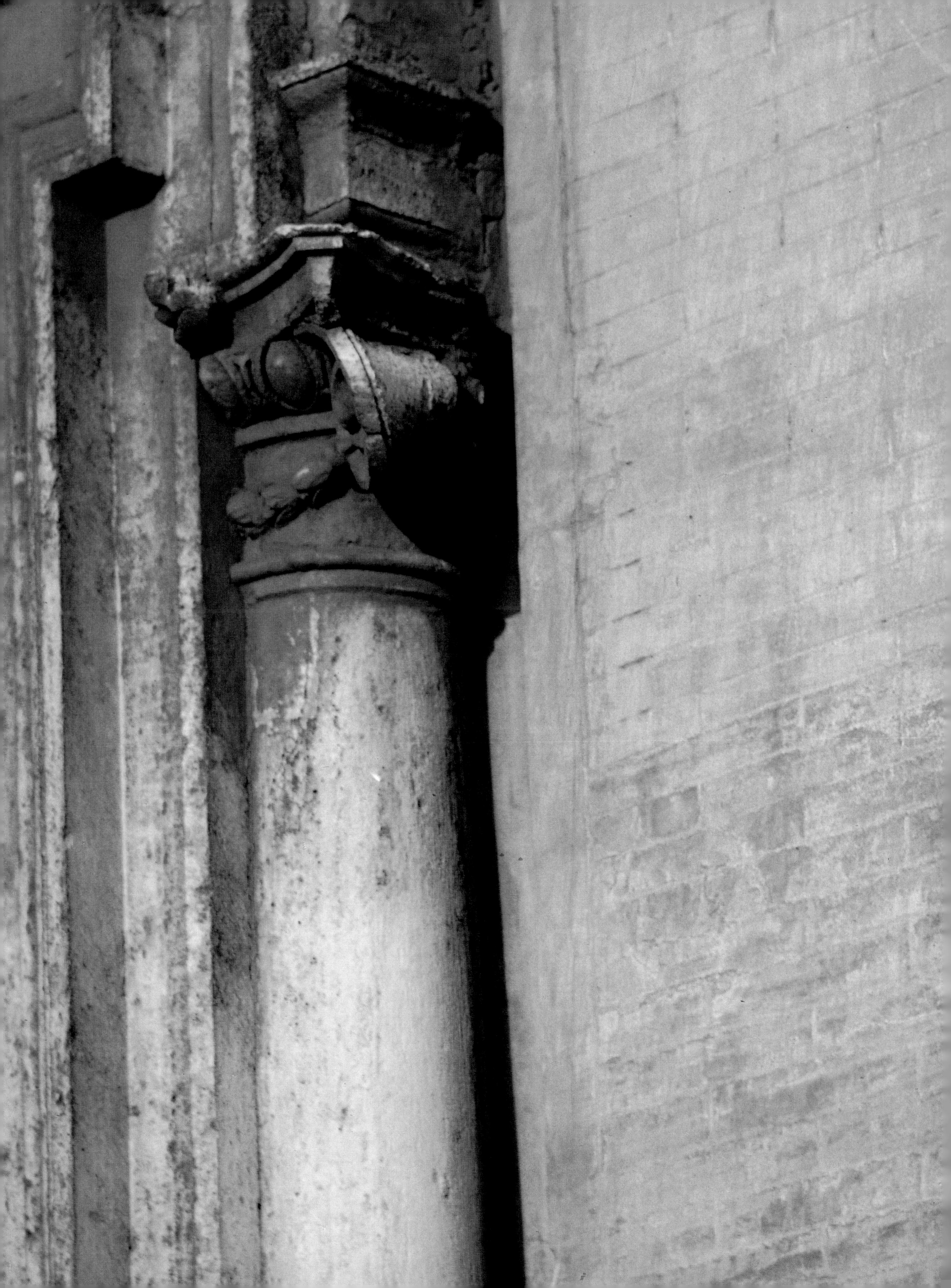

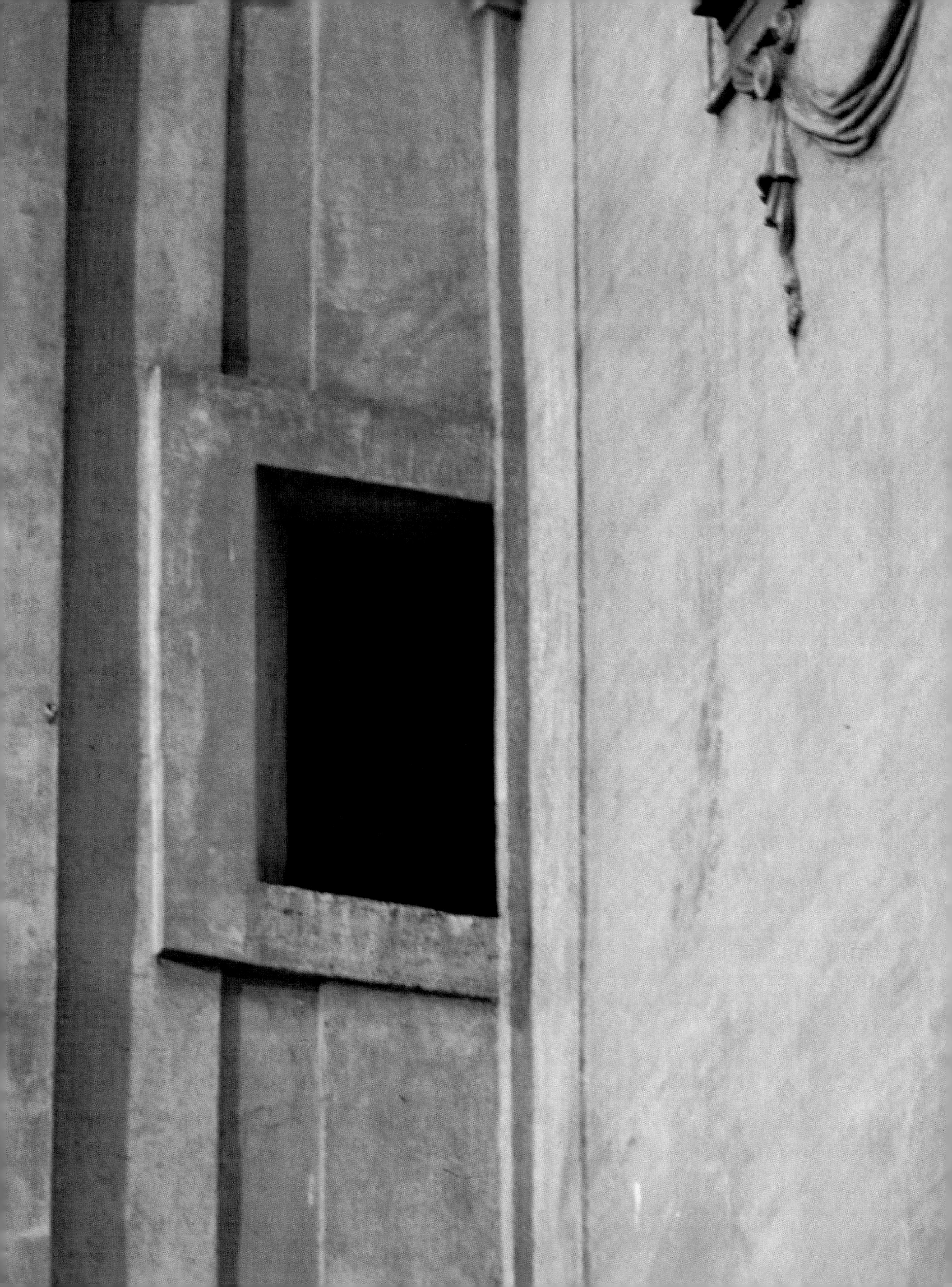

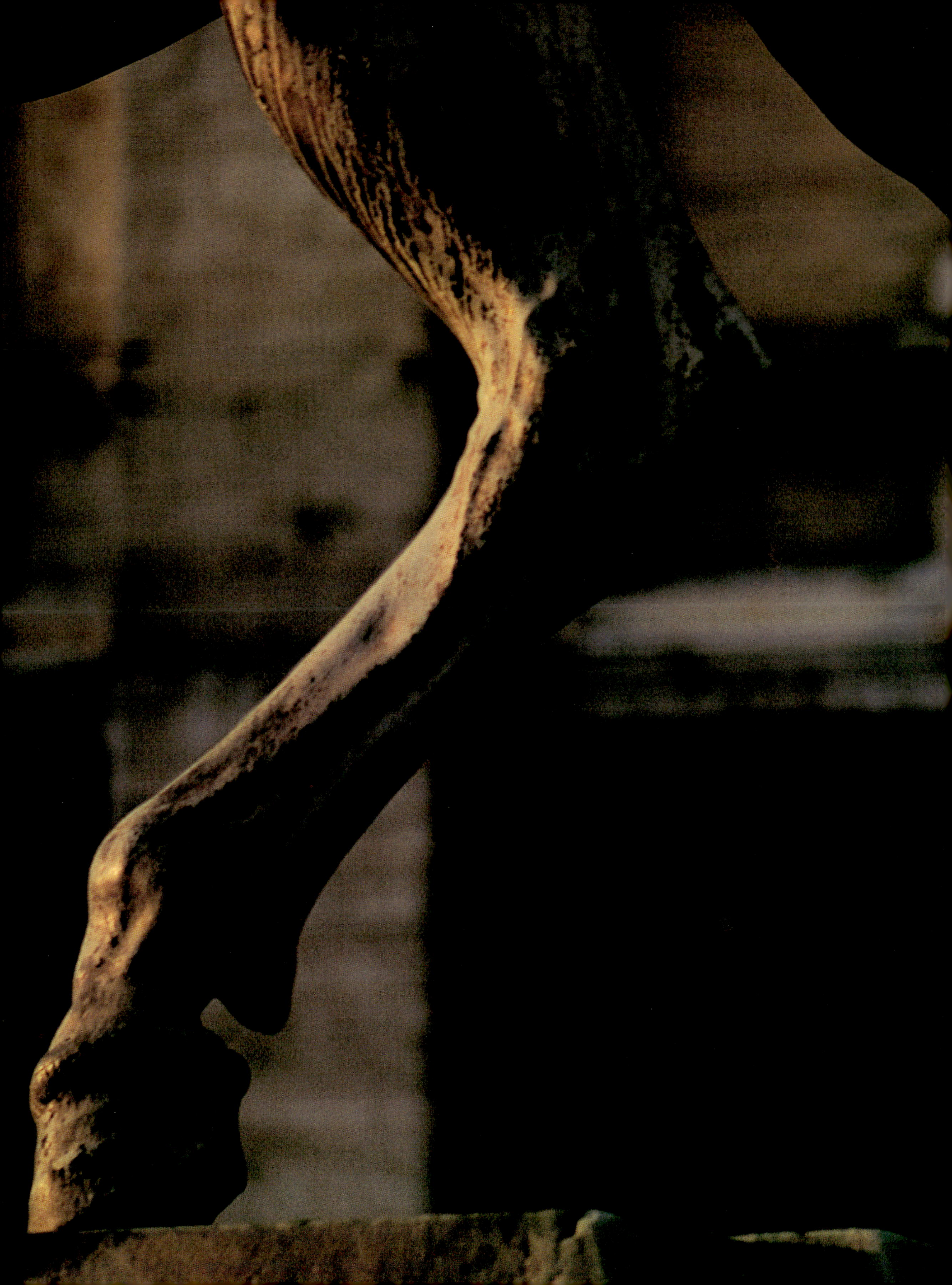

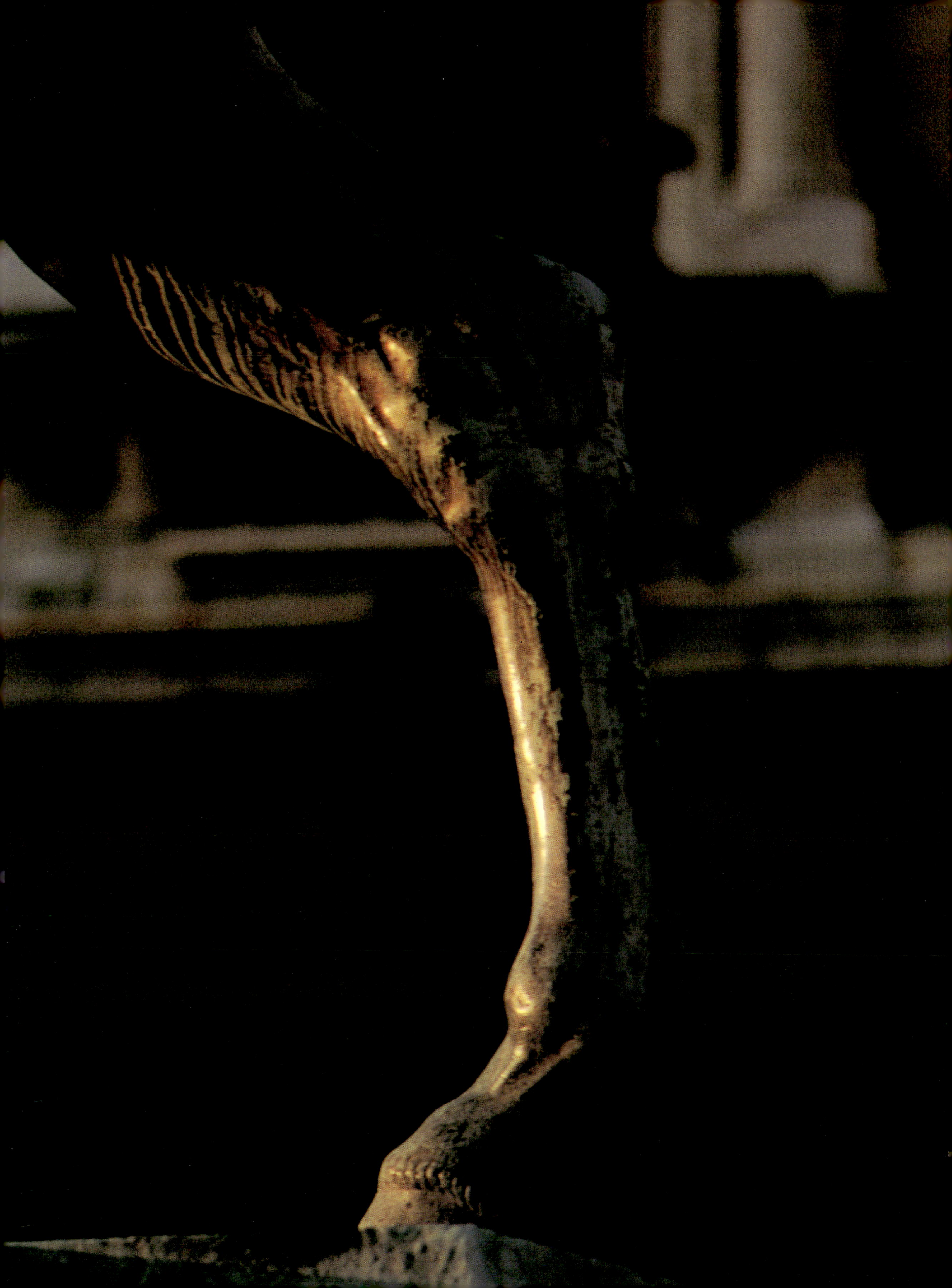

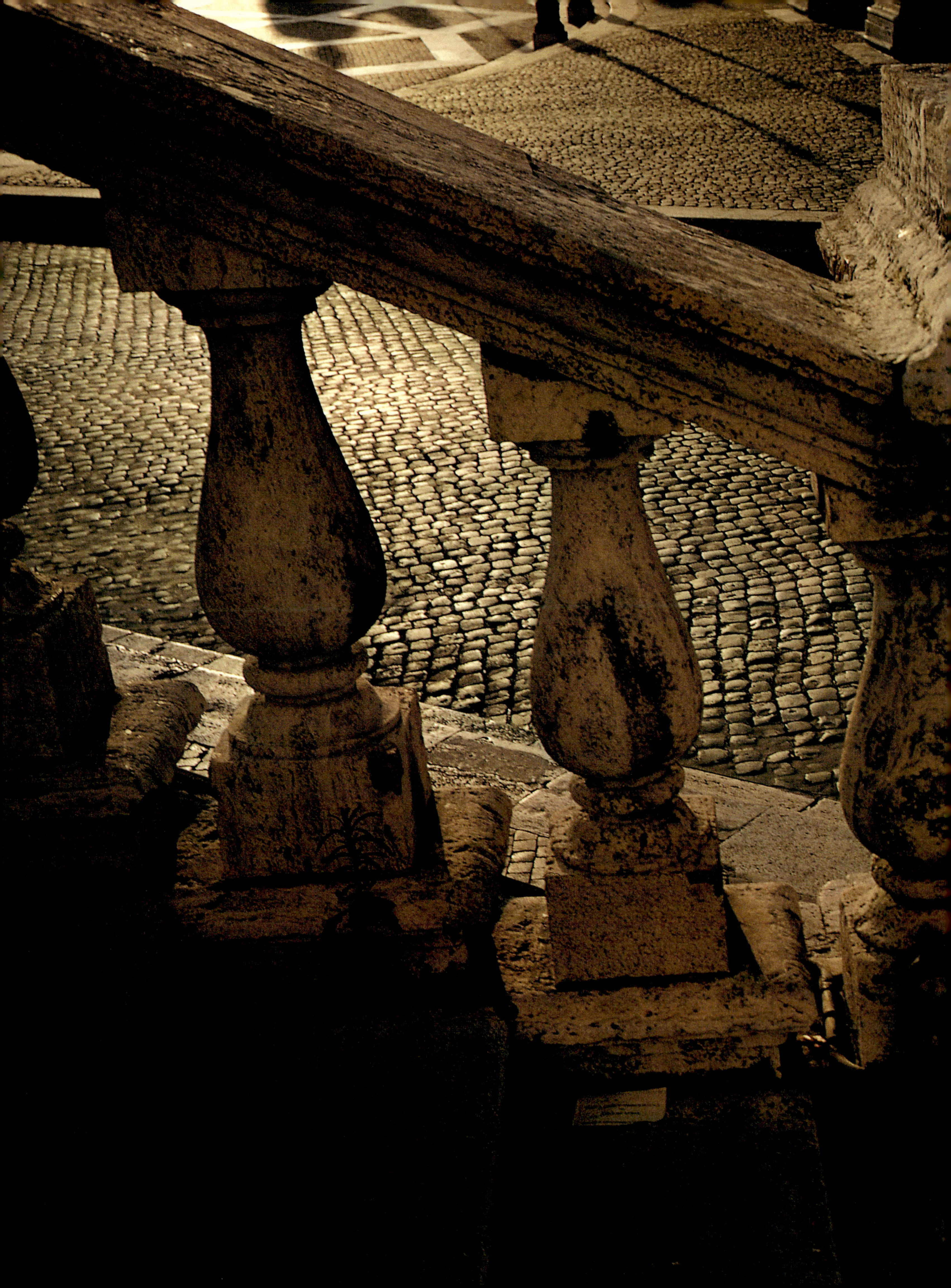

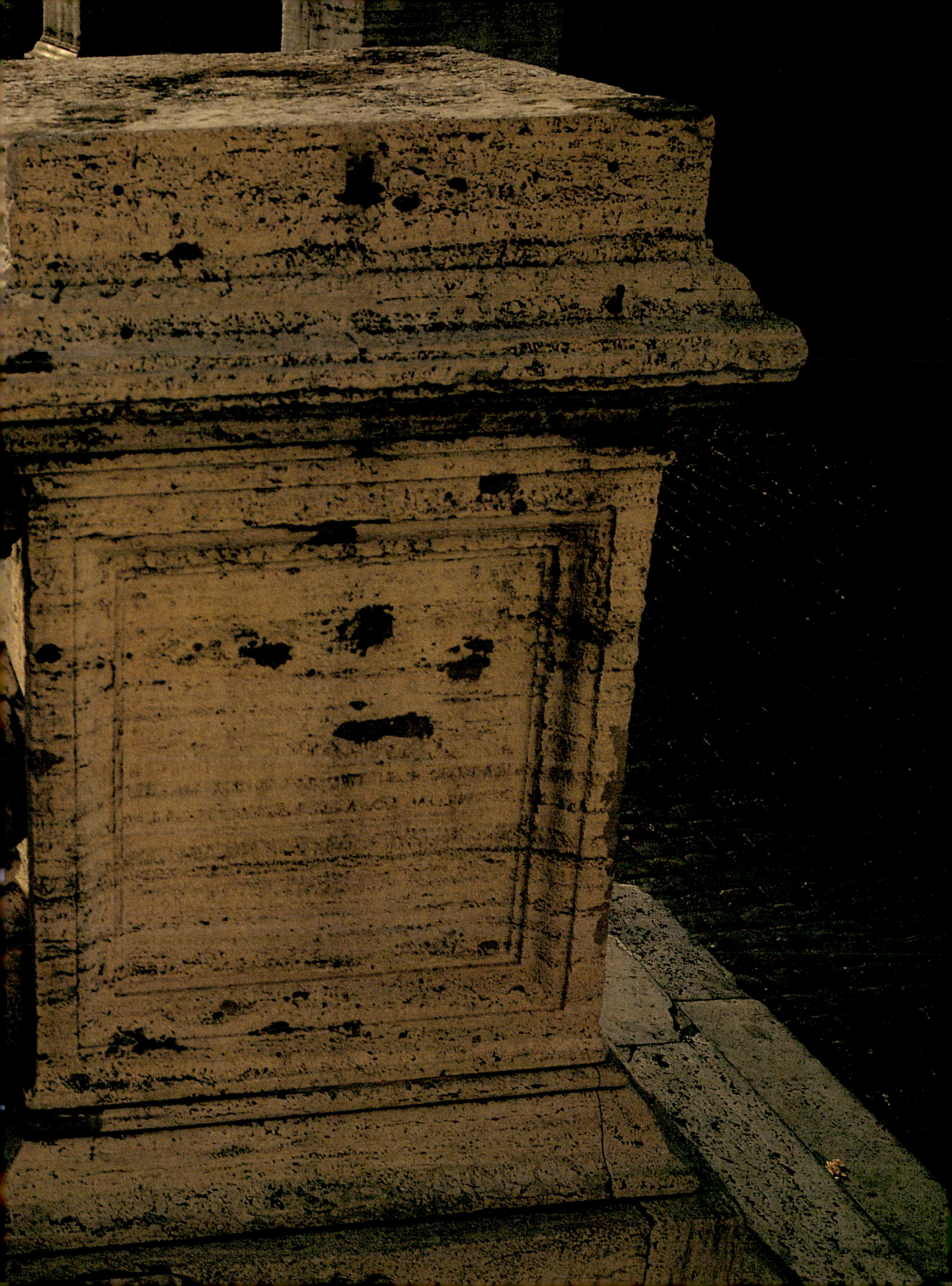

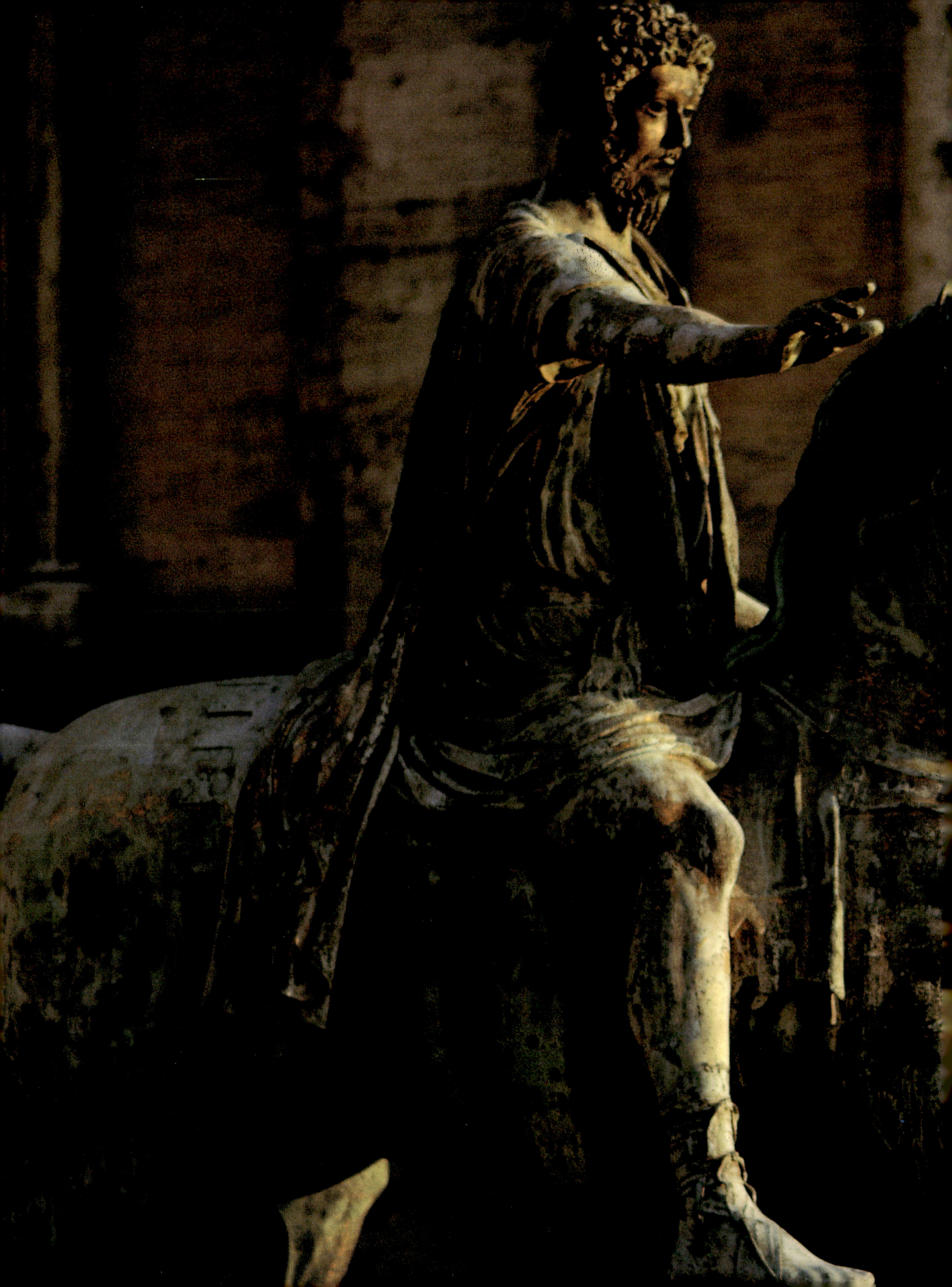

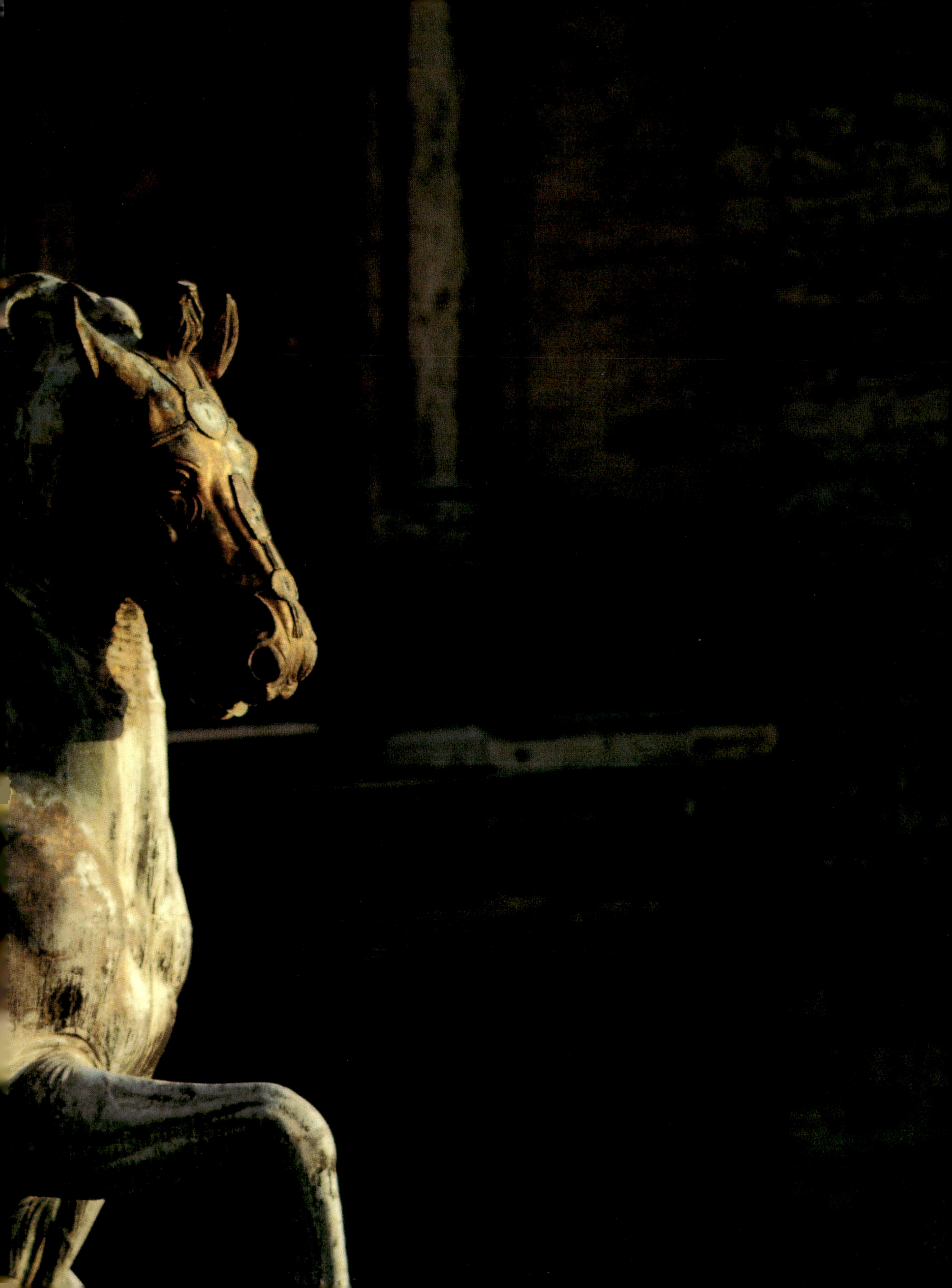

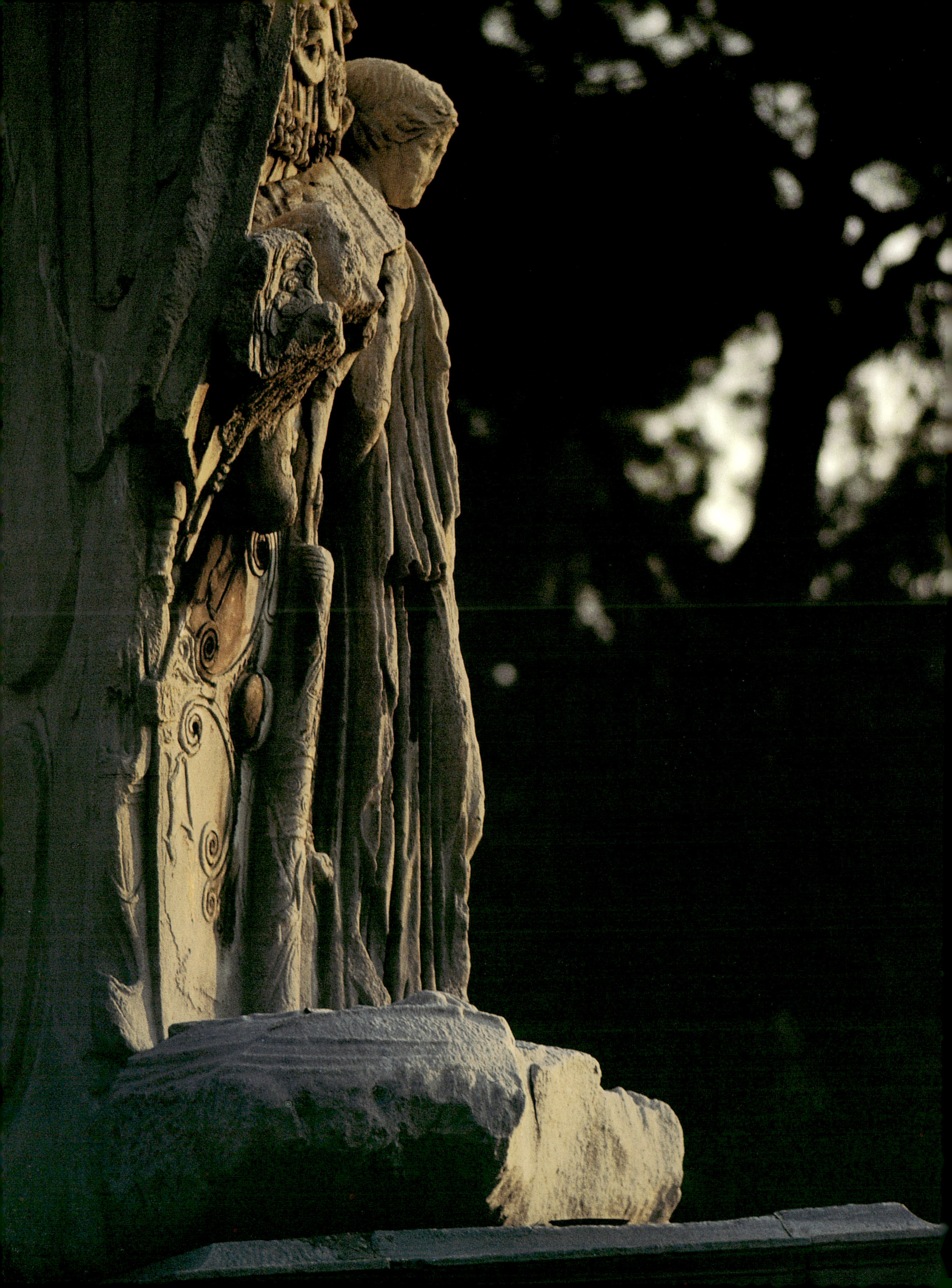

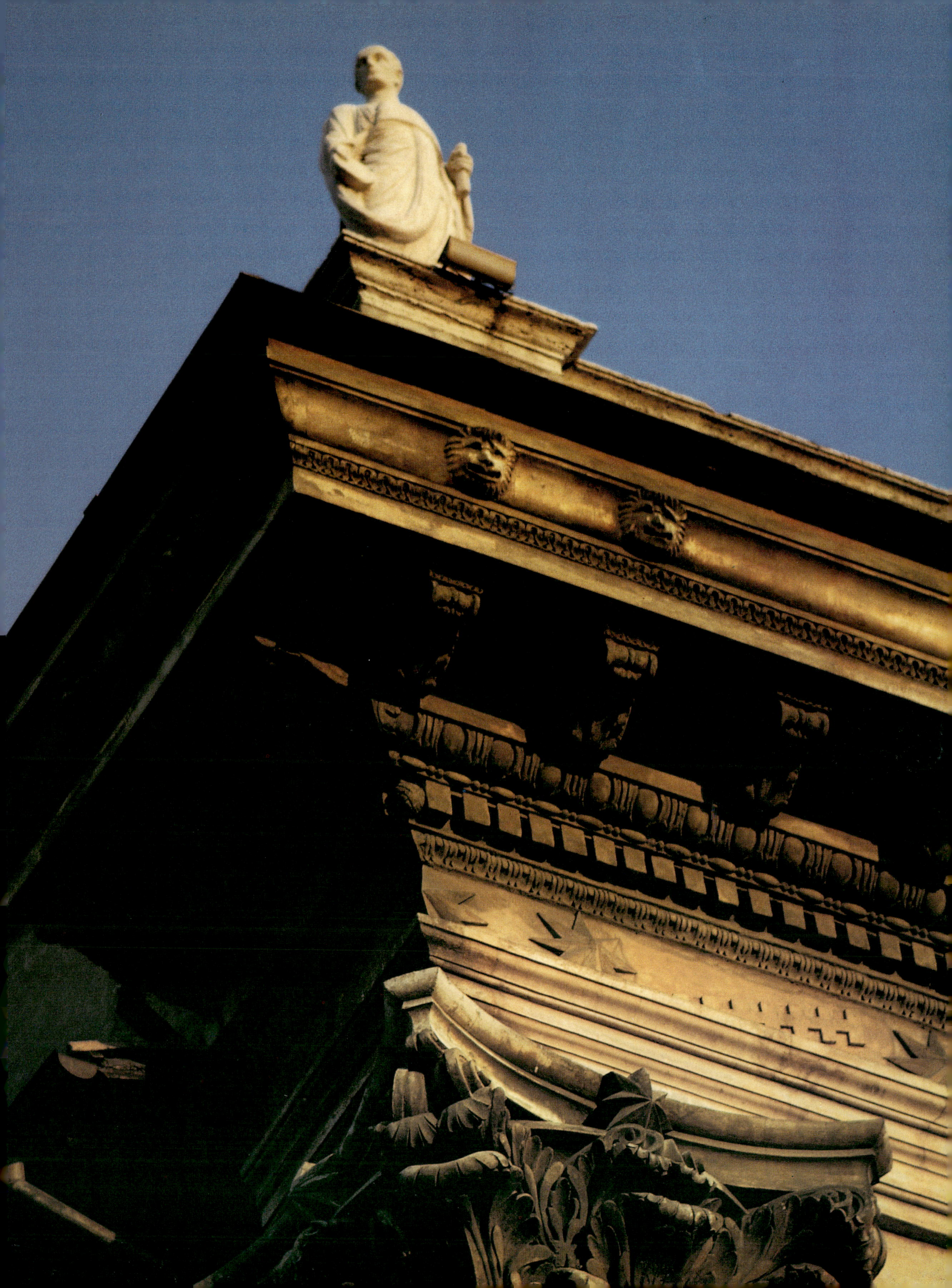

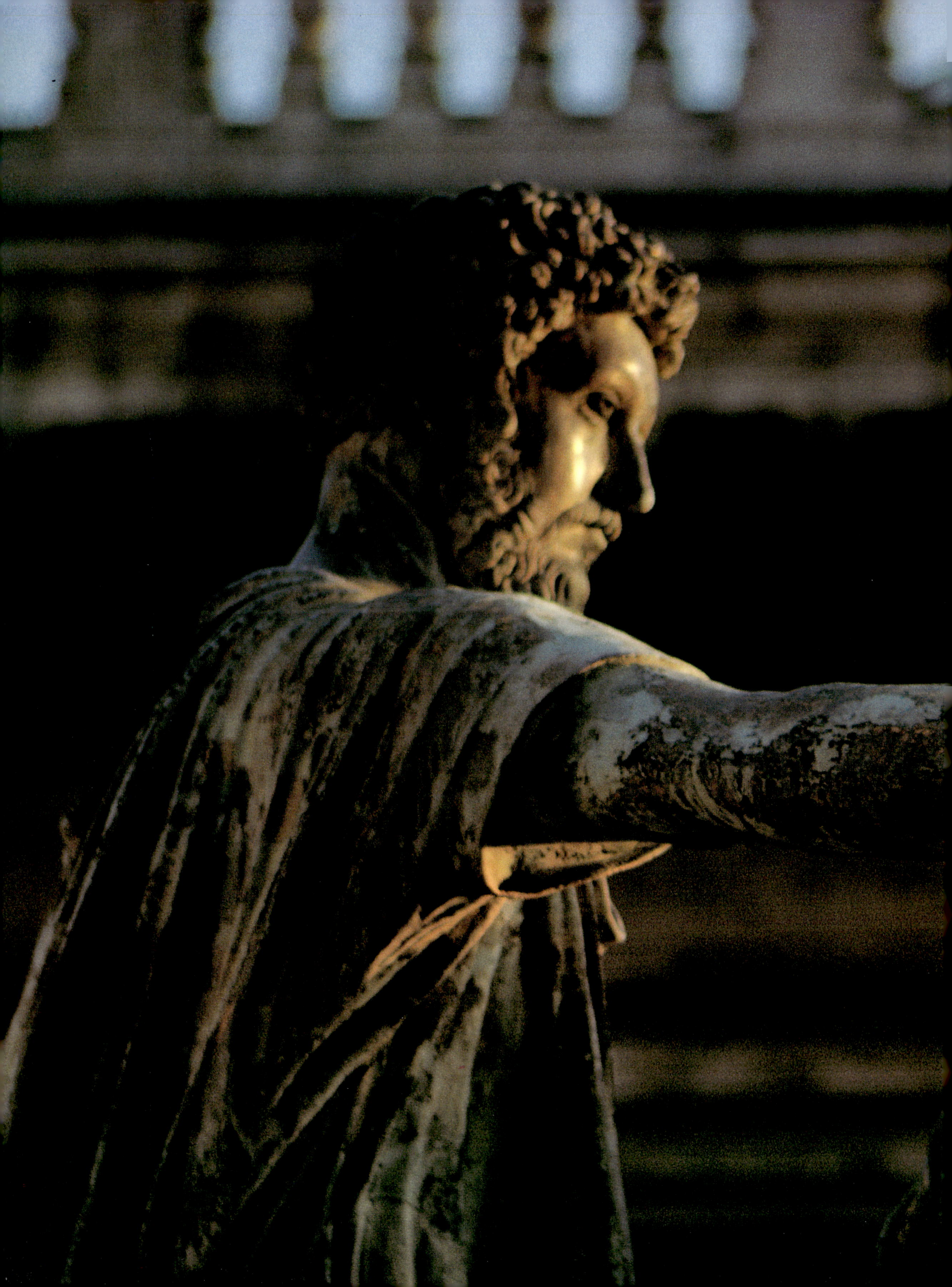

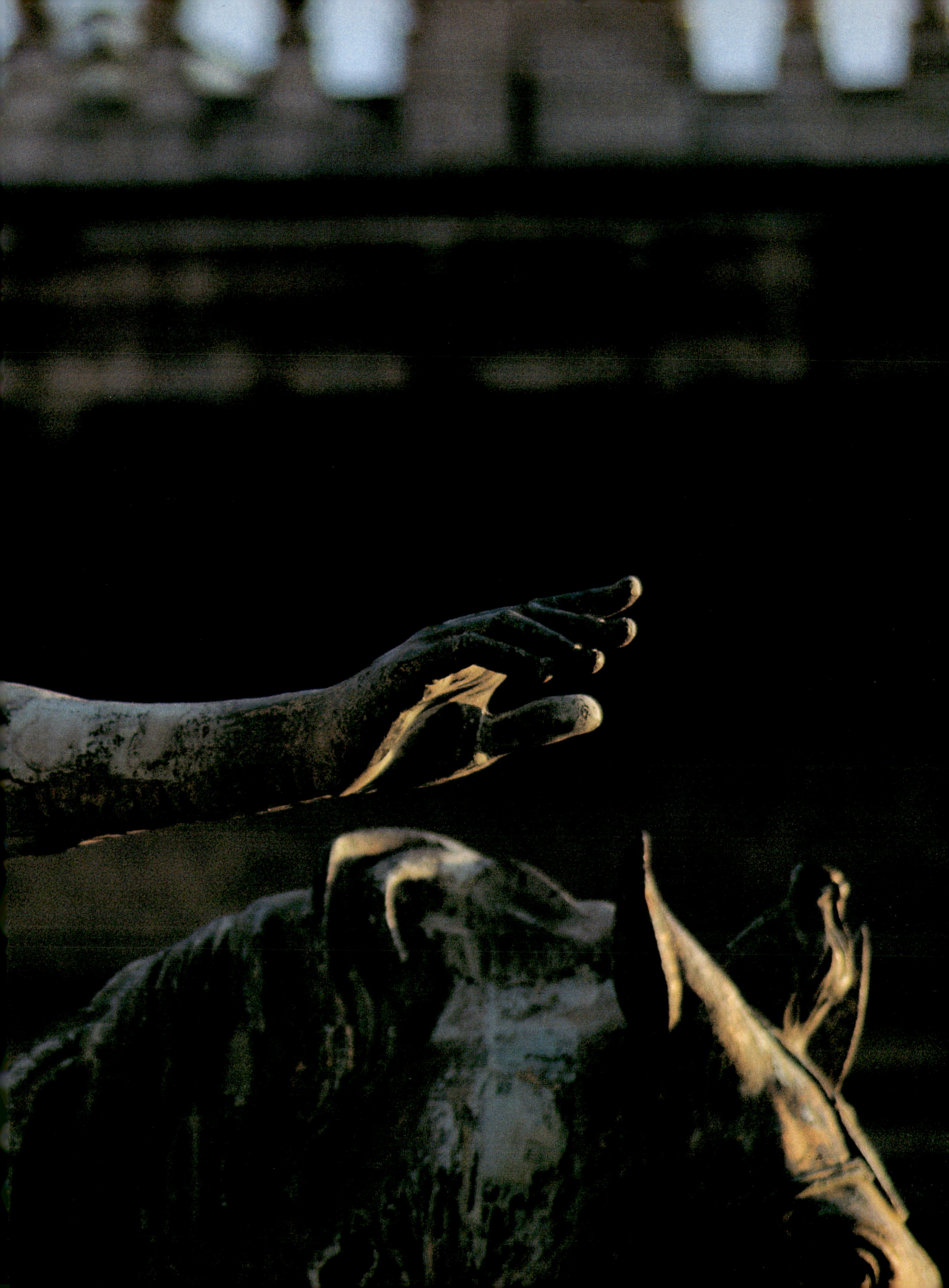

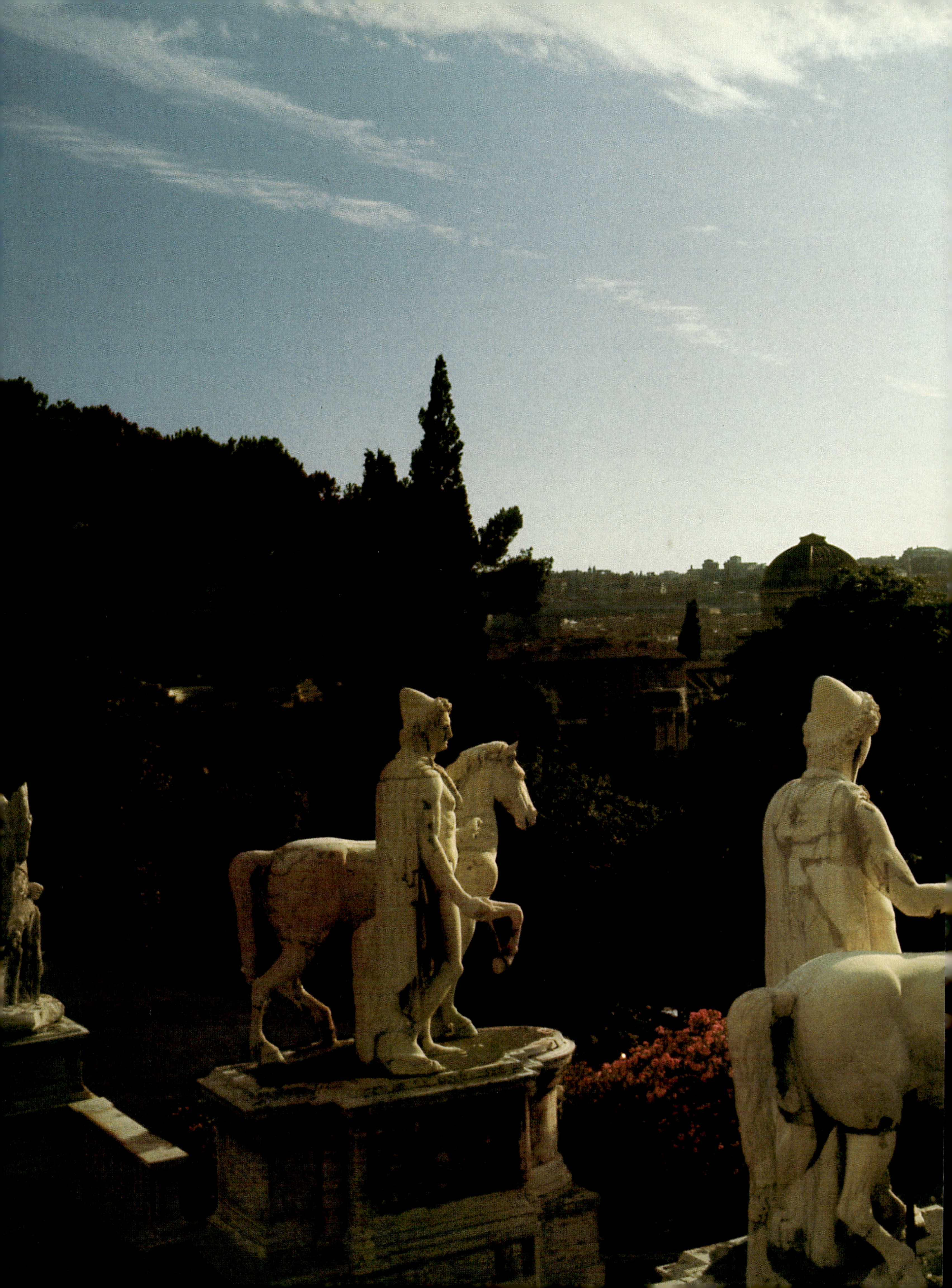

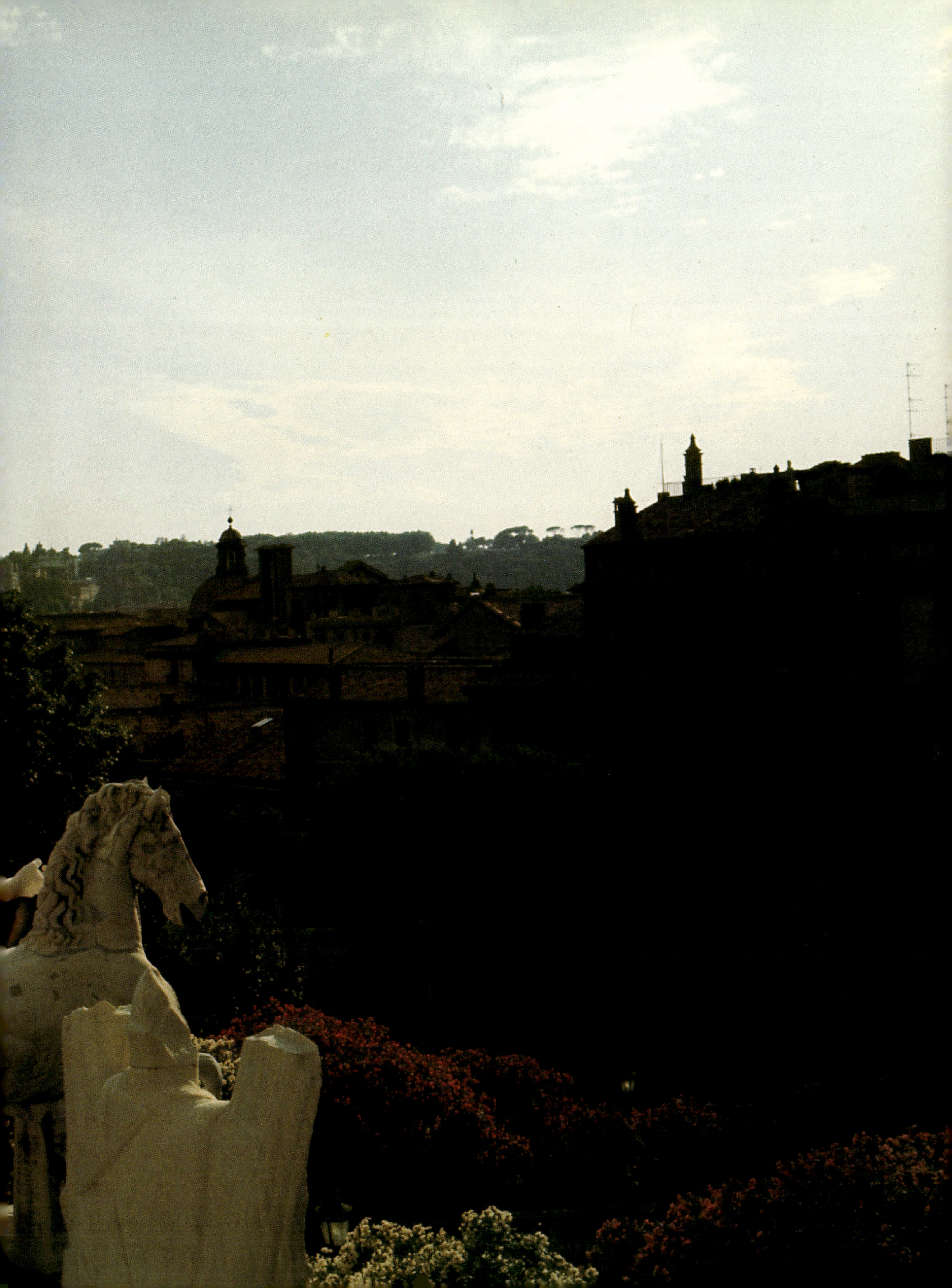

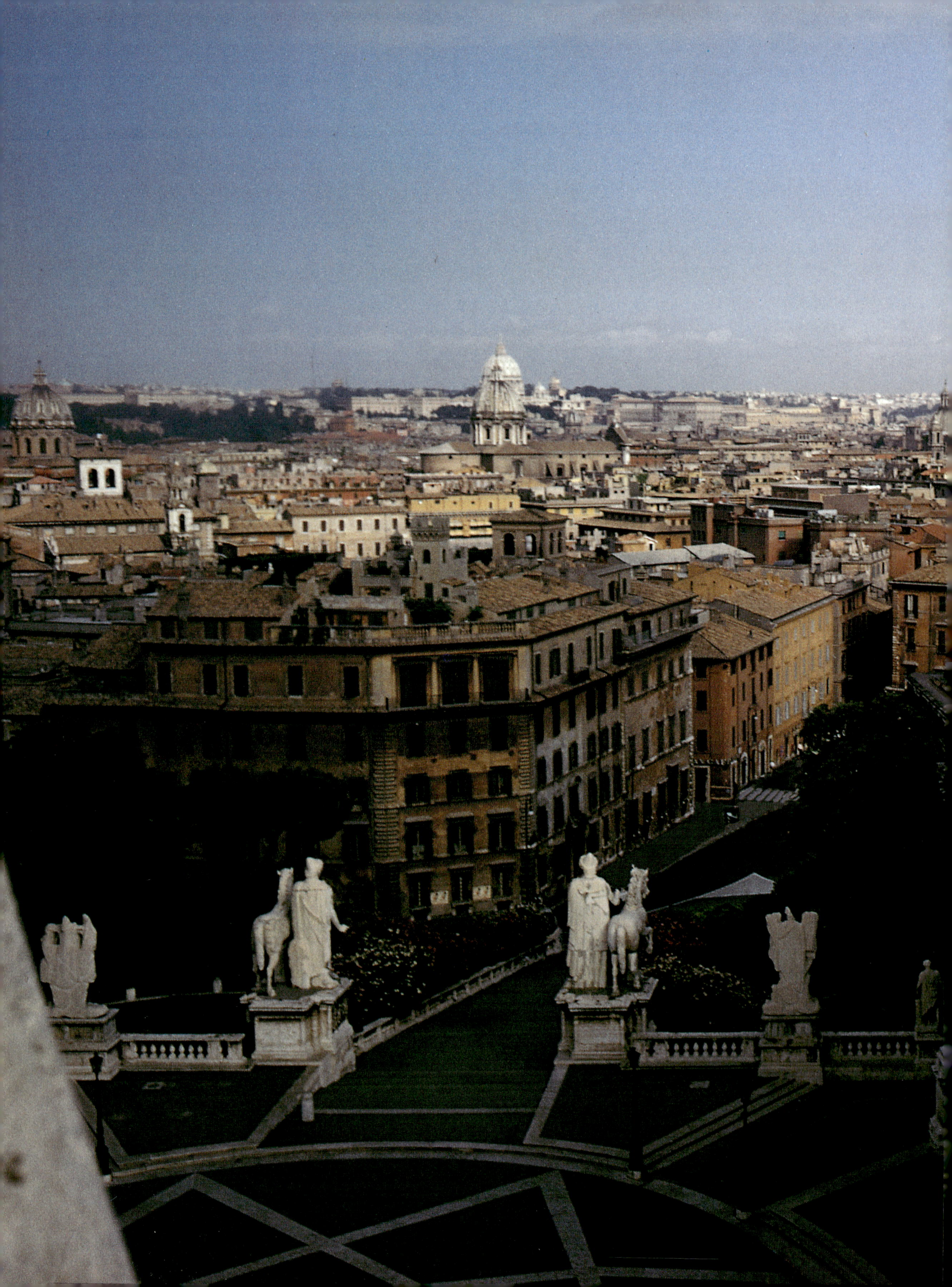

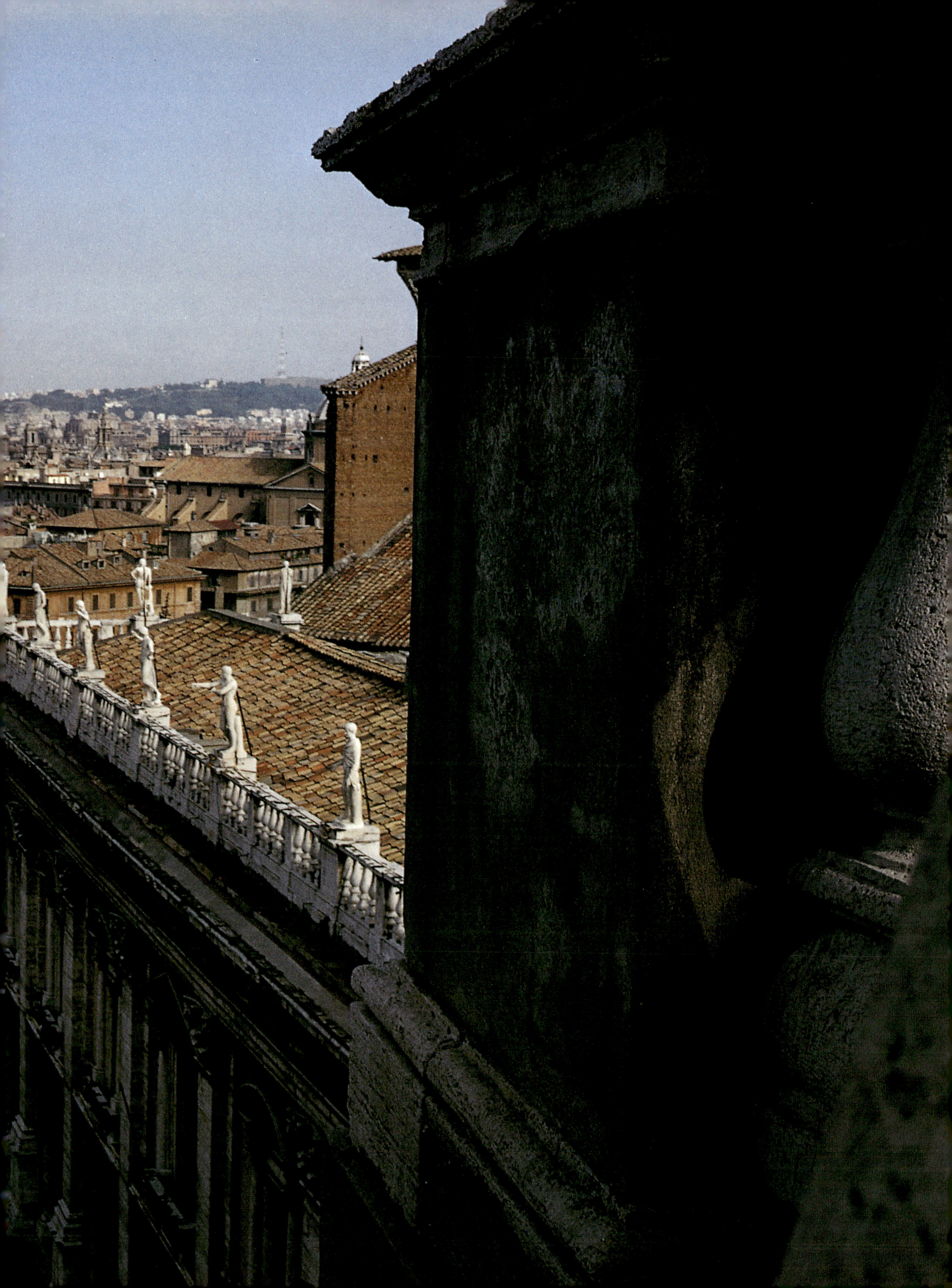

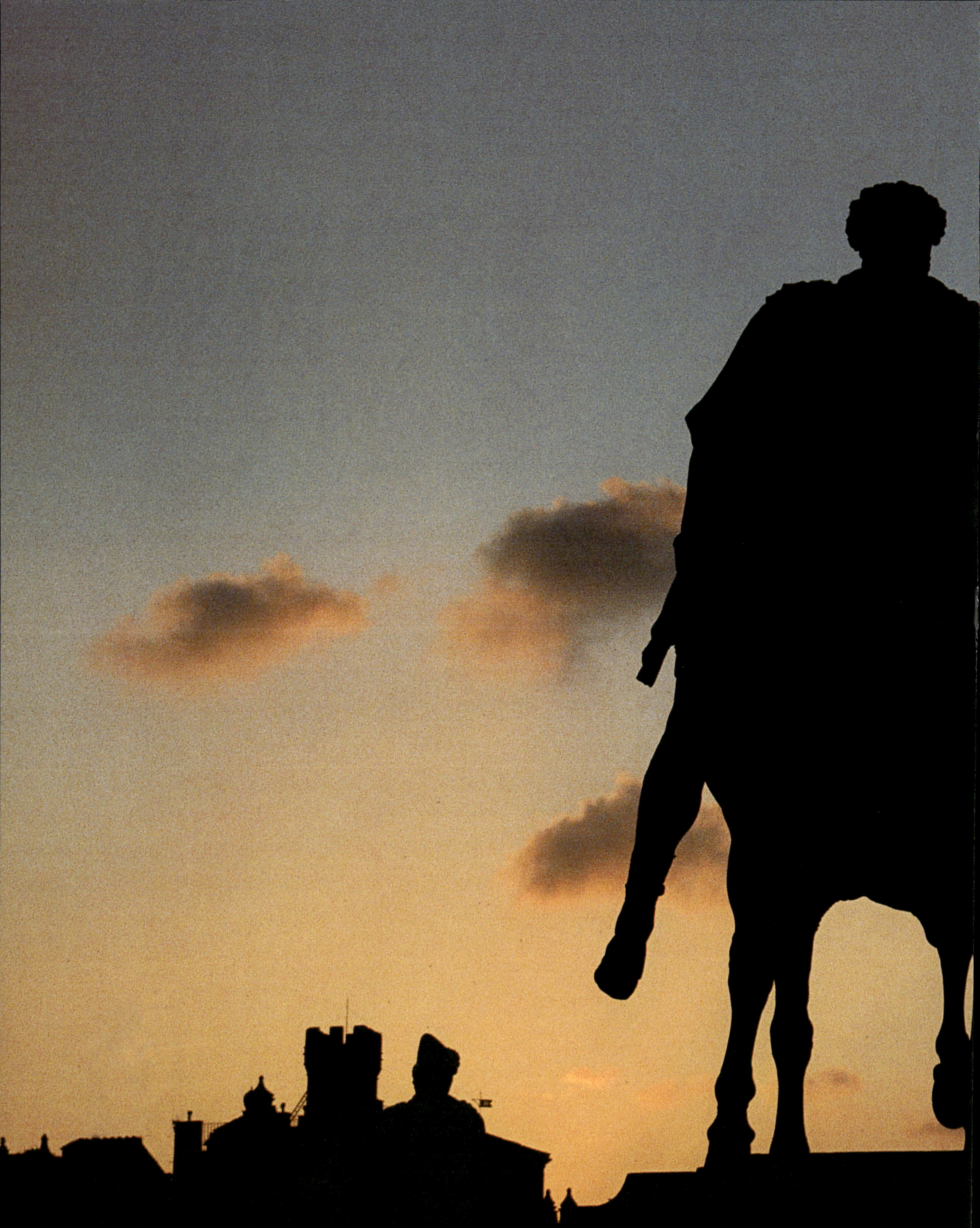

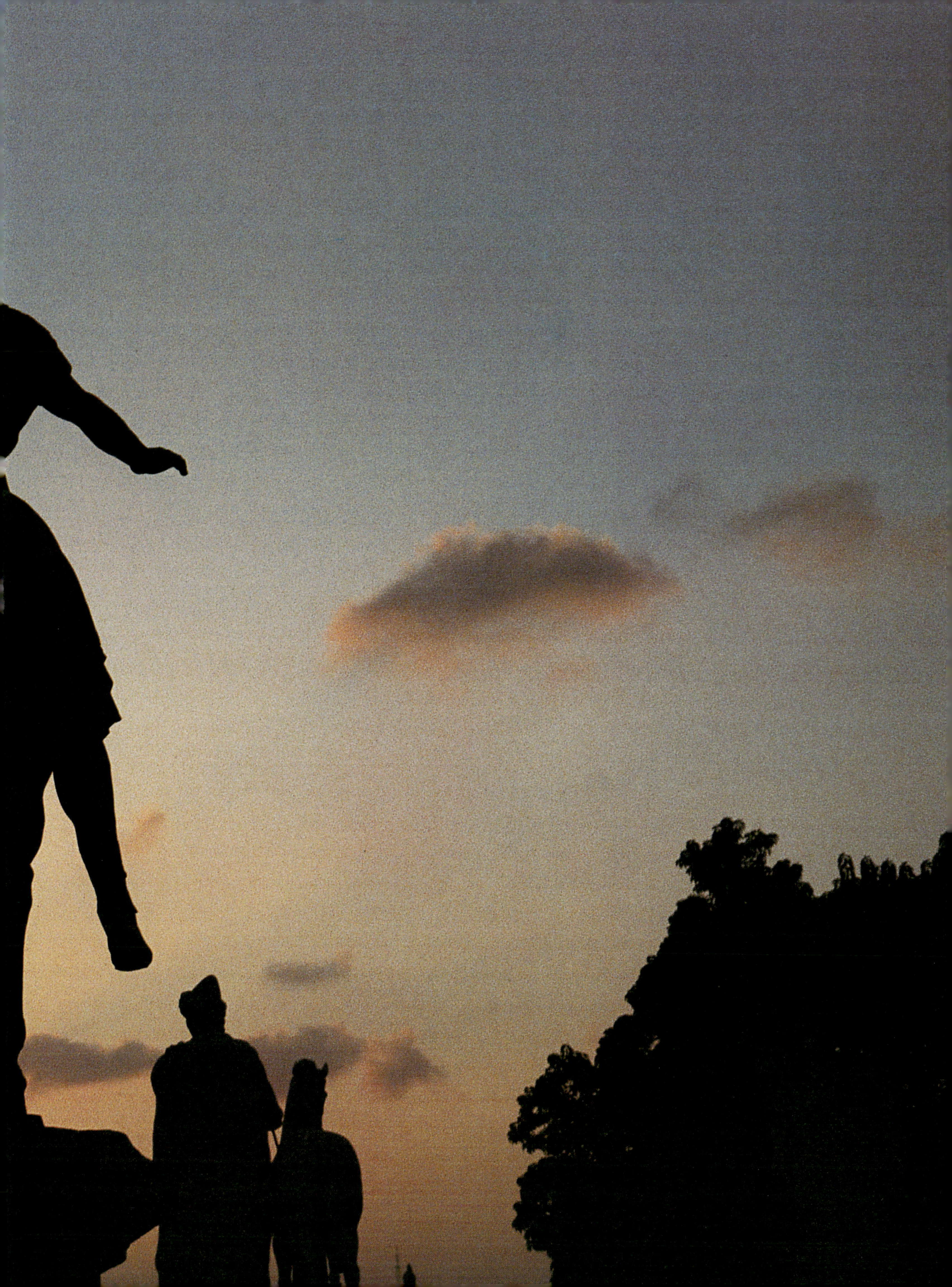

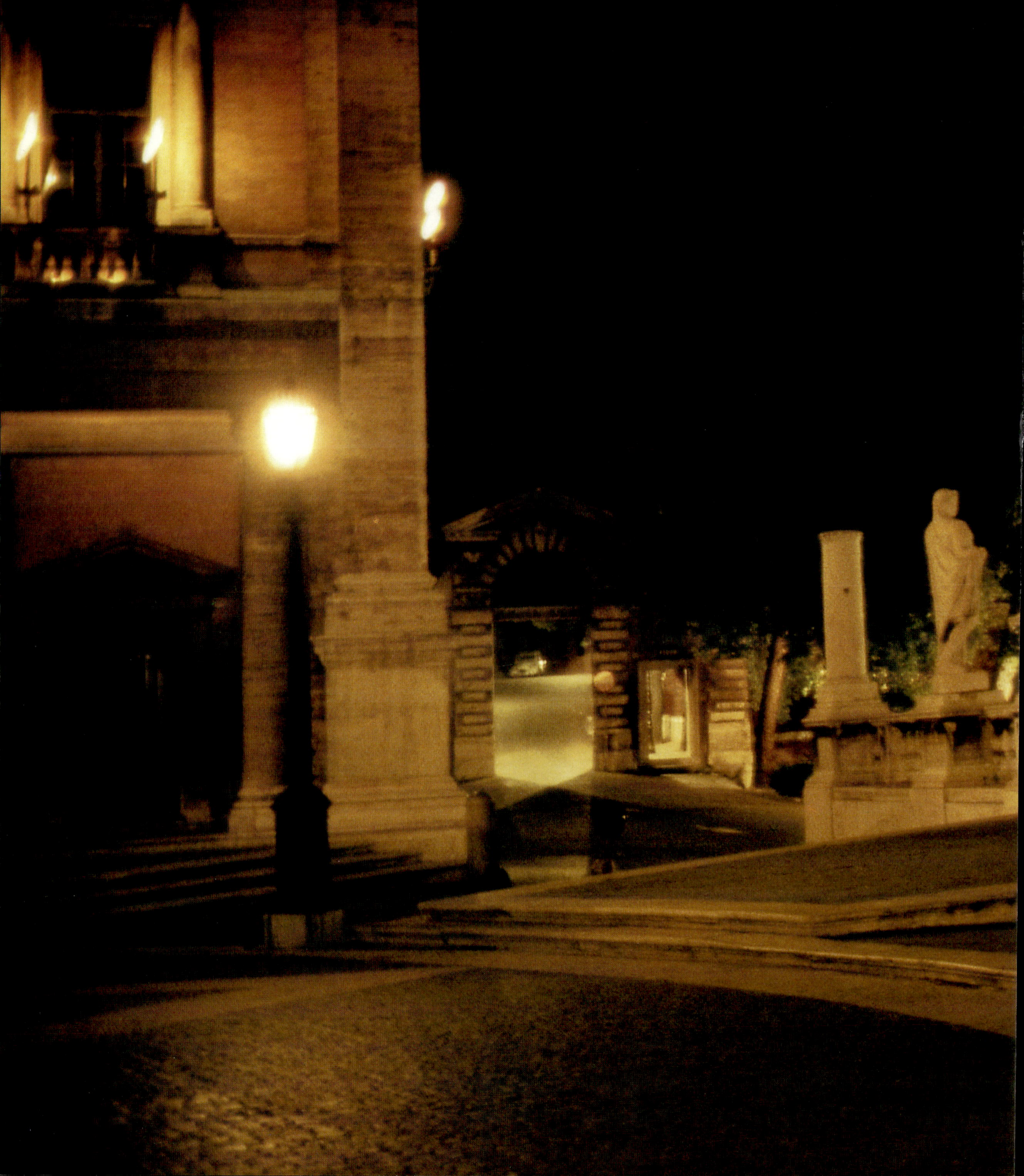

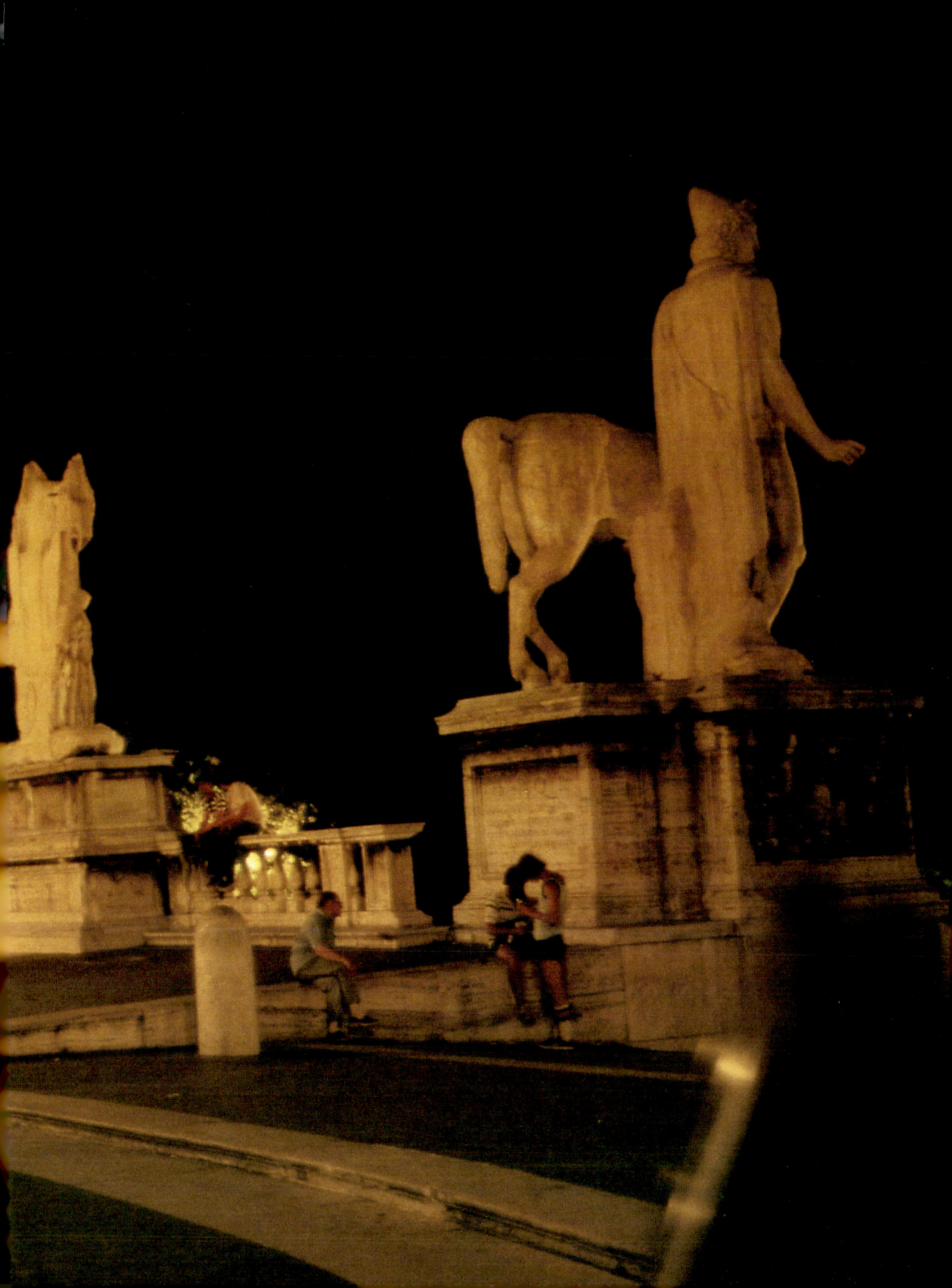

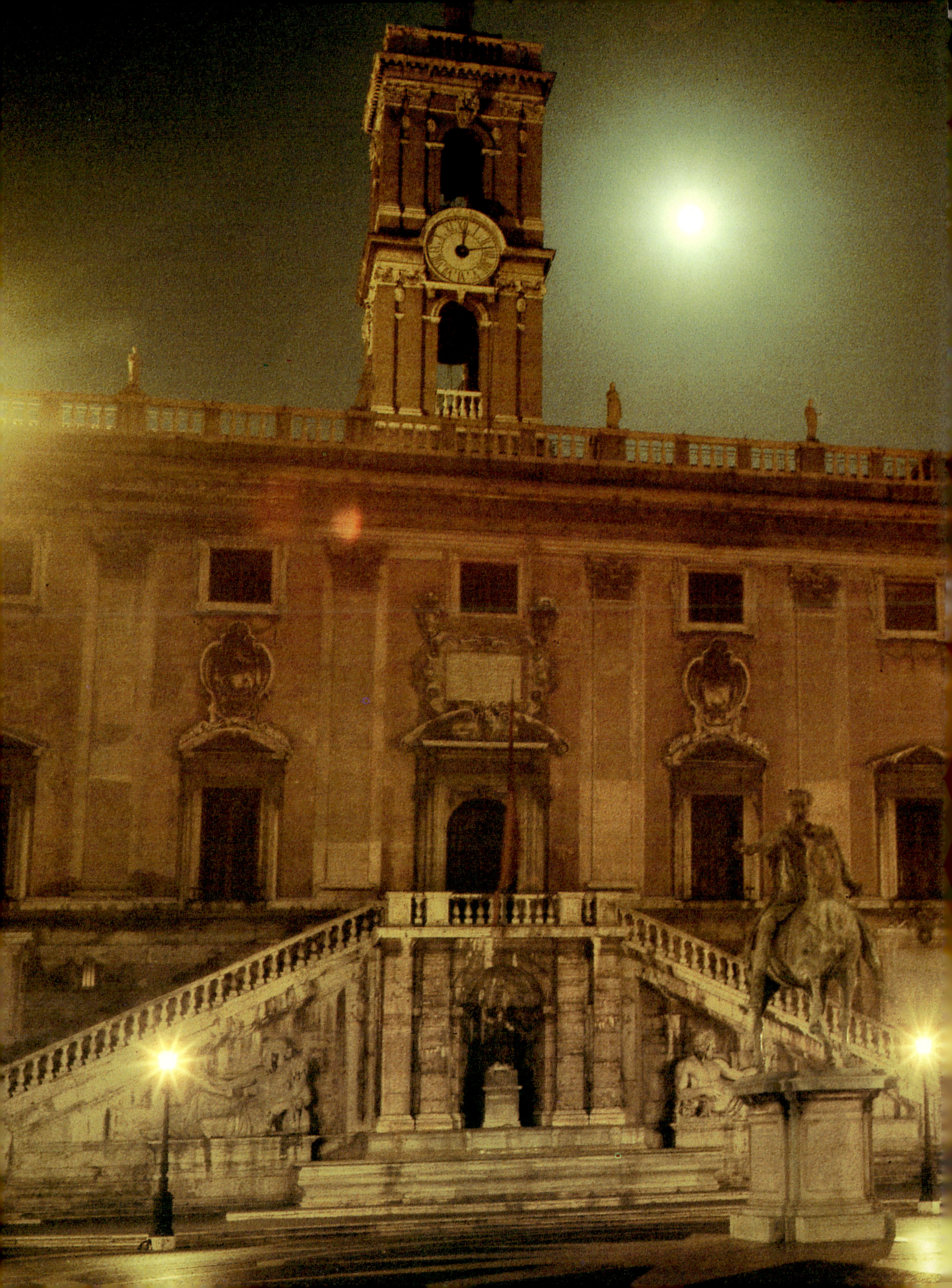

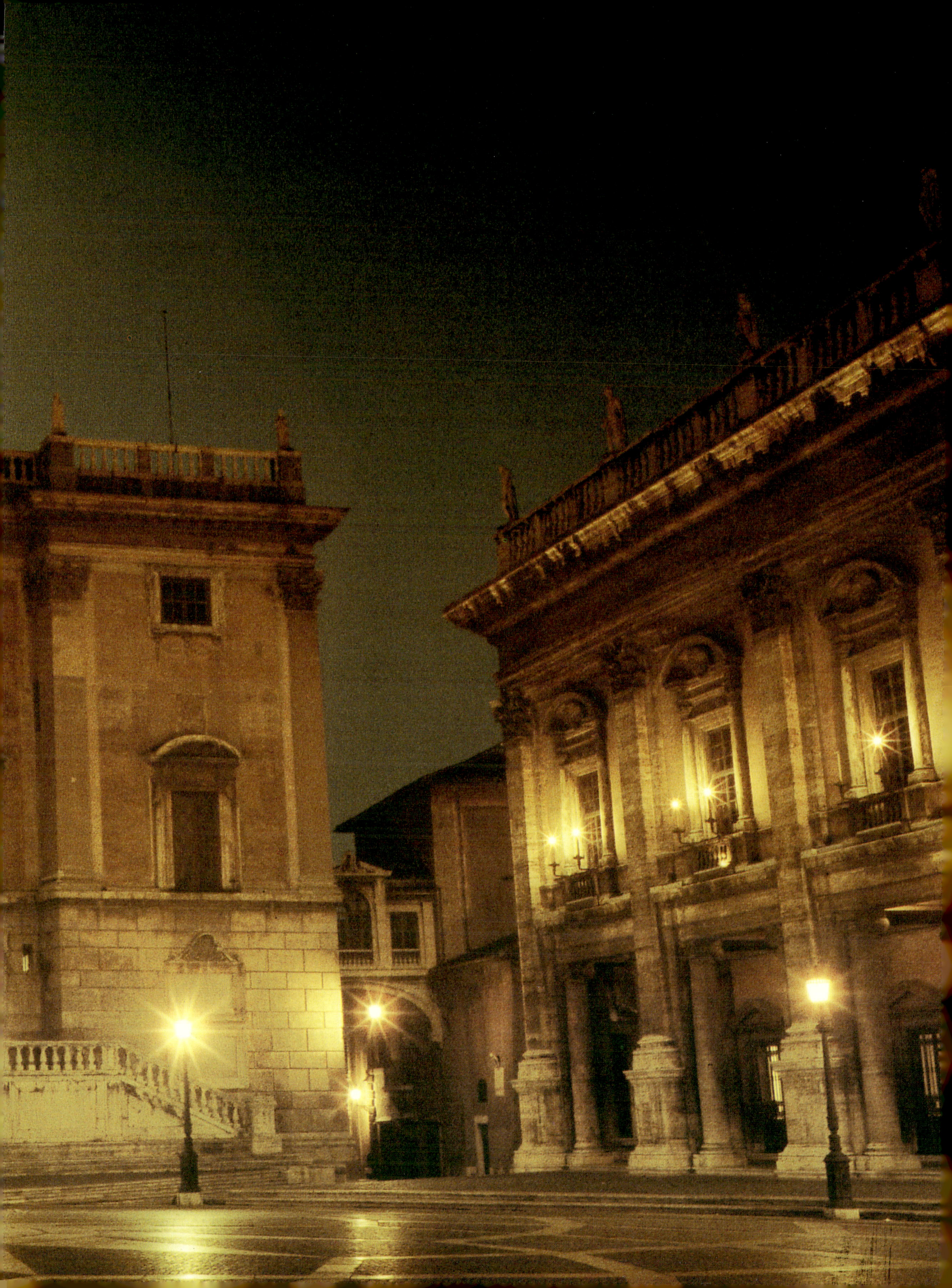

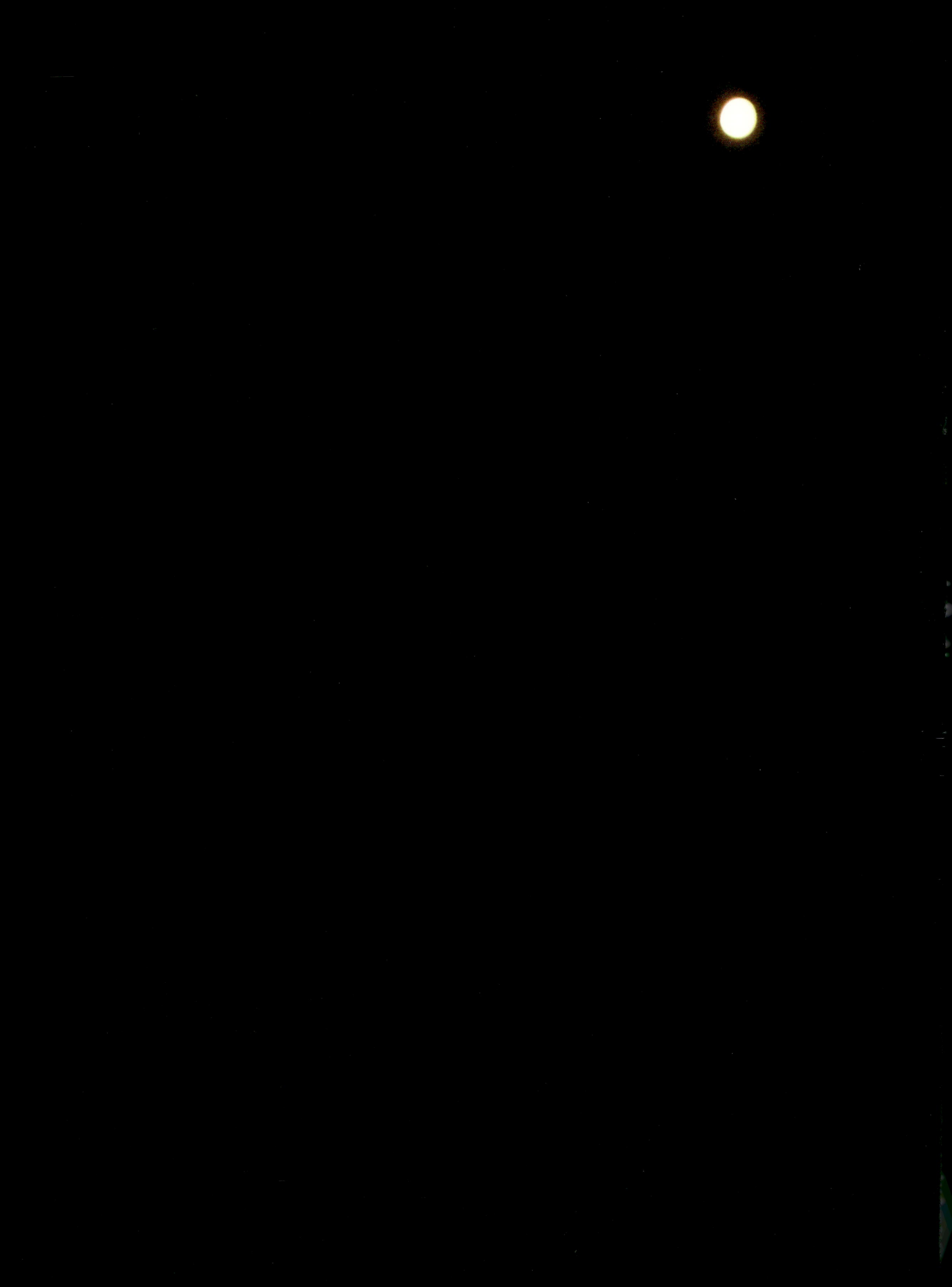

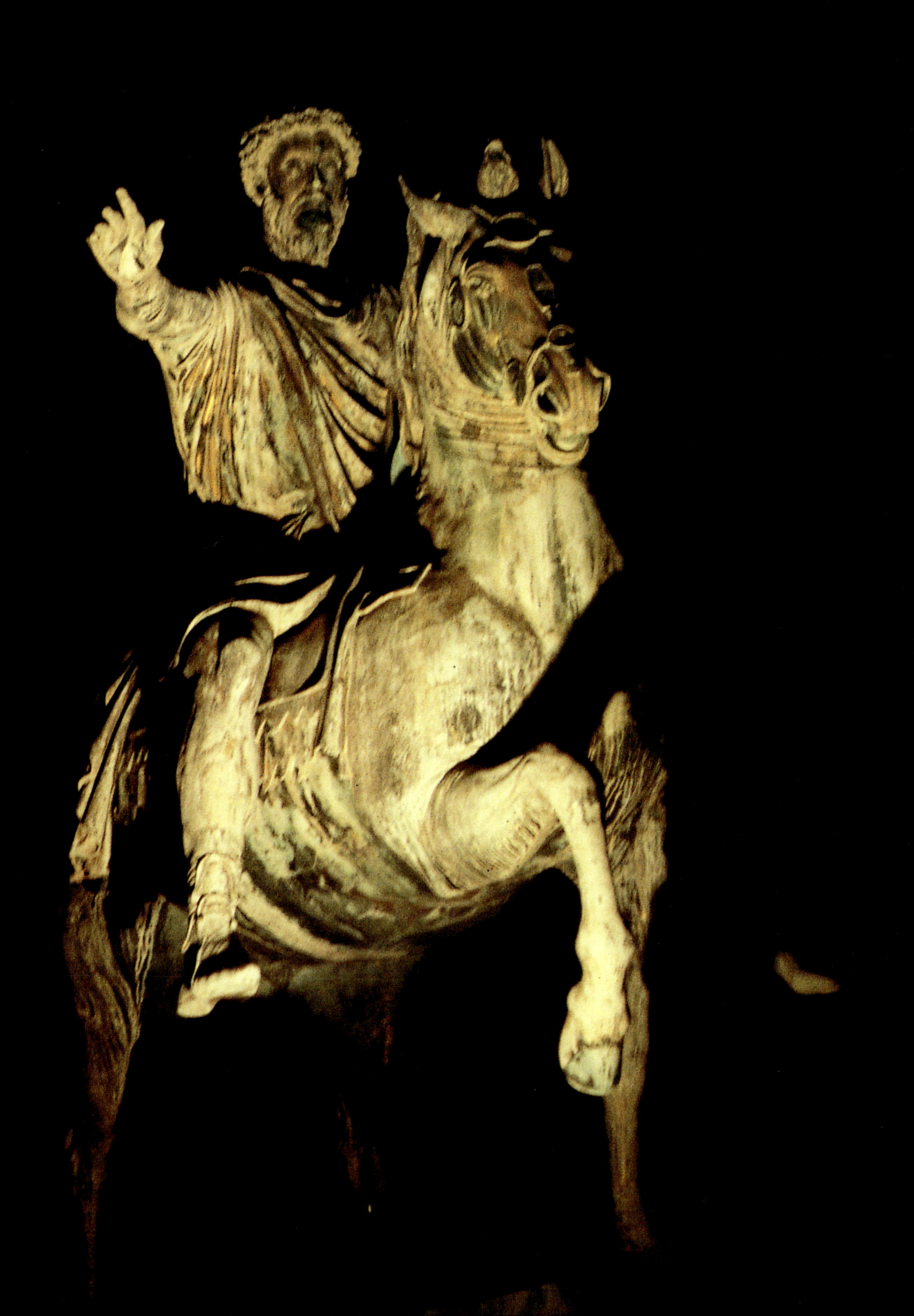

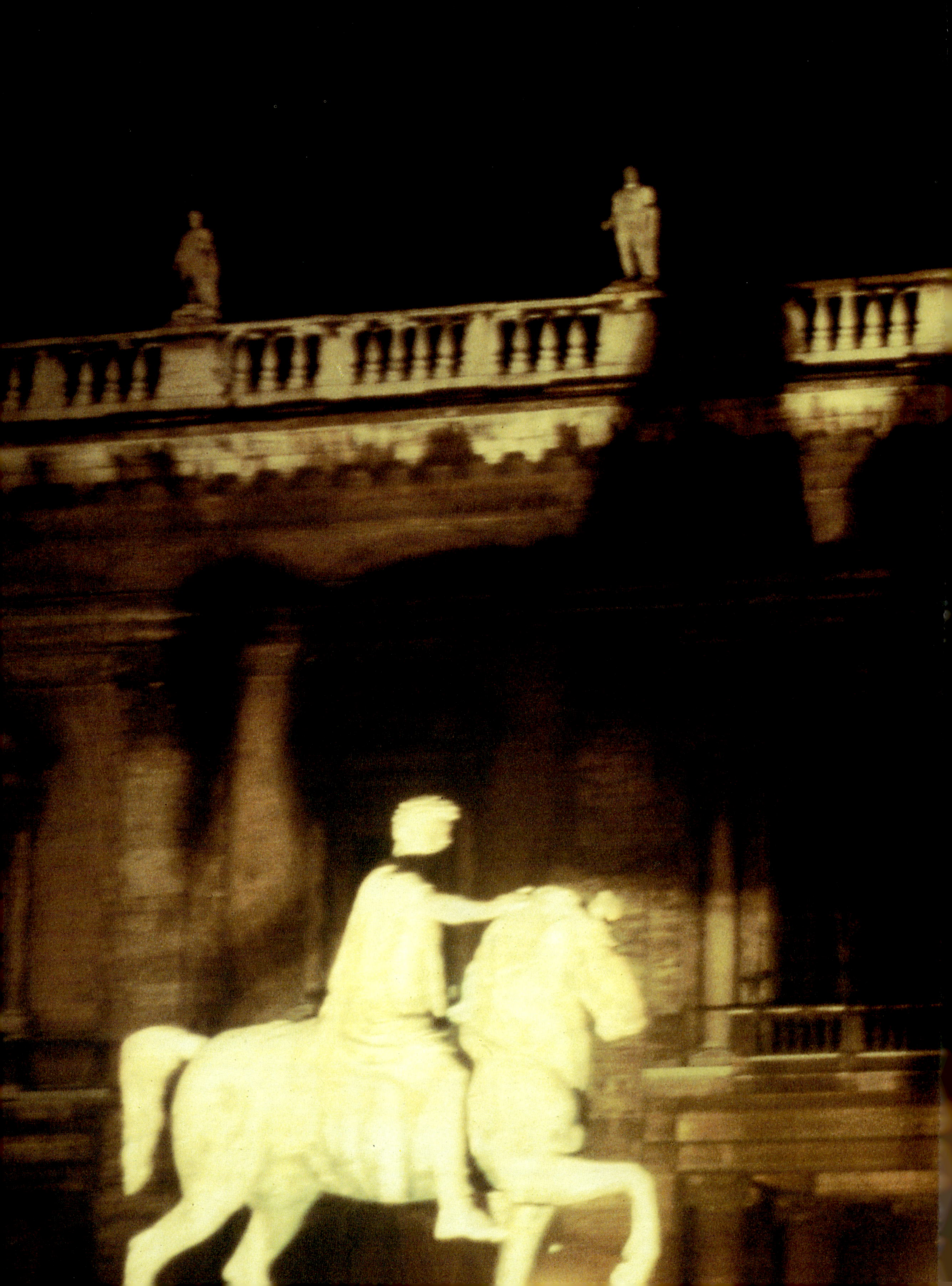

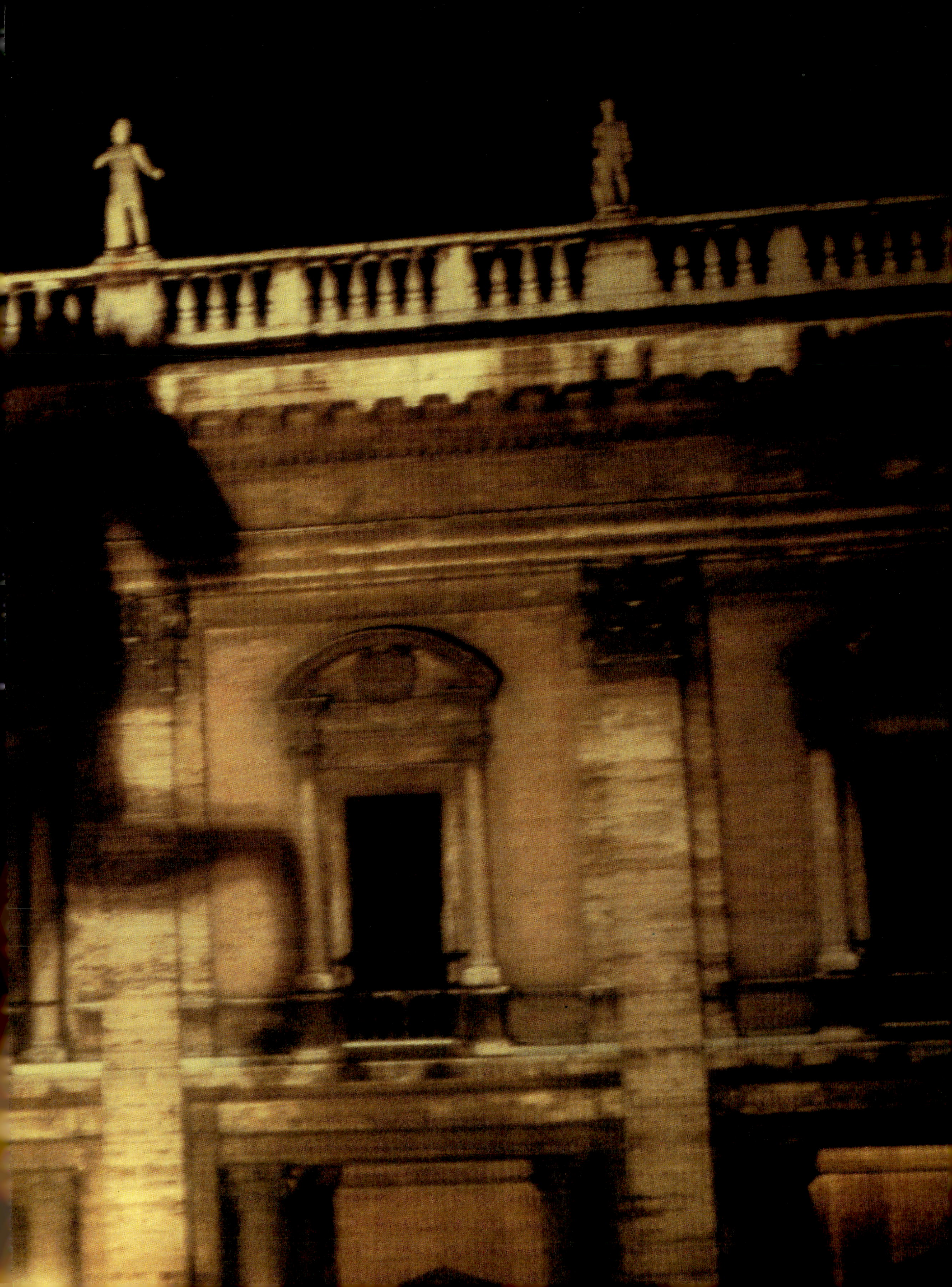

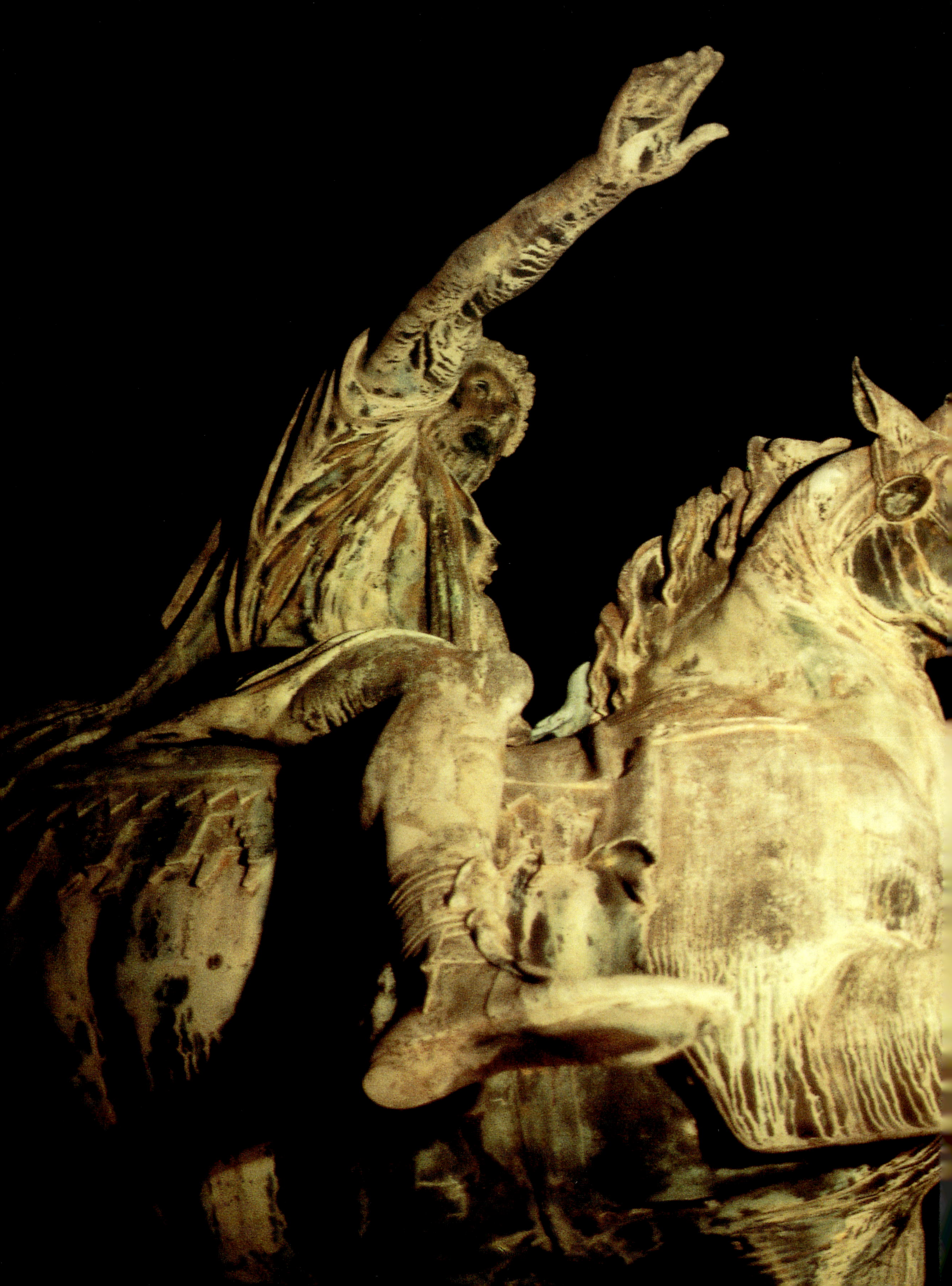

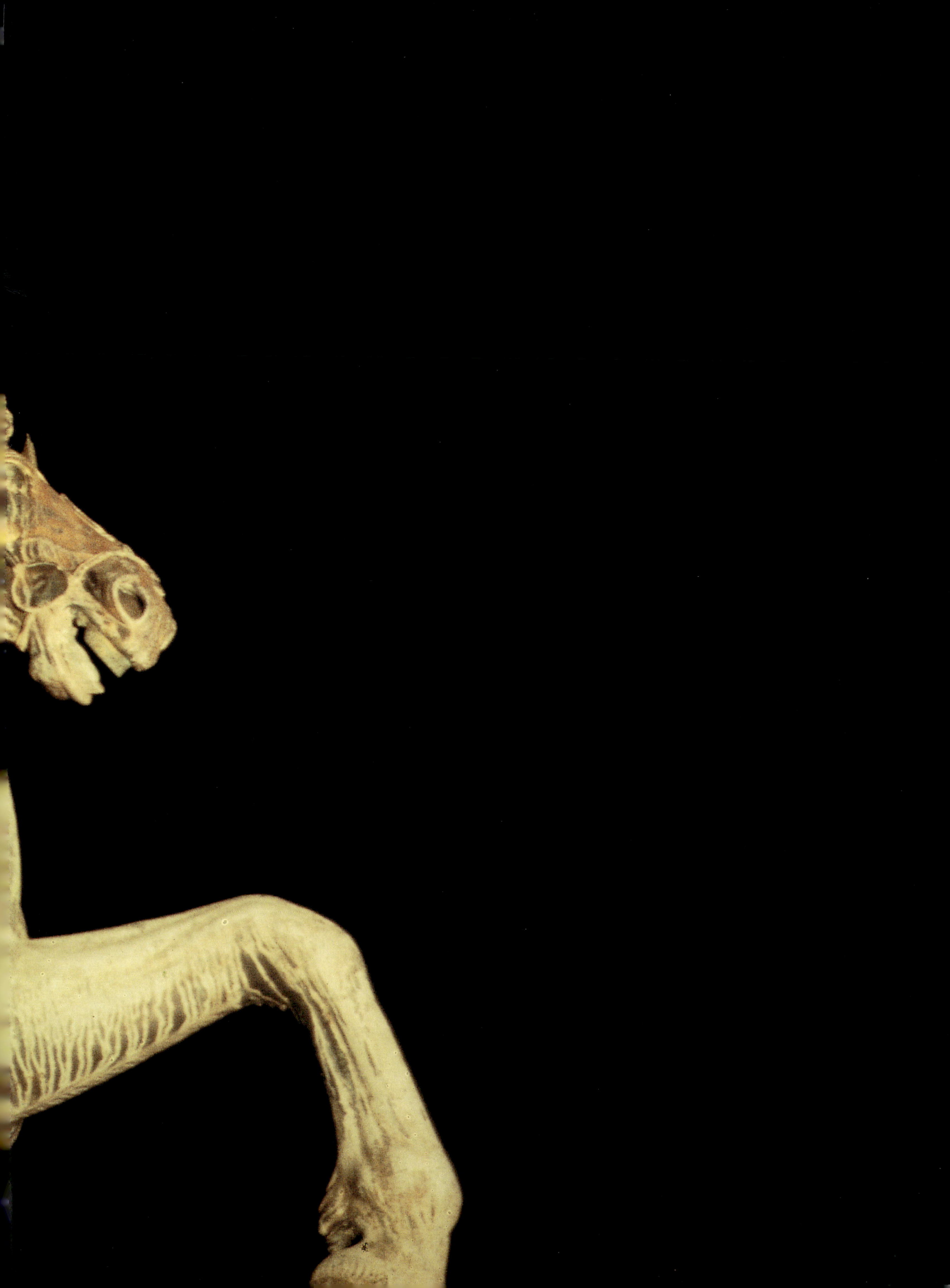

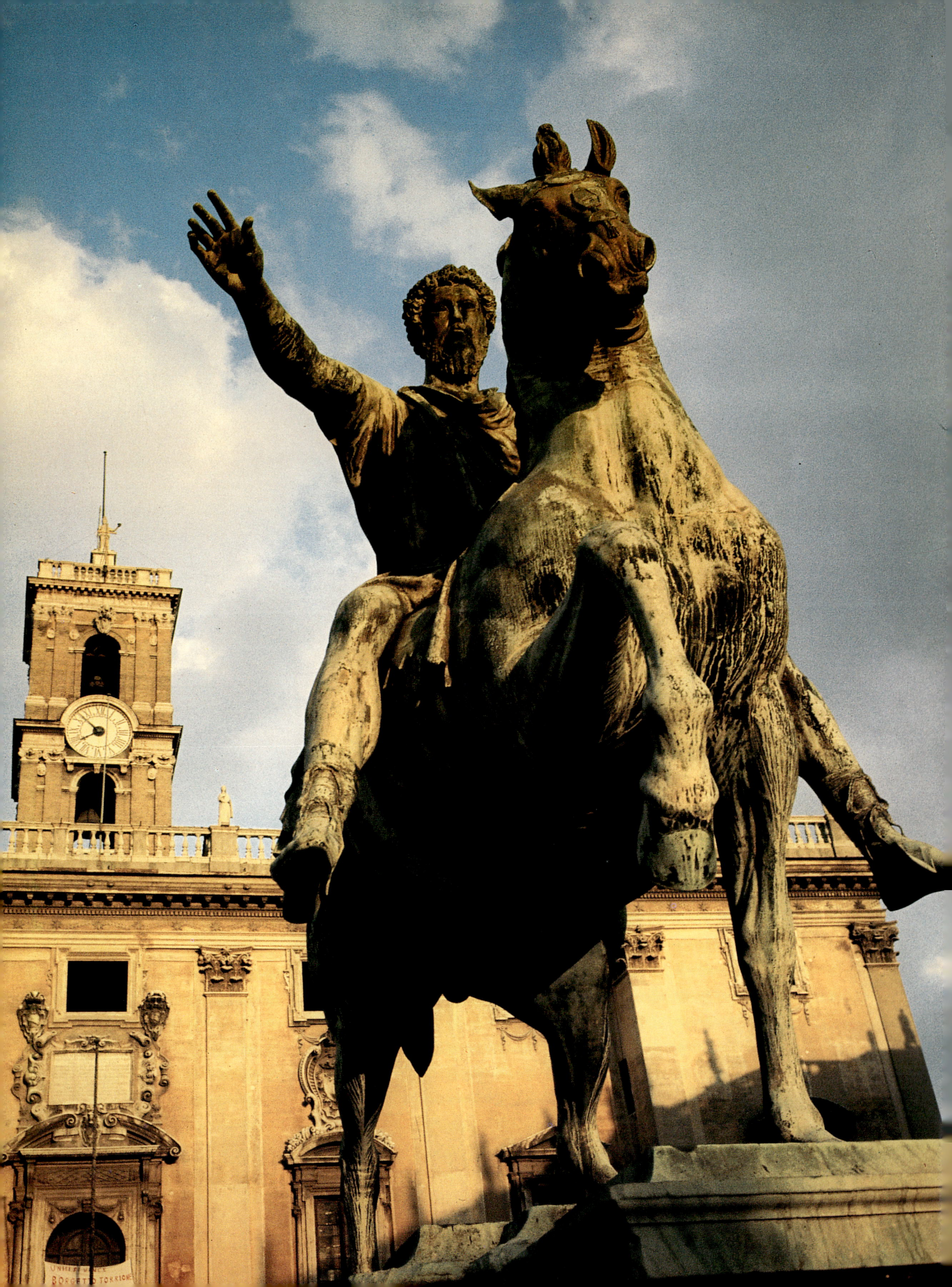

# The Campidoglio: A Historical Perspective

by DIANE KELDER

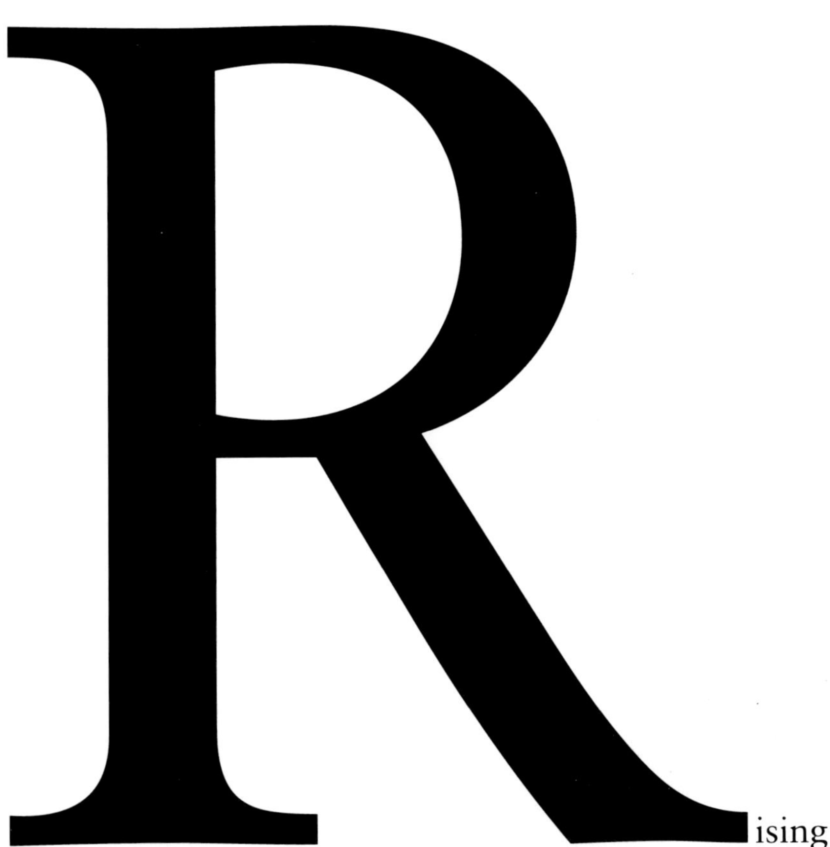ising high above a warren of crowded streets, the Capitoline Hill (the Italian word "Campidoglio" is likely a corruption of the Latin *Capitolium*) is the smallest of Rome's seven hills, encapsulating in its legends and monuments the city's nearly three-thousand-year history. On its two peaks the principal Roman deities, Jupiter, Juno, and Minerva, were worshiped and the most solemn state ceremonies were enacted. The hollow area between the peaks, now the Piazza del Campidoglio, was once called the *Asylum,* perpetuating the legend that the city's founder, Romulus, welcomed refugees and exiles from surrounding communities there.

From Rome's remote beginnings as a group of hill settlements through its long domination of the Western world, the Campidoglio maintained its religious and civic importance. Despite barbarian invasions and centuries of subsequent decline, its fame survived, inspiring the author of the *Mirabilia Urbis Romae,* a twelfth-century travel guide, to remind his readers that it had been "the head of the world, where consuls lived and governed the earth. Its face...was covered with high walls...and marvelous carved work...." This evocation of ancient splendor contrasted starkly with the desolation to which it had been reduced: where magnificent temples had stood, goats grazed in indifference. Yet the memory of its past was so vivid that in 1143, when the inhabitants of Rome rebelled against the pope, they assembled on this historic spot. Determined to restore the sovereignty of the Senate, they constructed a palace on the site of the Tabularium (78 B.C.), which had housed the archives of the Roman Republic.

However, their dream of self-governance was shattered by generations of popes who reduced the power and number of the elected senators and the *conservatori,* or magistrates, who assisted them, until only a token senator remained in 1358.

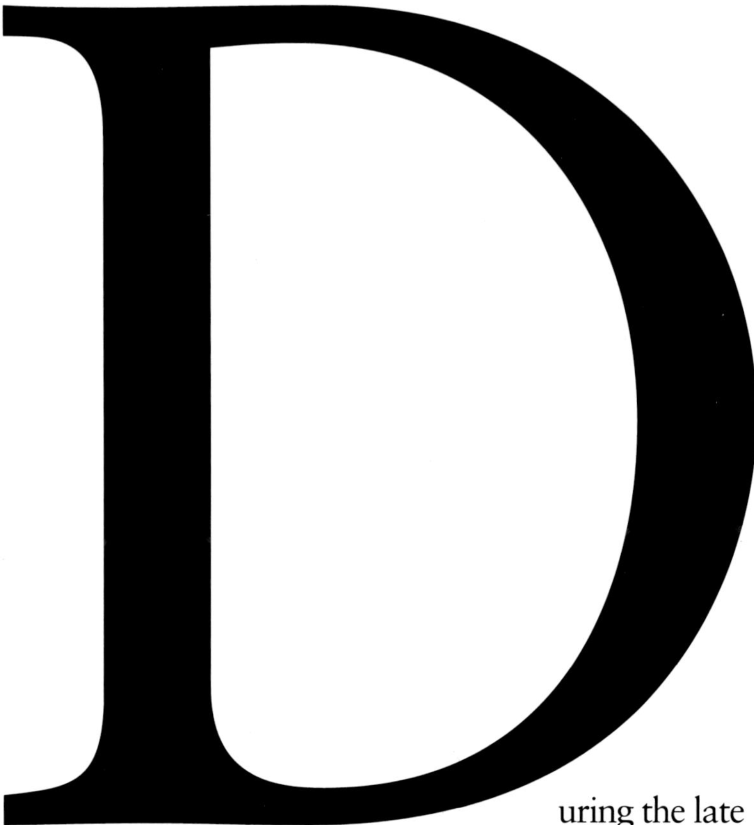uring the late fifteenth and early sixteenth centuries the grassy knolls and the medieval structures built for the Senate and *conservatori* gradually assumed the appearance of a bizarre sculpture park, as antique statues—gifts of Pope Sixtus IV and his successors—were casually deposited in their midst.

The felicitous decision to transform this random assemblage into a coherently organized architectural complex worthy of the Campidoglio's ancient status and function was prompted by the visit of Europe's most powerful ruler, the Holy Roman Emperor Charles V, in 1536. Pope Paul III planned to honor Charles for his recent victories over the Turks by reinstating the triumphal procession of the Caesars that traditionally culminated on the Campidoglio. Following Renaissance practice, temporary architecture symbolically proclaiming the solemn character of the occasion was erected in its open space. But after the Emperor's vast cortege proceeded along the historic route through the Forum Romanum, the steep path leading to the hill proved insurmountable, forcing the cancellation of the remaining ceremonies. It is likely that Paul III's dissatisfaction with this unprogrammed turn of events as well as his recognition of the urgent need for an appropriately impressive civic center influenced his determination, the following year, to move the celebrated equestrian monument of Marcus Aurelius from its centuries-old location near the Lateran Palace to the Campidoglio. First mentioned in the tenth-century *Liber Pontificalis Ecclesiae Romanae,* the statue was cast sometime after Marcus Aurelius became emperor in 161 A.D. It was long thought to represent the first Christian Emperor Constantine, a pious misconception that spared it from the zealous vandalism that befell so many "pagan" art works.

Thus papal pride initiated a glorious new chapter in the history of the Campidoglio, which was now graced by the presence of one of Rome's greatest rulers, admired as much for his humane ideals and philosophic writings as for his military or administrative accomplishments. Paul and the civil authorities confided the task of devising a plan for coordinating the surrounding space, renovating the extant buildings, and creating a ceremonial access worthy of this initiative to Michelangelo, who was then engaged in painting the *Last Judgement* fresco in the Sistine Chapel.

In the absence of definitive evidence such as autograph drawings, scholarly efforts to determine the specific features of Michelangelo's plan for the Campidoglio have relied on literary sources, notably the lengthy description in Giorgio Vasari's *Vite* (1568), as well as the visual testimony of contemporaneous drawings and prints by other artists. An etching published in 1569 by Etienne Dupérac bears the inscription "View of the Capitol from the model of Michelangelo Bonaroti [sic] himself." In the center of the print is the refurbished Palazzo del Senatore with its double staircase. It is flanked on the right by the classicizing façade of the Palazzo dei Conservatori and on the left by the Palazzo Nuovo, an edifice designed by Michelangelo to match the Palazzo dei Conservatori and provide symmetry to the piazza. As the focal point of this manifestly theatrical ensemble, the equestrian monument was situated at the center of a complex decorative and symbolic scheme of paving stones radiating from the tips of a twelve-pointed star. Envisioned as a vast terrace facing the modern city, the open end of the new Piazza del Campidoglio featured an imposing balustrade and a terraced ramp framed by colossal statues of the Dioscuri. Hampered by a lack of funds, work on this ambitious project proceeded slowly. After Michelangelo's death in 1564, some of his grandiose and costly designs were abandoned or modified by his successor, Giacomo della Porta. The façade of the Palazzo del Senatore was completed by Giralomo Rainaldi, who took charge in 1602, and the Palazzo Nuovo, destined to house the first public collection of ancient sculpture, now the Capitoline Museum, was finished in 1654.

From the late seventeenth century until 1979, when the nearby explosion of a terrorist bomb prompted the enclosure of the equestrian monument for safe-keeping and restoration, visitors who ascended the terraced ramp or *cordonata* and passed between the towering figures of the Dioscuri were greeted by the breathtaking spectacle of the horse and rider silhouetted against the golden backdrop of the Palazzo del Senatore. Poised on the roof balustrades of the surrounding buildings like marble actors, antique deities, athletes, and rulers declaimed the continuity of past and present, of sacred and civic that is inscribed within the space of the piazza. In 1981, the equestrian monument was removed to the Central Institute for Restoration. A few years ago, it returned to the Campidoglio. Not, as one might have hoped, to reaffirm the splendid equilibrium of Michelangelo's inspired conception, but to occupy a glass-walled room in the Capitoline Museum, where it is visible only from the courtyard. The empty pedestal still awaits the arrival of a promised replica.

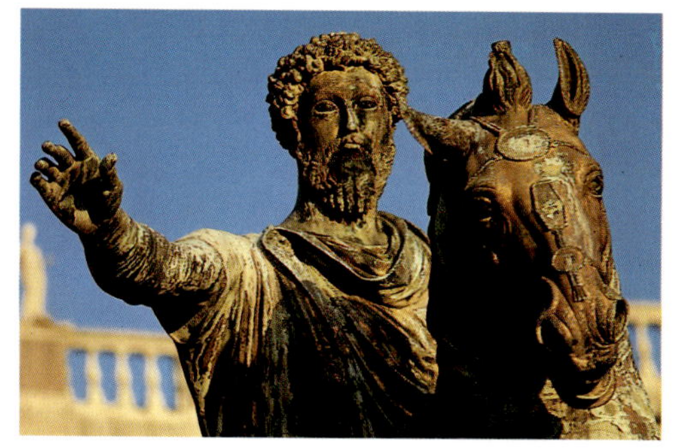

Wearing a simple tunic and riding cloak, the Emperor appears as the restorer of peace, an image consistent with the objectives of his reign. His sensitive features are framed by thick, curly hair and a carefully trimmed beard, a fashion introduced by Hadrian in emulation of the Greeks. Legend has it that when the bronze figures are again invested in their original gold, the end of the world will be proclaimed by a voice speaking from the forelock between the horse's ears.

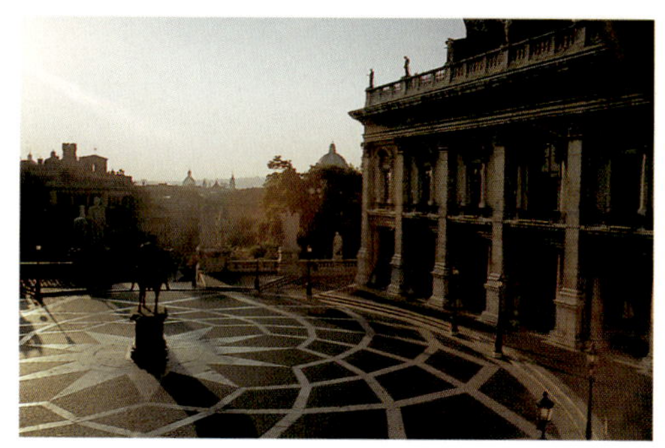

Michelangelo intended the piazza and its surrounding architecture to function as a permanent stage set for the Emperor on his horse. The Palazzo Nuovo, which became the Capitoline Museum in 1734, faithfully echoes the design of the Palazzo dei Conservatori on the opposite side, thus reinforcing the palpably theatrical dimensions of the space.

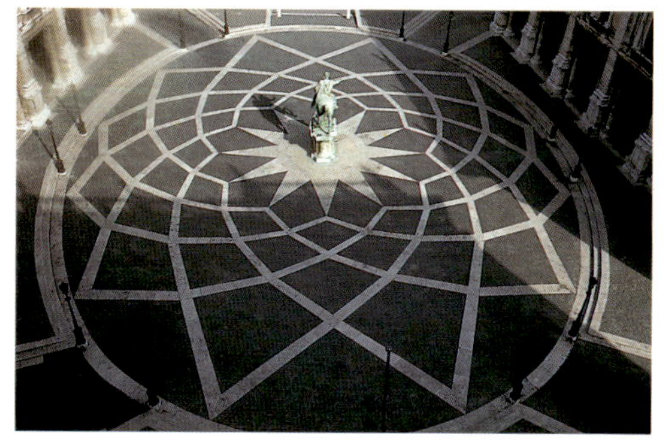

For the pavement of the piazza's trapezoidal space, Michelangelo conceived an oval design dominated by a twelve-pointed star intended to heighten the sensation of convexity at the center and to harmonize the proportions of the monument with those of the surrounding architecture. The pavement design was not realized until the 1940s.

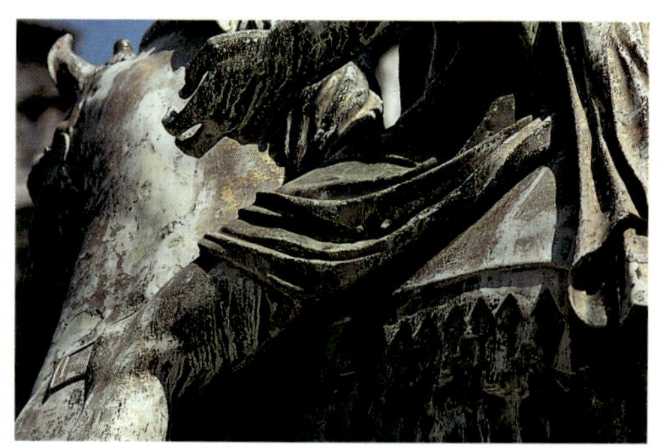

Even in this manifestly public monument, the second-century Roman sculptor's dedication to the scrupulous rendering of his subject's anatomical details is evident. While certain scholars argue that the beautifully articulated left hand of the emperor once held a scepter or globe, others maintain that it simply grasped the reins of his spirited horse.

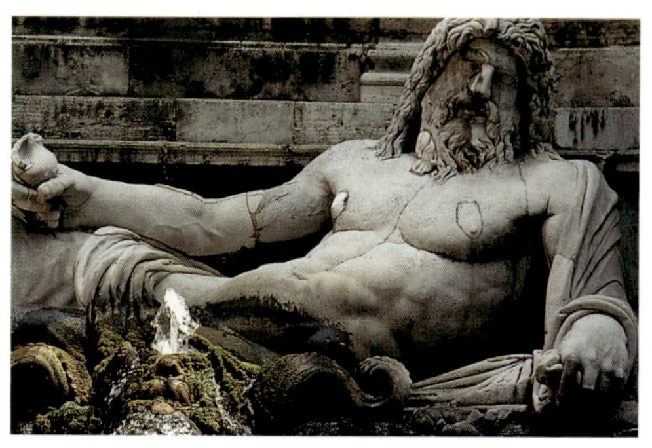

Among the ancient works moved to the Campidoglio in the sixteenth century, this reclining deity symbolizing either the ocean or a river god rested against a wall beneath the church of Santa Maria in Aracoeli before being placed in the courtyard of the Capitoline Museum. Its popular name is Marforio, and it belongs to an exclusive group of so-called "talking statues" to which citizens affixed messages of a political or satirical nature.

Romulus, the legendary founder of Rome, and his twin brother Remus were believed to be the sons of Mars and the vestal virgin Rhea Silvia. Abandoned by their mother's disgraced family, the infants were nursed by a she-wolf, an animal sacred to Mars and a traditional symbol of Rome. This celebrated bronze statue of the wolf is said to date from the sixth century, B.C. The twins were added some two thousand years later.

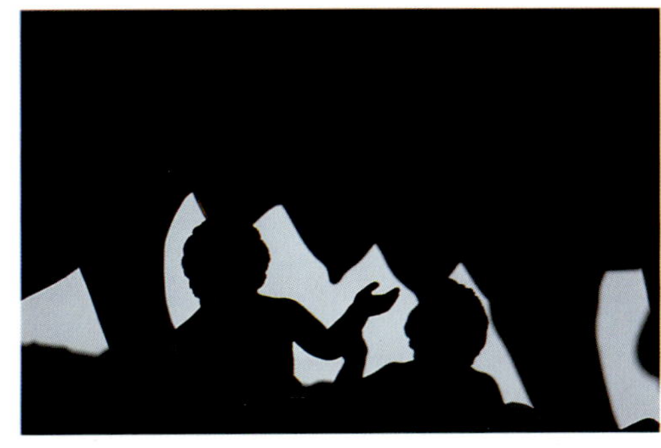

The highest peak on the Capitoline Hill was the Arx, or citadel, where Juno's temple stood. Here, the Emperor Augustus saw a vision of Mary and the infant Christ and heard voices proclaim it the altar of heaven. Nearly six hundred years later, the church of Santa Maria in Aracoeli was erected on this site. The imposing flight of marble stairs was built in 1348 in gratitude for the city's having been spared the ravages of the Plague.

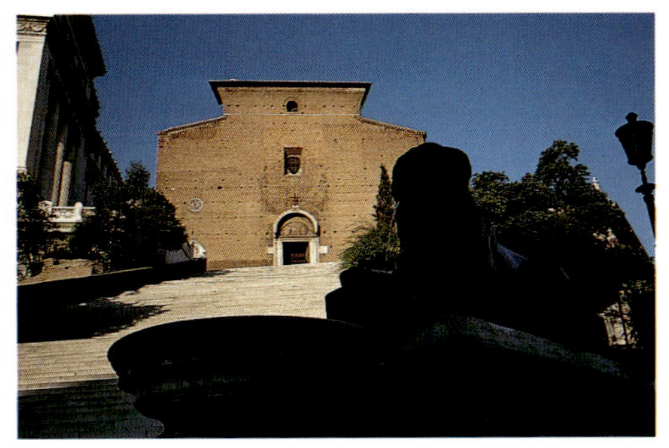

Traces of surviving gold leaf only partially convey the monument's original splendor. Yet it was not always treated with reverence. According to popular tradition, the medieval tyrant Cola di Rienzo celebrated a victory over his enemies by giving a huge banquet at which the horse served as a fountain. Wine and water issued from his flared nostrils.

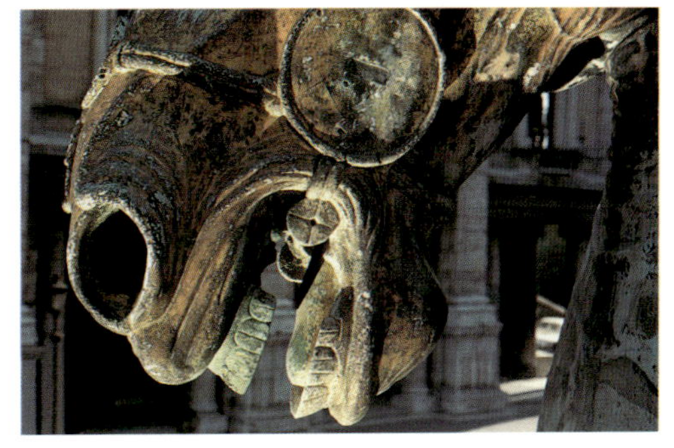

A gift of Pope Sixtus IV, these fragments of the forty-foot statue of Constantine that once stood in the basilica that bears his name were brought to the Campidoglio in 1471. The pronounced stylization of the features and the fixed gaze of the first Christian emperor prefigure the spiritualizing and hieratic art of the Byzantine Church.

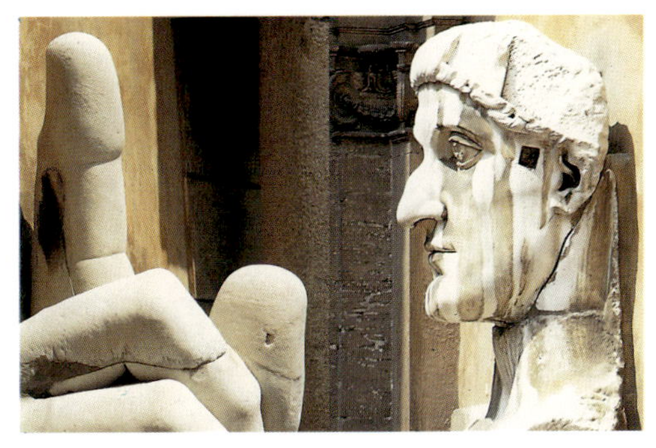

Portrait busts such as these in the Capitoline Museum provide a visual history of the statesmen, philosophers, soldiers, and poets whose contributions were to distinguish Roman civilization. Influenced by late Hellenistic art and by the *imagines* (clay, wax, and wooden funerary masks), they project a sense of uncompromising realism.

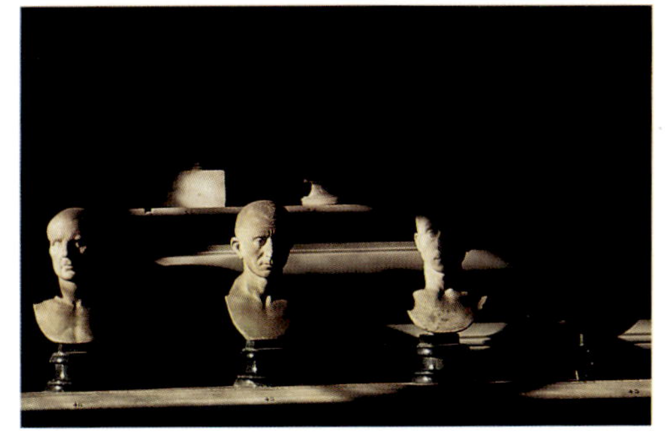

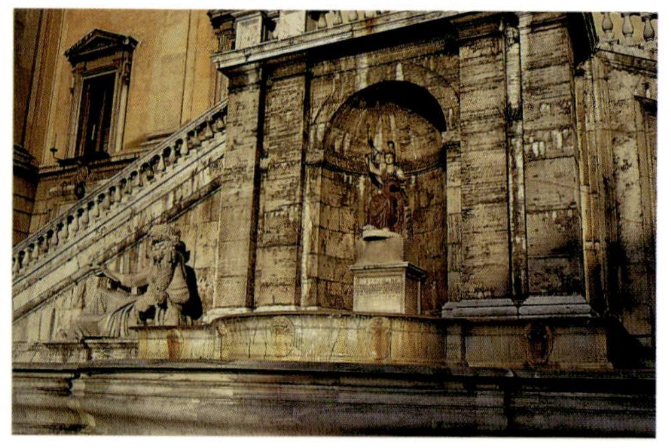

Michelangelo's design for the double staircase called for the inclusion of three monumentally scaled ancient statues: Jupiter, the supreme deity of the Capitoline Hill, was to have stood in the center, flanked by recumbent figures symbolizing the Nile and Tiber rivers. The fountain, which gracefully coordinates the figures, was designed by Matteo Bartolani in 1588.

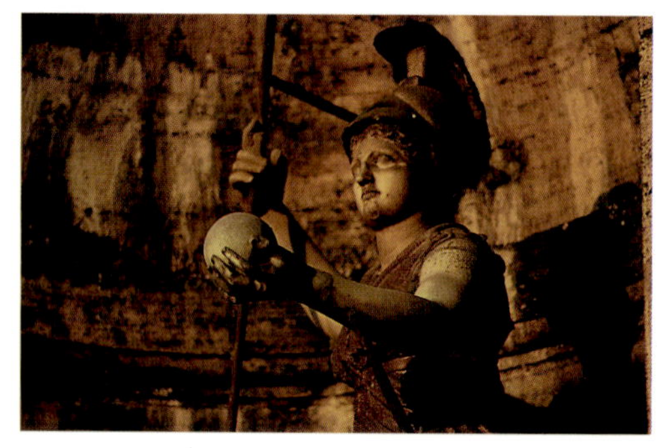

After Michelangelo's death in 1564, his intended sculptural ensemble in front of the Palazzo del Senatore was altered. The standing Jupiter was replaced by a symbolic personification of Rome. Dressed in a robe of porphyry, this helmeted goddess assumes the martial attributes of Minerva.

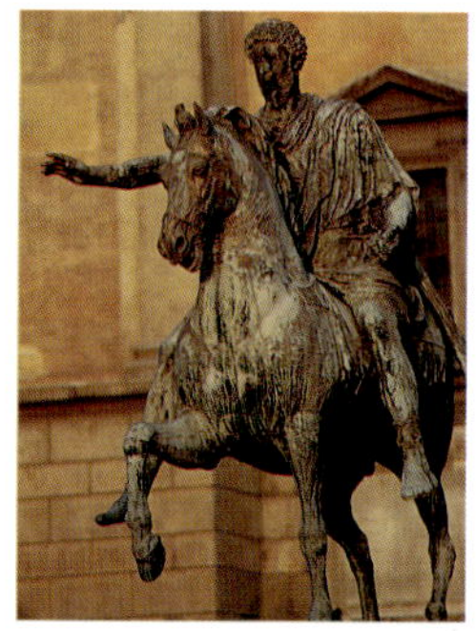

The sole survivor of at least twenty-two equestrian monuments that were recorded in Rome during the last years of the Empire, Marcus Aurelius and his horse are fourteen feet high and tweleve and a half feet long. An outstanding feature of the work, imitated by countless sculptors since the Renaissance, is the dramatic visual counterpoint of nervously animated horse and calm, authoritative rider.

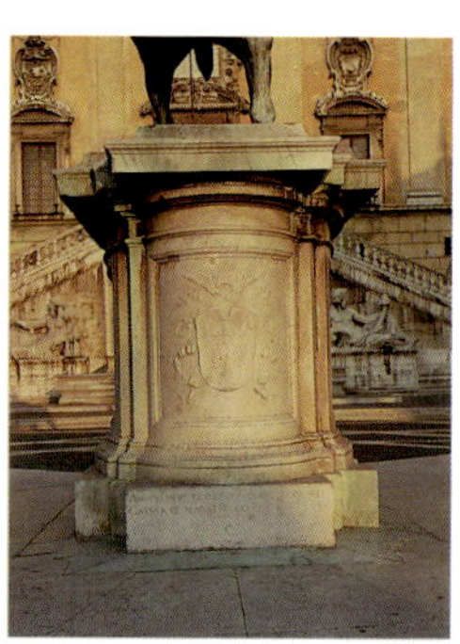

Michelangelo initially opposed Paul III's decision to move the equestrian monument from the Lateran to the Campidoglio. When it finally arrived in January 1538, the sculpture was placed on a large, rectangular marble slab. Realizing that its shape and proportions were unsuitable, Michelangelo designed a graceful curvilinear base whose commemorative inscriptions and coats of arms honor the pope and the civic authorities.

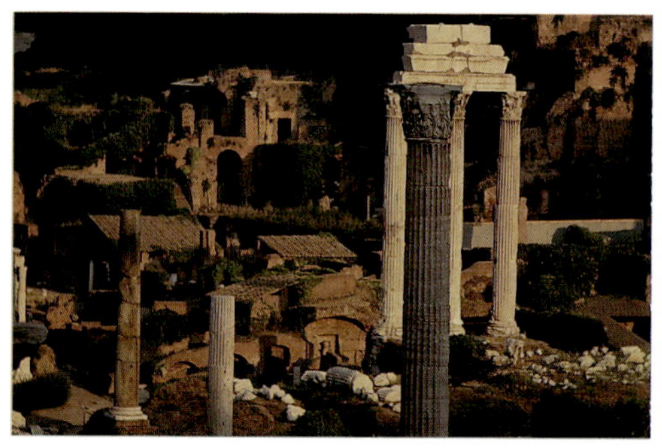

Once the pulsating center of city life, the Forum Romanum is situated at the southwestern edge of the Capitoline Hill. Surviving fragments of the architrave and three towering columns poignantly suggest the grandeur of the large temple that was dedicated to Castor and Pollux in 484 B.C.

Above the ornate entrance to the great hall of the Palazzo del Senatore, Giacomo della Porta wove a complex decorative motif integrating civic emblems with the coat of arms of the reigning Aldobrandini pope. The scroll honors Martino Capelletti, who held the title of Senator in the late sixteenth century.

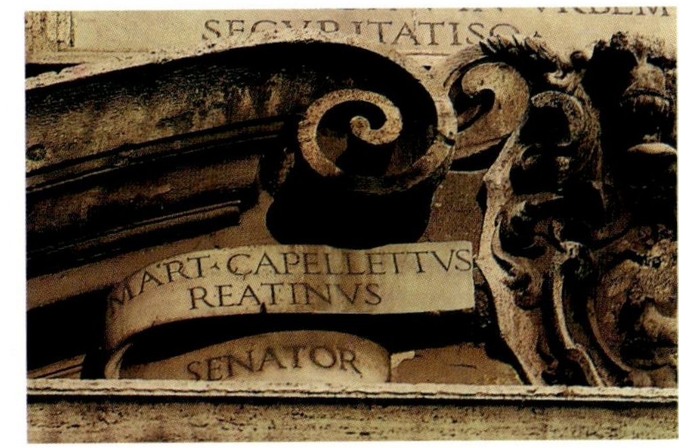


The colossal statues of Castor and Pollux, the Dioscuri, were probably placed on the balustrades at the top of the *cordonata*, or terraced ramp, in the 1580s. Venerated as protectors by the ancient Romans because of their intervention in a decisive battle with the Latin League (496 B.C.), the Dioscuri were said to have flown to the city on their snow-white horses to announce the joyous news.

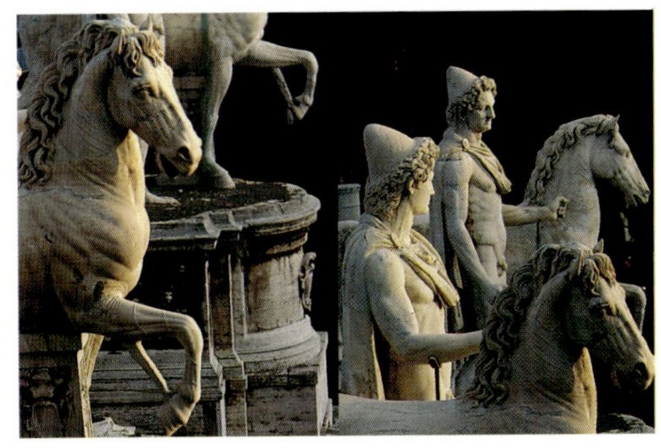

The remarkable sensation of harmony and continuity that pervades the Piazza del Campidoglio is enhanced by the presence of antique statues of deities and athletes on the roof balustrades of the palaces. They are aligned with the pilasters of the façades below.

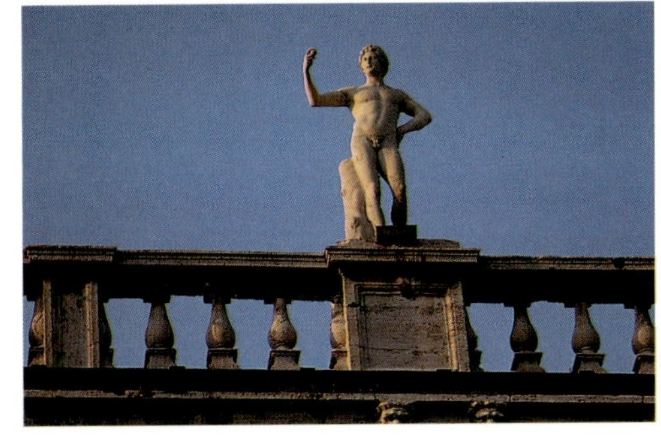

Roman sculptors relied on Greek models and techniques. The indirect lost-wax process employed in the casting of the bronze figures involved the separate fusion and subsequent soldering of their parts. Laboratory analysis has revealed that a total of thirty-two pieces were combined to create the horse and rider.

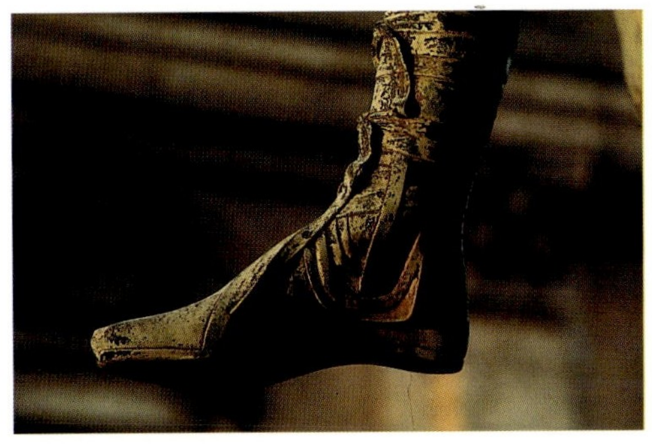

Behind the walls of the renovated Palazzo del Senatore are vestiges of its ancient and medieval past. Michelangelo intended to create a new façade of travertine, the same material that was employed in the other buildings, but his successor altered his design and substituted sandstone and tufa, later painted in the yellow-orange that has come to be identified with Rome.

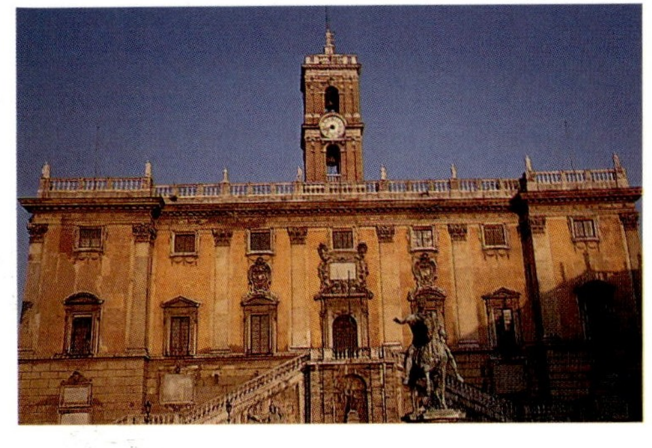

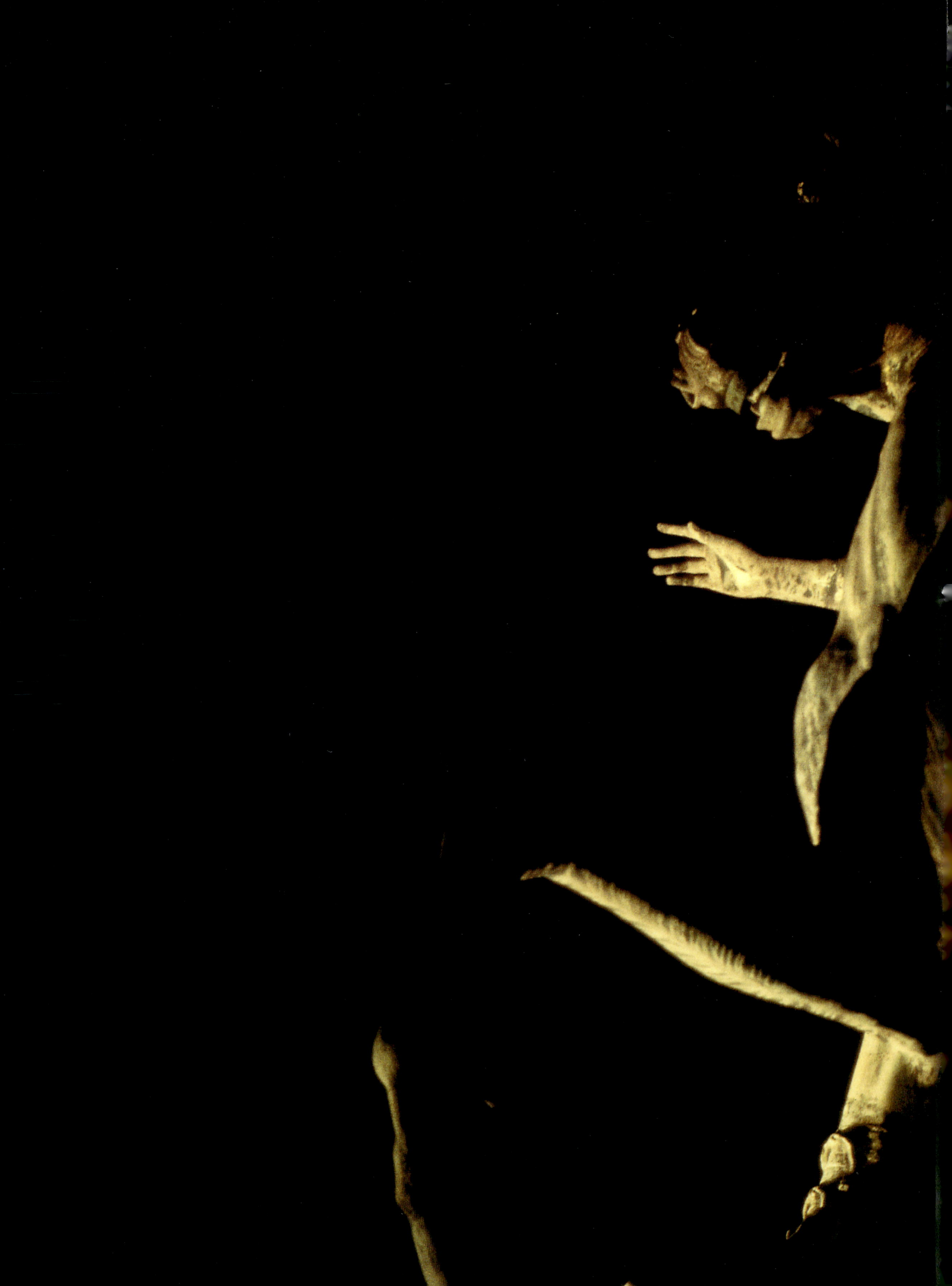

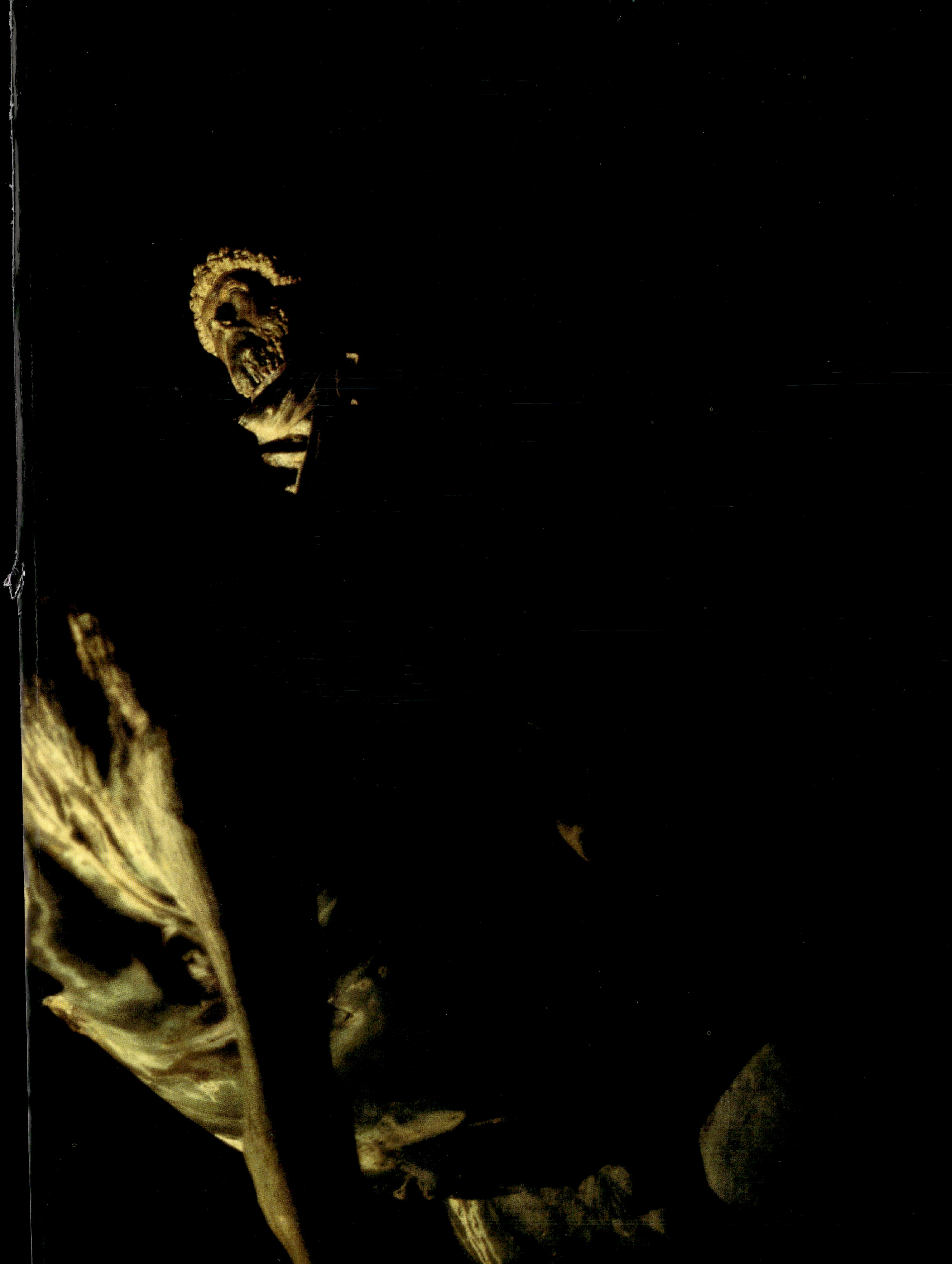

*ILLUSTRATIONS*

***Page 29:*** Francisco de Hollanda.
Statue of Marcus Aurelius before
modification of the base (1538 – 1539).

***Front endpaper:*** Anonymous.
View of the Campidoglio, ca. 1560.

***Back endpaper:*** Étienne Dupérac.
Michelangelo's plan for the Campidoglio (1569).


Printed by Amilcare Pizzi, Milan, Italy


Published in the United States by Random House, Inc.,
New York, and simultaneously in Canada by
Random House of Canada Limited, Toronto.

Library of Congress Cataloging-in-Publication Data
Liberman, Alexander.
Campidoglio : Michelangelo's Roman Capitol/
Alexander Liberman, Joseph Brodsky.
p. cm.
ISBN 0-679-43052-0
1. Capitoline Hill ( Italy)—Pictorial works.
2. Rome ( Italy)—Buildings, structures, etc.—Pictorial works.
3. Marcus Aurelius, Emperor of Rome, 121–180—
Statues—Italy—Rome —Pictorial works.
I. Brodsky, Joseph. II. Title.
NA 4415. I82R655 1994
799' . 445632–dc20 94–13750

98765432 24689753 23456789
First Edition

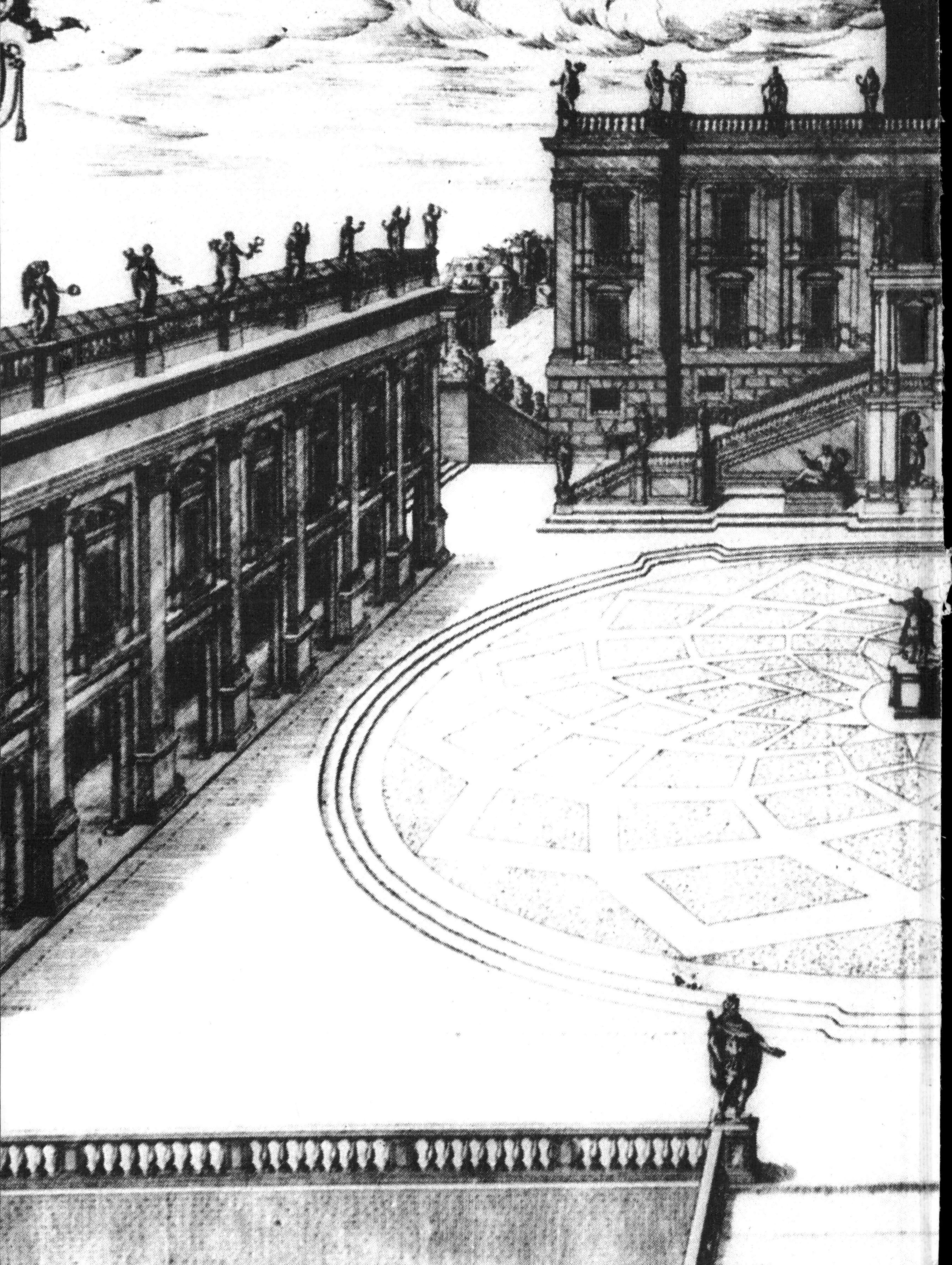